CLARENDON ANCIENT HISTORY SERIES

General Editors

The aim of the CLARENDON ANCIENT HISTORY SERIES is to provide authoritative translations, introductions, and commentaries to a wide range of Greek and Latin texts studied by ancient historians. The books will be of interest to scholars, graduate students, and advanced undergraduates.

AESCHINES

Against Timarchos

Introduction, Translation,
and Commentary by

Nick Fisher

OXFORD
UNIVERSITY PRESS
Great Clarendon Street, Oxford OX2 6DP
Oxford University Press is a department of the University of Oxford.
It furthers the University's objective of excellence in research, scholarship,
and education by publishing worldwide in

Oxford New York

Athens Auckland Bangkok Bogotá Buenos Aires Cape Town
Chennai Dar es Salaam Delhi Florence Hong Kong Istanbul Karachi
Kolkata Kuala Lumpur Madrid Melbourne Mexico City Mumbai Nairobi
Paris São Paulo Shanghai Singapore Taipei Tokyo Toronto Warsaw

and associated companies in Berlin Ibadan

Oxford is a registered trade mark of Oxford University Press
in the UK and certain other countries

Published in the United States
by Oxford University Press Inc., New York

British Library Cataloguing in Publication Data

Data available

Library of Congress Cataloging in Publication Data
Aeschines.
[Against Timarchos. English]
Against Timarchos / Aeschines ; introduction, translation,
and commentary by Nick Fisher.
p. cm. — (Clarendon ancient history series)
Includes bibliographical references.
ISBN 0-19-924156-2
1. Speeches, addresses, etc., Greek—Translations into English.
I. Fisher, N. R. E. (Nicholas Ralph Edmund) II. Title. III. Series.
PA3823 .A27 2001
885'.01—dc21   00-066915

ISBN 0-19-814902-6
ISBN 0-19-924156-2 (Pbk.)

1 3 5 7 9 10 8 6 4 2

Typeset by Regent Typesetting, London
Printed in Great Britain
by T. J. International
Padstow, Cornwall

PREFACE

Aeschines' speech against Timarchos, the published version of his prosecution speech in the trial of 346/5 BC, is an extremely important text from a climactic period of Athens' political history, the time when the city had agreed to make peace with Philip II of Macedon, and was immediately deeply divided over the wisdom of the peace and the motives of those who had argued most vigorously for it. Aeschines, who was facing a major trial for his part on the embassy, brought charges against his leading prosecutor, Timarchos, which included the allegations that in his younger days he had permitted acts of disgraceful sex to be performed on his body by a succession of men for material rewards.

The history of the treatment of this speech by classical scholars seems to have been determined above all by its high sexual content (albeit purposely inexplicit and tantalizing); also influential has probably been the view, prevalent alike in ancient and modern times, that Demosthenes, his great rival, was both a better orator and a nobler and braver defender of Athenian freedom.

Until the last thirty or forty years, the story of this speech is one of remarkable neglect. Some Greek texts of Aeschines have been produced (though there has been as yet no Oxford text); only one English translation has been available (the Loeb by Charles Adams), though Christopher Carey has just produced one in the new series of translations edited by Michael Gagarin. Most striking is the fact that there has been no commentary, with or without the Greek text, on this speech in any language (and as yet too no detailed modern commentary on either of his other two speeches). Until the 1960s, those who had to comment on the trial and Aeschines' arguments against Timarchos commonly resorted to vague or euphemistic allusions, rather than engage in the details and reliability of the accusations: the tendency was either to condemn Aeschines out of hand for gross muckracking, or (as e.g. in the 1872 Paris thesis of Ferdinand de Castets on *Éschine l'Orateur*) to assume the truth of the allegations through a patent disinclination to examine them closely.

Since the 1960s the 'sexual revolution' and the development of feminism, gender studies, and theories of sexuality, have inevitably produced massive interest in Greek sexual norms and behaviour and gender relations, and a preparedness to discuss all these matters with welcome and complete openness. No one has contributed more to this, and no one has done more to bring out the importance of Aeschines' speech against Timarchos for our understanding of Greek sexuality and its connections with Greek politics, than Sir Kenneth Dover: much of his *Greek Homosexuality* (1978) constitutes a partial, yet extremely acute and sensible, commentary on those aspects of the speech. Since then the many books and articles which have engaged in the many heated debates on Athenian laws and attitudes to homosexuality have given deserved prominence to the interpretation of passages from this single text: one might mention in particular books by Michel Foucault, Jack Winkler, David Halperin, David Cohen, and James Davidson (see the survey of the issues in sections 6–7 of the introduction). But a detailed historical commentary on the whole of the speech still has much to offer to a proper assessment of its major importance for these and many other issues in fourth-century Athenian political, social, and cultural life; there is much too to be said about the rhetorical strategy of the speech and the reasons for the success of the prosecution.

Some of the ideas explored here, especially in the introduction, have been presented to audiences in Oxford, Cambridge, Manchester, Lampeter, Princeton, New York City, and at the 1998 APA Meeting at Washington; I am grateful to all those present for many helpful comments. My colleagues in the Department in Cardiff have offered me constant support and good humour, and permitted me a period of leave in 1998. For more detailed assistance and encouragement, for reading drafts of the introduction, and/or for sharing new work with me, I am especially indebted to Paul Cartledge, John Davies, James Davidson, my daughter Kate Fisher, Mark Golden, Clifford Hindley, Stephen Lambert, Sian Lewis, Lloyd Llewellyn-Jones, Lene Rubinstein, Emma Stafford, Victoria Wohl, and Hans van Wees. My greatest academic debt is to David Whitehead, one of the editors of the Clarendon series: for long he showed exemplary patience towards a tardy author, and he returned my lacunose and error-strewn draft with remarkable alacrity and with a generous wealth of valuable suggestions at all levels for its improvement, all of which, gratefully, I have tried to adopt. None of the above is in any way responsible for the weaknesses which remain. Finally my deepest debt, as always, is to Sarah Fisher, my wife, and our children Kate, Matthew, and Rebecca, for their constant love and support and their tolerance of the disruption *Timarchos* has brought to our family life.

CONTENTS

ABBREVIATIONS

Throughout the Introduction and Commentary, references to sections in the speech *Against Timarchos* are given in bold. References to secondary literature in the Introduction and in the Commentary (when cited more than once) are given by the surname of the author and date of publication, and full details are provided in the Bibliography. Works cited only once in the Commentary are usually given a full reference in that place. Journal titles mostly follow the conventions of *L'Année philologique*. The following abbreviations include those for standard commentaries on Greek texts, collections of fragments and standard works of reference, as well as those for classical texts and journals.

Ael. *V.H.*	Aelian, *Varia Historia*
Aesch.	Aeschines
AHB	*Ancient History Bulletin*
AJAH	*American Journal of Ancient History*
AJA	*American Journal of Archaeology*
AJP	*American Journal of Philology*
And.	Andocides
Apuleius, *Apol.*	Apuleius, *Apology*
Ar.	Aristophanes
Ach.	*Acharnians*
Eccl.	*Ecclesiazusae*
Kn.	*Knights*
Lys.	*Lysistrata*
Thesm.	*Thesmophoriazusae*
Arch. Delt.	*Archaiologikon Deltion*
Arist.	Aristotle
Ath. Pol.	*Athenaion Politeia* = Constitution of the Athenians
Hist. Anim.	*History of Animals*
Pol.	*Politics*
Rhet.	*Rhetoric*
Arnott, *Alexis*	*Alexis: the Fragments: A Commentary*, by W. G. Arnott. Cambridge, 1996

Ath. Mitt.	*Mitteilungen des deutschen Archäologischen Instituts: Athenische Abteilung*
Athen.	Athenaeus
Aul. Gell.	Aulus Gellius
BCH	*Bulletin de correspondance hellénique*
BICS	*Bulletin of the Institute of Classical Studies*
C&M	*Classical et medievalia*
CAH²	*Cambridge Ancient History.* 2nd edn. Cambridge, 1990–
Callim.	Callimachus
fr.	fragments
Carey, *Lysias*	Lysias, *Selected Speeches*, ed. C. Carey. Cambridge, 1989
Carey, *Neaira*	Apollodoros, *Against Neaira* [*Demosthenes 59*] translated with an Introduction and Commentary by C. Carey. Warminster, 1992
Carey & Reid	*Demosthenes: Selected Private Speeches*, ed. C. Carey and R. A. Reid. Cambridge, 1985
Cicero, *de opt. gen. orat.*	Cicero, *de optimo genere oratorum* = *on the best type of orator*
Phil.	*Philippics*
CP	*Classical Philology*
CQ	*Classical Quarterly*
Davies, *APF*	*Athenian Propertied Families.* Oxford, 1971
Dein.	Deinarchus
Dem.	Demosthenes
Develin, *AO*	*Athenian Officials 684–321BC*, by R. Develin. Cambridge, 1989
DHA	*Dialogues d'histoire ancienne*
Diod. Sic.	Diodorus Siculus
Diog. Laert.	Diogenes Laertius
Dion. Hal.	Dionysius Halicarnassius
Dein.	*Deinarchus*
Dem.	*Demosthenes*
Dunbar, *Birds*	*Aristophanes' Birds*, ed. Nan Dunbar. Oxford, 1995

Etym. Magn.	*Etymologicum Magnum*
Eur.	Euripides
Alc.	*Alcestis*
Her.	*Herakles*
Or.	*Orestes*
Phoen.	*Phoenician Women*
Suppl.	*Suppliant Women*
Eusebius, *Hist.*	Eusebius, *Histories*
FGH	*Die Fragmente der griechishen Historiker*, ed. F. Jacoby. Berlin, 1926–30, Leiden, 1940–
Fornara	C. Fornara (ed.), *Archaic Times to the End of the Peloponnesian War. Translated Documents of Greece & Rome 2.* 2nd edn. Cambridge, 1983
G&R	*Greece and Rome*
Gauthier	*Un commentaire historique des Poroi de Xénophon*, by P. Gauthier. Geneva, 1976
GRBS	*Greek, Roman, and Byzantine Studies*
Hansen, *Inventory*	'Updated Inventory of *Rhetores* and *Strategoi* (1988)', in M. H. Hansen, *The Athenian Ecclesia II: A Collection of Articles 1983–1989.* Copenhagen, 1989, 32–72
Harding, *Androtion*	*Androtion and the Attis: The Fragments Translated with an Introduction and Commentary*, by P. Harding. Oxford, 1994
Harding	P. Harding (ed.), *From the End of the Peloponnesian War to the Battle of Ipsus: Translated Documents of Greece & Rome 2.* Cambridge, 1985
Harpok.	Harpokration
HCT	*A Historical Commentary on Thucydides*, by A.W. Gomme, A. Andrewes, and K. J. Dover, 5 vols. Oxford, 1945–81
Hdt.	Herodotus
Hornblower	*A Commentary on Thucydides*, by S. Hornblower. Oxford, 1991

HSCP	Harvard Studies in Classical Philology
Hyper.	Hypereides
Athen.	Against Athenogenes
Eux.	For Euxenippos
fr.	fragments
Fun. Sp.	Funeral Speech
Lyk.	For Lykophron
IG I³	Inscriptiones Graecae. I. 1 and I. 2. 3rd edn. 2 vols. Berlin, 1981–84
IG II²	Inscriptiones Graecae. II–III 2nd edn. 5 vols. Berlin, 1913–40
Isocr.	Isocrates
Antid.	Antidosis
Areop.	Areopagitikos
Panath.	Panathenaikos
JDAI	Jahrbuch des Deutschen Archäologischen Instituts
JHS	Journal of Hellenic Studies
K/A	Poetae Comici Graeci, ed. R. Kassel and C. Austin. Berlin, 1993–
Kapparis, Neaira	Apollodoros, Against Neaira. A Commentary by K. Kapparis. Berlin, 1999
LEC	Les Études classiques
LIMC	Lexicon Iconographicon Mythologiae Classicae. Zurich and Munich, 1981–
LGPN	Lexicon of Greek Personal Names, vol II, by M. J. Osborne and S. G. Byrne. Oxford, 1994
LSJ⁹	A Greek-English Lexicon, by H. G. Liddell and R. Scott, 9th edn. revised by H. S. Jones. Oxford, 1940
Lyc.	Lycurgus
Lys.	Lysias
MacDowell, Meidias	Demosthenes, Against Meidias, ed. D. M. MacDowell. Oxford, 1990
ML	Greek Historical Inscriptions to the End of the Fifth Century B.C., ed. R. Meiggs and D. M. Lewis. 2nd edn. Oxford, 1988

Nauck[2] — *Tragicorum Graecorum Fragmenta*, ed. A. Nauck. 2nd edn. Leipzig, 1926

OGIS — *Orientis Graeci Inscriptiones Selectae*, ed. W. Dittenberger. 3 vols. Hidesheim, 1903

PA — *Prosopographia Attika*, ed. J. Kirchner. 2. vols. 2nd edn. Berlin, 1901–3

PAA — *Persons of Ancient Athens*, ed. J. S. Traill. Toronto, 1994–

Paus. — Pausanias

PCPS — *Proceedings of the Cambridge Philological Society*

Pindar *Ol.* — Pindar, *Olympians*

Nem. — *Nemeans*

Pliny, *NH* — Pliny, *Natural History*

Plat. — Plato

Phaidr. — *Phaidros*

Phd. — *Phaido*

Theait. — *Theaitetus*

Plaut. *Trin.* — Plautus, *Trinummus*

Plut. — Plutarch

Alex. — *Alexander*

Alk. — *Alkibiades*

Arist. — *Aristeides*

Dem. — *Demosthenes*

Lyc. — *Lycurgus*

Nik. — *Nikias*

Per. — *Perikles*

Phok. — *Phokion*

Sol. — *Solon*

Ps. Andoc. — Pseudo-Andocides

Ps. Arist. — Pseudo-Aristotle, *Problems*

Ps. Dem. — Pseudo-Demosthenes

Ps. Dio Chrysostom, *Orat.* — Pseudo-Dio Chrysostom, *Orations*

Ps. Plut. *Mor* — Pseudo-Plutarch, *Moralia*

Ps. Xen. *Ath. Pol.* — Pseudo-Xenophon, *Athenian Politieia* = *Constitution of the Athenians*

RE — *Real-Encyclopaedia der Classischen Altertumswissenschaft*, ed. G. Pauly and R. Wissowa. Stuttgart, 1894–

REG	*Revue des études grecques*
RFIC	*Rivista di Filologia e Istruzione Classica*
Rhodes	*A Commentary on the Aristotelian Athenaion Politeia*, by P. J. Rhodes. Oxford, 1981
RIDA	*Revue internationale des droits de l'antiquité*
RM	*Rheinische Museum*
Schol. Aesch.	*Scholia to Aeschines*
SEG	*Supplementum Epigraphicum Graecum.* Leiden, 1923–
TAPA	*Transactions of the American Philological Association*
TrGF	*Tragicorum Graecorum Fragmenta*, ed. B. Snell, R. Kannicht, and S. Radt. Göttingen, 1981–85
Theocr.	Theocritus
Theophr. *Char.*	Theophrastus, *Characters*
Tod II	*Greek Historical Inscriptions*, ed. M. N. Tod. vol. II. 2nd edn. Oxford, 1947
Virg. *Georg.*	Virgil, *Georgics*
Wankel	*Demosthenes: Rede für Ktesiphon über den Kranz*, by H. Wankel. Heidelberg, 1976
Worthington	*A Historical Commentary on Dinarchus*, by I. Worthington. Michigan, 1992
Xen.	Xenophon
Hell.	*Hellenica*
Lak. Pol.	*Lakedaimonion Politeia* = *Constitution of the Spartans*
Mem.	*Memorabilia* = *Memoirs of Sokrates*
Oik.	*Oikonomikos*
Poroi	*Poroi* = *Revenues*
ZPE	*Zeitschrift für Papyrologie und Epigraphik*

INTRODUCTION

The varieties and pressures of human sexual desire have always caused major problems for governments and voters, especially in those societies which put high ideological value on stable family structures and the production of legitimate children, who should inherit their fathers' properties and take their place as members of the community. States often attempt to regulate sexual relations, usually justifying this by appeal to what is believed to be 'human nature', required by god(s) or by the 'universal laws' of all societies. Yet the history of societies demonstrates tremendous variations between what, in these areas, is thought of as natural, honourable, or in accordance with divine law, and what is not; while within individual societies, different people hold different views and have different tastes. Further, societies are often full of contradictions and undergo radical change (as has been especially evident in Western societies in the last hundred years). The frequency, origins, and moral worth of homosexual desire and behaviour have been especially problematic and contentious for many societies; but their approaches have been remarkably various. The complex patterns of approval of, tolerance for, and hostility to differing types of same-sex relationships and sexual practices found in Greece, so markedly different from Christian and contemporary post-Christian societies, continue to attract interest and controversy.

It is further noticeable (and seems to have been especially notable in Western Europe and North America in the last forty years or so) that a good many leaders of democratic societies have themselves displayed a particular tendency to break the very rules governing sexual behaviour and financial regulations which they have a major part in introducing or implementing. It may be that those driven by the craving for glory and the excitement and risks of political life are not only subject to greater temptations of wealth and power, but are also impelled by excessive energy in their private lives and subject to curious cravings to take extra risks. Since they are usually supposed to lead by example, and often tempted into proclamations of the need for morality and social control, their own lapses provoke outrage and cries of hypocrisy or treachery. Our recent experience of complex political and sexual allegations and scandals has shown how revealing they can be of a society's political preoccupations, its anxieties about human sexuality, and its consciousness of changing perceptions and values.

Fourth-century democratic Athens had its equally revealing scandals. The trial of Timarchos in 346/5[1] on the charge of unsuitability for public life because of his shameful past is perhaps the most spectacular example. Aeschines' prosecution speech has more to tell us than any other single source about Athenian laws and attitudes to homosexual behaviour and relations, and about Greek understanding of the 'construction' of human sexuality and their peculiar sets of moral norms and anxieties; it can also help us to understand the nature of the general political, cultural, and moral crisis perceived in Athens in the 340s and 330s, which was faced with a real challenge from Philip II of Macedon to its political freedom and to its cultural hegemony in Greece.

The Trial and the Characters

1. THE POLITICAL BACKGROUND OF TIMARCHOS' TRIAL

This trial arose directly from the intense political disagreements and personal rivalries between some of the ten prominent Athenians who had served on a crucial embassy to Macedon. In the spring of 346 the Athenians had reluctantly agreed to negotiate peace and an alliance with Philip II of Macedon, as his gains in Thessaly and elsewhere, and the last stages of the Sacred War, were bringing him ever more clearly into a position of power, influence, and authority in central Greece.[2] The making of

---

[1] All three-figure dates are BC unless otherwise indicated. Dates of this double form (346/5) reflect the facts that the Athenian official year ran from midsummer to midsummer, and the name of the main or 'eponymous' archon at Athens was the standard way of indicating year-dates inside Athens, and frequently used by contemporary and later historians and chronographers.

[2] Treatment here of the complex political and military issues between Athens and Philip will necessarily be brief and sketchy. For good recent accounts of these complex events from Philip's perspective, see Ellis (1976), Hammond and Griffith (1979), and Cawkwell (1978); on the Sacred War, Buckler (1989); from Aeschines' perspective, E. M. Harris (1995); from Demosthenes', Sealey (1993); on the relations and motives of the individual politicians, and the issue of 'bribery', also Mitchell (1997); a good collection of articles is Perlman (1973) (ed.).

the Peace of Philokrates involved an immensely confusing and complicated set of negotiations and changes of positions, and the ten Athenian envoys were throughout embroiled in mutual suspicions, hostilities, and recriminations. In no time at all the disagreements produced major political trials before the Athenian popular law courts. Our primary sources are the various lawcourt speeches involved, primarily this prosecution of Timarchos by Aeschines, the prosecution of Aeschines for misconduct on the Embassy by Demosthenes in 343 and his defence (Demosthenes 19 and Aeschines 2), and the prosecution in 330 by Aeschines of Ktesiphon for his proposal to honour Demosthenes with a 'crown', which is in effect an attack on Demosthenes' whole career, and his reply (Aeschines 3 and Demosthenes 18). Our texts, the published versions of what each said in court in 343 and 330, which they themselves subsequently circulated for their contemporaries and for posterity to read,[3] are naturally full of lies, evasions, and misrepresentations on both sides: as a result, we, like no doubt very many ordinary Athenian citizens, have very little chance of penetrating these radically conflicting accounts to achieve a clear view of the course of events, the negotiating positions adopted, and the motives of the chief characters.

After the Peace of Philokrates was approved by the Athenian assembly, the same ten envoys who had negotiated the peace went again to Pella to see it sworn and ratified. Delays in making contact with Philip (May–July 346) were exacerbated by fresh divisions between the envoys. Some, especially Philokrates of Hagnous[4] and Aeschines of Kothokidai,[5] spread hopes that Philip would effect a settlement of the Sacred War that would spare the Phokians and be unfavourable to the Thebans. Others, including Demosthenes,[6] doubted Philip's intentions and feared the consequences of establishing a group of anti-Theban states in Boeotia dependent on Philip. When the envoys returned, an atmosphere of mutual hostility and fear existed, and those more sceptical of Philip's good will towards Athens, led by Demosthenes, lost no time in attacking the over-optimism of those who were fostering hopes of a settlement of the war favourable to Athens' interests.

---

[3] On the issue of widespread revision of speeches for later circulation, see e.g. Dover (1968: 167–9), Worthington, 36–9.

[4] *LGPN* 76; *PA* 14576 + 14599; Hansen, *Inventory* 62.

[5] *LGPN* 54; *PA* 354; *PAA* 115030; Hansen, *Inventory* 34–5.

[6] *LGPN* 37; *PA* 3597; *PAA* 318625; Hansen, *Inventory* 41–3.

Some such allegations against Philocrates and Aeschines were probably made by Demosthenes at a meeting of the *Boule* (Council of 500) (Dem. 19. 17–19). The assembly on 16th Skirophorion 346 (early July) which received the reports of the envoys, refrained from voting them the honours and thanks usual in such circumstances, perhaps because they could see major disagreements between them, and expected further trouble when they each, as individuals, presented their accounts (Dem. 19. 31–2). They also passed a motion extending the alliance with Philip, and sought to assist a settlement of the war by proposing that the Phokians give up control of the sanctuary at Delphi to the Amphiktyons (which Demosthenes, 19. 48–51, represents, unfairly, as a complete surrender of the Phokians to Philip).[7] It was also agreed to send a third embassy to Philip, on which Demosthenes refused to serve. Aeschines initially declined to go, claiming illness (faked, according to his enemies), and so was enabled to watch Demosthenes' movements; his brother Aphobetos, who testified to his illness, was chosen to go instead.[8]

As the third embassy was preparing to leave, and some sort of settlement of the Sacred War was clearly imminent, the quarrelling between the ambassadors intensified, and the first legal move was made. Demosthenes and a friend and supporter, Timarchos, who was on the Council that year, launched a little later in July 346, at the presentation of the envoys for their accounting (*euthyna*), a prosecution against Aeschines for misconduct on the embassy (*parapresbeia*).[9] The central allegation was that he had taken bribes from Philip to betray Athens' interests, when he claimed that Philip had given him undertakings that he would settle the war without either destroying the Phokians or giving further power to Thebes. Aeschines' opponents alleged that all the time he was aware of Philip's contrary intentions (Dem. 19. esp. 257–8; *first hypoth. to Aesch.*, 2). It seems clear that he and other envoys had accepted varied gifts of hospitality in gold from Philip (Demosthenes had ostentatiously suggested using the money to ransom Athenian prisoners). It was alleged later that Aeschines had received a grant of land at Pydna, a city on the

---

[7] Cf. Cawkwell (1962); E. M. Harris (1995: 89–91).

[8] Dem. 19. 121–30; Aesch. 2. 94–6, with Cawkwell (1962); E. M. Harris (1995: 167–8).

[9] On the date, *scholia* on Aesch. 1. 169, Ellis (1976: 270–1). On the details of the *euthuna* procedure and the complaint against Aeschines, Piérart (1971: 560–4).

Macedonian coast between Methone and Dion.[10] It was further alleged that this estate brought Aeschines an income of 3000 drachmai a year (Dem. 19. 166–8, 145, and cf. 314; *scholia* to Aesch. 1. 3).[11] The issue then became whether Aeschines accepted generous 'gifts' in the conscious knowledge that he was damaging Athens' interests by serving Philip's, in which case the gifts could be classified as 'bribes', and treasonable, or whether, as most scholars now tend to believe, he was genuinely deceived by Philip's subtle manipulations.[12] When the case eventually came to court in 343, the Athenian jury narrowly decided that Aeschines had not colluded for gain; he was acquitted by only thirty votes (*second hypoth. to Aesch.*, 2; Plut. *Dem.* 15; Ps. Plut. *Mor.* 840c).

Aeschines' first, and as it turned out successful, response was to bring an anticipatory retaliation against Timarchos. The precise move he chose may well have come as something of a shock to his opponents. It was a very common practice, and a clear indication of the personal nature of Athenian politics, that those engaged in intense political conflict in assembly or courts would seek to damage their opponents by prosecuting them (or arranging for friends or political allies to prosecute them) on what might be regarded as allegations of personal or private offences.[13] What was less usual about Aeschines' attack was that the charge, and most of the allegations, concerned activities alleged to have taken place some decades earlier, when Timarchos was still a young man.

The process started with a proclamation (*epangelia*: see **32, 81**), brought right at the end of Skirophorion, the last month in the Attic year 347/6, that Timarchos was not fit to be an active citizen, e.g. by holding public office, speaking in the assembly, or

[10] Originally a Greek colony, under Macedonian control at least from the time of Archelaos, Pydna was among the places seized by Timotheos, perhaps in 360/59, and reannexed by Philip *c.* 356, with the help of some internal support, and, perhaps, by using a supposed secret 'deal' with the Athenian *boule* to allow him Pydna if he returned Amphipolis. See Dein. 1. 4; Dem. 20. 63; Diod. 16. 8, 2. 6–7; Theopompos, *FGH* 115F30; and Hammond and Griffith (1979: 230–1). That the estate was at a place about whose loss to Philip still produced resentment at Athens might make the gift yet more offensive.

[11] Cf. Davies, *APF* 547, who is inclined to accept some at least of these and later allegations of corruption, E. M. Harris (1995: 85–6, 189), who is inclined to dismiss them all as unsubstantiated Demosthenic allegations; and Hammond and Griffith (1979: 337) and Mitchell (1997: 183), who point out that the gift of the land is at least a detailed charge.

[12] Cf. E. M. Harris (1995: 95–6), Hammond and Griffith (1979: 337), and Mitchell (1997: 154–7, 181–6) above all on the issues of gifts and 'friendship' between the King and Greek politicians.

[13] The point is made by Aeschines himself, **1**, and notes.

bringing court actions, because he had previously 'lived disgrace-fully' (**28**). The consequence was a jury trial. The whole process is called by Aeschines (**186**) the 'scrutiny of orators' (*dokimasia ton rhetoron*).[14] The four grounds of disgraceful living listed by Aeschines (**28–32**) are a) maltreating parents, b) military evasion or cowardice, c) having been a prostitute (*pornos*) or having lived off men as an 'escort' (*hetairesis*), and d) having devoured one's inherited estate. As Demosthenes was to say later (19. 286) and no doubt did say at the trial itself, Timarchos had been an active politician for some time, and no one had up to this point prosecuted him for his unfitness to appear as a speaker before the assembly and as a prosecutor in the courts. Aeschines took this course now, primarily on the twin grounds that Timarchos had 'prostituted himself' when younger and had dissipated his property. Of these two charges, the first occupies more attention in the speech, and has aroused the greatest debate in recent years (see sections 7 and 8 below, and on **37–117**), but the importance of the second should not be underestimated. The jury convicted Timarchos, and thus imposed permanent and total disenfran-chisement (*atimia*, literally dishonour) on him.[15] This result may well have been something of a surprise, especially to Timarchos and his supporters (see section 8 below).

2. THE DATE OF THE TRIAL

It is certain that the trial took place some time in the Attic year 346/5, between late summer 346 and spring 345. The precise date depends on the interpretation of certain allusions in the speech.

Aeschines' main aim would have been to ensure that the trial of Timarchos took place before his own for misconduct on the embassy; but as that did not in fact reach court until three years later in 343, it does not follow that Aeschines must have sought to bring the trial on as soon as possible. Harris argued that to be on the safe side, he would have done just that, and the trial should

---

[14] On the accuracy of Aeschines' citation of the crucial law, see on **28**.

[15] On the penalty of total *atimia*, which includes permanent inability to participate in politics or the ritual life of the city, indeed to appear in public places such as the *agora*, or in court, cf. Aesch. **134**, 3. 176; Dem. 19. 257, 284; Hansen (1989b: 267); S. C. Todd (1993: 365), and Allen (2000: 202–5, 230–2) on this punishment as the imposition of public silence and deprivation of male honour. For the possibility that such *atimia* might be rescinded, see also below, p. 23.

probably be placed in the latter part of 346 rather than early in 345;[16] but Aeschines might have delayed a little, or been frustrated by his opponent. In ways which are not entirely clear, both parties to a legal action might hold matters up; one means was by requesting an adjournment, on grounds of illness or absence from Attica, which the other might or might not oppose. If a case were delayed, it may have been up to the other litigant to attempt to reinstate the case.[17] Of course, in important political trials such as these, each side would seek to bring it on at the best time for them, as new events might affect their personal standings or the popularity of their policies. Hence delays were frequent. In the case of the Embassy trial, Demosthenes suggests (19. 107, 257) that Aeschines was responsible for long delays, in the wish to choose the best time to undergo his scrutiny; the Crown case was delayed for six years until 330, presumably until Aeschines felt the moment had arrived when he might get a retrospective condemnation, in effect, of Demosthenes' whole career.

There are two places in the speech where Aeschines refers to events that took place 'the other day' (*proen*). One, Demosthenes' report to the Council (**168**), took place on 13th Skirophorion 346 (= early July). The other is a reference to a comedy performed at the Rural Dionysia in the deme of Kollytos, where there was a topical joke at the expense of 'big Timarchian whores'; this could in theory be either the rural Dionysia of the previous year, winter 347/6, or the current year, winter 346/5. E. M. Harris (1985) argues it could easily be the earlier year, and the date of the trial still no later than late autumn 346; but the older view in favour of the later year, restated by Wankel (1988), also has some force. One point is that a joke at a rural comedy is more likely to fade between December/January 347/6 and late summer/autumn 346 than is a statement made by Demosthenes at a highly charged meeting of the Council over a period of about six months or so (July 346 to early 345); but one could argue against that if such a reference and audience reaction had occurred, Aeschines would be very keen to use it, and describe it as 'recent'. Another argument is that a comic reference which could be taken to re-open memories of Timarchos' alleged early career is more likely to have taken place while the trial was known to be pending than before Aeschines had reactivated (or even created) awareness of

---

[16] E. M. Harris (1985: 378–80).   [17] Cf. Harrison (1968–71: II, 154–6).

his nickname as 'the prostitute' and his youthful excesses (see section 8 below). If that is right, it increases the possibility, at least, that Aeschines' portrait of these excesses was not necessarily based on widespread and current gossip. A stronger point is perhaps that in **77–8** Aeschines refers to the recent sequence of deme-investigations and court trials which had been provoked by Demophilos' measure commanding all demes formally to review their citizen-lists (the *diapsephisis*). This took place during the archon year 346/5 (Dem. 57; Isaeus 12), and is likely to have lasted a matter of some months, yet Aeschines (**77–8**, **114–15**) speaks of the whole process as essentially complete.[18]

The issue remains open. The balance of argument perhaps slightly favours dating the trial early in 345; on the other hand it cannot be pushed any later. It must have taken place before the affair of Antiphon, and the rejection by the Areopagos of Aeschines as an Amphiktionic ambassador to plead their case on the Delian temple dispute (Dem. 18. 132; Dein. 1. 63; Plut. *Dem.* 14; Dem. 18. 134–6);[19] otherwise Aeschines is unlikely to have been so consistently fulsome in his praise of the Areopagos' decisions (1. 81–5).

3. AESCHINES' CAREER TO 345 BC

Aeschines' father, Atrometos,[20] a member of the small deme Kothokidai (north of Eleusis, in the foothills of Mt Parnes), left his three sons little in the way of wealth or distinction of birth. All Aeschines can say on the question of birth is that his father 'was by birth a member of the phratry which shares use of the same altars as the Eteoboutadai, from which comes the priestess of Athena Polias' (2. 147); this implies no special distinction in itself, but rather that his family were 'ordinary' members of a phratry which was ancestrally linked to the ancient *genos* of the Eteoboutadai:[21] Atrometos, who was born *c.* 436 (2. 147), and died when he was

---

[18] Wankel (1988); Harris' response (1995: 202, n. 52) focuses on the swift initial decisions taken in each deme (one or two days, cf. Dem. 58), and argues that the process of appeals would not need to wait until all the demes had met; but even so a large number of appeals could well have taken months rather than Harris' 'several weeks' to work through the courts.

[19] Cf. Ellis (1976: 131–2), E. M. Harris (1995: 121, 169–71).

[20] *LGPN* no. 3; *PA* 2681; *PAA* 225105.

[21] Davies, *APF* 544 f.; Bourriot (1978: 1057–60); Lambert (1993: 55).

ninety-five *c.* 342/1, had been, his son alleges, an exemplary fighter in the cause of the democracy. The language used of these prewar activities is revealing. 'It befell him when he was young . . . to train with his body'; 'he showed manly excellence (*aristeuein*) in the dangers' (2. 147), and especially 'My father, whom you (sc. Demosthenes) slander, though you don't know him, nor saw him during his prime of life (*helikia*), what quality of man he was' (2. 77): all this suggests that he is presented as not only a fit and brave soldier, but also a notable athlete, famed for his physical skills and probably also his youthful beauty. Aeschines further claims that his father lost his property during the war, and was exiled, along with several hundreds of other Athenians, when the Thirty Tyrants were in power in Athens (2. 77, 147). Going first to Corinth, accompanied by his wife, he then distinguished himself as a mercenary soldier in Asia, before returning to Athens in time to help in the restoration of the democracy (2. 78, 147, cf. 3. 191–2).[22]

His wife came from a rather more distinguished and wealthier family. The career of her brother, Aeschines' uncle, Kleoboulos,[23] is recorded on his gravestone, as well as gaining a mention in Aesch. 2. 78; he earned renown both as a participant, apparently as general, in a sea-battle, probably late in the Corinthian War, and as a public seer (2. 78; *SEG* XVI 193).[24]

Atrometos then apparently worked as a schoolteacher, an employment poor in pay and status in Athens, though Demosthenes exaggerated its ignominy grossly and with increasing wildness, first in the Embassy speech (19. 249), and later in the Crown speech, where Atrometos has been transformed into a slave called Tromes (8. 129). His wife's name is given by Demosthenes as Glaukothea,[25] and she was the daughter of one Glaukos of Acharnai.[26] She becomes the subject of increasingly ludicrous allegations in Demosthenes' rhetoric: that she performed

---

[22] On such exiles, Strauss (1991: I, 61–71). There are grounds for doubting this story (Schaefer 1985–7: I², 194; E. M. Harris 1995: 22–3), especially that the rule of the Thirty was too brief to allow for an extended spell of mercenary service in Asia, and opportunities for such service are attested from 403 onwards; it is at least possible he was exiled by the Thirty, returned to play a (minor) role in the democratic restoration, and went off again rather for economic reasons (cf. Davies, *APF* 544–5).

[23] *LGPN* no. 3; *PA* 8558; Hansen, *Inventory* 52

[24] Cf. Daux (1958: 364–6); Bourriot (1978: 1373–5); Bourriot (1995: 436–7).

[25] *LGPN* no. 1; *PAA* 275915.

[26] *LGPN* no. 19; *PA* 2996; *PAA* 276200.

mystery initiation rituals into religious *thiasoi* (19. 199–200, 249, 281) in the later speech identified as those of Sabazios (18. 258–60), and that she acted in effect as a prostitute (18. 129–31). Possibly some priesthood she may have held formed the origin of these slurs; there may also have been be a connection with her brother's activities as a seer.[27] Aeschines boasted in 330 that his father would often describe to his son political events of the city that he had lived through (3. 191–2).

Our trust in the breadth and reliability of Atrometos' oral history is not increased by the fact that, when he needed a brief account of the events between the Persian Wars and the amnesty, Aeschines lazily had recourse to the wildly inaccurate account perpetrated by Andocides, which bears clear traces of Andocides' own aristocratic family traditions (Andoc. 3. 3–9; Aesch. 2. 172–6).[28] It seems likely, however, that the father may have nourished in his sons two ambitions: to recoup the family's finances and to participate in public life. It was probably not by accident that their early jobs gave them skills and experience which served them well in their later political careers.

The years in which Aeschines and his two brothers Philochares[29] and Aphobetos[30] were born are disputed, and solution of the problem depends on the interpretation of various data in this speech. Aeschines claims (**49**) that he and Misgolas, allegedly one of Timarchos' lovers, are the same age and were ephebes together (see note there), whereas Timarchos, of course, is markedly younger than both, despite the fact that Aeschines, but not Misgolas, has grey hair and looks his age. The manuscripts at this point report Aeschines as saying that he and Misgolas were 'in their forty-fifth year'. If this is right, they would have been born *c.* 390. But at another point (**109**) Aeschines describes Timarchos' activities on the Council of 500 in the archon-year of Nikophemos (361/0), in which case, on the generally accepted view that Councillors had to be 30,[31]

[27] Schaefer (1885–87: I², 197–8); Parker (1996: 159); S. R. F. Price (1999: 116). That we may know her name (if Glaukothea is not an insulting nickname) is a result of Demosthenes' insults; Aeschines naturally adhered to the practice of not naming a respectable woman in a public utterance, but Demosthenes deliberately expresses his contempt by naming (or misnaming) her, as he does by giving Atrometos a slave-name. See Schaps (1977).   [28] Cf. Thomas (1989: 101, 119).

[29] *LGPN* 22; *PA* 14775; Hansen, *Inventory* 62.

[30] *LGPN* 1; *PA* 2775; *PAA* 242605; Hansen, *Inventory* 39.

[31] On which see, however, Develin (1985).

Timarchos must have been born by *c.* 391, and if Aeschines is telling the truth in **49**, the number 45 given by our manuscripts for his and Misgolas' ages must be corrupt. That view has been argued by Lewis (1958: 108), and accepted by Davies (*APF* 545–6); they suggest that Aeschines and Misgolas (and hence also Nausikles, Aeschines 2. 184) were born between six to ten years earlier, *c.* 399–6.[32]

The counter-argument has been well put by E. M. Harris (1988), who argues, rightly, that orators would tell quite shameless lies if they thought they could get away with them, and that it is indeed important to Aeschines' case that Misgolas was a few years older than Timarchos, and thus in a position to have been his lover (*erastes*) and to have 'kept' him in a homosexual relationship. He suggests that Aeschines was indeed lying, and that he, Misgolas, and Timarchos were in fact much the same age (*c.* 45 in 346); and hence that the other two did not form, at least, a normal homosexual pair of unequal ages (see section 7), and indeed could just as well have been merely 'good friends' all the time.[33] Further, to imply that Timarchos was about 40, or even younger, if he was in fact about 45, makes the alleged youthful offences closer in time to the trial and increases the sense of shame Aeschines is trying to foster at the apparently seedy nature of Timarchos' physical condition (**26**). Such a misrepresentation is perfectly possible, and comparable cases can be suggested.[34] Aeschines was taking a risk in thus understating Timarchos' age: he does himself provide the relevant information for Timarchos' age at 346/5, by reminding the jury of Timarchos' service in the Council in the archonship of Nikophemos. But this would only be damaging on the assumption that some jurors at least would remember the age-limit, how long ago Nikophemos was archon and the events recorded by

[32] Lewis and Davies make some use also of Apollonius' *Life of Aeschines.* 2.12 (Dilts), that Aeschines died at the age of 75 (in 322 BC); but this is too suspiciously round a number to be of any use (cf. Whitehead 1986b: 313–14, Worthington, 264).

[33] If this is correct, one might wonder why Aeschines did not choose to accept that the two were about the same age, and argue that this made their sexual relationship even more objectionable (as Golden 1984: 321 mistakenly claims he does argue). Presumably Aeschines thought this would not be so easily believed by the jury, nor did it fit the picture of Timarchos he is so carefully constructing.

[34] Cf. E. M. Harris (1988); uncertainty and disputes over people's ages is not unlikely, in the absence of documentary material such as birth certificates, and a tendency to judge ages by appearance rather than documentation (cf. the procedure of the Council in judging those allegedly of age by inspecting them naked (Ar. *Wasps* 578, Arist., *Ath. Pol.* 42. 1).

Aeschines in that year, and do the simple sum; or else that Timarchos would take time to point this out and be believed. The risk was worth taking. It would have been possible, and important, for Timarchos to assert, and provide witnesses to testify to his age relative to that of Misgolas; whether he did take time to try to do this we do not know. Harris points out that what seem to be easily falsifiable claims are made by Demosthenes against Aeschines, which he did in fact refute adequately, by having official state documents read out (Aesch. 2. 5, 62, 89–96, cf. 135, and 3. 24, 75); as Thomas has shown, Aeschines was highly unusual (see also below) in his use of state documents to prove precise chronological points. As a further argument for accepting Aeschines' birth date as *c.* 390, Harris points to Aeschines' failure to cite military service before *c.* 363, which might be odd if he came of age *c.* 378 (see below); Lane Fox (1994: 136–7) adds that Aeschines' claim that he and Demosthenes were the two youngest of the ten ambassadors (2. 25, 108) is more plausible if they were something like six years apart rather than ten to sixteen. On balance, it is best to accept the date for his birth suggested by our text of **49**, *c.* 390, and its implications for our understanding of the gross lies Aeschines and the other orators thought they could get away with, and often did (see now Robertson 2000).

Growing up in their father's school may well have given Aeschines and his brothers a broader grasp of the skills of literacy and a broader knowledge of literature than was normal for non-élite Athenians.[35] Both Aeschines and his younger brother Aphobetos first spent periods acting as clerks, and perhaps first as junior clerks, though that may be merely Demosthenes' exaggeration, who greatly relished taunting Aeschines with this ignoble and almost slavish profession.[36] As full clerks they received pay and their keep in the *tholos*, the round building where the standing committee (*prytaneis*) were fed and lived (Dem. 19. 249). This work, though again not of high status, had the great advantage of giving them valuable direct experience of the political system, and daily contacts with politicians.[37] In particular, it may well have alerted

[35] Cf. Aeschines' pride in his quotations from Homer, Solon, and so on, and his concern to claim a proper understanding of literary culture, Bourriot (1995: 437–8), Ford (1999).

[36] See Dem. 19. 70, 95, 98, 200, 237, 249, 314; 18. 127, 209, 261, and also Ps. Plut. *Mor.* 840a–b, Libanius, *Hyp. Dem.* 19, and Develin, *AO* p. 297. The nature of these posts is described at Arist. *Ath. Pol.* 54 (cf. Rhodes *ad loc.*, and Rhodes 1972: 139–41).

[37] The first of the ancient lives of Aeschines (3; not a reliable source in general) seems to

Aeschines to the rhetorical use of documents in the public records.[38] It seems clear that in fact Aeschines and his brothers had no formal higher education in rhetoric or philosophy, despite some ancient traditions placing him as a pupil of Isocrates, Plato, Leodamas, or whoever;[39] instead Aeschines and Aphobetos may have made useful contacts (e.g. with Euboulos or those in his circle) while serving as clerks.

Two of the brothers also enjoyed successful military careers.[40] Aeschines gives an account of his own military services to Athens, in response to a sneer of Demosthenes' in the Embassy speech (2. 167–70, cf. Dem. 19. 113—probably Demosthenes had expatiated more on this in the original speech). He claims that on coming of age he served as an ephebe among the frontier guards (*peripoloi*).[41] He next cites his participation in a Peloponnesian campaign defending the Phliasians against the Argives in 366.[42] Next he cites successive campaigns including the major one in Mantineia (362)

support this idea of useful contacts: 'being clear-voiced, he served as secretary to Aristophon and Euboulos, and gained experience by reading the decrees and laws he began to speak in public, and being well-favoured, he stood out from his contemporaries'. But it seems a little implausible that a *grammateus* would 'serve' specific politicians, and the reference to individual leaders is probably an inference from the sneer at Dem. 19. 162.

[38] Thomas (1989: 69–71), doubted by Lane Fox (1994: 140–1). But his examples where Demosthenes cites some laws and a decree—from a speech (24) attacking the terms of a specific law, where you would especially find detailed quotations—do not match up to Aeschines' use of earlier decrees to establish precise chronological points, nor does he explain away the allegations of grubbing among documents that Demosthenes levels at Aeschines (e.g. 18. 206–9).

[39] The scholia on 1. 4 observe against the connection with Plato that whereas Aeschines uses the standard tripartite division of constitutions, Plato used either two or five; in itself no argument, but the conclusion is right.

[40] On the treatment of this theme in Aeschines' speeches, Bourriot (1995: 438); Burckhardt (1996: 238–9).

[41] On the importance of ephebic patrols in Athenian defence of their territory in the early fourth century cf. Xen. *Poroi*, 4. 51–2 and Gauthier, 190–5; Ober (1985: 90–5); Munn (1993: 31–2, 188–9); Hunter (1994: 151–3); Sekunda (1992: 323–9); Burckhardt (1996: 32–3). Mitchel (1961: 357) and Sekunda (1992: 329) suggest accepting the manuscripts' *synarchontas* ('fellow-officers') in 2. 167 rather than Bekker's emendation *archontas*, and the consequence that Aeschines served, perhaps in a third year, as a commander (taxiarch) of the ephebic patrols; but one might have expected Aeschines to make a bit more of such an appointment.

[42] Aeschines cites as his commander a mercenary leader, Alkibiades, whereas Diodoros mentioned Chares as the commander; perhaps the reason for the variation is that Aeschines was currently critical of Chares (2. 71, cf. Dem. 8. 30). On the contribution of this passage to the solution of whether Xenophon, *Hell.*, 7. 2. 18–20 and Diodoros (15. 75) are referring to the same or different battles or skirmishes near Phlius, see W. E. Thompson (1983: 303–5), and Stylianou (1998), on Diod. 15. 75. 3. Aeschines seems clearly to be describing a victory over Argives.

and two in Euboia (357, 349/8: on which see **113** and notes). The eldest brother, Philochares, seems to have made his way up essentially through military service, initially under Iphikrates, to be three times general between 345 and 342 (2. 149). On the other hand, the youngest, Aphobetos, after his spell as a clerk, was appointed to a post in charge of finances (presumably under, and perhaps at the suggestion of, Euboulos), and then served in summer 346 as ambassador in Aeschines' place to Philip, and on an embassy to the King of Persia, some time before 343 (Aesch. 2. 94, 149).[43]

The next profession Aeschines adopted was that of actor. Our information about this comes largely from Demosthenes' attacks on him (and later elaborations based on them), and have equally to be treated with extreme caution. Demosthenes attacked Aeschines' thespian career ruthlessly,[44] and most extravagantly and recklessly in the later speech. In 343 he claimed that Aeschines always played the third-actor parts (*tritagonistes*), such as tyrants,[45] in troupes led by the actors Theodoros and Aristodemos (19. 247); and in 330 he argued that he acted with the so-called 'roarers' Simylos and Sokrates, earned more picking up the fruit thrown at the performance than by his fees for his 'all-out war with the audiences', and in particular 'murdered the part of Oinomaos' playing the Rural Dionysia at Kollytos (18. 261–2, 180). Further alleged details of this episode are to be found tacked on to the end of one of the *Lives* of Aeschines; here it is stated that 'Demochares, Demosthenes' nephew, if one should believe him when he is speaking about Aeschines, claims that Aeschines was the third actor for Ischandros the tragic poet, and that when playing Oinomaos, and pursuing Pelops, he had an ugly fall, and was picked up by Sannion the chorus-trainer' (*Life of Aeschines* 7: on Sannion, see Dem. 21. 58–9). If this story does go back to Demochares, it is, as the *Life* itself points out, a most doubtful source.[46] We do not have to believe anything more than that

[43] See Develin *AO*, pp. 351, 323, 350.

[44] See Stefanis (1988: no. 90), cf. O. J. Todd (1938), Pickard-Cambridge (1968: 132–5); Ghiron-Bistagne (1976: 158–9, 307).

[45] Demosthenes' rhetorical point here is to set up the argument that Aeschines would have been familiar with Kreon's speech in Sophocles' *Antigone*, in order to use Kreon's words against him: cf. Pickard-Cambridge (1968: 141, n. 2).

[46] Dorjahn (1929/30: 225); further, Ischandros is otherwise known as an actor and politician, not a tragedian, and elsewhere it is Sophocles' *Oinomaos* (Pickard-Cambridge (1968: 50, n. 5).

Aeschines acted for some time with the highly respected actors Theodoros and Aristodemos, probably each in charge of their own troupe, and *perhaps* that something amusing happened at that one production at the theatre in Kollytos (see on **157**). One should certainly doubt the story of a spectacular and decisive failure. Equally dubious is the more general view that failure to achieve success as an actor was the main reason he left the profession, as has been claimed by many scholars.[47]

On the contrary, it would be better to recognize that acting provided Aeschines with excellent opportunities to hone his rhetorical skills and make useful money and contacts, preparatory to an entry into Athenian politics. Successful acting would have offered valuable training for the memory, gesture, voice, and delivery, for which Demosthenes has to admit he became famous (Aesch. 2. 157; 3. 21, 228; Dem. 19. 199, 216, 285–7, 336–40; 18. 129, 285, 259–60, 308).[48] Equally, a number of famous actors, some of whom had performed with Aeschines, were beginning to play a notable part in public life, and the status of the profession, while remaining somewhat raffish for some (see Ps. Arist. *Probl.* 30. 10, 956b), was markedly on the increase. Aristodemos, with whom Aeschines had acted, was sent as an ambassador to sound out Philip's preparedness for peace (winter 347/6) 'because of his acquaintance with him, and the good will towards the craft' (2. 15); he was also one of the ten ambassadors on the later embassy to Philip (2. 52; *2nd Hyp. to Dem.* 19. 4).[49] Neoptolemos of Scyros, a major star who acquired great wealth, also played a prominent political role with Aristodemos, using his contacts with Philip to persuade the Athenians to listen to his offers (Dem. 5. 6–8; 19. 12; 18, 94, 315); Demosthenes argues that he did so treacherously, and ended up absconding with all his wealth to Philip's court.[50] Ischandros the Arkadian actor, described by Demosthenes as 'the

---

[47] E.g. O. J. Todd (1938: 36–7); some, perhaps insufficient, scepticism, in Pickard-Cambridge (1968: 135, 141); and see Easterling (1999: 156–8).

[48] Cf. Ghiron-Bistagne (1976: 158–9); Hall (1995: 46–9); and on the voice, Easterling (1999).

[49] According to Schol. Aesch. 2. 15, Aristodemos came from Metapontium in S. Italy, in which case he must have been given citizenship, to be an envoy, cf. Stefanis (1988: no. 332); M. J. Osborne (1981–3: II, 172); *PAA* 168590; Hansen, *Inventory* 37.

[50] Stefanis (1988: no. 1797). *LGPN* 1; *PA* 10647; Hansen, *Inventory* 62. Probably not a naturalized Athenian: M. J. Osborne (1981–3: III–IV, 124); Easterling (1997: 218–22; 1999: 161–3).

second actor (*deuteragonistes*) of Neoptolemos' (Dem. 19. 10),[51] spoke on Aeschines' invitation in Athens against Philip's intrigues in the Peloponnese, claiming to act on behalf of the Arkadians.

Thus famous actors were now, thanks to the repute of the classic Athenian dramas, able to make good year-round livings, performing not only in the city and rural festivals in Attica but also throughout the Greek world and at the courts of avidly phil-Hellenic rulers such as the Macedonian Kings.[52] They were rewarded with higher status and immunity from hostile action, and could if pressed use their presentational skills and contacts to plead the case of their city, or of their patrons. Whether Aeschines himself performed such a role before becoming a full-time politician is not attested, and doubtful; otherwise Demosthenes would probably have alleged illicit deals struck at that time with Philip, instead of concentrating his fire on Aeschines' third-actor, and third-rate, performances in the rural Dionysia. On the other hand, Aeschines' reluctance to allow any such thoughts to enter the jurors' minds may help to explain why he refrained totally from responding to these allegations. But he may well have made some initial contacts with politicians or courtiers while performing with his colleagues in or outside Attica, which increased his ambitions to enter full-time politics. He may also have made considerably more money out of his acting than Demosthenes allows.

Aeschines continued to serve in the hoplite army, and with distinction. He claims (2. 168–9) to have fought in both of the expeditions to Euboia (357 and 348), and in particular to have made a brave showing in the second campaign as a member of a picked corps of experienced soldiers (*epilektoi*).[53] He fought especially bravely in the battle of Tamynai, where he was crowned, and was also selected for the honour of reporting the

[51] The word *deuteragonistes* here must surely have some theatrical reference, even if only as an appropriate metaphor for two actors, against Pickard-Cambridge (1968: 133); it is easier to suppose that Demosthenes is reminding the jury (or alleging) that Ischandros had acted with Neoptolemos than claiming they were now acting politically together, given that Ischandros was seeking to arouse anti-Philip feelings, while Neoptolemos was about to plead Philip's cause; their political opposition may be part of Demosthenes' point. The phrase should not be read as 'Ischandros, son of Neoptolemos, supporter of Aeschines', as e.g. Cawkwell (1960: 418); Ghiron-Bistagne (1976: 185, 333); Stefanis (1988: no. 1303); *LGPN* 1, given their different origins as well as opposing political lines.
[52] Cf. on the significant spread of dramatic performances across the Greek world, Taplin (1993; 1999).   [53] On this campaign, also on **113** below.

victory back home, for which he received another crown (2. 168–9); it is also possible that his selection as a herald owed something to his actor's memory and voice, as well as to his heroics on the field.[54] He is likely to have formed contacts which would last with the leading general of the campaign, Phokion, and at the same, perhaps through him, with Euboulos. The decision to fight in Euboia, in preference to giving assistance to Olynthos, was a victory for the policy favoured by Euboulos over that of Demosthenes. Both Phokion and Euboulos spoke as advocates for Aeschines in the Embassy trial (2. 183).[55] It was very soon afterwards that Aeschines made his debut as a political speaker and ambassador, in 348, following Ischandros' appeal and supporting Euboulos' attempt at a major diplomatic initiative to create an anti-Philip coalition through the Peloponnese. Despite powerful speeches before the Arkadian assembly at Megalopolis, the initiative came to nothing (Dem. 19. 10–12, 302–6; Aesch. 2. 79).[56]

His fame as an actor and his good showing as a soldier may have brought him into contact with the family with which he made an extremely advantageous marriage; this could well also have eased his path into politics. He married a daughter of Philodemos of Paiania,[57] whose uncle Philokrates[58] appears on the obscure '*diadikasia* documents' of *c.* 380, which list pairs of men who exchange a position with each other and are probably men of the propertied classes, though the precise significance of the documents is disputed (*IG*² II 1929 line 18).[59] Demosthenes alleged (18. 312) that Aeschines' wife's brother Philon left five talents to Aeschines; while this is likely to be a considerable exaggeration, he must have been known to be much richer than Aeschines, and rich enough for this not to be completely ludicrous. Demosthenes (19. 287) makes a point of insulting Aeschines' two brothers-in-law, and attributing nasty nicknames to them, whereas Aeschines defends them (2. 150–2).[60] One of the brothers-in-law, evidently

[54] On the campaign, cf. Brunt (1969), Tritle (1988: 81–9); on these honours, Gauthier (1985: 120, n. 135) (though he seems to place the battle of Tamynai erroneously in the 357 campaign) and S. Lewis (1996: 54–5).

[55] Another associate at this time and later was probably Meidias, Demosthenes' particular enemy: cf. on **114**.

[56] Cf. Cawkwell (1960); E. M. Harris (1995: 50–1 and 156–7).

[57] *LGPN* 41; *PA* 14494.

[58] *LGPN* 121; *PA* 14625.

[59] Cf. Davies (1981: 133–50); Rhodes (1982: 13); Gabrielsen (1994: 70–1).

[60] On the identities and nicknames of the brothers-in-law, E. M. Harris (1986).

Philon,[61] Demosthenes calls 'the disgusting Nikias, who hired himself out to Egypt with Chabrias', indicating by this soubriquet that as a soldier and commander he was no match for the famous fifth-century general; whereas Aeschines defends him as an excellent and solid hoplite soldier (as opposed to an effeminate *kinaidos* like Demosthenes, see section 7, and on **131**). It is conceivable, if speculative, that Philon's service as a mercenary soldier with Chabrias in Egypt provided the link between Aeschines and his wife's family; Phokion, who served in many of Chabrias' campaigns (and tried to protect his dissolute son Ktesippos from his vices), was probably a friend of Aeschines at least from the time of the Euboian campaign.[62] The other brother-in-law is called by Demosthenes 'the accursed Kyrebion, the man who appears in the revels in the Dionysiac processions without a mask' (see on **43**), but he was actually called Epikrates,[63] and was indignantly defended on the charge of inappropriate behaviour by Aeschines. 'Kyrebion' (bran-man) is the nickname of a well-known 'parasite', the subject of many jokes in comedy quoted by Athenaeus, and allegedly the dedicatee of a food book written by another noted parasite, Chairephon (see Athen. 244a, and cf. Alexis 173 K/A). It is not clear whether Epikrates and the 'parasite Kyrebion' are one and the same, and Aeschines' brother-in-law was often mocked for his alleged love of food, wit, and scrounging dinners (see Athen. 242d, and see Arnott on Alexis 173 K/A), or whether Demosthenes has created a sudden nickname for Epikrates by associating him with a separate, already famous, gourmet (so E. M. Harris 1986).

Aeschines was thus a relatively late entrant into the world of the political and social élite at Athens (at least in his late 30s), and had to face some contempt and snobbery from those already established there (played up for all it was worth by Demosthenes). Socially, he and his brothers and brothers-in-law seem to have sought to participate as fully as possible in the world of the *gymnasia*, literature, and the pursuit of young men, as he admits readily himself (**135–41**, see also **155–7**, **189**, and 3. 216), where he has to repel the expected allegations of inconsistency between his prosecution of Timarchos and his own activities.[64] The

---

[61] *LGPN* 158; *PA* 14862.

[62] On all this, cf. Davies, *APF* 543–5; E. M. Harris (1995: 31–3).

[63] *LGPN* 104; *PA* 4908; *PAA*.

[64] Schaefer (1885–7: I², 212); cf. also Ober (1989: 281–3), who argues plausibly (though

impression given by Demosthenes' attack on Aeschines and his family, when working up a sense of outrage that Timarchos had his life ruined by the trial, is that while Aeschines' own conduct with boys in the *gymnasia* could allow some general sneers, there were no detailed horror stories to retail; there was more mileage to be got, as seen above, from attacks on his brother Aphobetos and his brothers-in-law Philon ('Nikias') and Epikrates ('Kyrebion') (19. 287–8). According to Aeschines (3. 216), Demosthenes was intending to make some renewed attacks on his own pederastic career in 330; such allegations are missing from the published version of the Crown speech. He himself remained staunchly proud, at times to the point of gaucherie, of his achievements in attaining and defending his conception of Athenian culture and morality: a nice example is provided by his idiosyncratic list of deities and abstractions to which he appeals at the conclusion of the Embassy speech (3. 260)—'Earth, Sun, Virtue, Intelligence, and Culture'.[65]

Following the failure of the appeal to other Greek states, especially in the Peloponnese, Athenian public opinion coalesced to agree to overtures from Philip for peace negotiations, and early in 346 Aeschines had won sufficient support for his rhetorical and diplomatic skills that he was appointed to the First Embassy, on the nomination of his old friend Nausikles, who had been his fellow-ephebe (2. 18, cf. 2. 184, 3. 159).[66] During the long and complicated periods of negotiations, all the Athenian ambassadors came to accept, with varying degrees of enthusiasm, that peace and alliance with Philip was the best option; Philocrates and Aeschines were those who were most easily persuaded that peace with Philip would bring benefits, and had to bear the major criticism from Demosthenes and his friends.[67]

His political career after Timarchos' trial need not be surveyed

---

Lane Fox 1994: 138 has doubts) that his determination to seem a member of the gymnastic élite is also reflected in a fondness for athletic analogies and metaphors: see on **176**. Also Bourriot (1995: 435–8), and Golden (2000: 169–71). Allegations about an inappropriate relationship with a younger, pro-Macedonian politician, Pytheas were made in a speech of Deinarchos', fr. VI. 14 Conomis, cf. on **42**.

[65] Cf. Demosthenes' attacks on his 'tragic' cries, and cultural pretentions, 18. 127–8, Kennedy (1963: 239) and Wilson (1996: 320–2). Ober (1989: 182–4) points out that Demosthenes is also, in a rather more mock-modest way, proud of his superior education (e.g. 18. 256–8, contrasting it with Aeschines' acting as his father 'slave').

[66] Cf. Cawkwell (1960); Ellis (1976: 105–7); E. M. Harris (1995: 50–3).

[67] Good recent narrative in E. M. Harris (1995: chs. 4–5).

here. It was dominated as far as we can see by the need first to defend his position on the peace as it became increasingly fragile, and second by his continuing rivalry with Demosthenes, culminating in his eventual attempt to have Demosthenes' whole career judged a failure by the case over the Crown, which came to court eventually in 330. After his failure there, Aeschines retired from public life, perhaps suffering the penalty for failing to win a fifth of the votes in a public trial. The ancient lives, and Pseudo-Plutarch, tell inconsistent stories (none very convincing) of a retirement to teach rhetoric (or even grammar in a school) in Rhodes, and a final grudging compliment on Demosthenes' superior rhetorical skills.[68]

4. TIMARCHOS' CAREER

Timarchos' father, Arizelos, of the deme Sphettos,[69] is alleged to have been a rich man who deliberately kept his wealth invisible, and sold some of his properties to avoid paying liturgies (**101**). We have virtually no evidence for his career or family connections beyond this speech and the later exchanges between Aeschines and Demosthenes. As we saw above, Timarchos must have been born at least by 391/0, as he was on the Council in 361/0.[70] The one area of common ground between Aeschines and Demosthenes is that the youthful Timarchos displayed an unusual physical attractiveness (Dem. 19. 233); we may suspect, though Aeschines chose not to labour the point, that he was something of an athletic star at the *gymnasia* (his uncle was a trainer; see on **101**) and attracted admirers there. Arizelos died while Timarchos was still young (**103**). Aeschines lists a series of alleged lovers with and off whom Timarchos is supposed to have lived (**42–76**). Many (though very probably not all) may well have in fact been his friends and political associates as well; this was certainly the case with Hegesandros and his brother Hegesippos (see on **54–71**), perhaps with his fellow-demesman Phaidros of Sphettos, who was a general in 347/6 (see on **43**). Aeschines alleges that his first significant lover was the doctor Euthydikos, and Timarchos lived with him under the pretext of learning his profession; it may (or

---

[68] *Lives*, 1. 5–6, 2. 12, 3. 2–5, and Ps. Plut. *Mor.* 840c–e.
[69] *LGPN* 1; *PA* 1617; *PAA* s.v. 162070 + 162075.
[70] *LGPN* 36; *PA* 13636; Hansen, *Inventory* 59–60.

may not) be the case that Timarchos did briefly contemplate medicine, though at some probably early stage (perhaps as early as 364/3, see on **107**) he must have decided to become a politician, probably encouraged by the friends he had made in his youthful leisure activities, The absence of any attack on his preparedness to fight in Athens' campaigns may suggest that he had a fairly acceptable record on that score (see below on **37–116**). By 346/5, he was an established, middle-aged politician, who had been on the *boule* in 361/0, a *logistes*, an official of the Confederacy on Andros, an inspector of the mercenary troops on Euboia in 348, a prominent member of the *boule* again in 347/6, at the time of the debates on the Peace, a proposer of (allegedly) more than a hundred decrees, and a frequent prosecutor in the courts.

In politics between *c.* 348 and the trial in 346/5, Timarchos can plausibly be seen as working first with Hegesippos and then with him and Demosthenes. Conceivably, if speculatively, his activities in charge of moneys for mercenaries in Euboia had something to do with Hegesippos' later motion (*IG* II^2 125) criticizing those who had acted illegally on the campaign, and perhaps also the view associated with Demosthenes that more emphasis should be paid to Philip's activities at Olynthos (see on **113**). By 347/6 he had become very closely associated with Demosthenes, as well as with Hegesippos and Hegesandros, in opposition to Philip. As a member of the *boule* in 347/6 he made proposals on the assembly, though Aeschines does his best to hide the issues behind the display of Timarchos' raddled body and obscene double entendres at his expense (see below section 7, on **26, 80–5**). Timarchos appears to have struck martial poses and discussed the rebuilding of fortifications ('towers' and 'walls'); to have had a proposal concerning rebuilding or tidying-up of the Pnyx discussed (adversely) by the Areopagos; and according to Demosthenes, to have proposed the death penalty for any who conveyed arms or naval equipment to Philip (19. 286). By this time, as a natural ally for Demosthenes, and as a vigorous, experienced, but still youngish orator and politician with anti-Macedonian sympathies, he was happy to assist the dissident ambassador in his attacks on his former colleagues. Unfortunately, Aeschines' ultra-personal counterattack turned out to be a surprising success.

Timarchos' political career presumably was destroyed by this case, as Demosthenes claimed a couple of years later, despite his appeal to his old mother and his children (see Dem. 19. 283; nothing is said of his wife).[71] There is a hint of a possible reappearance in public life, but not a happy one. The late lexicographer Harpokration (s.v. *Autokleides*) claims that these 'excessive pederasts' (listed in **52**) were also mentioned by Aristogeiton in his 'Against Timarchos'. The Suda (a Byzantine dictionary) also reports (s.v. *Aristogeiton*) that he wrote a speech against Timarchos, and (s.v. *Timarchos*), suggests that he prevented Timarchos from acting as a guardian (*epitropos*). The Byzantine bishop Tzetzes (in his notoriously unreliable *Histories* or *Chiliades*, VI 104)[72] appears to be able to paraphrase some of Aristogeiton's arguments against Timarchos, indicating, in the same manner as Aeschines, that someone who uses the parts of his body as a woman, and does all the most hated acts, must not be trusted with an 'office'. In theory this might be before the present trial, since after the trial Timarchos was in a state of total *atimia*.[73] Aeschines suggests (**105**) that Arignotos, his blind and infirm uncle, was first looked after by guardians (*epitropoi*), but then neglected by Timarchos when he became of age; conceivably Aristogeiton succeeded, perhaps only temporarily, in preventing Timarchos from exercising any control over his uncle, by exploiting rumours of sexual debaucheries as Aeschines did later. But it is perhaps difficult to see Aristogeiton active as early as this; his first dated appearance is during the time of the Chaironea campaign in 338.[74] It may be more likely that after the conviction, Timarchos was acting quietly as a guardian of another member of his family. Those afflicted with total *atimia* might still perhaps engage in life inside their families, but their inability to bring legal actions, or enter the *agora* or the sanctuaries, made them extremely vulnerable to enemies. He might then have been denounced as an unsuitable guardian by

[71] Ps. Plut. *Lives of the Ten Orators, Mor.* 840 f. claims, citing Demosthenes, that Timarchos hanged himself on leaving the court, but this seems likely (contra e.g. Sissa 1999: 156) to be a dramatic exaggeration of Demosthenes' language in the Embassy speech, that Aeschines had 'removed' and 'destroyed' Timarchos (19. 2, 285).

[72] On his work, cf. N. G. Wilson (1983: 94–100); RE s.v. Tzetzes.

[73] On which see Hansen (1976: 54–67).

[74] References to his career in *LGPN* 4; *PA* 1775; *PAA* 168145; Hansen, *Inventory* 36–7. See the general attacks on him mounted in Dein. 2, and the two speeches attributed to Demosthenes (25 and 26). Sealey's attempt to attach him to the family of Aristogeiton the tyrannicide of Aphidna is unlikely, given the occurrence of the name in many demes, and the failure of his attackers to contrast his behaviour with the honours of the tyrannicides: see Davies, *APF* 476.

Aristogeiton. This orator, who claimed to be the 'watchdog of the people' but was frequently and naturally traduced as a sykophant, would have been able to recycle much of Aeschines' material, including references to 'womanish' practices and to the 'wild men' like Autokleides. This is perhaps the more likely scenario.[75] There is a possibility (though not very likely in my view) that Timarchos won a reprieve from his *atimia*, either because of a special plea made to the assembly (under the procedure attested at Dem. 24. 45), or because of a general amnesty: on these see Hansen (1976: 68–9). We have no idea how frequently individual reprieves were granted, and the only possible general amnesty which might help Timarchos would be the one proposed by Hypereides in 338/7 BC along with a mass enfranchisement of slaves, at the height of the emergency after the defeat at Chaeronea. The proposal was challenged by Aristogeiton using a *graphe paranomon*, and though Hypereides was acquitted, the proposals were apparently never implemented (Hyper. fr. 32–6, cf. Hansen 1974: 36–7). At all events there is no sign that Timarchos was able to rebuild his political career. Another fragment, from a speech against Timarchos attributed to Deinarchos by the Roman grammarian Priscian (18. 26), may also come from such a trial; it had the appropriate opening 'he was very frightened to appear before you'.[76]

5. DEMOSTHENES AND THE DEFENCE

It appears from our speech (**94** and **117–19**) that Demosthenes was at least master-minding the defence strategy and supplying arguments for Timarchos (and allegedly revealing some of them in advance to people in the *agora*). Many arguments against Demosthenes later in the speech, and especially **173–6**, seem to imply further that he was confidently expected to make a strong appearance speaking for Timarchos as a fellow-advocate (*synegoros*). Aeschines takes great trouble to warn the jury against being

[75] Cf. Schaefer (1885–7: II², 337, n. 2); and Blass (1898: III 2., 149).

[76] A funerary *lekythos* (Clairmont (1993–5: 3. 342) shows three members of a family, a seated female and two males and names the men as Timarchos and Zelias, both sons of Arizelos, and the woman as Deipyle, daughter of Timarchos: this may well have recorded our family, and so give us the names of Timarchos' brother and daughter. Which is the deceased is not clear; Clairmont suggests that it is more likely to be the younger brother Zelias. See also *PAA* s.v. 162070 and 162075.

diverted by Demosthenes from the central issue of Timarchos' offences on to the current political issues. Demosthenes in the Embassy speech (19. 241–3) explicitly refers to Aeschines' elaboration of this strategy, as he claimed how Demosthenes would later boast of his triumphing in 'filching' the case away from the jury (and Demosthenes tries to turn the argument back against Aeschines in the trial of 343). Many have asserted even so that Demosthenes certainly, or probably, did not appear himself, despite Aeschines' careful anticipation, because no evidence of a defence speech exists, and because in many places in the Embassy speech Demosthenes counters arguments used in the prosecution of Timarchos.[77]

Against this one should state first that, as Rubinstein will show in detail, lengthy supporting speeches by *synegoroi* for both prosecution and defence were very frequent in the Athenian courts, especially in public cases, and there is no reason in principle to doubt that Demosthenes and 'the General' made significant contributions to Timarchos' defence. One can also suggest that it would have seemed defeatist and treacherous for Demosthenes not to appear for Timarchos, and would enable Aeschines to claim that he had frightened him off; while arguments which had been used to no avail in the defence of Timarchos might easily be repeated or even sharpened in the Embassy speech. And Demosthenes would also be unlikely to draw attention to his failure to appear, by repeating as he did Aeschines' argument about the strategy he was going to use. That the case was lost is sufficient reason why we hear nothing of a later circulation of Demosthenes' defence speech; many of Demosthenes' defenders earlier in this century give the impression that they preferred to believe that he managed to avoid appearing in such an 'unsavoury' trial, in support of such an unattractive defendant.[78] There is no good reason to doubt that Demosthenes appeared for Timarchos, to share directly in the humiliation and anger of the defeat.

[77] e.g. Beloch (1912–27: III, 532); Pickard-Cambridge (1926: 302); Ellis (1976: 275, n. 16); Schaefer (1885–7: II², 342) was non-committal; Dover (1978: 39) and Rubinstein (forthcoming) assert, and E. M. Harris (1995: 104–6) implies, that Demosthenes did appear.
[78] e.g. Pickard-Cambridge (1926: 302).

The Main Issues

6. HOMOSEXUAL RELATIONS IN CLASSICAL ATHENS

Aeschines' speech is in fact our best source for Athenian laws regulating sexual behaviour between males, for the varieties of such behaviour in classical Athens, and for the values and attitudes that citizens professed in public on such matters. Both prosecution and defence agreed to place the case in the context of a more general debate on the moral education of the young, and the proper part to be played in it by 'noble' erotic relations between men and youths in the settings of the *gymnasia*, wrestling grounds, *symposia*, and places of rhetorical and philosophical education. Hence this speech has played a central part in the intense discussion of these topics which began over two decades ago with Dover's pioneering work,[79] and was given greater prominence by Foucault's influential and provocative *History of Sexuality* and his interest in variations in the 'moral problematization of pleasures' in the development of Western cultures.[80]

Dover established some fundamental points about the standard patterns and norms involving homosexual behaviour in ancient Greece; parts of his presentation have come in for serious criticism (and his nuanced views have at times been misinterpreted).

First, ancient Greeks did not believe it to be a central part of people's 'identities' to be either heterosexual, homosexual, or bisexual; hence they lacked any conception that such identities might be either given from birth ('in the genes'),[81] or at any rate fixed by the end of adolescence. In fact both the term 'homosexual', and the idea of a fundamental division of people into such categories, seem not to have been clearly expressed and widely

[79] Above all in Dover (1978). Following Dover, I use 'homosexual' as well as 'same sex' applied to nouns such as 'acts' or 'behaviour, without any implication that the Greeks operated with a conception of 'individual homosexual identity', or that I adopt a more 'essentialist' than 'contructionalist' position.

[80] Foucault (1985; 1986), and his American followers, especially Winkler (1990a) and Halperin (1990) (cf. Halperin's introduction for an assessment of Dover's and Foucault's contributions); on Foucault, esp. the essays in Larmour, Miller, and Platter (1998) (eds.).

[81] In the last few years the alleged discovery of an identifiable genetic predisposition to a homosexual identity (the 'gay gene') attracted much excitement and controversy; the findings seem not to have been satisfactorily replicated (see e.g. discussions in Nye 1999: 285–305).

adopted before the late nineteenth century.[82] Ancient Greek texts do not apply such labels, nor do they assume that if a person has a preference for sex with either males or with females, he or she is likely to feel distaste or loathing at the thought of sex with the other. They tend to assume that both desires are common and natural, and found often with comparable force in the same person, though, ideally at least, to differing degrees at different stages of life. So the assumption that most or all males are 'naturally' likely to feel sexual desire for other males, especially boys or young men, as well as for women, is found in comedy (e.g. Ar. *Clouds* 1071–4; *Wasps* 578; *Birds* 137–42; *Frogs* 55),[83] history (e.g. Thuc. 6. 54, 8. 74), and law-court rhetoric (e.g. Lys. 3. 4–5, 40, 43, 4. 7).[84] The way Aeschines describes the general interest the people as a whole took in attractive young athletes, and his attribution to Solon of the view, which he endorses, that free men should be positively encouraged to pursue youths at the *gymnasia*, while slaves may not (**136–40**), demonstrates that he shares that position in theory, as he admits he does in his own practice, and also, importantly, that he expects such a view to be very widely held among the jury.[85]

Secondly, accepted Greek cultural values tended consistently to select one type of homosexual relationship as especially common and natural, to such an extent that it could be argued (**136–40**) that it was positively encouraged by the laws of Athens: the relationship between an adult male, especially one still young, in his 20s or so (often called the *erastes*, the lover) and a younger male in his teens (generally known as the *eromenos* or the *paidika*, the boyfriend). An excellent forensic use of this assumption appears at an important point in the speech (**49**), where Aeschines argues, almost certainly falsely, that contrary to appearances Misgolas is a bit older than Timarchos, and *can* therefore have been his lover.[86]

---

[82] Hence Halperin's influential essay, 'One Hundred Years of Homosexuality' (1990: ch. 1).

[83] Cf. Dover (1978: 135–53); views that comedy generally disapproved of homosexual acts, or pederasty, as élite activities (recently Hubbard 1998) are misleadingly over-simple.

[84] cf. Dover (1978: 60–8).

[85] This view is far too deeply embedded throughout the speech for it to be plausible to suppose, as do most recently Hubbard (1998) and or Sissa (1999: 156–8), that it was put in to appeal only to a minority of more élite jurors, or was inserted by Aeschines in the published version, to appeal to the educated reading public, rather than to the jury; see also below pp. 58–60.

[86] Cf. above pp. 10–12. See Dover (1978: 16, 84–7), and a great deal of other material, above

Such relationships, pursued above all initially in the social settings of *gymnasia* and evening *symposia* and banquets, seem to have played a major part in Athenian cultural life. I shall argue below for the view that by Aeschines' time these practices were not restricted solely to small, closed worlds of Athenian élites; rather, as suggested by the crucial passage at **132–40**, 'noble', and even 'democratic', pederasty was widely held to have long been an essential element in Greek culture from Homer onwards. For Athenian citizens the 'role-models' were the democracy's founding fathers, the tyrant-slayers and lovers Harmodios and Aristogeiton.[87] As access to gymnastic and sympotic culture widened, so the concomitant pederastic emotions and relationships may also have become more widely admired and imitated.

Two rival theories currently contest the question of the origins of Greek homosexual patterns, and especially the privileging of this type of relationship. One theory imagines a long-term historical process, which began with closed initiatory rituals involving formalized homosexual pair-bonding. Such rituals have been discovered in a great many societies (especially in New Guinea and parts of Africa), and their complex varieties of initiation rituals and sexual practices have been analysed by anthropologists. In many such societies (including many Stone Age communities in New Guinea) there is no question of any conceptions of 'homosexual identity'. The assumption is rather that to grow into men, and to become warriors, fathers, and members of the community, all boys must endure painful ritual beatings or nose-bleedings, and repeatedly take in the semen of older males (orally or anally); next they will take their turns as the 'lovers', before they marry and propagate. In practice in these New Guinea societies the initiatory sexual acts (oral or anal) could involve loving relationships, and at least some older partners enjoyed the sex acts and continued the practices well after they were supposed

all perhaps the Socratic writings of Plato and Xenophon. The same assumption is made by the problematizing of exceptions, e.g. Xen. *Anab.* 2. 6. 28, where Xenophon includes among his adverse comments on the Thessalian Meno, one of the generals on the 10,000 expedition, that he had a boyfriend who was bearded when he was still without a beard. Cf. also Theopompos' outrage at Macedonians who had anal sex with adult male 'companions', some with beards, some with shaved bodies (*FGH* 115F, 225); and Golden (1984: 321–2). On Alkibiades' constant and pervasive subversions of all these norms, see above all Wohl (1999: 365–80).

[87] On their importance in this 'democratic ideology', see notes on **132**, Stewart (1997: 69–75), and Wohl (1999: 355–9).

to stop; but it must be emphasized that the practices were in general strongly age-delimited, and not seen as essentially individual choices, preferences, or tendencies.[88]

The argument that some sort of comparably age-determined and secretive rites of passage originally existed among many or most Greek-speaking peoples (as also among some other Indo-European peoples), might sometimes at least involve homosexual pairings, and were the ultimate source for the various later forms of more optional, non-universal forms of pederasty and homosexual relations, rests both on some items of evidence and on a general argument that one might envisage elements of continuity as well as change in the archaic period.

Attention focuses above all on the relatively isolated island of Crete. There was a belief current in fourth-century Greece that male homosexuality originated and remained strong in Crete (e.g. Plato, *Laws* 636a–b, 836b; Arist. *Pol.* 1273a23–6;[89] the fourth-century historians Ephoros, *FGH* 70F149, quoted by Strabo 10. 4. 21, and Timaeus, *FGH* 566F144). Some scholars argue for interpretations of certain Bronze Age Minoan cups (especially the so-called Chieftain Cup) and later early Iron Age bronze figures and statuettes, above all from Kato Syme, in terms of a continuity of institutions of male bonding and initiation into men's clubs (the *andreia*).[90] As early as the eighth or early seventh century we seem to find a man called 'Lover of boys' (Paidophila)—a *pithos* from Phaistos of *c.* 700 is inscribed with words probably to be interpreted as 'the possession of Erpeidamos son of Paidophila' (*SEG* 26. 1050, 29, 831). This suggests some sort of socially accepted love of boys. Myths and rituals based at Phaistos and elsewhere have also been argued with some plausibility to suggest well-established rituals of transvestite initiation rituals and perhaps sexual bonding between older and younger males.[91] Literary

[88] Cf. the descriptions and analyses in Herdt (1984; 1987; 1994). On rites of passage in general the classic work was van Gennep, *Les Rites de Passage* (Paris, 1909; Eng. tr., London, 1960).

[89] I am not convinced by one reason Aristotle offers for the Cretan system's encouragement of male seclusion and homosexuality, namely as a birth-control mechanism (cf. Leitao 1995: 143), and even less by the elaborate reworking of this idea as the major explanation for Greek pederasty by Percy (1996).

[90] Koehl (1986; 1997); some criticisms in Halperin (1997: 41–4).

[91] Cf. the wide-ranging and interesting article of Leitao (1995: *passim*). On initiatory myths and connections with pederasty, see Sergent (1986a; 1986b) (at times too positive); Dowden (1992).

sources and archaeological and epigraphic material alike suggest that men in many Cretan cities in the archaic period spent much of their time in the men's clubs (*andreia*), which formed systematic parts of the cities' organization.[92] Finally Ephoros preserves an impressively detailed account of initiation rituals in Cretan cities, whereby boys spent periods together in herds (*agelai*) and were trained to hunt, run, and fight; then each hoped to be selected by a young 'lover', who carried him off in a staged 'rape' to spend two months away hunting and copulating in the country, and on return gave him presents which may plausibly be taken to mark a successful transition to manhood: an ox and a cup (to sacrifice, and drink, as an adult in the male clubs), and military clothing.[93] It must be admitted that Ephoros' account is disappointingly generalized, as if all Cretan cities had the same customs in the fourth century, which is clearly unlikely. It may reflect the some-what idealizing and over-simplifying approach common in fourth-century theorizing, according to which Crete and Sparta were conservative societies which preserved ancient traditions. One must recognize too that the development of myths and rituals, in Crete as elsewhere in Greece, may often have intruded homosexual elements into existing accounts.[94] But it seems hard to deny some long-term continuities here between the impression of rituals given in these later sources and some ancient ritualized social practices.

Rock-cut graffiti from Thera (probably sixth-century) record that individual acts of homosexual couplings took place, often combined with praise of boys' qualities; they have been found very close to the terrace of a temple of Apollo, and some are associated with dedications to Apollo Delphinios, an aspect of the god which is associated in many places with young men and initiatory myths. All this strongly suggests that more than merely casual boasts of sexual contacts or conquests was involved on

[92] On Cretan *andreia*, J. B. Carter (1997); Lavrencic (1988). Cf. also the interesting abdominal guard (*mitra*) inscribed with the duties and privileges of the community scribe (the *poinikastas*) published by Jeffery and Morpurgo-Davies (1970), with Viviers (1994) for the suggestion that the building at Afrati where the object was found was the *andreion* of the Cretan city of Dattala.

[93] See Bremmer (1980; 1990); Cantarella (1992: 3–12); Ogden (1996b: 123–5); Stewart (1997: 27–9); Calame (1999: 96–9, 101–9). Patzer's attempt (1982) to see official or approved Greek 'love of boys' as fundamentally initiatory or educational with few or no sexual acts or emotions involved is, however, unconvincingly reductionist .

[94] Cf. Dover (1978: 185–96; 1988: 115–34).

archaic Thera; on the other hand their very publication, and the probable expression of personal feelings of pride or hostility, suggests that the transition to more overt and individualized pairings has already begun.[95]

The contrary view argues that evidence for continuities back to homosexual behaviour in initiatory rites is insufficient, and cannot explain the sudden presence across most of Greece of open and optional homosexual love, especially among the leisured élites. This view also lays great weight on the supposed absence of explicit or implicit references to homosexual love or sex in the earliest surviving Greek poets, Homer, Hesiod, and Archilochus. When we do find, from *c.* 600 on, male erotic poetry based on the symposion (Alcaeus, Solon, Theognis, and Anacreon) we find no sign of male initiatory practices (though arguably female rites and homoerotic expressions may be seen in the poems of Sappho of Lesbos and Alcman of Sparta);[96] instead we find culturally approved expressions of homosexual or pederastic desire, pursuit, and love. At the same time pederastic courtship and sex acts become rampantly widespread in ceramic iconography in the sixth century. This is then presented (but not really explained) as a new phenomenon in the development of the leisure activities of Greek aristocracies, which is associated with other developments in Archaic Greece. For example, access to free women outside marriage is limited, and there is intense interest in competitions, display, and athletics; in this period the athletic contests take their standard Panhellenic shape in the early sixth century, and athletic nudity is introduced, and there were major opportunities for young adults, in the relative absence of formal education, to be involved in the socialization of boys and youths.[97]

My preference would be to deny the exclusivity of these competing explanations, and combine elements of both. It seems implausible to suppose that there was no connection at all between the very marked privileging in the archaic and classical periods of the asymmetrical and educational aspects of one form

[95] Cf. *IG* XII 536–56; Cantarella (1992: 7–8); Calame (1999: 105–9); for the (in many ways) similar fourth-century graffiti found on sea-side rocks, near a fort, on Thasos, and one in the tunnel leading to the stadion at Nemea, cf. Garlan and Masson (1982) and Calame (1999: 106); for the 'casual' interpretation, cf. Dover (1978: 123, 195).

[96] Above all Calame (1997: *passim*).

[97] Above all Dover (1978: 185–203; and 1988: II, 115–34); cf. also Percy (1996); on athletic nudity, Bonfante (1989), McDonnell (1991).

of homosexual relations above others, and the hints of earlier initiatory practices. Evidence for those may not be as solid as one could wish, but such as there is does help to explain the prevalence of, and social approval for, just this educational pattern of pederastic relationships, which become evident in so many different areas of Greece.[98] It can be argued with considerable plausibility that Homer shows at least awareness, albeit expressed with delicacy and reticence, of homosexual desire, for example in Zeus' interest in Ganymede, and also of the possibility of extraordinarily intense, loving emotions between men (primarily Achilles and Patroklos). There are grounds too for suggesting that these may be seen as having a sexual dimension and perhaps even a hint at physical expression (see on **141–50**, Aeschines' attempt to argue a similar point).[99] It has also been suggested that Hesiod alludes to the prevalence of homosexual desire among his agricultural workers.[100] Homer, and perhaps Hesiod, like the earliest rock graffiti, may reflect the beginnings of a social shift from a concentration on secretive initiatory bondings to more openly acknowledged relationships.

But it is equally important to emphasize that the much greater openness of expression in poetry and art from the early sixth century must indeed reflect the development of strikingly new patterns in different parts of Greece. In some places, especially Crete and Sparta, what look like quasi-initiatory, age-determined, and standard, homosexual relations can best be seen as part of a 're-institutionalization' of ancient customs to fit new structures and new political needs of these communities. In Sparta the increasingly rigorous upbringing designed to create homogeneous Spartiate fighters to cope with the problems of helot-control was probably aided by the use of homosexual pair-bonding.[101] For the Cretan institutions described by Ephoros, the constant warfare between the cities mentioned by Aristotle (*Pol.* 1269a1) may be relevant; Ogden has noted that a successful pair of lovers in Ephoros' description may stay together in the army after completion of the initatory process.[102]

---

[98] Bremmer (1980; 1989; 1990), Calame (1999: 101–9).

[99] Clark (1978); Ogden (1996b: 123–5).

[100] Poole (1990).

[101] Cf. esp. Cartledge (1981) on Spartan pederasty; the process of formation of the social institutions of the classical Spartan state may have taken much longer to complete; cf. e.g. Hodkinson (1998).   [102] Cf. Ogden (1996b: 117).

In many other cities, the development of overt, formalized expression of love for boys among élite men at leisure arguably reflects the breakup into voluntary groupings of the more structured rituals, which had been, by common consent, rarely spoken about in public, though probably widely known. For Athens, there are a number of rituals and associated myths that have plausibly been held to suggest initiatory practices (the myths later often came to involve Theseus as a proto-ephebe). The institutions which may have been involved, the phratries, along with some form of military training for youths known (certainly by the fourth century, and probably at least from the sixth century) as ephebes, went through many transformations. But by the fifth century any systematic homosexual bondings linked specifically to the phratries or to ephebic training appear to have disappeared.[103] Instead, the needs of members of the archaic aristocracies to love and care for younger boys came to be expressed in the more overt proclaiming of the educational value of loving and affectionate relations between youth and boy, centred on the optional settings of the *gymnasia*, the games, and the *symposia*. Initially, it seems, restricted to the culturally dominant wealthy aristocrats engaged in hunting, athletics, and drinking, these practices acquired the characteristic complex of romantic idealization, of lovers' competitive rivalry, stylized pursuit, and expression of their emotions in love poetry. As a consequence they imposed on the boys some very delicate decisions: to which of their suitors, if to any, should they grant their favours, in exchange for the presumed educational or social advantages?[104]

But even in the sixth century, other forms of homosexual relations besides those between élite young men and adolescent boys/youths (the 'pederastic model') existed. The pictures of courtship in black- and early red-figure Attic vases (roughly between 570 and 470) predominantly display older bearded youths approaching, giving presents (such as cocks and hares) to, touching genitals or intercrurally copulating with younger beardless (and apparently unexcited) youths. This all seems to fit well

---

[103] Cf. Vidal-Naquet (1986a and b), Calame (1996). See, however, the more sceptical account of phratries and initiation in Lambert (1993). Ogden's valuable survey of Greek homosexuality in military contexts does not seem to me to find satisfactory evidence for *systematic* homosexual bondings in the ephebic training or in the Athenian army (1996b: esp. 125–35).

[104] Cf. Bremmer (1990); Calame (1999: esp. 23–38).

with much of the literary evidence which indicates that relationships were expected to be asymmetrical in ages, should involve as
inducements presents rather than cash, and should avoid anal sex,
and any suggestion of sexual pleasure for the boys.[105] Yet there are
important variants. A few black-figure vases (especially by the pot-
painter known as the 'Affecter') show courtship between two
beardless boys, or two bearded young men, both cases where it is
not at all clear which is the older. Other black-figure vases show
men with greater interest in the boys' buttocks than touching
genitals, or give indications of both partners with signs of erec-
tions, or boys visibly responding warmly, with kisses or other signs
of affection. A very few show or strongly suggest anal intercourse;
one in particular, doubly anomalous, shows a beardless youth
anally penetrating a bearded man.[106] Red-figure vases down to *c.*
450 show fewer variations in modes, and, for reasons which are
not at all clear, explicit scenes of sexual activity, whether homosexual or heterosexual, tended to go out of fashion after that
date.[107]

How far this can take us is not clear, as our understanding both
of the conventions of these artefacts and of their markets is
seriously incomplete. The great majority of Attic vases, including
the explicit ones just mentioned, have been found in Etruria, not
in Greece, but whether all which reached Etruscan graves
were explicitly aimed at Etruscan markets, or only some (and if so,
how do we decide which ones), is hotly disputed.[108] Even so,
some doubt seems to be cast on the complete dominance of the
pederastic/educational model in representations in the archaic

---

[105] Cf. on in general Dover (1978); on the pictures, especially Shapiro (1981), Koch-
Harnack (1983), Kilmer (1993a), and for analysis of the complex polarities between presents
and cash in texts as well as in iconography, von Reden (1995: ch. 9), pointing out that males
offering money to boys seem more acceptable in gymnastic than in sympotic contexts; cf.
also Fisher (1998a: 97–8). Satyrs on the other hand may engage in all forms of sexual or
bestial activities.

[106] Hupperts (1988); de Vries (1997); Kilmer (1997a: 15–26). The convention of showing
couples, often of similar ages, under the same cloak may well be a decorous way of indicating intercourse; see Koch-Harnack (1989). Cf. also for casual sex between coevals,
Theopompos the comic poet fr. 29 K–A; Dover (1978: 87), and below on **10–11**.

[107] Though it is worth noting the red-figure bell-krater by the Dinos Painter (*c.* 420s)
(Dover 1978: no. 954*, 87, 99; Kilmer 1993a: 23–5, 183), where a very keen boy climbs on to
a chair to sit on another boy (or perhaps youth) with an erection, apparently for anal, or
perhaps intercrural, copulation; their headdresses suggest the licence of a festival, perhaps
the Anthesteria (von Blankenhagen 1976).

[108] e.g. Spivey (1991), Sparkes (1996).

period. One might in any case suspect that in a society which for whatever historical reasons placed an extraordinary high cultural value on one particular form of pederastic relationship (and allowed many controlled opportunities for the display, admiration, and discussion of naked male bodies), many other types of homosexual relationships or casual sex acts would be tolerated, at least by many, and in any case would certainly occur with great frequency.

By the period of full Athenian democracy, as our literary sources become more abundant, Athenian society itself became more complex, and increasingly contained many contradictory ideologies and values. As the speech given to Pausanias in Plato's *Symposion* explained, this was especially true of same-sex relations. On the one hand, homosexual desire was almost universally seen as natural for any man; on the other all respectable men were under strong social pressures to marry, settle down, and produce heirs for their households and for the city. The age by which marriage was expected seems to have been around thirty. Hence exclusively homosexual practice and refusal to marry would arouse condemnation on the grounds that one was betraying both one's family and the city, and confirmed bachelors are very rare.[109] These parameters provide room, and reason, for those Athenians who had the necessary attractiveness and inclinations, or those who were put under the appropriate social pressures, to spend early portions of their lives as boyfriends, lovers, or both, before settling down, marrying, and perhaps entering politics. Aeschines' speech provides the best evidence that these patterns, if conducted without 'disgrace', can be presented as 'noble love', and an essential part of Athenian culture: as a pattern which ordinary Athenian citizens might hope for themselves or for their sons (see section 8 below).

But other patterns and other preferences are also presented by the speech, as by other evidence, as both common and not unacceptable, without the issue of an exclusively homosexual 'identity' being explicitly raised. So Timarchos is attacked for his

---

[109] e.g. Solon fr. 27. 9–12; Dein. I. 71; Lyc. fr. 96 Conomis; Golden (1990: 98, 108–10); on age at marriage, also Verihlac and Vial (1998: 214–16), emphasizing individual variations. Euripides' Hippolytus is an excellent example of a fictional youth whose attempts to avoid marriage and sex, and stay permanently an 'ephebe', antagonized Aphrodite and caused disaster (though a preference for male lovers is not suggested); cf. Dowden (1989: 113–15); Cairns (1993: 316–19); Calame (1999: 7).

acceptance of a great many male lovers, yet his own preference was allegedly for extravagant fun and gluttony with girl-pipers and *hetairai* (esp. **42**), and he appears to have married and had children (Dem. 19. 287).[110] On the other hand, Misgolas, one of his lovers, maintained until well into middle-age his exceptional preference for slender musicians and singers (**41**, a *prohaeresis*).[111] Aeschines himself admits a still active life pursuing youths, getting into fights and writing poetry, when the same age as Misgolas, also well into middle-age (**135–6**).[112] Agathon and Pausanias in Plato's *Symposion* form the most plausible example of an intense asymmetrical partnership which grew into an affectionate and lasting relationship well into both their adulthoods.[113] In his conclusion (**195**) Aeschines addresses all those who have such an inclination to avoid citizen youths and instead 'hunt easily-caught youths', i.e. non-citizens; he does not urge them to give the practice up. Plato himself apparently did not marry, and like some of these other men has been labelled a 'homosexual';[114] certainly his work displays a passionate and abiding interest in the possibilities for 'noble' and serious homosexual love (not excluding some physical expression) to lead towards philosophical commitment and understanding, above all in *Symposion* and *Phaidros*. In the *Laws*, however, a much more condemnatory attitude to any physical form of homosexuality is adopted.[115] Plato is also often

[110] Sissa (1999: 153–60) seems to suggest that Aeschines' arguments that Timarchos' character and body have been marked for life by having 'sold himself' for sex 'against nature' (**185**), and pursued his pleasures, are enough to label him (and the others involved in the case) 'homosexual' or 'a gay man'; this ignores the insistence throughout the speech that Timarchos shamelessly accepted what his lovers wished to do to him solely to pay for his own different pleasures.

[111] Whether he married and had children is unclear; Aeschines chooses to treat him kindly. There are also the 'wild men' listed at **52**, cf. Dover (1978: 37–8).

[112] About which he—necessarily—shows less embarrassment than the apparently even more elderly speaker of Lys. 3, whose passions have led him into fights and a difficult lawsuit.

[113] Cf. also the picture of Agathon as an effeminate, shaven, adult who still enjoyed anal penetration (*euryproktos*) in Aristophanes' *Thesmophoriazusae*, Dover (1978: 140–4). *Phaidros'* examples of famous couples in his speech do not always fit the major pattern either; cf. on **141–4** on Achilles and Patroklos, and Hubbard (1998: 71).

[114] e.g. Wender (1973); Vlastos (1973: ch. 1). On whether it is in general appropriate to call, with due qualification, those with varying degrees of 'preference' for same-sex relationships 'homosexuals' or 'gay men', cf. e.g. Boswell (1980); Halperin (1990); Thorp (1992), and with reference to Rome, Richlin (1994); Richlin (1997) (ed.); and Williams (1999).

[115] For analyses of the value of pederastic relationships for Plato's philosophy, and his rejection in the *Laws*, e.g. Dover (1978: 153–68); Vlastos (1973: 1–42; 1987); A. W. Price (1989: chs 2 & 3).

supposed to present, in 'Aristophanes' speech' in the *Symposion*, an 'essentialist myth', which assumes, and then purports to explain, an accepted division of men and women into (roughly in equal proportions) homosexuals and heterosexuals;[116] but there are good grounds for supposing that these assumptions underlying the myth serve complex Platonic agendas in the work, and are not to be taken as straightforward representations of possible Greek beliefs in the sexual identities of heterosexuals and homo-sexuals.[117]

In conclusion, one might say that that there were probably very few males indeed who would have said they were exclusively lovers of males, but there were those who consistently preferred sex with males (or certain types of younger males) to sex with women through much or all of their lives, some very passionately or with great commitment. There were those who were very keen on romantic attachments, and sex, with younger males at certain periods of their lives; and in general a relatively high level of actual homosexual sex probably occurred, much of it casual. This activity may have been especially frequent in the leisured classes, but was found pretty widely in the rest as well. But there were a good many conflicts, variations, and moral problematizations throughout the society as well, and the easiest way to approach these are through a consideration of the laws and the moral values discussed in our speech.

7. HOMOSEXUAL RELATIONS AND THE LAW

The prevailing form of these relationships assumed asymmetrical relationships, in which the younger partners were described as boys (*paides*), youths (*meirakia*), or young men (*neoi, neaniskoi*). There must have been issues of parental or legal protection for boys who were not yet of an age to be responsible for their own decisions. Aeschines claims there was a coherent set of laws designed by the lawgiver Solon, to protect the boys against attack or abuse at schools and *gymnasia* (**9–11**, and see also **187**), against being forced into prostitution by pimps or fathers, and against *hybris*,

---

[116] e.g. Boswell (1980: 54); cf. D. Cohen (1991a: 190–2), with a different emphasis, seeing 'Aristophanes' presenting an argument against social disapproval of males with a preference for their own sex, as also Thorp (1992).

[117] See Carnes (1998), and also Ludwig (1996).

deliberately insulting or dishonouring behaviour. Aeschines claims
these laws might among other things protect boys and youths
against rape or under-age seduction or prostitution (**13–18**). Much
later he cites laws forbidding slaves from exercising in *gymnasia* or
from being the lovers of free boys (**138–40**). The laws cited are
probably rather more of a rag-bag of provisions of different dates
than the allegedly planned 'Solonian' programme, but some of
them at least may well go back to the sixth century.[118]

Many of Solon's more certainly genuine laws and constitutional
reforms, as well as his poems in justification of his reforms (e.g. frr.
4–6), show a persistent concern for the maintenance of status-
distinctions, the protection of the honour and appropriate status
of the citizens, and the stability of the family. Some more personal
poems display an interest in the ideals of pederasty; see fr. 24.5–6,
and especially fr. 25 West, a couplet apparently giving a standard
picture of the erotic man: 'while [or until] he loves a boy (*paido-
philesei*) in the delightful flower of youth / desiring thighs and
sweet mouth'.[119] Politically Solon divided the citizens into four
income-classes, with appropriately graduated duties and office-
holding opportunities for each; many laws protected the weaker
members of families, and their inheritance patterns, or showed
concern for the preservation of physical or social boundaries.[120]
The public suit (*graphe*) of *hybris*, designed to protect the honour of
all, but especially of male citizens, against all forms of serious
abuse (and especially violence or sexual abuse), fits these patterns
very well, and is very likely Solonian, or at least sixth-century.[121]
Also probably Solon's are the laws forbidding slaves access to the
gymnasia or to be lovers of free boys and arguably thereby indicating approval for pursuit of boys at the still essentially aristocratic *gymnasia*. They are also mentioned by Plutarch (*Solon* 1), the
text contains an archaic-looking word (*xeraloiphein*), and the
content suits Solon's concern to maintain the slave/free boundary
at the social setting where they would certainly come into
contact.[122] The other laws cited may conceivably have a Solonian

---

[118] See notes on **6–36** and **138–40** below, and D. Cohen (1991: 175–82); Cantarella
(1992: 27–36, 42–4, 51–3); Ford (1999: 243–4).

[119] Quoted by Plut. *Amat.* 751b, cf. his *Life of Sol* 1. 2; Athen. 602e; Apuleius, *Apol.* 9.

[120] See esp. Murray (1980); P. B. Manville, *The Origins of Citizenship in Ancient Athens*
(Princeton, 1990), Ch. 5.

[121] So argued by Murray (1990b) and Fisher (1990), and also Fisher (1992: ch. 2).

[122] Cf. Murray (1990b), and Golden (1984: 317–18); Kyle (1984; 1987: 22–3); Mactoux
(1988).

origin, at least, but may well contain later elaborations (see notes). The fundamental point is perhaps that Athenian legislation in these areas is above all concerned with issues of status, honour, and shame: the central question is what exactly is it that constitutes shameful behaviour in both partners to a homosexual relationship.

There is no evidence on how often, if at all, these laws designed to protect the younger boys against sexual abuse or prostitution resulted in prosecutions. In principle Athenian fathers might *claim* that any sexual act by an outsider, against their permission, with a son not yet of age (or indeed an unmarried daughter) rendered the seducer or rapist liable to a charge of *hybris* against the offender, conceived as a gross insult to the father and family. D. Cohen has argued that this in effect constituted a notion equivalent to 'statutory rape' designed to cover all sex with minors. But evidence is lacking for widespread awareness of such a general interpretation of the legal offence of *hybris*, and, as Golden and Cantarella have pointed out, 'Pausanias' in Plato's *Symposion*, when he is arguing the case for the more noble love of youths presided over by the pair of Ouranian Aphrodite and Ouranian Eros, which prefers youths beginning to grow beards and acquire discretion, over the 'commoner' or 'demotic' love of younger, foolish boys, suggests that there 'should be a law' preventing such love of boys (181d–e). He does not suggest that such a law in effect exists, but is not implemented (though he does praise the noble love for being without *hybris*).[123]

In practice, fathers, and the slaves appointed to watch over and protect boys (*paidagogoi*), must have tried to ensure their charges did not 'yield' too easily to unsuitable lovers, while respectable and controlled would-be lovers of boys under eighteen no doubt were supposed to proceed with caution and seek the approval of their fathers.[124] Prosecutions of one's teenage son's lover where

---

[123] D. Cohen (1987: 6–8; 1991a: 176–80); objections in Cantarella (1989: 160–5; 1992: 42–5); Golden (1990: 58–62). On the value to Aeschines of his arguments about *hybris* see on **16–17**.

[124] Cf. the emphasis on the approval of Lykon for Kallias' love of Autolykos in Xenophon's *Symposion* (1. 8–11), in contrast, evidently, to the presentation of the relationship in Eupolis' *Autolykos* attacking Kallias as a rich keeper of parasites, Lykon as an effeminate parasite, and Autolykos as 'well-bored', presumably buggered by Kallias (fr. 48, 58, 61, 64 K–A; Dover 1978: 146–7); and contrast the fantasy of Ar. *Birds* 137–42, where an ideal city is one where a father remonstrates with his old family friend for not immediately kissing, embracing, and tickling the testicles of his good-looking, freshly bathed son, where

the issue was persuasion by gifts or by money, not rape, would have seemed a very risky procedure. Conviction would be difficult, especially on what was regarded as the very serious charge of *hybris*, and the publicity might well be more likely to increase family shame than to save it.[125] One might, however, suspect (though there is no evidence) that the younger the boy, the greater the likelihood of a stronger desire to prosecute, and a better chance of success.[126]

Once Athenian boys had come of age and registered in their demes (see on **18**), at around eighteen, the only sexual acts likely to bring *immediate* legal penalties were rapes or seductions of citizen wives or daughters, or perhaps, as above, rape of young free boys. To engage in homosexual relationships, as senior or junior partner, or as an equal, or even voluntarily to engage in prostitution (*porneia*) or be an escort (*hetairesis*) was not in itself illegal (though Aeschines often asserts the contrary, see on **72, 87, 163–4**; Dover 1978: 31–3). Such relationships were open, as the speech fully reveals, to a great deal of gossip, scandal and disrepute, especially directed at the junior partners, but so far from being illegal, they could be the subject of legal contracts (see on **158–64**) and taxes were levied on male as well as female prostitutes (see on **119–20**). A major reason was the general liberal principle of the Athenian democratic system, that its citizens should be free to live 'as they please'; the most famous expression of these values comes in Pericles' Funeral Speech (Thuc. 2. 37. 3).[127] The Athenians had a conception of 'private life' which should be left alone by the laws, provided the honour of other citizens, or the interests of the state, were not attacked. The moral problematics of homosexual relations only became of interest to the laws if those who could be held to have 'lived shamefully', that

the joke is I think that normally one would have to proceed much more cautiously and work hard to be thought worthy of such approaches (rather than, as Hubbard 1998: 54–5, supposes, fathers from the perspective of comedy would wholeheartedly resist any such propositions to their sons).

[125] Cf. Fisher (1990; 1992: 50, 81–2); R. G. Osborne (1985b: 50). Part of Sokrates' strict judgements in Xenophon's *Symposion* (8. 19–21) envisages a practised seducer of boys who assigns what he desires to himself, not caring that this brings the greatest shame on the boy, and alienates his family from him, but there is no hint that they might resort to the law.

[126] For attempts to divide boys and youths into differing categories in this area, cf. Dover (1978: 84–7); Cantarella (1992: 30–44); Golden (1990: 58–62).

[127] Cf. also Thuc. 7. 6. 2; among the philosophers, Arist. *Pol.* 1317a40–b14; Plat. *Rep.* 577b, and the orators Lys. 26. 5, Isocr. 7.20. See Wallace (1994; 1996) and Hansen (1996a).

is, it seems, had engaged in prostitution or *hetairesis*, later sought to exercise *active* citizenship—for example by proposing motions, speaking in the assembly, bringing a law suit, or standing for office. Hence while the law's interests in the 'private morality' of youths may seem illiberal and in tension with the praise of the 'negative freedom,'[128] it can also be seen as 'democratic' and 'egalitarian', as it imposes a higher standard of personal morality on those who enter public life, who choose to seek the extra honours and financial rewards which may derive from success in addressing, and representing, the city.

It appears from Aeschines' speech that two procedures might then be used; but the crucial point here is that these procedures were not immediately operable, but could only come into operation if the youth with a doubtful past entered serious politics. Aeschines might in fact have prosecuted Timarchos by a public indictment (*graphe hetaireseos*) on the grounds of having been a prostitute though a citizen and over the age of sense and knowledge of the laws: in which case he might allegedly have been liable to the death penalty (see **20**, and also Dem. 22.30 ff.). Aeschines claims to have used an alternative procedure which he calls the 'scrutiny' (*dokimasia*) of orators (**26–32**).[129] Under this procedure 'anyone who wishes'—in fact a personal enemy or someone currently engaged in a political struggle, like Aeschines—might challenge the man's eligibility to speak or be otherwise politically active (*epangellein dokimasian*) (**32, 81**), as Aeschines did at the assembly at which Timarchos' proposal about the Pnyx was under discussion. This then led to a hearing before a jury. Timarchos was accused primarily on two of the four counts of inadequate behaviour as a male and an active citizen (see section 5, and below on **37–116**), and clearly the sexual charges were the more significant.

Several important questions remain: what did the law mean by *porneia* and *hetairesis*, and what was necessary to prove it? And why did the law bear down on youths who commit these offences if and only if they then engage in public life? Why did it impose higher standards of *sophrosyne* and *eukosmia* solely on the powerful, the members of the honour-seeking, political élite?

As far as we can tell from Aeschines, the law gave no further

---

[128] Cf. e.g. Thomas (1994: 119, 124–5); Lane Fox (1994: 144–5).
[129] On doubts about Aeschines' accuracy, cf. Lane Fox(1994: 149–51).

definition of *hetairesis* or *porneia*, and in that it was entirely typical of the Athenian approach to lawmaking. Nor did it indicate whether their use in homosexual relationships was at all different from that in heterosexual (see **13, 19, 29**). The main issue of debate in homosexual contexts concerns whether the distinction between *porneia*, *hetairesis*, and a proper relationship, is based more, or entirely, on the types of payment or advantage accruing to the 'boyfriend' or on the performance of certain specific sexual acts. Involved in this debate is the precise meaning and moral denotation of certain expressions applied to the participants. It seems to me that the defining element in being a *pornos* in texts of this period is pretty clearly and consistently seen in terms of selling oneself, one's body, or one's sexual favours, nearly always for hard cash, and from a frequently changing cast of clients; *hetairein*, to be the male equivalent of a female *hetaira*, or the relationship of *hetairesis*, is harder to define or to distinguish exactly from *porneia*, but involves rather appearing to be a 'friend' and 'companion', while being thought to be benefiting materially from one or more (often longer-term) sexual association(s).[130] In contrast to both, a 'good' boyfriend is in a relationship of friendship and affection, and benefits rather from valued advice and guidance, perhaps by some presents, but not in terms of cash of a living. In contemporary terms, one may compare a distinction between *pornoi* as 'whores' or 'rent-boys', and those in *hetairesis* as 'escorts'; the parallel is not exact, as 'escorts' nowadays seem to be classier and hence more expensive sexual partners than rent-boys, but also involved in what are usually also short-term arrangements. So in the translation I usually render *pornos* as 'prostitute' or, in some places, where a more colloquial tone seems appropriate, (e.g. **157**), as 'whore' ('rent-boy' seems too low a register, given Aeschines' extravagant care to avoid appearing to break the rules of decorous language for the court). I usually translate, with reservations, the female *hetaira* as 'escort' or 'escort-girl', *hetairein* and *hetairesis* of males as 'be an escort' and 'escortship'. Comparison of two crucial passages in the speech (**51–2** and **119–20**) seems to make it clear that to take pay or live off one man while 'doing

---

[130] Dover (1978: 20–2); on the fluid distinction in relation to women and men, esp. Davidson (1997: *passim*). See also Kurke (1999: 175–221), who traces possible origins of the term *hetaira* in the context of the archaic *symposion*, and explores the distinction in terms of the opposition between the cash commodification of *porneia* and the friendship and 'mutual favours' of *hetairesis*.

this thing' might be enough for a charge of *hetairesis*, while to sit in a house, take pay for sex and pay the whores' tax, certainly demonstrated *porneia*; but the distinction is fluid, and depends on one's argument. If, as Timarchos was alleged to have done, one is thought to have lived with and off a succession of men over a considerable period of time, though not necessarily ever receiving specific sums of money for particular acts, one gives the opportunity to an enemy to argue with some plausibility that such behaviour merited being called *porneia*, not just *hetairesis*.

There is little or no indication that the law named specific sexual acts, nor that Aeschines felt he had to make it utterly unambiguous what acts Timarchos had allowed to be performed; he prefers to make repeated play of the need to maintain decorum of language, and express reluctance even to use a term which the law itself uses, *pornos* (see above all **37–8, 40–1, 45, 51–2, 74–6**). If it was crucial to argue that anal or oral sex was involved, one suspects that Aeschines would have made it clearer which acts he was delicately alluding to, by reference for example to 'rear parts' or 'mouth'.[131] In that sense, then, it is not correct to claim that submission to bodily penetration, in any type of relationship, was clearly indicated by the laws as behaviour which constituted the offence of *hetairesis*.[132] If an enemy had reason to suppose (not in itself very likely) that an otherwise socially approved couple who engaged in an apparently loving and educational relationship had also performed buggery, and the younger one then went into politics, it seems unlikely that he would calculate that he would have much of a chance of a successful prosecution under the *hetairesis* rule.

On the other hand, Aeschines does makes constant, allusive references to 'the thing' or 'the act', as if everyone knows what he means. This is best explained by a set of common assumptions which made a close, *de facto*, connection seem plausible between mercenary arrangements and certain sex acts, especially buggery.

[131] Cf. also Cantarella (1992: 48–53); Davidson (1997: 177, 219–21, esp. 253–6); Calame (1999: 139–40), all suggesting (with different emphases) that it is the 'prostitution' issue that matters for the law, not the nature of the acts. Aeschines comes closest to implying that a specific act was in itself illegal at **40–1**. He is more explicit in reference to Demosthenes' mouth at 2.99–100; and may hint at sexual 'bending down' at **187**.

[132] e.g. D. Cohen (1987: 9; 1991a: 181): 'at Athens public submission to such intercourse as required of Melanesian initiates (i.e. anal or oral penetration in an approved initiatory bonding) would [or, in the later publication, 'could'] result in disenfranchisement'. Dover was generally more circumspect, though 1978: 103 comes close.

The assumptions (see **40, 52, 69**) are that the man who pays for the arrangement can insist on whatever acts he prefers; that anal sex is what homosexual lovers usually want, and that 'good boys' should not, as *pornoi* would, agree to 'present their bottoms' to their lovers for money (Ar. *Wealth* 149–56). It is interesting that the next lines of that play add the usual comic addition which works to collapse the vital distinction between good and bad boys, by assuming that even the good ones are persuaded to accept buggery by agreeable and generous presents. It is in general the assumption of comedy (esp. Ar. *Clouds* 1085–104) that all boyfriends are 'wide-bummed' (*euryproktoi*).[133] The fact that the vast majority of vases which display what look like 'normal' homosexual pairs engaging in sex shows face-to-face genital handling or intercrural sex (for which the Greek term was evidently *diamerizein*, 'to (do it) between the thighs')[134] supports the view that this, if anything, was what, in much polite discourse, noble lovers were supposed to do. The relative infrequency of the younger partners displaying either much of an erection or much facial sign of excitement (though as recent work is emphasizing, there are significant exceptions to this picture) supports the view found in some of the literary sources, namely that good boys did not seek sexual enjoyment from an affair (put very strongly by Sokrates in Xen. *Symp* 8. 21–3).[135] Sokrates' view, much of the time, in both Plato and Xenophon, was that noble lovers should, if they can manage it, avoid physical copulation with the boys they love;[136] but this was an extreme view.[137] Most believers in the traditions of noble love and the importance of distinguishing this from a shameful sort would insist, one suspects, not so much on a rigid avoidance of any orgasmic intercourse, nor even on the strict avoidance of penetration, as on more fluid notions such as mutual consent, affection, honest persuasion, and respect for the boy's

[133] Dover (1978: 99, 140–7). Cf. also Amphis 15K–A, where the cynical character does not believe that any lover only loves his boyfriend's character, ignores his looks (*opsis*), and is really *sophron*. On the meaning of *euryproktos*, below pp. 45–9, and Davidson (1997: 176–7).

[134] Dover (1978: 98).

[135] Cf. also Plat. *Phaedr.* 255d; Dover (1978: 52–3).

[136] Cf. Dover (1978: 159–61); Hindley (1999: 79–80); the loving philosophical couple in the *Phaidros* may have a momentary lapse into temptation, brought on by mutual affection and excitement, and be tolerated; but it is better if this is avoided.

[137] Hindley (1999) argues plausibly that Xenophon's personal views were more tolerant of 'respectful' physical love than is his Sokrates, above all in *Symp*. 8; Plato's *Laws* show him ending in a more extreme position yet.

interests and reputation. Whether boys agreed to intercrural, even anal, sex, and whether they also permitted (or encouraged) masturbation,[138] or enjoyed anal sex, was for many understood to be matters left to the couple, who should keep outsiders guessing.[139] The greater the numbers of lovers a boy or youth was supposed to have had, the greater the grounds for believing that he was living with and/or off one or more lovers. The more he went on living like this while becoming an older youth, or even an adult, the more the assumption would be that there was no delicate and sensitive negotiation and mutual respect between the pair, but the lover with the wealth would insist on whatever acts he preferred, and that they would be performed 'in *hybris*', or 'with shame'.[140]

For these reasons Aeschines builds his case above all on the narrative he constructs. It highlights a long series of men Timarchos had been involved with once he, as a *meirakion*, had reached the age of sense and knowledge of the laws: Misgolas; Kedonides, Autokleides, and Thersandros the 'wild men'; Antikles; Pittalakos; and Hegesandros. It dilates on the lovers' houses he had lived and been available in, and dwells on some famous scandals, involving illegal and violent acts by some of his lovers, notably Hegesandros. On the back of these narratives he throws out repeated (and unsubstantiated) assertions that all these lovers naturally called the shots, and insisted on the performance of shameful, self-hybristic, and degrading acts (which cannot of course be named explicitly) for which Timarchos voluntarily sold his body and to which he subjected himself.

One may separate out in analysis the issue of self-control and mastery of one's own body from that of the moral values of specific acts. In all cases there may have been issues of the disgraceful assimilation of a citizen male to those of lesser status—women, barbarians, or slaves. For boys who were about to assume

---

[138] The interesting passages (esp. Ar. *Ach.* 591–2; *Kn.* 963–4) relegated by Dover to his Appenda (1978: 204) ('because I could not explain [them]'; but he does a good job), suggest that if those engaged in homosexual rape would be likely to handle their victims' penises, kinder lovers would do the same; to say nothing of what one might in practice expect of vigorous adolescents fond of their lovers, cf. also de Vries (1997).

[139] Cf. Dover (1978: 106–9), whose caution here has not always been noticed; Vlastos (1987).

[140] Cf., in addition to Aeschines' defence at **136–40**, esp. Pausanias' speech in Plat. *Symp.*, the 'non-lovers' speeches in Plat., *Phaedr.*, and Xen. *Symp.* 1. 10. See also Cantarella (1992: 18–20); Hindley (1999: 89).

(or had just assumed) citizen-status to allow a lover to dictate sexual terms could be seen as accepting a shameful surrender of control to another merely for gain, an inappropriately mercenary exchange of one's supposedly inviolable body. This risked the assimilation of their behaviour and characters to those of women, who have less choice in such matters, and even more to those of slaves, who were legally debarred from loving boys (see on **138–9**) and had often to serve their master's sexual demands. It is noticeable how 'decent' lovers often emphasized how they chose to 'enslave themselves' to their boyfriends (e.g. 'Pausanias' in Plat. *Symp.* 183a; Xen. *Mem.* 1. 2. 11; the motif is found as early as the pederastic poems in 'Theognis' Book II, e.g. lines 1235–8, 1305–10, 1337–40, 1341–50, 1357–60). One advantage of this was to counter any suggestion that they may be inappropriately in control. For the older males, most no doubt already enrolled as citizens, to adopt a position of abasement, competing with rivals and pleading for 'favours', making offers and promises, even taking up a relatively submissive, knees bent, position in intercrural sex, could pass as an acceptably paradoxical pose, and did not seriously damage their civic status. More importantly this apparent reversal of power relations often masked reality, and constituted a useful defence for the lovers against the charge of abuse of superior age and power, and treating their free boyfriends as women or slaves, and for the boys against the more serious charge of slavish surrender.[141]

What then was so objectionable and sensitive about the sexual acts which Aeschines alludes to but will not mention? It seems uncontroversial that in some sense 'anal intercourse' is central, but how that is to be interpreted is a complex and hotly debated question. A view which has become widespread, perhaps standard, especially since the books by Dover, Foucault, Winkler, and Halperin, puts heavy emphasis on a simple division between those who penetrate with the penis and those who passively accept it. This is built up into a 'phallocratic' theory of Greek culture (and a specifically Athenian, democratic, version of it) which links citizen status with active exercise of the phallos,[142] and

---

[141] See esp. Golden (1984; 1990: 58–9).

[142] Evidence for these attitudes comes, *inter alia*, from the frequency of phalluses, and phallic imagery, on Greek vases, on the stone images of bearded, phallic Herms at the point where Athenians' private houses met the street, and from comic passages asserting

stigmatizes those free males who receive a penis inside them as losing masculinity, by being 'soft' or 'passive'.[143] This view then interprets certain crucial terms of abuse applied to deviants in this light. *Euryproktos* (wide-bummed) is held to be applied especially to those noted as accepting (many) lovers because habitual buggery was supposed permanently to distend the anus; *lakkos* (cistern, tank—see on **84**) and *lakkoproktos* (tank-arse), similarly denote those with widened anuses; *katapugon*—'down the arse'—(usually) denoted those who passively accept anal sex; and a *kinaidos* (which seems to take over from *katapugon* as a sexually charged term of abuse, see on **131**) is seen as an effeminate male most importantly characterized as one who submits to regular penetration. This view supposes that what is especially objectionable in moral terms is that by passively accepting penetration these characters assimilate themselves to women, who are expected to be penetrated and to be inferior, and to slaves; occasionally this position can be designated as 'against nature' (see on **185**).

Recently this view has come under sustained challenge, above all by Davidson (1997), essentially as monolithic and obsessed with the single issue of penetration, phallic power, and submission. He points out, correctly, that many of the texts describing individuals as *euryproktoi, kinaidoi,* and so on, focus not on passivity but rather on their capacity to find sexual pleasure in the anus, and on an insatiable appetite for this pleasure. This can be discussed as a physiological problem, as by Arist. *EN* 1148b15–49a20, and [Arist.] *Probl.* 4. 26, or seen as an unacceptable or disgusting way to choose to live, as by 'Kallikles' and 'Sokrates' in Plat. *Gorg.* 493a–4e, where the life of the *kinaidos*, endlessly seeking to satisfy his apparently disgusting desire, like scratching an itch, revolts even the amoralist Kallikles. The notion of insatiability is applied equally to other pleasures, such as food, drink, and gambling. Similarly, *euryproktos* and *lakkos* may indicate not so much the forced widening of the anus by constant buggery as the capacity of a 'lewd' youth to widen or contract it himself to increase his pleasure and his capacity to be 'filled up'. For Davidson and

'Solon's' democratic spirit as displayed by the provision of cheap brothels for all (Philemon 4 K/A; Dover 1978; Halperin 1990: 102–4).

[143] Cf. Winkler (1990), more strongly; Halperin (1990); Stewart (1997: 156–71). On the *kinaidic* styles of dress, posture, gesture, etc., cf. Winkler (1990: 46–54); Thornton (1997: 99–110); Gleason (1995: 62–70).

others what is thought wrong about being buggered was not passivity and humiliation, but lewd and insatiable pleasure-seeking, comparable to the nymphomania often attributed to women.

This analysis undoubtedly adds important and neglected elements to a complex picture, perhaps gives a more realistic picture of the enjoyments some may have experienced, and certainly reflects better many hostile beliefs about what '*kinaidoi*' did and why. But it does not necessarily make the alternative account redundant. 'Passivity' or 'moral cowardice' may not be the only sources of moral error in this area; yet Davidson has not discussed or disposed of all the evidence for a deep-rooted association of phallic assertiveness and display with masculine status, nor has he in my view accounted adequately for the focus of so much sexual hostility in relation to homosexual acts on those who accepted being buggered. There is plenty of evidence (*pace* Davidson 1997: 169) that many Greeks saw anal rape and forced masturbation in certain circumstances as a means of asserting power or inflicting revenge: see for example Ar. *Ach.* 592; *Knights* 355, 364, 962–4; *Thesm.* 157–8 and Theocr. 5. 40–4, and also the supposed 'radish' punishment which might be inflicted in reassertion of his lost masculinity by a wronged cuckold on an adulterer (see on **185**). Further, the so-called 'Eurymedon vase' does in my view demand a political interpretation. It shows a naked Greek (captioned as saying 'I am Eurymedon', meaning perhaps the personification of the major victory which the Greeks inflicted on the Persians in the early 460s at the river Eurymedon),[144] striding forwards holding his erect (or half-erect) penis as if about to penetrate a terrified Scythian/Persian figure (who is captioned saying: 'I stand bent over'). This should be read as a political statement, which perhaps asserts something like 'we can bugger the Persians as we did at Eurymedon, because they are softies and gagging for it', implying perhaps a variety of ways in which Greeks can now dominate and exploit the Persians.[145] Davidson may be right that

[144] On who utters which caption, the personification of 'Eurymedon', and the ethnic associations of the victim, see most recently Smith (1999: esp. 135–9).

[145] For all Davidson's sophisticated arguments (1997: 170–1, 180–2), it is hard to believe that an Athenian vase featuring 'Eurymedon' as a sexually aggressive Greek and a soft Oriental, in the 10–20 years after the battle, would not convey a political meaning. Cf. Kilmer (1997b: 135–8); Cartledge (1998: 56–7); Humphreys (1999: 130–1), and most fully now Smith (1999).

other cultures, including Roman, have been more dominated by images of phallic power, but he seriously underrates their significance in Athens. The choices of the *kinaidoi* may be found especially objectionable because they found excessive pleasure in forms of sex more appropriate for women (or slaves) than free men, as also in feminine styles in dress, hair, etc.; but those who accepted the commands or requests of other men for penetrative sex in exchange for money are also subjected to much obloquy.

In our speech it is significant that Timarchos is not described as a *kinaidos*; Demosthenes, however, who is not exactly presented as a 'shameful boy', is called a *kinaidos* for his frilly clothes and ambivalent sexual habits with his youthful pupils (see on **131**). Throughout his life Timarchos was allegedly devoted to a variety of pleasures, but was not, it seems, especially effeminate in appearance, and he is criticized for having no qualms about performing what his lovers demanded of him, not for actively enjoying it as a form of sex (see esp. on **41–2**, and also **76, 95**).[146] Nonetheless the emphasis in Aeschines' abuse towards the end of the speech of his opponent's 'most shameful' (if unspecific) sexual offences is focused on Timarchos' selling himself for self-degradation (*hybris*), on how he, with his male body, was guilty of 'bending down to the acts of shame', 'committing women's offences', 'committing *hybris* against himself contrary to nature' whereas an adulterous woman offends 'in accordance with nature' (see **185–7**). If he did not agree to the shameful acts for his pleasure, but for the money to spend on other pleasures, the point must be that the acts themselves should be seen as shameful and unnatural for men, because they put the man in the place of the woman (**185, 187** and notes; see also **37, 41**). The point is made forcefully in two other forensic denunciations: Hypereides fr. 215 Jensen, a fragment surviving only in Latin, argues (rather as does Xen. *Oik.* 7. 20–34) that Nature has distinguished the male and the female and given them their specific tasks and duties, yet his opponent had abused his body in a feminine way; and Deinarchos VI. 14 Conomis, where the alleged former boyfriend of Aeschines himself, Pytheas, is accused of 'doing or

---

[146] Davidson (1997: 254–7) acknowledges this, but also contemplates the idea that Aeschines may hint at times (but does not specify where) that Timarchos may 'enjoy his job', because he's sex-mad, not because he enjoys being a sex-object.

enduring whatever was proposed to him by Aeschines' (see also on **42**).[147]

The situation for the younger partners was admittedly extremely complex (as was recognized) and arguably to the point of incoherence or contradiction.[148] The issues of the nature of the relationship (loving and educational, or based on sex, or sex and money), and of the acts through which it was expressed could not be easily separated in the discussion of particular cases. The law focused on the 'mercenary' issue; and observers were no doubt inclined to allow their feelings one way or the other about that to colour their speculations and their judgements about the acts the pair might be performing. Thus one might suppose—following the model of a neat division between good and bad youths at **155–8**—that if the relationships generally were felt by outsiders to be within the limits of acceptability (which were of course not easy to define), relatively relaxed attitudes might be adopted. If there seemed to be not too many lovers (see **52**), and not too many gifts or inappropriately extravagant lifestyles (see **75**), if the clothing worn or the mannerisms adopted were not too bizarre, and there were not too many gratuitous displays of affection, then one suspects that relatively little damage might occur: the questions of whether they stuck to kisses or intercrural sex, what the junior partner got out of it, and in particular whether anal sex was involved, or whether they switched sexual roles, need not have gone beyond relatively harmless gossip. Polite or friendly discussions might wish to assume they had not, more cynical observers, or enemies, would adopt the tone found in comedy and assume the opposite.[149] Neither group would feel so far that the law should be involved at any stage. But if circumstantial evidence suggested the junior partner was 'selling' himself too easily, from excessive desire either for the sex itself, or for other pleasures and advantage, gossip would be the more intense and hostile, and prejudices about the nature of certain acts be invoked; but only if the youth

---

[147] Cf. Winkler (1990a: 61). D. Cohen (1987; 1991a: 187–8), and Hubbard (1998: 64–6), may make too much of this line of denunciation, in their attempts to paint a picture of fairly widespread hostility to the whole practice among many Athenians; on the other hand Davidson only refers to Pamphilos' allegation that Timarchos was Hegesandros' 'woman' (**111**, see note), and seems nowhere to consider why Aeschines here condems the offences as womanish and against nature.

[148] Cf. esp. Dover (1978: 106–9).

[149] Cf. the sensible discussions of Dover (1978); Vlastos (1987); Halperin (1990; 1995: 47–8).

later went into politics would even the threat of legal action arise, let alone a prosecution.[150]

Yet this dichotomy is of course far too neat. It assumes (as does Aeschines) an agreed, *ex post facto*, decision of the community on the youth's behaviour, whereas in fact, in many cases, disagreements and doubts would persist, and become affected by later events and relationships; it also assumes that the decision down which path to go was clear-cut at the time. During their erotic careers attractive youths faced difficult decisions whose effects would be hard to predict. As they contemplated whether to get involved in this sort of activity at all, how to respond to flattering attentions, how many lovers to encourage, how far to go with lovers, and when to switch from being a beloved to pursuing a boy as a lover,[151] they should have been aware of the dangers. Not only did they risk incurring contemporary shame and gossip, but they had to contemplate the unpredictable consequences of hostile gossip, and later threats of prosecution, which might possibly hamper their careers and status at any time in the future, and could even ruin them. If they had rival lovers competing for their attentions, they had to balance competing claims (attractiveness, wealth, intelligence, connections, and fame). They had also to calculate the dangers of playing the field too long, or rejecting one suitor for another, if one was too importunate, jealous, unhelpful, or violent. The gap between sensibly looking for the best and most valuable lover and appearing to behave like a mercenary 'escort' might seem slight; yet overstepping this almost invisible line might yet turn out to have been crucial, especially as the same facts and relationships would be very differently interpreted by friends and enemies, both at the time and later. Naturally disappointed lovers would make the most effective ene-

---

[150] Cf. also Omitowoju (1997: 5–7 and n. 19). Gossip might extend to adverse comments or jokes in comedy (cf. **157**). But the infrequency of comic references to current athletic or gymnasium stars, and the caution claimed by Ar. *Wasps* 1023–4, *Peace* 762–3, may suggest comic poets did try to avoid spreading uncertain gossip about possible bad boys, while constantly peddling the line that all future politicians were *euryproctoi* (cf. Sommerstein 1996: 331 and his lists; some of those he labels 'pathics' may of course be gymnastic stars, as well as the certain case of Autolykos).

[151] Cf. the picture of Kritoboulos (son of Kriton) in Xen. *Symp.* 4. 10–16, still attractive to many older men, including Sokrates, but himself the passionate, and noble, lover of Kleinias (son of Axiochos), whom he had first begun to fancy when they were both at school (4. 23–4); the relative growth of their facial and back hairs seems to be intended also to suggest that they are very close in age (cf. Davies, *APF* 336).

mies. The parodic speech Plato gives to 'Lysias' in the guise of the cunning suitor who claims not to be in love points up the many difficulties lovers and ex-lovers can cause for those boys who fear 'the established *nomos*, lest, when people find out, shame results' (*Phaidros* 231e). *Nomos* is usually, and rightly, interpreted to mean primarily 'established social values' here, but it may perhaps also convey a hint of a possible later prosecution under the law. As the speech makes clear, the danger to their reputations would come especially from over-emotional and passionate lovers blabbing of their conquests, creating enemies, among the boy's own parents or outside the family, through their jealous possessiveness, or reacting with vindictive hostility when their passion has cooled (*Phaidros* 231–4c).[152] Equally indicative seems to be Aristophanes' amusing claim that he never abused his sudden position as a famous poet either to try to pick up boys at the *palaistra* or to agree to attack someone's boyfriend (*paidika*) in a comedy when requested by the disgruntled lover (*Wasps* 1023–8).[153]

It is time to face the fundamental question of why these bizarre laws against adult citizen prostitution or *hetairesis* were explicitly directed solely at those who (subsequently, often much later) entered active political life.[154] Both Aeschines (esp. **195**) and Demosthenes (22. 30) confirm that this fact was well understood. Allusion is made to these laws as examples of Athens' excellent traditions at Isocr. 12. 139–40 (composed *c.* 342–339). Other laws in the Athenian system were also reserved specifically for use against the '*rhetores*', as Hypereides (*Eux.* 7–9) argues *à propos* of the legal procedure of the *eisangelia* law; he observes that as the *rhetores* claimed to derive extra honours and other benefits from political activities, they deserve to be subjected to greater risks.[155] Even so

---

[152] Good illustrations of all these points can also be found in the *Erotic Essay* attributed to Demosthenes, (esp. 17–21), a valuable document from the later fourth century whether written by Demosthenes or someone else.

[153] I would read this denial as a claim by a newly famous man to be refusing himself an understandable temptation (cf. Fisher 1998a: 97), rather than a claim to be sticking to one's common roots by displaying populist hostility to the pederastic ethos, as Hubbard (1998: 50–1).

[154] This point is properly highlighted by Winkler (1990a: 59–61). D. Cohen's treatment of these themes regularly speaks inaccurately of such illegitimate relationships 'disqualifying future citizens', which ignores this vital restriction (e.g. 1987: 8–9; 1991).

[155] On the honours politicians sought and received, and the widespread recognition, increasingly built into the official language of honorific inscriptions that 'love of honour' (*philotimia*) was the proper motive for public office and service, cf. on **129**, **195–6**, and Whitehead (1983 and 1993).

the offences envisaged under this procedure, at least properly and normally according to Hypereides, were essentially offences which the *rhetores* alone would be likely to be in a position to commit.[156] The procedure Aeschines calls the *dokimasia rhetoron* set up a group of preliminary qualifications which could be held, by a jury, to be so important that shameful failure in these areas of private life rendered the perpetrator unsuitable for the extra responsibilities of public life.

One common factor uniting these disqualifications may be identified as a failure in the primary functions or civic duties of a male citizen in relation to his military duties, his family responsibilities, and his sexual life (see on **28–32**). Another point constantly made in justification of these rules is the well-worn argument that any one who has shamed his parents, destroyed his inheritance, betrayed his courage and manhood, or sold his own body in shameful sex, would have no qualms about selling his country to the highest outside bidder. Another argument was that to have such people as the city's representatives brings it into disrepute (see **26, 65, 67**).[157] Also used was the argument that sexual deviants are somehow polluted, and may defile the sacred wreaths worn by officials (see. **19, 54, 95, 188**). One may, however, also go beyond all these common positions and, following up Hypereides' point, suggest that these laws fit into broader patterns of encouragement and control between the mass and the élite: the people encouraged the ambitious and active members of the élite to earn their rewards of extra honour and extra wealth, not only by forcing them to greater expenditure through liturgies, but also by forcing them to meet higher standards of personal morality, even though this was at the expense of some infringements of the Athenians' general ideals of personal freedom. Further, the mechanisms by which this control was exercised required prosecution to come from another (inevitably prominent) citizen, as did a great deal of the legal and political system; this kept the élite divided by their internal competitions, hatreds, and feuds. The show trials provided public entertainment and amusement both for the mass juries and for the bystanders who crowded the areas of the courts.[158] It is going too far to conclude that the so-

---

[156] Cf. also Hyper. *Dem.* 24–5, on differential penalties for bribe-taking; Hansen (1989: 213–14, 268–71).   [157] Cf. Winkler (1990a: 56–7).

[158] Cf. the analyses by Ober (1989); Foucault (1985); Winkler (1990a).

called *dokimasia rhetoron* had little to do with sex, and was almost entirely to do with élite competition and its harnessing by the people to maintain their control and amusement.[159] The moral concerns for male independence, for the maintenance of a masculine role, and for control over one's desires in the areas of sex and money, along with the demonstration of courage, family feeling, and care for property and inheritance, were all genuinely felt throughout the citizen community. But the crucial point is that they also felt it right to make these moral failings legally problematic only for the ambitious élite.

The dangers of prosecutions should not be exaggerated. Besides the Timarchos case, Aristophanes refers to an apparently successful prosecution of Gryttos by Kleon (*Knights* 876–9);[160] we find in Demosthenes' speech against Androtion the promise to bring a prosecution on such a charge against Androtion (22. 21–4), and in Aeschines' speech the report of a comparable threat against Hegesandros allegedly made by Aristophon of Azenia, which apparently had the desired effect of stopping his attacks on him (**64**, and see notes). It may well be that public, or private, threats to bring such a charge were much more frequent, and effective, than prosecutions which came to court. This raises all the more urgently the question of Aeschines' success.

8. 'BIG TIMARCHIAN WHORES': AESCHINES' STRATEGY AND ITS SUCCESS

The case was a triumph for Aeschines. His enemy, an established, middle-aged, well-connected politician who had held many offices, was disenfranchized and his career was ruined. If we can trust the published version of what he said in his prosecution of Aeschines in 343, Demosthenes believed that there was political mileage to be extracted from an attempt at exciting sympathy for the dishonoured Timarchos. He mentions Timarchos' aged

---

[159] So Winkler (1990a: 60–1); against, partly rightly, but also exaggerating the hostility to anal penetration as such, Thornton (1998: 258, n. 110).

[160] *LGPN* i. This allegation (whether factual or invention) is overlooked by Keuls (1995), in her otherwise simplistic and implausible argument that legal and social hostility to pederasty only began in the fourth century, primarily as a result of Democritus' medical theories. See also the accusation levelled by Andocides against Epichares, one of his prosecutors in the mysteries trial of 400 or 399 (Adoc. 1. 100), that Epichares was not eligible to plead in the courts because of his self-prostitution.

mother and his children, and arouses indignation at the spectacle of Aeschines, despite his own disgraceful public and private record, and those of his relatives, playing so heavily the role of the moral reformer (*sophronistes*), claiming that the *sophrosyne* of the nation's youth was in danger and that his prosecution would improve things (19. 283–7). Demosthenes' public reaction suggests two things: first, that the verdict could be presented as a surprise and an outrage, given Timarchos' long and hitherto unchallenged career in public life, and the complete absence of witnesses (19. 241–4); and second that what seemed to be the crucial argument leading to this travesty of justice could plausibly be said to be the serious concern assumed by Aeschines for the morality of the young.[161] One must note, however, that Demosthenes used the opportunity of this response to make a strong personal attack on the moral behaviour of Aeschines and his relatives; and one should also remember that some of the jurors may have been as much or more influenced by the other major allegations in the speech, how Timarchos has 'eaten up' his property, maltreated his family, and engaged in many acts of political corruption. Another cause of surprise at the result—then as now—is the wholly justified belief that the speech adduced nothing in the way of reliable evidence or witnesses, above all for the allegations of youthful sexual misconduct. This lack of human witnesses explains why Aeschines places such emphasis on the 'general knowledge' about Timarchos shared by all the jury, and why he built up the divinity and reliability of Report (*Pheme*) as a witness, going so far as to claim that it would be impious not to believe a Report which was found spread throughout the *polis* (see on **125–9**).[162] This section will examine aspects of Aeschines' presentation of Timarchos' character and reputation, and his heavy concentration on an alleged moral crisis, and suggest reasons why this strategy may have been so successful.

Historians primarily interested in the issues of the peace of Philokrates and the settlement of the Sacred War often infer from the verdict the contemporary state of public opinion towards these issues, and suggest that Demosthenes had not yet managed

---

[161] Notice also Aeschines' proud and defiant riposte at 2. 180 to Demosthenes' charge (19. 283–7).

[162] Cf. also on gossip in general in Athens, and the crucial importance of accepting it as reliable in this case, above all Hunter (1990; 1994: ch. 4).

seriously to undermine Aeschines' credibility as a non-corrupt politician and ambassador.[163] It is true that the speech is much concerned to undermine Demosthenes as the man likely to be commanding the defence and the main man behind the prosecution of Aeschines' over the embassy (see notes on **119–35, 131, 170–5**). But Aeschines' strategy was to avoid any serious discussion of the embassy and the peace. Philip, the embassy, and the Phokians are alluded to only to be explicitly declared completely out of bounds. Recent events are used only as the basis for the personal attack on Demosthenes' conduct on the embassy and back in Athens, his lack of culture and *savoir-faire* in his allegations about the boy Alexander and Aeschines' alleged attentions to him,[164] his dubious relations with his rhetorical pupils (including the murder allegations over Aristarchos), his frilly clothes and *kinaidia*, and his supposed demonstration of his power in diverting from issues of personal morality to foreign policy.[165] Instead of focusing on the political issues, Aeschines forces the jury to contemplate unpleasantly lurid images of his two opponents, as part of his more general aim to win a conviction on moral grounds, not on the political grounds of the value of the peace or his own repute.

As well as offering narratives of Timarchos' past, the speech purports to present a powerful image of the apparently respected politician who was in reality an unreconstructed, and unreconstructable, degenerate. Attention is focused both on his body and on his name. Early in the speech the jury is 'reminded' of Timarchos' current physical appearance, carrying the imprint of his shameful past so vividly that it is impossible to take him seriously, or attend to his arguments. Aeschines presents a picture of Timarchos' performing 'all-in fighting routines naked in the assembly' (**26**), and claims that the sight of his body ruined by drink and debauchery was so offensive that it caused sensible men to veil their heads in shame that the city was using such men as him as advisers. By this dramatic means, one of the crucial arguments of the case is presented in a vivid picture; simultaneously

---

[163] e.g. Ellis (1976: 128); E. M. Harris (1995: 105–6).

[164] An agreeably retaliatory reversal of the terms Aeschines has earlier claimed the 'General' will use against him: see on **131**.

[165] See notes on **166–6**, and above all the excellent analysis of Davidson (1997: esp. 260–7, 306–8).

the jury sees Timarchos the politician but is prevented from hearing what he was talking about. They are permitted to see merely his raddled body shamefully and gratuitously exposed.[166]

The theme of Timarchos' significant nickname is subtly developed in concert with his appearance to reinforce the idea that he can never be taken seriously, as the riddle of his name is teasingly explored and explained at strategic points throughout the speech. A nickname could be said to fall within the sphere of the 'goddess' *Pheme*, a form of common speech or gossip which reliably reflects an important truth of the individual's character. It is first mentioned, on the occasion of Timarchos' naked assembly display, as a sobriquet as well-known as Aristeides', though of opposed meaning, and so well known that neither needed to be spelt out (**26**, see notes).[167] Another reason for assumed diffidence becomes clearer when, at the crucial point (**52**) where Aeschines claims Timarchos' succession of lovers entitles him to use the *pornos*-term, not just *hetairesis*, he makes a great to-do about actually uttering the word (though he had used it when allegedly citing a law in **29**).[168] An extra, humorous, point would be picked up by those who have realized that it is precisely this word which is his nickname. If any have not yet got this point, a further clue comes in the next visual portrait of Timarchos' unsuccessful displays in the assembly, as the debate on the Pnyx rebuilding dissolves into a string of double entendres and helpless laughter at **77–80**, and the argument is put that the people had in effect on that occasion already voted on the question of whether Timarchos had been a '*pornos*'. As part of the full-scale praise of *Pheme* the reliable and revered goddess, it becomes at last explicit that Timarchos' nickname is recognized by the jury to be precisely *ho pornos*, the whore, just as Demosthenes' nickname, *Battalos*, means the 'Arse' (and not the 'stammerer', as Demosthenes likes to say is the meaning of his nickname: see on **131**). When they hear the

---

[166] According to Dem. 19. 286, Timarchos was energetically proposing motions stipulating the death penalty for those who carried arms or naval equipment to Philip. Cf. notes *ad loc.*, and Davidson (1997: 261).

[167] The addition of 'the so-called Just' is probably a later gloss, see note. Aeschines evidently liked this ploy, as 'Aristeides the just' is also alluded to in both Aeschines' other speeches: see 2. 23, and esp. 3. 181—where he makes a similar contrast between Aristeides' nickname and Demosthenes' of Battalos, cf. on **131**.

[168] Cf. his reticence just before on the statement he has written for Misgolas to confirm under oath, forbearing to put in 'the actual name of the act that Misgolas used to commit with him' (**45**).

name Timarchos (a name borne by a good many Athenians) they ask 'Which Timarchos? The whore (*pornos*)' (**130**)?

This point recurs, and some evidence for this audience reaction is presented, when Aeschines brings into the argument the difference between Timarchos and his namesake, the pretty but respectable nephew of Iphikrates. The alleged fact that a jibe at a 'recent' comedy at the rural Dionysia mentioning 'big Timarchian whores' was understood by all to be to Timarchos is proof that Timarchos is evidently 'the true heir of this practice'. As the whore *par excellence* of his generation, he cannot now leave the ranks of the self-prostituted, because he has chosen to register into their 'property-group' (*symmoria*) and cannot (as a slave) desert to the life-styles of the free men (see notes on **157–9**). His nickname, this suggests, is a deliberately self-inflicted designation (because it accurately reflects his life), which cannot be removed. Aeschines further suggests that Demosthenes may try to mitigate the effects of Timarchos' nickname (as he does in his own case), by the argument that it was because Timarchos was pretty (*horaios*) that he had acquired an unpleasant nickname through slanderous distortion (**126**).

Further confirmation that Demosthenes could not avoid making concessions on this issue, and had to admit both that Timarchos' youth had aroused suspicion and that he had recently been behaving foolishly, comes in the embassy speech (Dem. 19. 235; and cf. also 251):

So then, Aeschines did not prosecute this man (sc. Phrynon), because he sent his own son to Philip to his dishonour; but if an individual on his point of adulthood were better than another in appearance, and if he then, not anticipating the suspicion which would arise from his looks at that time, lived his life after that rather more energetically, that was the man (sc. Timarchos) whom Aeschines brought to trial on grounds of having prostituted himself (*peporneumenon*).

If in fact Timarchos had been referred to as 'the whore', even before Aeschines first announced the prosecution, however unfairly, this may help explain the attitude of a good many of the convicting jurymen; especially if the comedy mentioned 'Timarchian whores' had been performed in winter 347/6, rather than the following year (see above pp. 6–8).[169] On balance it seems

---

[169] But the *hypothesis* asserts that 'from this trial people called *pornoi* 'Timarchuses'; this

unlikely that the allegations about double entendres in the assembly in the Pnyx debate, and the nickname *ho pornos*, were entirely made up after the laying of the charge, and probable that allegations about Timarchos' relations with Misgolas, Pittalakos, and Hegesandros had been dredged up by his personal and political opponents for a decade or more.[170] But many jurors may well have been unaware of them, or had forgotten them; Aeschines worked hard to make them seem familiar and reliable.

But Aeschines had not only to persuade the Athenians of the reliability of the rumours, but more importantly that they mattered enough to ruin a career, especially if such prosecutions were rare. Of course he deploys for all they are worth the usual arguments (summarized above): the threat to Athens' reputation that one of their representatives was deficient in the qualifications of masculine citizenship; the probability that one who so betrayed such ideals against his family, his inheritance, and his own body would also be treacherous and corrupt in public life; the allegations that scandals in Timarchos' actual political career confirmed this expectations (and these parts of the case may well also have carried considerable weight). But more was surely needed. As we have seen, Aeschines also works hard to elucidate and defend the vital, if somewhat subtle and shifting, distinction between 'noble love', which he also calls 'democratic', disciplined (*sophron*) or moderate (*metrios*), and the shameful, degrading, enslaving, and self-hybristic behaviour of those who had too many lovers, were living off them, and consented to whatever sexual acts they demanded. Demosthenes later suggested that what especially carried weight—wholly mistakenly—with the jury was Aeschines' strategy in planting himself on the high plateau of moral ground with his assertion that Athens' young were in present danger of corruption: (19. 287).

It is very important to take seriously here the surprising fact

may be based on the comic joke referred to in **157**, on the assumption, very possibly correct (cf. Wankel 1988), that this joke was made in the winter of 345, while the charge had been made and the trial was awaited.

[170] Cf. e.g. Demosthenes' allegations against Androtion (Dem. 22.30 ff, alluded to by Aesch. 1. 165, see note). Suspicion that this damaging nickname was a careful creation of Aeschines since his decision to prosecute Timarchos cannot quite be erased. Lanni (1997) has pointed to the large crowd of bystanders in important trials like this (cf. on **77, 117, 173**), who might vocally confirm or deny allegations of what all Athenians are supposed to 'know'; but of course many of the most vocal bystanders would be partisans of one side or the other.

that Aeschines presents his opponent, the so-called 'General', as sharing with him important basic assumptions about this vital distinction (**131–40**, see notes). They agree that proper homosexual relationships were an essential part of Athenian culture, to be found in Homer and among the democratic founding fathers Harmodios and Aristogeiton, and that all Athenians understood this ideal; they agree that to participate in such relationships was part of the proper aspirations of many ordinary Athenians, whether for themselves or for their attractive sons (see especially **134**, and also **156–7**).[171] Some have recently disputed the plausibility of this picture, holding that other evidence compels the view that the emotional homosexual relationships that blossomed in the *gymnasia* and the *symposia*, and produced jealousies and fights, in all of which Aeschines admits he participates, remained pretty much the preserve of upper-class or leisured groups, and would be regarded as alien by the majority of jurors, who would not imagine themselves or their sons as likely to be involved, and would find any actual sexual expressions of these relationships with distaste. Hence they seek ways of evading the implications of this argument.[172]

This approach, in my view, underestimates the coherence of the speech. The suggestions that the speech is somehow deliberately incoherent, because it is aimed at two separate audiences,[173] or that this section praising 'noble and democratic love' was added in the published version, for the more educated reading public,[174] are neither necessary nor convincing. 'The General's' argument is that Aeschines, whose own pursuit of boys, fights, and poetry are coarse and unsophisticated, can only assume (like the comic poets) that all relationships are of the 'wrong' sort, and so assumes that Timarchos' relationships were

---

[171] Cf. Dover (1978); Winkler (1990a: 64); Cantarella (1992: 21–2); Fisher (1998a: 100–4).

[172] e.g. Ober (1989: 257, but also 283); S. C. Todd (1990a: 166).

[173] See Sissa (1999: 155–7), who accuses Aeschines of being inconsistent and incoherent in his attempts, first to maintain a distinction between 'a good and a disgusting homosexual eros', love against money, and second to claim that the bad eros involves acting against (male) nature; she tries to explain this in terms of two audiences, with two radically opposed sets of attitudes, those represented by the 'General' and the élites, defending the noble form, and the mass of Athenians, happy to accept the whole sexual business as distasteful. But it better fits Aeschines' strategy throughout the speech, and the rest of the evidence as well, to assume many, perhaps most, Athenians appreciated and tried to maintain this delicate, and perhaps strictly untenable, balance.

[174] See Hubbard (1998: 66–8).

shameful; and the effect of a conviction in the case would be to diminish the people's understanding and sympathy for the 'noble love'. Aeschines' clear response is that it is the 'General' who is displaying a snobbish contempt both for him and for the jury, in attributing to them a lack of understanding of the niceties of the cultural phenomenon. He thus identifies his cultural level with the jury, admitting his own, not too impressive origins; he claims that he has (like his brothers) managed to gain admittance to full-scale participation in gymnastic life and in the concomitant pederastic affairs, fights, and erotic poetry, and fully understands the importance of the distinction (and, I think one can assume, implies that he engages in restrained and consensual forms of 'proper' sex);[175] and finally he agrees with 'the General' that *all* men do and should long for their sons to be attractive and to attract attention, from lovers and from observers at large (**133–6**). This is supported by the later picture of the interest all citizens took in the achievements and careers of the prettiest youths (**157–9**).[176]

Further, and equally important, it is not in fact at all implausible that such views could be widely held, and that they have probably been increasing over the previous half-century or so. One may point first to the constant exposure to large audiences of attractive, naked citizens and foreigners, running, boxing, wrestling, posing in the 'manhood' (*euandria*) contests, jumping on and off chariots, at the games and at the innumerable other festival competitions at varying levels.[177] Displays of beautiful youths exercising or engaged in courtship, or sex, or simply named as *kalos*, on a good many Attic vases may also testify in the late archaic period both to visual tastes and perhaps to general interests in the named beauties, though interpretation of the possible targets of these images and namings remains very controversial.[178] In the more democratic period from the time of Kimon

---

[175] Cf. Dover (1978: 42–5); Hindley (1999: 89–90).

[176] Cf. also Winkler (1990a: 63–4).

[177] On the significance of athletic nudity in arousing the admiring 'gaze' of the general public, as well as the desire of individual would-be lovers, Bonfante (1989); Bossi (1995); Stewart (1997: 33–4, 67); and in relation to the praise poems of Pindar, see Instone (1990); Steiner (1998). On the *euandria*, cf. Crowther (1985); Neils (1994): Fisher (1998a: 92, 98); Goldhill (1998: 108, 114).

[178] Cf. Kilmer (1993b); Slater (1998); Lissarrague (1999) and P. J. Wilson (2000: 254–6). Much commoner than the labelling of a specific painted beauty on the vase as *kalos* is the simple inscribing of words 'the boy's lovely' or 'you're lovely' (*ho pais kalos* and *kalos ei*), inviting the viewer(s) (e.g. at a *symposion*) to apply the label appropriately.

and Pericles onwards, official sculptural representation (most famously the Parthenon frieze) may present the youthful 'citizen' as a frozen, often naked, unaroused, beardless youth or ephebe; the sculptures encouraged an eroticized but sanitized gaze at images which are idealized but not necessarily to be seen as aristocratic or heroized: rather visions of naked loveliness combined with decorum and order, *sophrosyne* and *kosmiotes*, with signs of arousal strictly under control.[179] Such representations as ideals may well have encouraged hoplite fathers to send sons to the *gymnasia*, and train for the ephebic and other festival contests, albeit with evident fears of possible adverse consequences; opportunities certainly existed for considerable athletic participation, in the *ephebeia*, and in the festivals for fairly large numbers of young men of middling citizen families.[180] I have also argued more speculatively that the formation of homosexual relationships at the *gymnasia* and its associated cultural activities between richer lovers and talented and/or attractive youths of less favoured families may have been an additional cause of greater mobility into the athletic, political, or leisured élites of fourth-century Athens.[181]

Of course the view that 'all' jurors nourished ambitions for their sons' admiration and advancement through successful gymnastic and pederastic exposure may be largely ideological, as may be comparable flattery of jurymen as slave-owners or as effectively controlling their women's capacity to move outside the household, and as representations of them as *eisphora*-payers almost certainly is.[182] But they may also make some sense in a fairly mobile society full of contradictions, where access to a leisure class was increasing, while there were relatively limited opportunities for really serious luxuries even for the rich. Hence many middling citizens may in fact have been open to persuasion that the delicate moral choices open to boys or youths pursued by older lovers might yet face their own sons or those known to them, or they might at least hope so; and they may therefore be more likely to

---

[179] Cf. Stewart (1997: 63–85); R. G. Osborne (1998a; 1998b); other aspects of the democratization of the ideal Greek body in Humphreys (1999).

[180] Cf. R.G. Osborne (1993); Kyle (1992; 1996); Fisher (1998a).

[181] Fisher (1998a); for similar arguments for varied participation at *symposia* and other drinking and eating settings, Fisher (2000). The constant comic assertion that it is the young *euryproktoi* who become, in steadily increasing numbers (cf. esp. Plato Com. 202 K/A), the new politicians can be seen as the typically cynical response to this perception.

[182] Cf. e.g. S. C. Todd (1990a).

take seriously allegations about dangers of serious immorality at these settings. The spread of gymnastic and sympotic activities and associated culture, as well as the widening of other educational activities often attached to the *gymnasia*, which offered boys 'transferable skills' such as rhetoric and philosophy, may then all help to explain how this prosecution successfully evoked a widespread concern for the moral well-being of the nation's youth.

The growing threat to Athens' foreign interests and political independence from Philip and Macedonian power, and the protracted and uneasy debate on the best ways of facing it (the political issues that divided Demosthenes and Aeschines), are likely in principle to have stimulated a wider debate about the fitness of the polis' institutions, and the moral 'fibre' of the young. Major trials would provide occasions for such debates to surface, and their results would have their effects on their development. There is no doubt that the defeat at Chaeronea in 338 and the creation of Macedonian hegemony through the League of Corinth directly inspired a major reorganization of a great many aspects of Athenian life, the changes which we associate with 'Lycurgan Athens'. There is good evidence for significant signs of the debates beginning a little earlier, around the time of the trial, which need to be brought into the discussion of Aeschines' strategy and to the verdict.

First, there is the *diapsephisis* of 346/5, the complete revision of the citizen lists held by the demes, itself mentioned twice in the speech (**77–8, 114–15**), either the only one, or one of the only two, held between 451/0 and 322.[183] The decision to approve such an elaborate process (see Dem. 57. 49) must have reflected strong and widespread anger that money or illicit sexual liaisons were responsible for filling the demes illegitimately with metics, slaves, and sons of *hetairai*; the process itself, however, may have done nearly as much damage in allowing manipulators to expel their enemies, and by creating new grounds for feuds, as Euxitheos alleged happened to him in Halimous (Dem. 57 *passim*), and Aeschines alleged Timarchos somehow assisted his friends to perpetrate in Kydathenaion.

Second, another famous trial may be relevant. Apollodoros'

---

[183] Cf. Whitehead (1986a: 99–109). The doubtful case is that of 445/4, probably a general *diapsephisis*, but conceivably a very large rash of prosecutions for breach of citizenship rules in relation to the special grain distribution from Psammetichos of Egypt (see *scholia* on Ar. *Wasps* 718; Philochoros, *FGH* 238 F 119).

prosecution of Neaira (Ps. Dem. 59), part of his personal and political quarrel with Stephanos, probably occurred a few years later than Timarchos' trial.[184] Stephanos' sons had presumably survived the 346/5 scrutiny in their deme (whether or not a challenge was mounted then, it is not surprising that Apollodoros makes no mention of it); a few years later Apollodoros (and perhaps Demosthenes, who had been involved with Apollodoros at the start of this affair) felt the time appropriate to go for revenge on Stephanos by bringing the case against the apparently famous *hetaira*.[185] In the case the central issues are the boundaries of citizenship, marriage, and inheritance, and a major part of the speech is taken up with lurid sexual narratives. The success of the Timarchos case, following on the *diapsephisis* furore, as well as changing views about the desirability of the peace, may have encouraged them to think that moral denunciation of a *hetaira*'s career of sexual outrages and breaches of the citizenship rules would play well in the court. Unfortunately we do not know the result, though the case against Stephanos is also notably weak and rests on arguments about the parentage of the woman called Phano which would have been very hard to prove.[186]

Other evidence concerns the procedures and physical settings of some central democratic institutions. There were evidently allegations of widespread political bribery flying around at the time of our speech (see **86–7** and notes). Sometime around 340, the physical arrangements and admissions procedures for the major law-court complex underwent a highly elaborate reorganization (new fencing, complex allotment machines, juror identification tokens, and so on), in order further to minimize any possibilities of bribing juries as they entered the buildings.[187] A law passed just before our speech (**33–4**, see notes, and also Aesch. 3. 4), created a procedure whereby members of each tribe in turn

---

[184] On Apollodoros (*LGPN* 68; *PA* 1411; *PAA* 142425) see esp. Trevett (1992). The trial has been dated to *c.* 343–340; see Trevett (1992: 48–9); Carey, *Neaira* 3; Kapparis, *Neaira* 28–31, but see now Wallace (2000): 591. Cf. below on **186**, for similar arguments used in the two speeches.

[185] Stephanos, a minor politician (*LGPN* 33; *PA* 12887; Hansen, *Inventory* 59) had won a case against Apollodoros for having proposed an illegal motion in 348, and perhaps in 346 followed this up with a co-ordinated but unsuccessful attempt to convict him for homicide of a slavewoman. See Ps. Dem. 59. 1. 10, with Carey, *Neaira* 86–90 and Kapparis, *Neaira* 29–30, 174–8, 182–4. [186] See Kapparis, *Neaira* 31–43.

[187] See the detailed and convincing accounts, based on Arist. *Ath. Pol.* 63–9, and the archaeological remains, in Boegehold *et al.* (1995: esp. 36–41, 110–13).

were charged with keeping order, or reducing heckling and undignified behaviour in the assembly. Aeschines of course argues that this law was introduced as a direct response to Timarchos' shameful gestures and display of saggy flesh. Timarchos' other contribution to recent debates, on the Pnyx (**79–85**), allegedly produced a rash of double entendres which brought into collision two clashing worlds—the open, public, spaces of debate, and the dark haunts of prostitutes' houses and deserted places—and demonstrated that Timarchos' deep familiarity with the one in effect precluded his serious participation in the other. The assembly's laughter at Autolykos the Areopagite's confusion at the talk of 'quietness' and 'cisterns' (**83–4**) may also suggest popular concern at shady activities near the assembly-site; again Aeschines avoids making explicit the nature of the debate (see notes on **81**). But whether it was merely a relatively minor tidying up of unsavoury areas on the fringes of the Pnyx, or the beginnings of what would become the major rebuilding of Pnyx III,[188] the debate suggests that the people were already worried that the central decision-making space of the democracy should look and sound respectable, and that the major rebuilding of the public spaces and defences of the city associated with the Lycurgan period may have begun to be planned already in the mid-340s.[189]

This was also precisely the period when the Areopagos was asserting a more prominent and proactive role in political life. Aeschines mentions, obliquely, its role in the debate on the Pnyx (whatever line it may have taken), and shows it considerable respect (tinged with some gentle humour at its pompous representative Autolykos).[190] It seems to have played some part in investigating the religious aspects of the alleged participation by Neaira's daughter, as the wife of the Archon *basileus* Theagenes, in the 'Sacred Marriage' with Dionysos at the Anthesteria festival (Ps. Dem. 59. 80–4);[191] these are clear signs of its growing concern to protect Athens' moral and civic identity. Some time after this trial Demosthenes proposed yet greater supervisory powers to punish offenders to the body (Dein. I. 62–3) and there came, ironically

[188] So H. A. Thompson (1982); Hansen (1996a), and notes on **81**.

[189] Notice also that some of Timarchos' reportedly ambivalent phrases also suggest proposals to strengthen Athenian defences ('towers').

[190] Despite *his* own later troubles, the prosecution by Lycurgus of *c.* 338, Lyc. I. 53, fr. 9.

[191] Cf. Wallace (1985: 108–9); de Bruyn (1995: 124–5); Carey, *Neaira* 126–8 and Kapparis, *Neaira* 344–8.

enough, the serious snub to Aeschines over the Antiphon affair and the dispute with Delos at the Delphian Amphictiony.[192] Already in the years *c.* 346–340, then, the Areopagos commanded considerable respect, was given extra duties, and displayed a renewed vigour for the defence, the liberties, and the moral well-being of the city. After Chaeronea, it maintained its prominence and high profile, amid much controversy, as testified above all by the specific mention of it as a possible danger to the democracy in Eukrates' law about traitors of 337/6,[193] and the cautious approval offered to it by Lycurgus in 330 (1. 12, 52–4). Both Aeschines and Lycurgus interestingly combine guarded praise for the conservative, dignified, and stable court of the Areopagos, with equally guarded praise of some Spartan institutions and moral values.[194]

Finally, one of the major changes rightly associated with the Lycurgan years specifically set out to transform the training of the young, namely the reform of the *ephebeia* achieved, it seems, by Epikrates' law of 335/4.[195] Aeschines focuses throughout the speech on the message the verdict will send out to the young, and repeatedly claims that their *sophrosyne* and that of their guardians and teachers was in urgent need of protection and regulation. One can suggest then that the concern for current standards of education and upbringing offered to young Athenians (which both Aeschines and his opponents sought to tap into) helped to produce the major change in the *ephebeia*. The new ephebes after 335/4 had a far more systematic programme of military, civic, and cultic training and participation, in the Peiraeus, in the *gymnasia*, and then in the second year in the frontier forts, and, probably, a much more extensive set of activities in the city's festivals.[196] Their gymnastic training became more structured and controlled, in new premises.[197] Most notably, they came under the

[192] Cf. above p. 8, and see Carawan (1985: 124–32); Wallace (1985: 176–7); de Bruyn (1995: 126–8); E. M. Harris (1995: 121–2); Hansen (1983a: 194) dates Demosthenes' law immediately after Chaeronea.

[193] *SEG* 12. 87 (1952); Ostwald (1955); Wallace (1985: 180–4); cf. also Dein. 1. 62–3 on alleged contradictions in Demosthenes' handling of the Areopagos.

[194] Cf. Fisher (1994: 370–9).

[195] Lyc. fr. 25 Sauppe.

[196] Cf. Reinmuth (1971); Mitchell (1970); above all Humphreys (1985: 205–9), and also Sekunda (1990 and 1992).

[197] Humphreys (1985a: 207 and n. 32); Xen. *Poroi* 4. 51–2 complained in the mid-350s that while the ephebes had trained in *gymnasia*, organized by the gymnasiarchs, they did not spend enough time there.

control of new officials, who were given programmatically strict titles which echo, strikingly, the two key value terms for moral control and order used *ad nauseam* in our speech. Ten 'Regulators'—*sophronistai*—(one from each tribe), were elected by the people, each from a short list of three selected by the tribes 'from those over 40 who they believe to be the best and most suitable to have care for the *ephebes*'; and the people also elected one 'Director'—*kosmetes*—to be supreme commander of the whole body of ephebes (Arist. *Ath. Pol.* 42. 2). The titles ('very moralizing and Spartan in tone'),[198] the age-limits and the facts that the more technical aspects of military and gymnastic training were in the hands of the generals and specialist *paidotribai* and combat-teachers, all suggest that the function of the *kosmetes* and the *sophronistai* was above all seen as the protection of the ephebes ('young, handsome and conspicuous in their short distinctive cloaks')[199] from improper sexual attentions or behaviour, whether instigated by themselves or older pursuers. This particular aspect of the major ephebic reform must then be in part a response to a feeling, very much in accord with the views expressed so strongly in our speech, that increased guidance and protection were needed for the boys and the youths at publicly approved institutions such as schools, *gymnasia*, and liturgically managed festival contests.[200] The tightening of the *ephebeia* and the message of the new officials' titles and ages also gives good support to the view that Aeschines' speech picked up effectively on a growing mood of moral anxiety for the Athenian young, and perhaps also contributed to its spread.[201]

Thus, while the competing politicians may have treated their mutual moral assaults and hypocritical accusations of corruption, treachery, or a misspent youth as part of the game of politics, yet

[198] Hansen (1989: 301). Ironically and interestingly Dem. 19. 287 uses the term in mockery of the pose Aeschines (and his relatives) have adopted for the trial. See also notes on **6, 8, 22** on the use of *sophrosyne* and *kosmos* in the speech.

[199] Humphreys (1985a: 208).

[200] The extra age-limit of 40 for the *choregoi* of boys had been already established some time earlier in the fourth century (**9–12** cf. *Ath. Pol.* 56.3, with Rhodes *ad loc.*; both Alkibiades and the speaker of Lys. 21 (1–5) had so acted when less than 40. Cf also the narrative of Antiphon 6. 1–13, which shows the care a *choregos* for the boys' dithyramb in the late fifth century should take to avoid giving offence or alarm to their parents when recruiting and training the boys.

[201] More generally, a wider fourth-century debate over the content of education both in elementary schools and in the varied forms of post-school education, can be seen in Plato, Isocrates, and Aristotle (*Pol.* 8), and see Ford (1999: 243).

the Athenians could on some occasions, at least, still decide to take them with deadly earnestness. So they did at least in 345. We need not suppose they did so out of any particular approval of Aeschines; it can be seen as part of a set of confused yet insistent responses to the challenges facing their political and social systems. On this view, then, the verdict of the majority of the jury suggests that many of them did care about the preservation of the delicate boundary between, on the one hand, the legitimate homosexual pursuit of attractive youths, and the youths' decent acceptance of (not too many) lovers, and, on the other, the more ruthless pursuit of sexual gratification by the elders, and the youths' surrender of their bodies for 'mercenary' reasons which might mean that they, like Timarchos, might be known years afterwards as 'whores'. It was probably above all for these reasons that they decided to end Timarchos' career, and demonstrate that they believed it to be right to impose higher standards of civic, familial, and sexual morality on those active in political life. What counted for these jurymen in the Athens of the mid-340s was in part a not unreasonable sense of alarm for the future of their independence and their political system, and more generally a vague and confused fear for their culture, education, and the 'moral fibre' of their citizens. This fear, after the major defeat at Chaironeia, did much to produce Lycurgan Athens; previously it had played a large part in the ending of Timarchos' political career.

The Text and the Translation

9. SOURCES OF THE TEXT

I have translated the latest Teubner text, by M. R. Dilts (1997), and the main aim of the translation has been to convey Aeschines' arguments as clearly and accurately as I could. The primary basis of our knowledge of the text circulated by Aeschines, and collected in the Alexandrian libraries, is a number of medieval manuscripts, the oldest of which (*f*) dates from the late tenth century AD; also important are a number of other manuscripts (thirteenth to fifteenth centuries), which often share many readings and other characteristics, and are conventionally grouped under the label β, and a fifteenth-century manuscript designated D.[202] In a few places papyri discovered in the sands of Egypt, mostly written in the second and third centuries AD, make contributions. I comment on disputed readings only where they are of historical significance. Very brief, and often unreliable, 'lives' of the orator, and extracts from ancient commentaries (called the *scholia*) are included in the margins of some of the manuscripts (recently edited by M. R. Dilts); the information contained therein can at times be valuable, or at least worthy of consideration.

10. THE DOCUMENTS

Many manuscripts of our law-courts speeches include what purport to be the texts of the laws and testimony cited by the orator and read out to the court. Opinion is divided as to whether all of these citations are spurious, later compositions by students of rhetoric editing these texts in the Hellenistic or Roman periods, or whether only some of them are: there are some arguments for suspecting all documents in principle, but the prevailing view at present is that some may be genuine, and each case needs to be judged on its merits. In the case of this speech, the decision is easy: all the documents included are universally and rightly condemned as spurious. The general reasons are that these documents are only found in the set of later manuscripts grouped under the collective label β, not in the oldest manuscript, *f*; that documents are found only in the first part of Aeschines' speech 1 (the last comes at 1. 68); and that there is no room for any documents in the surviving papyri. Some of the more specific reasons for believing individual documents to be spurious are given in the notes.[203]

---

[202] For the manuscript tradition see Diller (1979).

[203] The last systematic discussion was a century ago, by Drerup (1898: esp. 305–8 on documents in Aeschines). Recent discussions: Carey, *Neaira* 20 and *passim*, Kapparis, *Neaira* 56–60, and MacDowell, *Meidias* 1990, 43–7, E. M. Harris (1992: 70–7) and see also my note on **16**, on the text of the *hybris*-law cited in Dem. 21. 47.

AESCHINES

Against Timarchos

TRANSLATION

(**1**) Not one of my fellow citizens, men of Athens, have I ever prosecuted in a public action, not one have I disturbed in an examination of office; on the contrary I believe that I have demonstrated myself to be a reasonable man in all such matters. Hence when I saw that the city was being greatly damaged by the defendant Timarchos who was speaking before the people contrary to the laws, and when I was myself in person being made a victim of a sykophantic prosecution—just how I shall reveal as my speech proceeds—(**2**) I concluded that it would be one of the most shameful things for me not to come to the aid of the whole city, the laws, you yourselves, and me. Knowing that he was guilty of the charges which you heard read by the Clerk of the Court a little time ago, I have brought this case of scrutiny against him. So it seems, men of Athens, that what is commonly said of public trials is indeed the case: private enmities do very often correct public affairs.

(**3**) It is not the city, it will be seen, that is responsible for this whole trial facing Timarchos; it is not the laws, not you the jury, not I; it is that man there who has brought it on himself. The laws proclaimed to him, because he had lived so shameful a life, that he should not speak before the people, thus imposing on him an injunction, in my judgement, not difficult for him to keep—in fact perfectly simple. It was open to him, if he had been sensible, not to play the sykophantic prosecutor against me. On these matters I hope to have spoken in a moderate way.

(**4**) I am not unaware, men of Athens, that what I propose to say at the start of my speech are things which you will clearly have heard from others in the past; but it seems especially timely for me to employ the same argument to you now. It is agreed that there are three forms of government in the world, tyranny, oligarchy, and democracy; tyrannies and oligarchies are governed by the characters of those in power, but democratic cities are governed by the established laws. (**5**) You should be aware, men of Athens, that it is the laws that protect the bodies of those living in a democracy and their system of government, but it is suspicion and armed guards which protect the affairs of tyrants and oligarchs.

Oligarchs and those who operate any type of unequal government need to be on their guard against those trying to overthrow their systems by the law of force; but you, who operate an egalitarian and legal government, must be on your guard against those whose speeches or styles of life are contrary to the laws. This is the source from which you will derive your strength, when you keep to your system of laws and do not find your system overthrown by those who systematically break the laws. (**6**) It is my view that it is our duty, when we are making laws, to have as our aim that we create laws that are well framed and suitable for our type of government; but it is equally our duty, when we have enacted the laws, to obey the laws we have established and to punish those who do not obey them, if the city's affairs are to be in a good state.

Consider, men of Athens, how much concern was shown for moral control by Solon, our ancient lawgiver, and by Drakon and the other lawgivers of those times. (**7**) First of all they legislated about the moral control of our boys, and they laid down expressly what habits a free-born boy was to adopt and how he was to be brought up; and secondly about the young men, and thirdly about the other age-groups in turn, not only in the case of private individuals, but also of the *rhetores*. When they had written these laws they left them in trust to you, and made you their guardians. (**8**) I would like now to develop my argument in the same manner which the lawgiver used in his laws. First I shall expound to you the laws which have been established on the subject of the orderly conduct of your boys, then the laws about the young men, and third those about the other age-groups in turn, not only in the case of private individuals but also of the *rhetores*. In this way I am sure that my arguments will be easy to understand. I would like at the same time, men of Athens, first to expound to you what the laws of the city say, and then after that to expound in contrast Timarchos' character; you will find that he has lived in a manner contrary to all the laws.

(**9**) First, the case of schoolteachers. They are those to whom as a matter of necessity we entrust our own children, and their livelihood depends on their behaving with self-control, and destitution results from the opposite behaviour. The lawgiver, however, seems not to trust them, and expressly prescribes, first, the time that the free-born boy should go to the school, and then how many boys may attend the school, and when they should go home. (**10**) He forbids the schoolteachers to open the schools, and the gymnastic teachers to open the wrestling-schools (*palaistrai*), before the sun has risen, and commands them to close them before sunset; thus he casts the greatest suspicion on occasions for solitary contact and on darkness. He prescribes which youngsters are able to attend the schools, and what ages they should be, and provides for an office that shall regulate the schools. He provides for the supervision of the slave-attendants, and for the regulation of the *Mouseia* in the schools and the *Hermaia* in the *palaistrai*; finally for the regulation of the company the boys may keep and of the cyclical choruses. (**11**) Under this heading, he prescribes that the *choregos*, the man who is going to spend his own wealth on you, must be over 40 years of age when he does this, in order that he may only be involved with your boys when he has already reached the most self-controlled time of his life. These laws will be read to you, so that you may know that the lawgiver believed that it was the well-brought-up boy who became the man useful to the city; but when the nature of a person receives a bad start right from his education, he thought that the result of such badly brought-up boys would be citizens similar to the defendant, Timarchos. [*To the Clerk of the Court*] Read these laws to the jury.

(**12**) *Laws*

[*The teachers of the boys shall open the schools not earlier than sunrise, and they shall close them before sunset. It shall not be permitted to any who may be older than the boys to enter when the boys are inside, unless he be a son of the teacher or a brother or a sister's husband. If any one enters against these regulations, he shall be punished by death. The gymnasiarchs shall not permit under any circumstances any one who has reached manhood to enter in the contests at the Hermaia; if he permits this and does not exclude them from the gymnasium, he shall be liable to the law concerning the corruption of free males. The* choregoi *appointed by the people shall have attained an age greater than 40 years.*]

(**13**) Next, then, men of Athens, he lays down laws to cover offences which, great as they are, are still, I believe, actually committed in the city. It was, after all, because improper acts were performed that the ancients passed their laws. The law states explicitly: if anyone hires a boy out to be an escort, whether the hirer is the father, the brother, the uncle, the guardian, or finally any one who has authority over him, the law does not permit an indictment against the boy himself, but against the man who put him out to hire and against the man who hired him, against the former because he put him out for hire, and against the latter, it says, because he hired him. The law makes the penalties the same for both, and adds that there is no necessity for a boy, when he has grown up, to support his father or provide him with a home, if that father has hired him out to be an escort; he must, however, bury his father at his death, and perform the customary rites. (**14**) Observe, men of Athens, how finely framed is this law: while the father is alive, it deprives him of the benefit of having produced a son, just as he has deprived his son of the right of free speech; but when he has died, when the man receiving a benefit is no longer conscious that he is being well treated, the law, and the demands of religion, command the son to bury him and perform the other customary rites.

What other law has the lawgiver established for the protection of your boys? There is the law against procuring, in which he has prescribed the heaviest penalties against any one who has procured a free woman or boy.

(**15**) And what other law? The law against *hybris*, which takes in all such offences in one summary clause. In that law it is explicitly written, that 'if anyone commits *hybris* against a boy'—and the man who hires a boy for his own use surely commits *hybris* against him—'or against a man or a woman, either free or slave, or if he does anything *paranomon* against any one of these persons', in such a case the law has provided for indictments for *hybris*, and prescribed the penalty of 'whatever the guilty party should suffer or pay'. [*To the Clerk*] Read the law.

(**16**) *Law*

[*If any of the Athenians commits* hybris *against a free boy, let the man in authority over the boy bring a* graphe *before the* thesmothetai, *writing down the penalty. Where the court condemns him, he shall be handed over to the Eleven and executed the same day. If he is condemned to a fine, he shall pay it in eleven days after the trial, if he be unable to pay immediately; until he has paid he shall be detained. There shall also be liable to these actions those who have offended against the bodies of slaves.*]

(**17**) Perhaps someone would wonder, on suddenly hearing it, why on earth in the law of *hybris* the phrase is included referring to 'slaves' as victims. If you think about this question, men of Athens, you will realize that this is the best provision of all in the law. The lawgiver was not concerned on behalf of the slave-servants; it was because he wanted to accustom you to keep well away from *hybris* against free people that he added the provision penalizing *hybris* even against slaves. In general, his view was that in a democracy the man who is a *hybristes* against anyone else at all was not a fit person to share in the political system.

(**18**) This point too I ask you all to call to mind with me, men of Athens, that the lawgiver at this point is not yet conversing directly with the person of the boy himself, but with those concerned with him, father, brother, guardian, teachers, and in general all those in authority over him. But as soon as anyone is registered in the citizen list, and knows the laws of the city, and is by now able to distinguish what is right and what is not, the lawgiver no longer addresses another person, but the man Timarchos himself. (**19**) What does he say? 'If any of the Athenians', he says, 'has acted as an escort, it shall not be open to him to become one of the nine archons'—because, I suppose, those officials wear the sacred wreath; 'nor to hold one of the priesthoods'—since such a person is of unclean body; 'nor to become an advocate for the public, nor to hold any office whatsoever, either in the community or abroad, whether the post be appointed by lot or by election'; (**20**) 'he may not act as a herald, or as an ambassador'—nor may he bring prosecutions against ambassadors or accept fees to act as a *sykophantes*; 'nor may he speak to any motion whatever, whether in the council or in the people's assembly'—even if he is the most skilful orator of all the Athenians. If anyone acts contrary to these provisions, he has provided indictments for being an escort, and imposed the heaviest penalties for the offence. [*To the Clerk*] Read this law to the jury also, so that you may know what laws there are established in your system, what fine and morally proper laws, and yet Timarchos has had the audacity to speak before the people, the man of whose moral character you are well aware.

(**21**) *Law*

[*If any Athenian acts as an escort, it shall not be open to him to be one of the nine archons, nor hold any priesthood, nor be a public advocate, nor hold any office, either in the community or abroad, whether the post be appointed by lot or by election; he may not act as a herald, nor be sent off to act as a herald, nor propose a motion, nor enter upon the publicly funded cults, nor appear wreathed in the collective wreath ceremonies, nor proceed inside the sprinkling bowls of the agora. If any one acts contrary to these prescriptions, if he is condemned of acting as an escort let him be punished by death.*]

(22) The lawgiver enacted this law to deal with young men who offend heedlessly against their own persons. The laws which I had read to you a little while ago related to boys. But the laws I am going to cite now concern the Athenians in general. When the lawgiver had finished with those laws he began to consider the manner in which we were to gather together in assembly and conduct our discussions on the most important matters. Where does he begin? 'Laws', he says, 'concerning good order.' He began first with moral self-control, on the grounds that the state where there is the greatest degree of good order will be the best managed. (23) So how does he command that the presiding officers should conduct the business? When the sacrificial victim has been carried round, and the herald has uttered the ancestral prayers, he commands the presiding officers to take the initial votes on matters to do with ancestral religious matters, dealing with heralds and embassies, and with secular matters; after that the herald asks 'Who wishes to speak of those above 50 years of age?' When they have all spoken, he then invites any one who wishes to speak from the rest of the Athenians who are entitled.

(24) Observe how well, men of Athens, this law is framed. The lawgiver was well aware, I think, that older men are in their prime when it comes to good judgement, while their boldness is beginning to leave them because of their experience of events. So, wishing to accustom those who have the best judgements, wishing it to be compulsory for them to speak on public affairs, since he found it impossible to address each one of them by name, he summons them to the platform under this general designation of their age-group, and urges them to address the people. At the same time he instructs the younger men to have respect for their elders, to let them, in all ways, act before them, and to honour old age, to which we shall all come, if we survive till then. (25) The older orators were indeed so well self-controlled, Pericles, and Themistocles, and Aristeides, the one who has a nickname so unlike that of Timarchos there [the so-called just], that something which we are all now accustomed to do, namely to speak holding one's arm outside one's cloak, seemed then to be a rather bold thing to do, and

they took care not to do it. I think I will point out to you a very substantial and real indication of this. I am sure that all of you have sailed over to Salamis and seen the statue of Solon, and you can yourselves bear witness that in the civic centre of the Salaminians Solon stands with his arm inside his cloak. This is a proper memorial and representation, men of Athens, of Solon's stance, of the manner in which he used himself to talk to the people of Athens.

(**26**) Consider then, men of Athens, how much Solon, and those other men that I mentioned just now, differ from Timarchos. They were ashamed to speak with their arms outside their cloaks, but Timarchos, not long ago, in fact just the other day, threw off his cloak and did all-in fighting routines naked in the assembly, and his body was in so dreadful and shameful a condition through drink and disgusting behaviour, that men of sound judgement covered their eyes, and were ashamed for the city, that we use such men as him as advisers. (**27**) It was because he envisaged this conduct that the lawgiver explicitly prescribed who were and who were not permitted to speak before the people. He does not keep away from the platform any one who does not have ancestors who were generals or even any one who works at some trade to support those he has to maintain; he invites such people very positively, and that is why he repeatedly asks 'who wishes to speak'.

(**28**) Who, then, did the lawgiver think should not be permitted to speak? Those who have lived shamefully; it is those men he does not allow to address the people. Where does he say this? 'Scrutiny of orators' he says, 'If any one addresses the people who beats his father or his mother, or fails to support them, or fails to provide a home for them', such a man he does not allow to speak. And quite rightly, by Zeus, I say. Why? Because if a man is mean towards those whom he ought to honour on an equal level with the gods, how on earth are other people going to be treated by him, how will the city as a whole be treated? Whom did he, in the second place, forbid to speak? (**29**) 'Or any one who did not go on those campaigns for which he was called up, or who has thrown away his shield', quite justly. Why? Well really, Sir, a city for which you do not take up your arms, or which you are unable through cowardice to defend, is not a city you can claim a right to advise. Whom does he discuss in third place? 'Or any one who has prostituted himself', he says, 'or acted as an escort.' For he thought that the man who had sold his own body in *hybris* would readily sell the common interests of the city as well. Whom does he discuss in fourth place? **(30)** 'Or any one who has consumed his ancestral goods, and whatever else he was heir to.' He thought that the man who had managed his own household badly would deal with the common affairs of the city in a similar way, and it did not seem to the lawgiver to be possible that the same man could be a rotten man in his private life and a good man in public life; nor did he think that the *rhetor* should come to the platform having prepared himself with words, but not with his manner of life. **(31)** In fact he thought very useful advice is given to the audience by one who is a fine and good man, even if he speaks poorly and simply; but words uttered by a debauched man, who has used his own body in a contemptible way, and consumed his ancestral estate shamefully, however well expressed, would not, he thought, bring benefits to their audience. **(32)** These are the men he keeps away from the platform, these the men he forbids to address the people. But if any one not only speaks contrary to these provisions, but actually makes sykophantic attacks and behaves disgustingly, and the city can no longer put up with such a man, he says 'Let any one of the Athenians who is entitled proclaim a scrutiny,' and he orders you to make the decision on these matters in a law court. So I appear before you in accordance with this law.

(33) These laws were enacted long ago, but you yourselves have added a new law now, after that fine all-in fighting routine which Timarchos gave in the assembly, since you were so very ashamed at the affair, to ensure that at each assembly one tribe shall be chosen by lot for the charge of the platform, to preside over it. What did the proposer of this law enjoin? He tells the members of the tribe to sit and to give support to the laws and the democracy, in the belief that unless we send in some help from somewhere against the men who have lived such lives we shall not be able even to hold debates about matters of the very greatest importance. **(34)** There is no benefit, men of Athens, in seeking to drive such men away from the platform by shouts; they have no sense of shame. We must break them of their habits by penalties; only in that way would they become bearable.

The Clerk shall read to you the laws that have been established on the subject of the good order of the *rhetores*. The law about the presidency of the tribes Timarchos there and other *rhetores* like him have indicted as being unsuitable, operating together; their aim is to enable themselves to go on living and speaking as they please.

(35) *Laws*

[*If one of the rhetores speaks in the* boule *or in the assembly not on the motion proposed, or does not speak on each separate item separately, or speaks twice on the same issue the same day, or utters abuse, or slanders some one, or interrupts, or when the business is being conducted gets up and speaks on a topic when not standing on the platform, or shouts approval, or manhandles the chairman, when the assembly or the* boule *is concluded, the presiding officers record his name with the* praktores *with a fine of up to 50 drachmai for each offence. If he deserves a heavier penalty, they may, fining him 50 drachmai, refer the matter to the* boule *or the first assembly. When the summonses are made, judgement shall be passed; if he is convicted on a secret ballot, the presiding officers shall record the verdict to the* praktores.]

(36) You have heard the laws, men of Athens, and I am confident that you think that they are excellent. But it is in your hands whether these laws are useful or useless. If you punish those who do wrong, the laws will be excellent and have authority, but if you let them lapse, they will be fine, but will have authority no more.

(37) I wish now, as I proposed at the start of my speech, to proceed, now that I have finished speaking about the laws, to investigate the character of Timarchos, so that you may know the extent to which it is at variance with your laws. I ask you, men of Athens, to forgive me if, compelled to speak about practices which are ignoble by nature, but which have been engaged in by the defendant, I am brought to utter some word which resembles Timarchos' acts. (38) It would not be just for you to criticize me, if I use plain language because I wish to inform you of the facts; you should much rather criticize the defendant. He happens to have lived his life so shamefully that it becomes impossible for a man describing his deeds to speak as he himself wishes without uttering some of these types of expressions. I shall, however, take every care to avoid doing this, just as far as I can.

(39) Observe now, men of Athens, how reasonably I am going to deal with Timarchos. All the offences which he committed when a boy against his own body, I shall pass over; let those acts

be invalid, like the acts committed in the time of the Thirty or before the archon year of Eukleides, or acts before any other similar date imposing a statute of limitations. The offences he has committed when already of sound mind and a young man, and when he knew the laws of the city, those are the acts about which I shall make accusations, and to which I believe it right that you should give very serious attention.

(40) First of all, when he was released from boyhood, he settled in the Peiraieus at the surgery of Euthydikos; the pretext was that he was a student of the profession, but in reality he had resolved to offer himself for sale, as the event showed. All those, whether merchants, other foreigners, or our own citizens, who made use of Timarchos' body, I shall willingly forbear to mention their names too, in order that people do not say that I am going into great detail in all cases. But those in whose houses he stayed, shaming his own body and the city, earning fees for that very thing which the law forbids one to perform, on penalty of losing the right to address the people, those men I shall give an account of.

(41) There is one Misgolas, men of Athens, son of Naukrates, of the deme of Kollytos, a man in all other respects fine and good, and one would not in any way find fault with him, except that he is phenomenally devoted to this pursuit, and is accustomed always to have singers to the lyre and lyre-players around him. I say this not in order to be vulgar but that you should be aware of the sort of man he is. So Misgolas, learning of the reasons why Timarchos was spending his time at the doctor's house, paid him a sum of money in advance, got him to move and kept him at his house, since he had a good body, was young and disgusting, and fitted for the act which he had made it his choice to perform and Timarchos his to endure. (42) Timarchos did not hesitate; he submitted to it all, though he was not in need of the requirements for a reasonable life. His father left him a very substantial property, which he has himself consumed, as I shall show as my speech proceeds. No, he did these things because he was a slave to the most shameful pleasures, fish-eating, extravagant dining, girl-pipers and escort-girls, dicing, and the other activities none of which ought to get the better of any man who is well-born and free. This polluted wretch was not ashamed to leave his ancestral home, to live with Misgolas, a man who was neither a family friend nor a man of his own age, but a stranger and a man older than

himself, and a man without any restraint in these matters, while Timarchos himself was in the prime of his youth.

(**43**) There were a good many disgraceful acts committed by Timarchos at that time; one in particular I wish to describe to you. It was the procession of the City Dionysia, and Misgolas, the man who had taken control of Timarchos, and Phaidros, the son of Kallias of the deme of Sphettos, were to process together. Timarchos had agreed to join them in the procession; they were spending time over their general preparations, but he did not return to join them. Misgolas, irritated at this, made a search for him with Phaidros, and when they received a message they found him in a tenement-house having lunch with some foreigners. Misgolas and Phaidros made threats at the foreigners, and told them to accompany them to the prison, because they had corrupted a free young man. The foreigners, frightened, ran off, leaving behind all their preparations.

(**44**) That all I am telling you is true, is known by all those who knew Misgolas and Timarchos at that time. I am indeed very glad that this lawsuit that has come my way involves a person not unknown to you, and that your knowledge of him concerns that very same practice about which you are going to cast your votes. On matters that are not known to a jury a prosecutor must, I suppose, make his demonstrations very clear indeed, but where the matters are all well agreed, I think that prosecution is not a very great business; one need only remind one's hearers of what they know.

(**45**) Nonetheless, although the affair is a matter of general agreement, since we are in a court I have written out a testimony for Misgolas, one which is true, and yet is also, I am persuaded, not uncultured; the actual name of the act that Misgolas used to commit with him, I am not including in my written testimony, nor have I written anything else which would lead to a penalty being imposed by the laws on a man who testified to its truth. What I have written are statements which will already be known to you when you hear it, and which bring no danger and no shame on the man who testifies to it. (**46**) So if Misgolas is prepared to come forward and testify to the truth, he will be doing what is right. But if he chooses to be 'summonsed' rather than to testify to the truth, then you will see the whole business. For if he, the man who committed the act, is ashamed and chooses to pay a fine of one thousand drachmai to the treasury so as not to have to show his face before you, but the man who had it done to him addresses the people, then indeed how wise was the lawgiver who debarred such disgusting persons from the platform. (**47**) But if he responds to the challenge, but resorts to the most shameless course of action, that of denial of the truth of the statement under oath, as a means of offering gratitude to Timarchos, and as a demonstration to the others of his type that he knows well enough how to keep secret on such matters, first he will do harm to himself, and second, there will be no advantage in it. For I have prepared a second testimony for those people who know that Timarchos over there left his ancestral estate and lived with Misgolas; though I suspect that I am embarking on a difficult task. The men I have to present as witnesses are not friends of mine, or enemies of theirs, nor those who are acquainted with neither them or us, but they are friends of theirs. (**48**) But even if they persuade these men too not to give evidence—and I do not think they will, at least not all of them—one thing they will certainly never be able to achieve is this: they will never annul the truth, never blot out the reputation that exist in the city concerning Timarchos, which is not something that I have fabricated against him, but which he has created for himself. After all, the life of a moral man should be so pure that it does not admit the appearance of a base accusation.

(**49**) I wish to make this point too in advance, in case after all Misgolas responds to the laws and to you. There are human natures which differ very greatly from each other in appearance, as far as their age is concerned; some who are actually young appear mature and older than they are, and others who have a great number of years seem altogether young. One of this type of men is Misgolas. He happens in fact to be of the same age as me and was a fellow-*ephebos*, and we are both now in our forty-fifth year. I have all these grey hairs, as you see, but he does not. Why am I telling you this in advance? So that you are not surprised when you suddenly catch sight of him, and have an idea like this in your minds: 'Herakles, this man is not much different from Timarchos in age.' Such is indeed the natural appearance of the man, and moreover he associated with Timarchos when he, Timarchos, was already a young man.

(**50**) So that I do not spend any longer on this, [*to the Clerk*] call now for me those men who know that Timarchos there lived in

Misgolas' house, then read the testimony of Phaidros, and lastly take please the testimony of Misgolas himself, just in case he is prepared, through fear of the gods, and in shame of those who know the truth as well as he does, and of the rest of the citizens and of you the jurors, to give evidence of the truth.

Testimony

[*Misgolas, son of Nikias, of Peiraieus, gives this testimony. Timarchos was in close association with me, the man who once was settled in the house of Euthydikos the doctor, and I have not ceased to have him in high regard from the time of my former acquaintance until now.*]

(51) If then, men of Athens, Timarchos there had remained with Misgolas, and never moved on to another man's house, he would have conducted himself with rather more moderation, if indeed any behaviour of this sort is 'moderate'; and I would not have been emboldened to bring any charge against him except that which the lawgiver mentions very plainly, simply of having been an escort. The man who does this thing with one man, and engages in the practice for payment, seems to me to be liable to just that charge. (52) But if, passing over those wild men Kedonides, Autokleides, and Thersandros, and telling you merely of those in whose houses he has been an accepted member, I remind you of what you know and demonstrate that not only did he earn his living from his body at Misgolas' house, but then did the same in another's, and then in another's, and moved on from him to yet another, then, surely, he will seem to you no longer to have been an escort; no—and by Dionysos I do not know how I can keep wrapping it up all day long—to have prostituted himself. A man who performs this act indiscriminately, with many men, and for pay, is a man who, it seems to me, is liable to this charge.

(53) So then, when Misgolas wearied of the expense and sent him away from his house, the next man to take him up was Antikles the son of Kallias of the deme Euonymon. This man is away in Samos with the klerouchs; so I shall pass on to what happened next. When the defendant Timarchos came away from Antikles and Misgolas, he did not admonish himself or take to better pursuits, but spent his days in the gaming-house, where the dicing-table is set up, and men set the cocks fighting [and play the

dice]. I expect that some of you have seen what I am talking about, or at least have heard of it. (54) One of those from that place of leisure is one Pittalakos, a public slave-fellow, a servant of the city. He was well off for cash, and, seeing Timarchos in that place, took him up and kept him at his house. He did not object to this, that polluted wretch over there, that he was about to humiliate himself with a public slave, a servant of the city; no, if he was going to acquire a financial sponsor for his foul debauchery, that was the only thing he looked for, and at no time did he show any consideration for what is fine and what is most shameful.

(55) The sort of offences, the sorts of acts of *hybris*, that I hear were committed by that person against the body of Timarchos were such that I could not possibly bring myself, by Olympian Zeus, to utter to you; the things that the defendant was not ashamed to do in action, I would not be prepared to speak clearly about in words to you and continue living. Anyway, at about that time, when Timarchos was staying with Pittalakos, a man came sailing back from the Hellespont—Hegesandros; I am sure that for some time now you have been surprised that I have not yet mentioned this character: so well known is the story I shall tell. (56) This man Hegesandros arrived, a man whom you know better than I. He happened to have sailed at that time to the Hellespont as treasurer to the general Timomachos of Acharnai; he came back having made very good use, it is said, of his general's simple generosity: he had acquired not less than eighty mnai of silver. In a way, too, he was not the least of those responsible for the ill-fortune which happened to Timomachos. (57) So, being flush with money, and visiting Pittalakos who was a dicing-companion of his, he saw Timarchos too, for the first time, there; he was pleased with the sight, desired him, and wished to take him up: no doubt he realized that his nature was very close in kind to his own. First of all he spoke to Pittalakos, asking him to hand Timarchos over to him; when he failed to persuade him, he applied himself to the lad himself, and did not need to waste many words, but quickly persuaded him. Indeed, in relation to this business, Timarchos' wickedness and infidelity are really remarkable, so that this very aspect of his character would properly arouse your hatred.

(58) When he had departed from Pittalakos' house, and had been taken up by Hegesandros, Pittalakos was very upset, I

believe, at having wasted, as he conceived it, so much money, and was full of jealousy at what was happening, and he kept visiting the house. When he was proving a nuisance, just observe the great force inflicted by Hegesandros and Timarchos. Drunk, on one occasion, themselves and some others with them, whose names I do not wish to mention, (59) they burst in at night into the house where Pittalakos was living. First, they smashed up his equipment and threw it all into the street, some shaking knucklebones, dice-boxes, and other dicing apparatus; the quails and cocks, of whom that thrice-miserable man had been very fond, they killed; finally they tied Pittalakos himself to a pillar and gave him the worst beating imaginable in the world, for such a long time that even the neighbours heard the outcry.

(60) On the next day, Pittalakos, extremely upset at the affair, came unclothed into the *agora* and sat down at the altar of the Mother of the Gods. A crowd came running up, as always happens, and Hegesandros and Timarchos took fright, in case their disgusting conduct became proclaimed throughout the city—an assembly was about to take place—and they ran up to the altar, they and some of their dicing-companions, (61) and surrounded Pittalakos and begged him to get up from the altar, saying that the whole affair was a drunken brawl; and Timarchos himself, then, by Zeus, not yet as unpleasant to look at as he is now, in fact still reasonable, played his part, touching the fellow on the chin and offering to do anything that might satisfy Pittalakos. In the end they persuaded him to get up from the altar, in the expectation that he would receive some portion of what was just. But once he had left the altar, they paid no more attention to him.

(62) The fellow took their *hybris* against him very badly, and brought an action (*dike*) against each of them. But when the case was coming to trial, observe another great blow inflicted by Hegesandros. Pittalakos was a man who had done him no wrong, but on the contrary had been wronged by him, and did not belong to him, but was a public slave, the servant of the city: still, Hegesandros tried to lead him off to slavery, claiming he belonged to him. Being thus in every sort of trouble, Pittalakos met with someone who actually was a very good man, one Glaukon of Cholargos; he sought to bring Pittalakos back into freedom. (63) After this the lodging of the legal actions took place. As time went

by, they handed the matter over for arbitration to Diopeithes of Sounion, a fellow-demesman of Hegesandros, and a man who once had relations with him, when he was in his prime; Diopeithes took on the case, but kept putting it off time after time, to do a favour to these men.

(64) When Hegesandros was beginning to come forward to your public platform, at the time when he was also engaged in his war with Aristophon of Azenia, which lasted until Aristophon threatened to bring against him the same formal pronouncement in the assembly which I have brought against Timarchos, and at the same time that his brother Hair-bun was beginning to speak regularly in the assembly, when, that is, these two men had the nerve to offer their advice to you on Greek politics, then finally Pittalakos lost confidence in himself, thought who he was, and with what sort of people he was engaged in fighting, and took a sensible decision (one must tell the truth): he held his peace, and thought himself lucky that he had not attracted some fresh disaster.

So then Hegesandros, who had thus won this splendid victory, without a fight, kept Timarchos at his house. (65) That what I say is true, you all know. Which of you has ever gone to the fish-stalls and not witnessed the expenditures of these men? Which of you, chancing on their street-revels (*komoi*) and fights, did not feel outraged on behalf of the city? Still, since we are in court, [*to the Clerk*] call for me Glaukon of Cholargos, the man who brought Pittalakos back into freedom, and read the other testimonies.

(66) *Testimonies*

[*Glaukon son of Timaios of Cholargos gives this testimony. 'I brought Pittalakos back into freedom when he was being taken into slavery by Hegesandros. Some time later Pittalakos came to me and said that he wished to send to Hegesandros and be reconciled with him, so that the suits would be dropped, the one which he was bringing against Hegesandros and Timarchos and the one which Hegesandros was bringing against him over the slavery. And they were reconciled.'*]

Testimony

[*Amphisthenes gives this testimony. 'I brought Pittalakos back into freedom when he was being taken into slavery by Hegesandros, and the rest.'*]

(67) Now I shall summon Hegesandros himself. I have written

out for him a testimony that is more decent than fits him, but is a little more explicit than the one I wrote for Misgolas. I am not unaware that he will refuse to swear to it, and will then perjure himself. Why, then, do I summon him to testify? The reason is that I wish to demonstrate to you the sort of men that this habitual practice produces, men who despise the gods, have contempt for the laws, and think little of all types of shame. [*To the Clerk*] Please call Hegesandros.

(**68**) *Testimony*

[*Hegesandros son of Diphilos of Steiria gives this testimony. 'When I sailed back from the Hellespont, I found Timarchos the son of Arizelos spending time at the house of Pittalakos the gambler, and arising from this acquaintance, I had a relationship with Timarchos, engaging in the same activity as I had previously with Leodamas.'*]

(**69**) I was not unaware that he would disdain to take the oath, Athenians; indeed I told you in advance he would. It is in fact perfectly clear, from the fact that he was not willing to give evidence, that he will soon appear for the defence. This is nothing surprising in this, by Zeus; he will take the stand, I suppose, trusting in the record of his life, as a fine and good man and a man who hates the bad—a man who does not know who Leodamas is, the man at whose name you gave a shout when the testimony was being read out.

(**70**) Well, then, am I to be led on to put it more explicitly than my own nature inclines me? You tell me, in the name of Zeus and the other gods, Athenians, a man who has shamed himself with Hegesandros, do you not think that he prostituted himself with the prostitute? What excesses of loathsomeness are we to imagine they did not commit when offensively drunk and on their own? Do you not think that Hegesandros, trying to wipe out his own notorious practices with Leodamas, which you all know about, will have made extravagant demands on Timarchos, so as to make what he did seem modest, in comparison with Timarchos' excesses?

(**71**) Yet, despite this, you will see, very soon, the man himself and his brother Hair-bun energetically and rhetorically come leaping up on to the stand and declare that what I am saying is a load of stupidity, and they will demand of me that I produce witnesses who will explicitly testify where he did it, how he did it, or who saw him do it, or the manner in which it was done: this, I believe, is a shameful thing for them to say. (**72**) I do not, after all, suppose that you are so forgetful that you do not remember the laws that you heard read out a little while ago, in which it is written that if any one hires any Athenian for this practice, or if any one hires himself out, he is liable to the greatest penalties, and the same penalties for each offender. What man is so foolhardy that he would be willing to give clear evidence of a sort that, as a result, if he told the truth in his evidence, he would show himself liable to the most extreme penalties? (**73**) So then the only possibility left would be for the man who endured the acts to admit what happened. But that is precisely the charge he is facing, namely that, after having done these deeds, he makes speeches in the assembly contrary to the laws. Is it your wish then that we let the whole matter drop, and inquire no further? By Poseidon, we shall really be running the city well if, when we ourselves know what actually happened, we shall forget about it unless some one comes forward to us here and gives explicit and shameless testimony of the facts.

(**74**) Look at the matter now with the help of some comparable cases; and they will inevitably have to be cases that are similar to Timarchos' habits. You see those men over there, sitting in their little huts, the ones who confessedly pursue the profession. Even so those men, since they have been brought by necessity to this, still put up some cover to hide their shame, and keep the doors shut. If anyone asked you as you went past in the street, what the fellow inside was doing at that moment, you would immediately name the deed, though you did not know the man who had gone in to the house; because you know the choice of profession of the man, you know the activity taking place as well. (**75**) In the same way, therefore, you should conduct your investigation of Timarchos, and not wonder whether anyone saw it, but whether the deed was done by him. After all, by the gods, Timarchos, what would you say yourself about another man being tried on this charge? What is one to say, when a youth, still quite young, leaves his father's house, and spends his nights in other men's houses—a youth of exceptional appearance; when he enjoys expensive dinners without making any contribution to them, and keeps the most expensive girl-pipers and escort-girls? When he goes dicing, and pays out no money himself, but another man always pays for him? (76) Is there still any need for divination? Is it not quite plain that the person who imposes such demands on other men must of absolute necessity himself be providing pleasures in exchange— *some* pleasures—for the men who have spent out the money in advance? I am at a loss, by Olympian Zeus, to know in what other more euphemistic way I may refer to the contemptible deeds that you have performed.

(77) Consider now, if you will, the matter in the light of some illustrations in the political sphere, particularly these activities on which you have recently been engaged. There has taken place the scrutiny on the citizen lists in all the demes, and each of us has submitted to a vote about our individual person, to decide who is really an Athenian and who is not. Now whenever I am present in the court and I hear the disputants pleading, I observe that every time the same argument carries weight with you. (78) Whenever the prosecutor says, 'Gentlemen of the jury, the members of the deme have taken their oaths and voted against this man, and they have done so not because some one brought an accusation against him or gave evidence against him, but because of their own personal knowledge', you immediately give a roar of approval on the assumption that the man on trial has no share in the city. Your opinion is, I suppose, that one does not need argument or evidence to prove what one knows perfectly clearly oneself.

(79) Well then, in Zeus' name, imagine this: if, as on the issue of birth, so on the issue of this style of life, Timarchos was required to undergo a vote as to whether he was guilty of the charge or not, and the case was being heard in the court, and Timarchos was brought before you as he is now, and it were not possible under the law or the people's decree either for me to make a prosecution or for him to make a defence, and if the herald who now stands by my side were to put the question to you in the pronouncement formula prescribed by the law—'The hollow ballot is to be used by those who decide that Timarchos has been a prostitute, and the solid ballot by those who decide that he has not'—how would you vote? I am absolutely certain that you would condemn him. (80) If one of you were to ask me 'How do you know whether we would condemn him or not?' I should reply: 'Because you have given your opinion freely to me, you have told me'. When, and where, each of you has done this, I shall remind you. It is every time that Timarchos mounted the rostrum in the assembly, when

he was on the council last year. If ever he mentioned *the repair of walls* or of a *tower*, or was describing how someone was being *taken off somewhere*, immediately you shouted out and burst out laughing, and you used yourselves to utter the correct name for the acts which you knew well that he had committed. (**81**) I shall pass over many of these incidents of some time ago; but I do want to remind you of what happened in the very assembly-meeting at which I proclaimed this legal process against Timarchos. When the Council of the Areopagos made its appearance before the assembly in accordance with the decree which the defendant proposed about the dwelling-houses on the Pnyx, the member of the Areopagos who made the speech was Autolykos, a man who has lived his life with honour, by Olympian Zeus and Apollo, and distinction, and in a way worthy of that body. (**82**) When, in the course of his speech, he said that the Areopagos council was opposing Timarchos' motion and he added 'on the subject of that deserted spot and the place on the Pnyx, you should not be surprised, Athenians, if Timarchos is more experienced than the Council of the Areopagos', at that moment you burst into uproar and said that Autolykos was telling the truth: you said that he was certainly experienced with those places. (**83**) Autolykos did not take in the point of your uproar, frowned severely, and, after a pause, went on: 'We Areopagites, Athenians, do not make accusations against people, or defences of them—that is not our ancestral tradition—but we do have this much sympathy for Timarchos; perhaps', he said, 'he thought that in this quietness there would be only little expense for each of you.' Once more, at the words 'quietness' and 'little expense', a greater uproar, amid much laughter, broke out among you. (**84**) And when he spoke of 'building-sites' and 'cisterns', you were unable to control yourselves. At that point Pyrrhandros came forward to rebuke you, and asked the people if they were not ashamed laughing in the presence of the Council of the Areopagos. You sent him off the platform, answering 'We know, Pyrrhandros, that we ought not to laugh in the Council's presence; but still the truth is so strong that it overcomes all men's calculations.' (**85**) I take it then that the people of Athens has given you this testimony; it would not be proper to convict the people of false testimony. If, then, when I do not say anything, you yourselves shout out the name of the acts which you know he has committed, it would surely be very odd that if I do mention them, you then forget them; and it would be odd that if there had been no trial against him, you would have convicted him, but now that the legal proof has been made, he is to be acquitted!

(86) Since I have mentioned the citizen-list scrutinies and the political acts of Demophilos, I wish now to cite another illustration on these matters. This very same man had previously brought in another political measure of the same type. He made accusations that there were those who were trying to bribe the assembly and also the law courts, as Nikostratos has also done very recently; some cases on these charges have been heard, others are pending. (87) Well now, by Zeus and the gods, if those defendants had resorted to the same defence as Timarchos and his advocates are using, and claimed that it was right that someone should give evidence on the charge, or else the jury should not accept it, then it would be an absolute necessity, as a result of that argument, that either one or other party would have to give evidence, one man that he gave a bribe, or the other that he received it, though there is the legal penalty of death for each of them; just as in this case, if someone hires an Athenian for *hybris*, or again if any Athenian hires himself out voluntarily for the shame of his own body. (88) Well, is there any one who would have given such evidence, or any prosecutor who would attempt such a manner of proof of his case? There is not. So what follows? Were those accused in fact acquitted? No, by Herakles, they were condemned to death, though they had committed, by Zeus and Apollo, a lesser crime than the defendant; those unfortunate men, who were unable to defend themselves against the combination of old age and poverty, the greatest of human evils, encountered this calamity, one which the defendant should encounter because he cannot restrain his own disgusting behaviour.

(89) Now if this trial were taking place in an appellate city, I would indeed have claimed the right to summon you yourselves as my witnesses, on the grounds that you are the people that best know that I am telling the truth. But if the trial is at Athens, and the same people—you—are both jurymen and witnesses of my arguments, the proper thing is for me to remind you of the facts, and for you not to disbelieve me. In fact it seems to me, Athenians, that Timarchos the defendant has got himself agitated not only for himself, but also for the other men who have engaged

in the same activities as he has. (**90**) For if this practice will go on, as it has been accustomed to be conducted hitherto, in secret, in lonely places and in private houses, and if the man who knows the facts best, namely the man who has disgraced one of the citizens, will be, if he testifies to the truth, liable to the most severe penalties; and if the man on trial, against whom is the testimony of his own life and of the truth, is to claim that he should be tried not on the basis of the facts which are known, but on the basis of witnesses; then that is the destruction of the law and of truth, and a clear road has been shown along which the greatest offenders will run off to freedom. (**91**) After all, what clothes-snatchers, thieves, seducers, homicides, or generally what men who have committed any of the most serious crimes and done it in secret, will ever then be brought to justice? For as it is, some of these men are caught in manifest guilt, and, if they confess, they are immediately punished by death, and others, who act in secret and deny the charge, are put on trial in the courts, and the truth will be discovered on the basis of the probabilities.

(**92**) Take as an example the council of the Areopagos, the most scrupulous legal body in the city. I have myself seen before now many defendants appearing in that Council chamber convicted, for all that they spoke very effectively and presented witnesses; and I know of others who won their cases though they spoke very badly, and had no witnesses in support. The Council members do not cast their votes only on the basis of the speeches and the witnesses, but also on the basis of their own knowledge and of their own investigations. That is the reason why this council retains its high reputation in the city. (**93**) Hence you too, Athenians, should make your decision in this case in the same way. First of all, let nothing have greater reliability in your eyes than what you yourselves know and what you are convinced of about the defendant Timarchos; second, consider the matter not in the light of the present, but of past time. After all, the words that have been spoken in the past about Timarchos and his prac- tices were spoken because they were true, but those which will be spoken today will be spoken because of this trial, with the inten- tion of deceiving you. Give your verdict therefore in accordance with the longer span of time, with the truth, and with what you yourselves know.

(**94**) But there is a certain speechwriter, the one who is devising the defence speech for him, who is saying that I am contradicting myself. According to him, it does not seem possible that the same man has both prostituted himself and has consumed his inheritance; he says that to have committed some offence in relation to one's body is the act of a boy, but to have consumed one's inheritance the act of a man. He also says those who bring shame upon themselves exact payments for the act. So he goes around the *agora*, expressing amazement and making a great show of it, at the idea that the same man could have been a prostitute and consumed his inheritance.

(95) If anyone really does not understand how this is, I shall try to define it more clearly. As long as the property lasted which had come with the heiress whom Hegesandros, the man who was keeping Timarchos, had married and as long as the money lasted which Hegesandros had when he came back from his journey with Timomachos, they lived in conditions of abundant and unstinting debauchery. But there came a time when these resources had been squandered, diced away, and gobbled up, and the defendant was getting past his youthful bloom, and no one, reasonably, would give him anything; but this man's revolting and unholy nature still longed for the same pleasures, and in his excess of uncontrolled desire he kept making demand upon demand, and was carried back to his daily habits. So then at that point he turned to the eating up of his inherited property. (96) In fact he did not only eat it up; if one may put it this way, he drank it down as well. For he sold each item of his property not for what it was worth, but, since he could not wait for a higher offer, or even for a suitable offer, but sold it for what it fetched on the spot. Such was his very pressing need for pleasure.

(97) His father left Timarchos a property from which another man would even have been able to perform liturgies, but which he was unable to preserve even for himself. There was a house behind the Acropolis, a piece of marginal land at Sphettos, another landed property at Alopeke, and besides some slaves working in the shoemaking trade, nine or ten, each one of whom brought in a rent of two obols a day, while the manager of them brought in three obols; there was in addition to these a woman skilled in *amorgina*-cloth who took her products to the market, and a man skilled at pattern-weaving; and there were men who owed him money; and some personal effects.

(98) That I am telling the truth, in this case at least, by Zeus, I shall provide witnesses for you who are going to give clear and explicit evidence; there is no risk, as there was previously, and no shame as well, for the man who gives true evidence. The house in the city he sold to Nausikrates the comic poet, and afterwards Kleainetos the chorus-master bought it from Nausikrates for twenty mnai. The marginal plot Mnesitheos of Myrrhinous bought from him, a large place, but allowed to run terribly wild by that man over there. (99) The piece of land at Alopeke, which was eleven or twelve stades from the city-wall, his mother supplicated and begged him to let alone, as I have heard, and not sell; let him leave that, if nothing else, for her to be buried in. He did not keep off even that land, but sold that too for two thousand drachmai. Of the slave-women and slave-men he kept not one, but sold them all. That I am not telling lies about this, I shall produce testimony to show that his father did leave these slaves to him, and if he denies that he has sold them, let him produce the slaves' bodies in open court. (100) That his father lent money out, which Timarchos has collected in and has spent, I shall produce as a witness for you Metagenes of Sphettos, who owed him more than thirty mnai, and paid to Timarchos what was still owing on his father's death, namely seven mnai. [*To the Clerk*] Please call Metagenes of Sphettos. First of all, read Nausikrates' testimony, the man who bought the house, and then take all the other testimonies which I mentioned in the same context.

Testimonies

(101) Now I shall demonstrate to you that his father possessed a not inconsiderable sum of money, which Timarchos has squandered. Fearing he would be liable to liturgies, his father sold the properties which he owned except the ones I have just mentioned, namely a piece of land in Kephisia, another in Amphitrope, and two workshops in the silver-mining areas, one in Aulon, the other near Thrasymos. I shall now tell you how he came to be so well-off. (102) There were three brothers, Eupolemos the gymnastic-trainer (*paidotribes*), Arizelos the defendant's father, and Arignotos, who is still living, an old man who has lost his sight. The first of these to die was Eupolemos, while the property was still undivided, and Arizelos, Timarchos' father,

died second; while he was alive, he had control over the whole estate, because of Arignotos' weakness and the accident to his eyes, and the fact that Eupolemos had died; he made an agreement with Arignotos and provided him with money for his support. (103) When Arizelos, Timarchos' father, died, for the first period, when he was still a boy, Arignotos received all reasonable support from the guardians. But when Timarchos became registered on the citizen list and took control of the estate, pushing aside this man, elderly and unfortunate, his own uncle, he made the estate disappear and gave Arignotos nothing of what he needed. He stood by and watched him reduced from such a large estate to accepting the payment given to the disabled. (104) The final and most terrible thing is this: when the old man failed to attend when the scrutiny took place for the disabled, and he then placed a suppliant bough before the Council pleading for his payment, Timarchos, who happened to be on the Council and one of the presiding officers on that day, did not think it right to speak up for him, but allowed him to lose the prytany payment. That I am telling the truth, call please Arignotos of Sphettos, and read his testimony.

Testimony

(105) But someone might perhaps say that Timarchos, after selling his ancestral estate, acquired another one somewhere in the city, and in place of the marginal plot and the land at Alopeke, the craftsmen and the rest, he has set up some business in the silver mines, as his father had done before him. No, he has nothing left at all, no house, no multiple-dwelling, no land, no slaves, no money out on loan, nor anything else from which men who are not criminals earn their living. All that is left to him, instead of his inherited goods, are debauchery, sykophancy, boldness, luxury, cowardice, shamelessness, the inability to blush at his shameful acts; with these resources he has become the worst and the least beneficial of citizens.

(106) It is not only his inheritance he has consumed, but also your common possessions, all those over which he had control. Timarchos has the age which you see for yourselves, yet there is no public office which he has not held at some time, though he was never properly appointed by lot or election, but bought his

way into them all contrary to the laws. Most of them I shall pass over, but I shall mention two or three. (**107**) He became an auditor, and did a very great deal of damage to the city by taking bribes from those whose term of office had not been honest, but especially by bringing sykophantic charges against those appearing for their audit who had done no wrong. He held an office in Andros which he had bought for thirty mnai, borrowing the money at nine obols for the mna, and so made your allies the source of supplies for his debauchery; and he revealed a level of wantonness in relation to the wives of free men as has never been shown by any one else. None of these men shall I summon here, to testify before many people about his own misfortune, on which he has chosen to keep silent, but I leave this to you to investigate. (**108**) But what can you expect? If there is a man who, at Athens, is a *hybristes* not only against other people but also against his own body, where laws exist, where you are watching him, where enemies are set against him, if this same man had obtained immunity from prosecution, power, and public office, who would expect that he would abstain from any of the most wantonly aggressive acts? By Zeus and Apollo, I have often before now wondered at the good fortune of our city, but I do this especially now, seeing that at that time no one appeared as a buyer of the city of Andros.

(**109**) Well, perhaps he was a poor official when operating on his own, but a reasonable one when with more colleagues. Anything but! This man, Athenians, was a member of the Council in the archonship of Nikophemos. To recount all the wrongs he committed in that year is not a suitable task to perform in just a small part of a day; the offences that are closest to the charge in the present trial, I shall describe in a few words. (**110**) During the same archon-year in which he was on the Council, Hegesandros the brother of Krobylos was a treasurer of the goddess' funds; they were engaged in stealing, collectively and very amicably, a thousand drachmai from the city. A reputable man, Pamphilos of Acherdous, discovered the affair; he ran up against Timarchos and was angry with him, so at an assembly he rose and spoke: 'Athenians, they are stealing from you, a man and a woman together, a thousand drachmai.' (**111**) When you expressed astonishment, about how it could be a man and a woman, and what the story was, he went on after a bit: 'Don't you understand what I'm saying? The man is Hegesandros over there, though he too used himself to be Leodamas' woman; the woman is Timarchos here. How the money is being embezzled, I will tell you.' He then gave an exposition of the affair, which was both very well informed and clear. Having instructed you in the matter, he said: 'So what is it, Athenians, that I am advising you to do? If the Council determines that he is in the wrong, leaf-votes against him, and hand him over to a law court, grant them their reward; but if it does not punish him, do not grant the usual reward, but hold the memory of this event against them on that day.' (112) When the Council then returned to the Council chamber, it leaf-voted to expel him, but restored him on the final vote. But, because it did not hand him over to a law court, or even expel him from the Council-chamber, though it grieves me to say it, I have to record that it failed to be granted the award. You should not show yourselves, Athenians, prepared, on the one hand, to be aggrieved with the Council and to deprive five hundred fellow-citizens of their crowns, because they did not punish Timarchos, while on the other hand, you yourselves let him off, and allow a man who was not a useful orator for the Council to be preserved for the Assembly.

(113) Well, perhaps that was his conduct in the offices appointed by lot, but he was better in the elective offices. But which of you does not know of his notorious conviction for embezzlement? You sent him as an inspector (*exetastes*) of the mercenary troops in Eretria; he, alone of the board of inspectors, admitted that he had accepted money. He made no defence on the charge, but immediately supplicated concerning the penalty, admitting he was in the wrong. You imposed a penalty of a talent on each of those who denied the charge, but one of three hundred mnai on Timarchos. And yet the laws prescribe that thieves who admit guilt are to be punished with death, while those who deny it are to be put on trial.

(114) Consequently, Timarchos had such contempt for you that he went straight on to grab two thousand drachmai at the time of the scrutiny of the citizen lists. He claimed that Philotades of Kydathenaion, a citizen, was a freedman of his own, he persuaded the demesmen to vote him off their list, he took charge of the prosecution in the law court, he took the sacred offerings in his own hand, he swore that he had not taken, and would not take,

bribes, he swore by the gods of oaths and called down destruction on himself; (**115**) and then he was convicted of having taken twenty mnai from Leukonides, the relation by marriage of Philotades, through the agency of Philemon the actor, money which he spent in a short time on Philoxene the escort, and thus gave up the case, and was shown to have perjured his oath. That I am telling the truth, [*to the Clerk*] please call Philemon who handed over the money, and Leukonides, the relation by marriage of Philotades, and read the copies of the agreement, in accordance with which he managed the sale of the case.

Testimonies: Agreement

(**116**) Well then, the character he has shown in relation to his fellow-citizens and his relatives, the shameful way in which he wasted his ancestral estate, and the way in which he accepted without a qualm the *hybris* against his own body, all this you all knew before I spoke, but my speech serves sufficiently to remind you of it. Two subjects remain for my prosecution: and I pray to all the gods and goddesses, first, that I may speak on these topics for the good of the city, as I have planned to do, and, second, I should like you to maintain your attention to what I am about to say and follow it intelligently.

(**117**) The first subject is a preparatory account of the defence which I hear is going to be offered; if I omit to do this, I fear that the man who makes promises that he can teach the young the art of words may by some deception lead you astray and bring disadvantage to the city. The second subject for me is an exhortation of the citizens towards moral goodness. I see that many of the younger men are present in the court, and many of the older ones, and that not a few people from the rest of Greece have gathered to hear the case. (**118**) You should not think that they have come to see me; no, much more they have come to find out about you, whether you not only know how to make good laws, but also whether you are capable of judging what is honourable and what is not; and whether you know how to honour good men, and whether you are willing to punish those men who make their own lives a disgrace for the city. I shall speak to you first about the defence speech.

(**119**) The over-clever orator Demosthenes says that you should either abolish the laws, or pay no heed to my words. He is amazed, he says, if you do all not remember that each year the Council farms out the prostitutes' tax; and hence those that have bought the tax do not merely estimate, but have exact knowledge of those who engage in this practice. When, then, I have had the nerve to bring this counter-accusation against Timarchos for having been a prostitute, so that he should not be able to speak in public, Demosthenes claims that this activity calls not for an accusation by a prosecutor, but for the testimony of the tax collector who collected this tax from Timarchos.

(120) In response to this, Athenians, consider whether I seem to you to be offering a simple and honest reply. I am ashamed on behalf of the city, if Timarchos, the people's adviser, the man prepared to serve on embassies the city sends to Greece, will not seek to clear his name over the whole issue, but instead will ask me to specify the places where he sat working, and the tax collectors, if any collected the prostitutes' tax from him. (121) For your sake, let him give up a defence of that sort. I shall suggest to you, Timarchos, an alternative line of argument which is honourable and just, which you will use, unless you are conscious of something shameful in your life. So then, have the courage to look straight at the jurymen and make a statement which is an appropriate one for a man who has been self-controlled in matters concerning his prime of life. 'Athenians, I have been brought up from boyhood and youth among you, and I engage in activities that are not unknown, but I am to be seen with you at the assemblies. (122) I believe that if my defence speech on the accusation on which I stand trial were being heard before any other jurymen, with you giving testimony for me, I should easily defeat the arguments of the prosecutor. After all, not only if I had actually committed any such act, but even if I seemed to you to have lived a life at all resembling the charges made by that man, I should think my life to be not worth living, and I should offer up my punishment as the defence for the city to make to the rest of the Greeks. I have not come here to plead for mercy, but you may use me as you will, if that is how I seem to you.' That is, Timarchos, the defence of a man who is good and self-controlled, a man with confidence in his past life, a man who reasonably has contempt for any slander. (123) But the defence which Demosthenes is persuading you to use is not the defence of an honest man, but of

a prostitute, disputing over the precise places involved. But since you are seeking refuge in the precise naming of dwellings, and you demand that we give proof of your activity in relation to the house at which you were sitting, when you have heard what I am about to say, you will not use such an argument again, if you have any sense. It is not, after all, particular houses or dwellings which give their epithets to the people who live in them, but it is the inhabitants who give to the places they live in the epithets appropriate to their personal pursuits. (124) Where many people hire out one house, and occupy it together, dividing it up, we call it a multiple-dwelling; where only one man lives there, a house. If a doctor moves into one of these workshops on the streets, it is called a surgery; if he moves out, and a bronze-smith moves in to the same workshop, it is called a smithy; if a fuller, a laundry; if a carpenter, a carpenter's shop; and if some female prostitutes and their pimp move in, from their activity it is immediately called a brothel. So the result is that you have made many dwellings into brothels through the facility of your activities. So I advise you to stop demanding where you engaged in this activity, and try to make a defence on the grounds that you did not do it.

(125) Another argument will arrive, it seems, composed by the same sophist. He claims that nothing is more unjust than Report, and produces evidence from the market-place, totally suitable for his own lifestyle. First he says that the multiple-dwelling in Kolonos which is called Demon's house is wrongly named, because it is not Demon's. He says that the so-called Herm of Andokides is not Andokides', but a monument of the tribe Aigeis. (126) He brings himself forward by way of a joke, wishing to appear an amiable man, able to be witty about his own activities. 'Unless I too should answer', he says, 'to the crowd, not when I am called Demosthenes, but Batalos, as I got that nickname from my nurse as a term of endearment.' So if, he argues, Timarchos was beautiful, and is mocked by slander based on that fact, and not because of his own actions, that is no reason why he should fall into misfortune.

(127) Well now, Demosthenes, in the case of monuments, houses, possessions, and all other non-speaking things, I do hear many and varied names applied, and never the same ones again. There are no fine or shameful actions inherent in the objects themselves; it is the man, whoever he may be, who happens to be

attached to them, who provides the name in accordance with the greatness of his own reputation. But in the case of the lives of men and their activities, an unerring report of its own accord spreads throughout the city. This reports private activities to the general public, and in many cases it actually gives a prediction about what is likely to happen. (128) So clear is this point which I am making, and far from a contrivance, that you will find that our city and our ancestors have established an altar to Report as to one of the greatest gods. You will find Homer often in the *Iliad* saying in advance of one of the events about to take place: 'And Report came to the army.' Again, you will find that Euripides reveals that this goddess is able to make clear the real natures not only of the living, but also of the dead. He says:

Report shows clear the good man even in the recesses of the earth.

(129) Hesiod too expressly represents her as a goddess, speaking very clearly to those willing to understand. He says:

Report does not ever die out completely, one to which many people give utterance. She is herself a goddess.

You will find that men who have lived decorously are admirers of these poems. All men who are ambitious for public honour believe that their reputation will be brought to them by the good report about them; but those whose life is shameful do not honour this goddess, because they think they have her as their everlasting accuser.

(130) Call to mind, therefore, gentlemen, what report you have about Timarchos. Is it not the case that as soon as the name is uttered, you ask the question: 'Which Timarchos? The whore?' Further, if I provided witnesses on a matter, would you not believe me? If I then provide the goddess as a witness, will you not believe her? She is someone it is not proper even to denounce for false witness. (131) Similarly in the case of Demosthenes' nickname, he is called Batalos, not wrongly, by report, not by his nurse; he has brought the name on himself for his effeminacy and his deviance. If someone were to take off you those fancy little cloaks and those delicate little tunics, which you wear when you are writing your speeches against your friends, and were to pass them around

and give them to the jurymen, I think that they would be quite uncertain, if someone had not told them in advance when doing this, whether they were handling the clothes of a man or of a woman.

(**132**) In the course of the defence there will mount up to the stand, as I understand it, one of the generals; he will have a laid-back manner, and a self-conscious air, giving the impression of a man well versed in the wrestling-schools (*palaistrai*) and their discussions. He will attempt to tear the whole basis of the legal contest to pieces, claiming that I have created not so much a trial as the start of an appalling denial of our cultural education. He will first bring forward your benefactors, Harmodios and Aristogeiton, describing their mutual pledges, and how this fact was a benefit for the city. (**133**) He will not refrain, they tell me, from mentioning the poetry of Homer and the names of the heroes; he will sing hymns to the friendship of Patroklos and Achilles which is said to have come into being through erotic love; and he will eulogize beauty, as though it had not long been celebrated as a blessed thing, if it happens to be combined with moral self-control. If, he says, certain men may slander bodily attractiveness, and thereby make it a misfortune to those who possess it, the result will be that you will contradict in your public vote what you say in your private prayers. (**134**) It would seem to him to be very bizarre, if you, when you are about to have children, all pray that your unborn sons may be fair and noble in appearance and worthy of the city, yet those that have been born, in whom the city may well take pride, if they are exceptional in beauty and youthful charm and if they arouse the desires of some men and become the objects of fights because of erotic passion, you are then to disenfranchise such men, on the persuasion of Aeschines.

(**135**) At that point, as I hear, he is intending to make a raid on me, and will ask me if I am not ashamed, since I make myself a nuisance in the *gymnasia* and have been the lover of many, to be bringing the practice into disrepute and danger. And finally, as certain people are telling me, in an attempt to reduce you to laughter and idle talk, he says he will display all the erotic poems which I have written to people; and he says he will produce witnesses to certain quarrels and blows arising out of this activity in which I have been involved. (**136**) Now I do not criticize erotic love that is just, and I do not say that those who are exceptional in beauty have prostituted themselves; nor do I deny that I have myself been engaged in erotic passion, and am still today; nor do I deny that the competitions and fights which arise from this activity in other people's cases have arisen in mine. As far as concerns the poems which they say I wrote, I acknowledge they are mine, but I deny that they have the character which they will, by distortion, impart to them

(**137**) I make this distinction: to love those who are beautiful and self-controlled is the condition of a generous and sympathetic soul, but to hire someone for money and to behave grossly with him I hold to be the act of a *hybristes* and an uneducated man. And I say that it is noble to be loved in a non-corrupting way, but it is shameful to be persuaded by the hire-fee and prostitute oneself. How big is the distinction between these two activities, how great is the difference, I shall try to inform you in the next part of the speech. (**138**) Our ancestors, when they were making laws to regulate men's practices and the necessities of nature, prohibited slaves from engaging in those activities which they thought free men ought to do. 'A slave', the law says, 'is not to exercise himself, nor to rub himself dry with oil in the wrestling grounds.' It did not also state: 'But the free man shall rub himself dry and exercise himself.' The reason is that when the lawgivers, observing the noble results that stem from the *gymnasia*, forbade slaves to share in them, they thought that on the same argument by which they were prohibiting slaves from it, they were exhorting free men to it. (**139**) Again, the same lawgiver said: 'The slave is not to be the lover of a free boy, nor to pursue him, or else he is to receive fifty lashes with the public whip.' But he did not prevent the free man from being a lover, from associating with or pursuing a boy, nor did he think that this brought harm to the boy, but saw it as a testimony to his self-control (*sophrosyne*). But, I think, while the boy is not his own master and incapable of judging who is really well-disposed to him and who is not, the lawgiver makes the lover be self-controlled, and makes him defer the words of affection until he has reached an older age and is capable of good sense. But to follow and look after the boy he regards as the greatest guard and protection for the boy's chastity. (**140**) That is the reason why the city's benefactors, men excelling in the virtues, Harmodios and Aristogeiton, were educated by their chaste and legitimate—whether one should call it erotic love or whatever one should call it—and it educated them to be of such a kind that those who praise their deeds seem in their encomia to fall well short of what those men achieved.

(**141**) Since you are mentioning Achilles and Patroklos, and Homer and the other poets, as if the jurymen were quite ignorant of culture, whereas you are the sophisticated ones, and look down on the ordinary people in your learning, well, so that you realize that we too have listened and learned something, we shall say a little about this as well. Since they are seeking to mention philosophers and to take refuge in the sayings expressed in verse, look carefully, Athenians, at those who are acknowledged to be good and sound poets, and see how great they thought was the difference between the chaste men who love those like themselves and those who have no control over their improper desires, and are *hybristai*. (**142**) I shall speak first about Homer, whom we rank among the oldest and wisest of the poets. He mentions Patroklos and Achilles in many places, but he keeps their erotic love hidden and the proper name of their friendship, thinking that the exceptional extent of their affection made things clear to the educated members of his audience. (**143**) Achilles says somewhere, when lamenting the death of Patroklos, as if remembering one of the things that most grieved him, that he had unwillingly broken the promise he had made to Patroklos' father, Menoitios; he had declared that he would bring Patroklos back safe to Opous, if Menoitios would send him along with him to Troy and entrust him to his care. It is clear from this that it was because of erotic love that he undertook the charge of Patroklos. (**144**) These are the verses which I am now going to recite:

> Ah me, it was an empty word that I sent forth on that day
> when I encouraged the hero Menoitios in his halls.
> I said to him that I would bring his famous son back to Opous,
> when he had sacked Troy and won his allotted share of booty.
> But Zeus does not bring all men's plans to completion.
> It was fated that both of us would stain red the same part of earth.

(**145**) Now it is not only here that he seems to be in distress, but he mourned so intensely for him, that though he learnt from his mother Thetis that if he did not go after his enemies, but let the death of Patroklos remain unavenged, he should go home and die of old age in his native land, but that if he took his revenge he would quickly end his life, he decided to put his pledge to the dead man above his safety. With such nobility of soul did he press on to take revenge on the man who killed his friend, that when all were trying to comfort him and persuade him to bathe and take food, he swore to do none of these things until he had brought Hector's head to the grave of Patroklos. (**146**) When he was sleeping by the funeral pyre, the poet says, the ghost of Patroklos stood before him, and roused such memories, and laid such commands on Achilles, at which it is right for us to weep over, and right for us to feel envious at their virtue and their friendship. He gave him these commands, after prophesying that Achilles too was not far from the end of his life: if it were possible, he should make provisions in advance, so that in the same way that they had grown up and lived together, so when they were both dead, their bones should lie in the same tomb. (**147**) Weeping, and describing the pursuits they had shared together in life, he says: 'Nevermore shall we, as before, sit together, alone and apart from all our other friends and deliberate about the highest matters,' thinking, I suppose, that this faithfulness and affection was what they would miss the most. So that you may hear these sentiments of the poet in the verse form itself, the clerk will read for you the verses on this theme that Homer composed. (**148**) Recite first the lines on the revenge on Hector:

> Well since, then, dear comrade, after you I shall go under the earth,
> I shall not bury you before I have bought here Hector's
> armour and head, your great-hearted slayer.

(**149**) Read now what Patroklos says in the dream about their sharing the grave, and about the pursuits they had shared together.

> No longer, alive, shall we, sitting apart from our friends
> and companions, lay our plans; the hateful doom
> opened up around me, that one which was allotted me at my birth:
> and destiny waits for you too, Achilles, like to the gods,
> to be killed beneath the walls of the well-born Trojans,
> fighting with the enemy for the sake of lovely-haired Helen.
> I shall tell you this one thing more, and you place it in your heart.
> Do not have my bones laid apart from yours, Achilles,
> but so that the same earth may cover you and me

in the golden urn which your mother has provided,
as we were brought up together in your house,
when Menoitios brought me, yet a little boy, from Opous
to your home after the grievous manslaying,
on that day when I had killed the son of Amphidamas,
as a child, not willingly, when angered over knucklebones.
Then Peleus the horseman received me into his house,
and brought me up kindly and named me your henchman.
So may the same vessel cover the bones of both of us.

(**150**) To show that it was possible for Achilles to be saved if he did not take revenge for the death of Patroklos, read what Thetis says:

'You will be a soon-dying child, according to your words.
For your death is prepared to follow straight after Hector's.'
To her replied then swift-footed godlike Achilles.
'So may I die straight away, since I was not going after all to defend
my companion when he was being killed, who was by far the dearest to
me.'

(**151**) Euripides, who was as wise as any other poet, and who understood that one of the most beautiful things is to love chastely, says somewhere, placing love in the list of things one prays for:

The love that leads to the chaste and to virtue
and is pursued as enviable by men of whom may I be one.

(**152**) Again, the same poet in his *Phoinix* sets out his views, when making the defence against the slander brought against Phoinix by his father, and trying to accustom men not to make judgement about people on the basis of suspicion and slander, but of their lives:

By now I have been a judge of many arguments,
and have taken cognisance of many points disputed
by witnesses, giving opposed views on the same event.
Then do I, as does each wise man,
reckon up the truth, by looking at each man's
nature, and at the way in which he passes the days.
Whichever man takes pleasure in company with the bad,

> I have never questioned, knowing that
> he is such as are the men with whom he pleases to be.

(**153**) Look, Athenians, at the sentiments that the poet sets out. He says that he has been a judge of many disputes, as you are now the jurymen, and he says that he made the judgements not on the basis of the testimonies, but of the habits, and the associations, of the people concerned; he looked hard at this point, at how the accused lived his daily life, the manner in which he manages his household, on the grounds that he would manage the city in a similar way, and with whom he liked associating; finally, he has no hesitation in stating that he is 'such as are the men with whom he pleases to be'. It is right then for you to employ the same reasoning as Euripides does in Timarchos' case. (**154**) How has he managed his household? He has consumed his inheritance, and having hired out his body, and taken bribes from the state, he has spent the lot, so that nothing remains for him except his shame. With whom does he like to associate? Hegesandros. What habits are the basis of Hegesandros' life? They are the habits as a result of which the laws forbid the man who behaves like that from addressing the people. What is it that I am saying about Timarchos, and what is the counter-accusation I am bringing? That Timarchos addressed the people as one who has prostituted himself, and who has consumed his ancestral property. And what oath did you swear? To cast your votes on just those issues on which the prosecution is based.

(**155**) So that I do not speak too long expounding from the poets, I shall now mention to you the names of some older, well-known men, some youths, and some boys, some of whom, because of their good looks, have had many lovers, and some of those still in their prime of life now still have lovers, but none of whom has ever undergone the same accusations as Timarchos. By contrast I shall on the other side give you names of men who have shamefully and openly prostituted themselves, so that you may remember the names, and assign Timarchos to the correct class. (**156**) First I shall state the names of those who lived as free and honourable men. You know, Athenians, Kriton the son of Astyochos, Perikleides of Perithoidai, Polemagenes, Pantaleon son of Kleagoras, and Timesitheos the runner, men who were the most beautiful not only of all the citizens, but of all the Greeks, men who had very many lovers of the greatest moral control; but still no one ever criticized them. (**157**) Again, of the youths and of those who are still even now among the boys, there is the nephew of Iphikrates, the son of Teisias of Rhamnous, the boy with the same name as the present defendant. He, good looking as he is, has kept so clear of disgrace that the other day at the Rural Dionysia, when comedies were being performed at Kollytos, and Parmenon the comic actor addressed an anapaestic verse to the chorus, in which there appeared 'some big Timarchean whores', no one understood the reference to be to the youth, but all took it as referring to you. So clear is it that you are the true heir of this practice. Again, Antikles the stadium runner and Pheidias the brother of Melesias. Though I could name many more, I shall leave it there, so that I should not appear to be giving them praise through desire to win their favour.

(**158**) When it comes to those who share the ways of Timarchos, wishing to avoid enmities I mention only those with whom I have least personal concern. Who of you does not know of Diophantos, known as the orphan, who brought the foreigner before the archon whose assistant was Aristophon of Azenia, and who accused him of having deprived him of four drachmai in relation to this activity? He cited the laws which command the archon to take concern for orphans, while he had himself violated the laws laid down about chastity (*sophrosyne*). Or who of the citizens was not annoyed at Kephisodoros, known as the son of Molon, for having ruined by his most dishonourable acts the perfect bloom of his appearance? Or Mnesitheos, known as the butcher's son? Or many others, whom I am happy to forget? (**159**) I have no wish to work through, bitterly, each of them by name; I would much prefer to be at a loss to name such men in my speech, because of my good will for the city. But since we have selected and gone through a number of each category, on the one side those who have been loved with moral self-control, and on the other those who commit offences against themselves, could you now answer me this question I put to you: to which category do you assign Timarchos, to those who are loved, or to those who have prostituted themselves? So, Timarchos, you are not to leave the group into which you have chosen to register and desert to the pursuits of the free men.

(**160**) If they then attempt to say that a man has not acted as an escort unless he was hired out with a contract, and they demand that I produce a written statement and witnesses for these things, you should remember, first, the laws about escortship, in which the lawgiver has nowhere made any mention of contracts. After all he did not investigate whether it was according to a written agreement that an individual had shamed himself, but in all ways, in order that practice becomes revealed, he commanded that any-one who had engaged in it should not share in the common affairs of the city. And rightly: anyone who when young stood aside from the ambition for noble honours because of his shameful pleasures, he thought should not be eligible to share in the honours when older. (**161**) Secondly, it is easy to demonstrate the naiveté of this argument. We would all agree on this point, that we make con-tracts with one another because of mistrust, in order that the man who has not broken the written agreement may receive judge-ment by the court's vote from the man who did. Therefore, if this activity needs a court case, then the assistance of the laws, as they are arguing, remains available to those who have acted as escorts according to written contract. But what would the arguments on each side appear to be? Think of this not just as something being described by me, but imagine you are seeing the affair taking place. (**162**) Assume a case where the man who hired a youth is in the right, and the hired youth in the wrong, and did not hold to the agreement; and assume also the opposite case, where the hired youth was reasonable and performing what was agreed, but the man who took the other's youth (*helikia*) and hired him has deceived him. And imagine that you are sitting as the jurymen. Now first, the elder man, when the water and the time to speak are his, prosecuting with energy and looking naturally straight at you, will say: (**163**) 'I hired Timarchos, Athenians, to act as an escort for me according to the written agreement which is deposited with Demosthenes'—for nothing prevents such a state-ment being made!—'But he does not carry out what was agreed.' And then he evidently goes into details to the jury, saying what such a person must do. Then will he not be stoned, the man who has hired an Athenian contrary to the laws, and will leave the court not only convicted of paying the sixth payment for his failure, but also of *hybris* in addition? (**164**) But in the other case where it is not he, but the one hired, who brings the action. Let him come forward and speak—or let the wise Batalos speak on his behalf, so that we may know what he is going to say. 'Jurymen, some one or other—it does not matter who—hired me to act as an escort (*hetairein*) for him for money, and I have done, and am still even now doing, everything in accordance with the written agreement, which the one acting as an escort must do; but he is breaking the contract.' Will he not then be met by a big outcry from the jury? Will not everyone say 'Are you then forcing yourself into the *agora*, are you putting a crown on yourself, are you engaged in the same activities as us?' So he will get no benefit from his contract.

(**165**) I shall tell you now how it has gained strength and become a custom to say that certain people have worked as escorts 'according to written agreement'. One of our citizens (I shall not give his name; I wish to avoid personal enmities), without foreseeing the consequences which I expounded to you a little earlier, is said to have served as an escort according to contracts deposited with Antikles. When he was no longer a private citizen, but went into public affairs and met with some abusive attacks, he caused the city to become accustomed to this expression, and that is the reason why people ask whether this practice take place according to written agreement. But the lawgiver did not give thought to the question of how the practice came about, but if a hiring took place by any means whatever, he fixed a verdict of shame upon the perpetrator.

(**166**) But still, though these issues have been thus clearly defined, many intrusions of irrelevant arguments will be discovered by Demosthenes. One might perhaps be less aggrieved by his malignant expressions when they are on the subject; but the points which he will drag in irrelevantly to the case, and doing damage to the city's just interests, at those it is certainly right to get angry. There will be a lot of Philip, and the name of his son Alexander will be mixed in with it too. After all, in addition to his other faults, Demosthenes is an uncultured and uneducated person. (**167**) To be offensive in a speech against Philip is boorish and untimely, but a lesser offence than the one I am about to mention. It is generally known that he is going to make disgraceful allegations against the man—he, who is himself no man; but when he insinuates disgraceful suspicions against the boy through fabricated ambiguities of language, he makes the city ridiculous. (**168**) In trying to damage the accounting, to which I am about to submit myself for the embassy, he says that when he was talking in detail the other day about the boy Alexander, how he played the lyre at a drinking party, and recited some speeches and made some sallies against another boy, and when he was revealing to the Council all that he happened to know about these events, then I, he says, became angry at the jokes at the boy's expense not as a fellow-member of the embassy, but as if I were a relation. (**169**) Now I have naturally had no conversation with Alexander because of his youth, but I do now have some praise for Philip because of the propitiousness of his statements. If he turns out to be the same in his actions to us as he now appears in his pro-nouncements, he will make praise of himself a safe and easy thing. I did rebuke Demosthenes in the Council-chamber, not because I was paying court to the boy, but because I thought that if you accepted that sort of talk the city would seem to be like him in its lack of decency.

(**170**) So in general, Athenians, do not accept the defence arguments that are irrelevant to the case, first because of the oaths which you have sworn, and second so that you are not thrown off course by a man who is a verbal manipulator. Going back a little, I shall begin to instruct you about this. When Demosthenes had spent his ancestral property, he went round the city on the hunt for rich young orphans, whose fathers had died, and whose mothers were managing their properties. I shall pass over many such cases, and mention just one of those who were treated terribly. (**171**) He spotted a wealthy household that was not being run well, in charge of which was a woman who was proud and lacked sense, while a young orphan, half-mad, was running the estate, Aristarchos the son of Moschos; pretending to be his lover, and inviting the young man to experience his generosity, filling him up with empty hopes, promising how he would straight away become absolutely the first of the orators, showing him a written list, (**172**) he turned out to be an initiator and teacher into such activities in such a way that as a result Aristarchos is in exile from his native land, Demosthenes has got his hands on, and has cheated him of, the three talents meant to keep him in the travels of his exile, and Nikodemos of Aphidna was killed violently by Aristarchos, poor man, who had both his eyes gouged out and his tongue cut out, the tongue with which he had addressed you freely, trusting in your laws and in you.

(**173**) So then, Athenians, did you put Sokrates the sophist to death, because he was shown to have educated Kritias, one of the Thirty who had overthrown the democracy, and will Demosthenes then beg off his companions from you, a man who inflicted revenges of that sort on private individuals who showed their popular concern by defending free speech? Some of his pupils, invited by him, have come to listen to the trial. He is making promises to them, doing deals for himself at your expense, as I hear, saying that he will transform the case and your understanding without your realizing it. (**174**) He will, he says, inspire confidence in the defendant, as soon as he comes forward to speak, and throw confusion in the prosecutor who will be terrified for himself. He will arouse so many outcries, such loud outcries, from the jury, as he throws in his accounts of my public speeches and criticizes the peace that was made thanks to Philokrates and me, that I shall not even face him in the court to defend myself, when I submit to the accounting for the embassy; he promises that I shall be content if I have to face a moderate fine, and not a capital punishment. (**175**) So do not by any means provide the sophist with the chance for laughter and entertainment at your expense; imagine you are seeing him returning home from the court, and putting on his airs at his young men's school, expounding how effectively he filched the case away from the jury: 'I carried them away from the charges against Timarchos and brought them over to be fixed on the prosecutor, and Philip and the Phokians, and I suspended terrors before the audience, so that the defendant started prosecuting, the prosecutor was on trial, and the jury forgot the issues on which they were the judges, and listened to issues on which they were not.' (**176**) But it is your job to stand in line together against this practice, and, following him closely at every point, do not let him at any moment turn aside, or hold on to arguments which are outside the contest; no, as at the horse races, drive him down the course of the case. If you do that, you will not incur contempt, and you will hold to the same opinion when judging that you had when making the laws; but if you do not, you will be thought to foresee that crimes are going to be committed and to be angry at them, but that when they have been committed, you no longer care.

(**177**) Well then, to sum it all up, if you punish the wrongdoers, your laws will be excellent and valid; but if you acquit them, the laws will be excellent, but no longer valid. I have no hesitation in speaking out freely to you, to explain why I say this. Why is it, do you think, Athenians, that the laws in place are excellent, but decrees passed by the city are inferior, and verdicts given in the courts sometimes incur criticism? (**178**) I shall lay out the reasons for this. It is because you establish the laws with a view to all aspects of justice, not for the sake of any unjust gain, or favour or enmity, but concentrating your minds purely on what is just itself, and on the public interest; and, I suppose, since you are intelligent, more so than others, you establish, naturally, very excellent laws. But in the assemblies and the courts, you often lose your hold on the issue itself, and are led astray by deceit and pretentious cheating; you have admitted the most unjust of all habits into your trials. You allow the defendants to turn round and prosecute the prosecutors. (**179**) When you have been dragged away from the defence speech, and have your minds all set on other matters, having fallen into forgetfulness of the accusation, you leave the court without having imposed a penalty on either party, neither on the prosecutor, since you were not given the chance to vote on him, nor on the defendant, since he has wiped away the existing charges against him by the other accusations, and escaped free from the court. Thus the laws are being slackened, the democracy is corrupted, and this custom is steadily gaining ground; the reason is that sometimes you readily accept an argument not accompanied by a morally good life.

(**180**) But not so of the Spartans; it is a fine thing to imitate virtues even in foreigners. When someone had made a speech in the Spartan assembly, a man who had lived shamefully, but was an exceptionally able speaker, and the Spartans, the story goes, were about to vote in favour of his motion, there came forward one of the Elders—whom they both respect and fear, and the office, called after their age, they regard as the greatest, and they appoint men to it from those who have been self-controlled from boyhood to old age: one of them came forward, it is said, and strongly chastized the Spartans, and denounced them in terms like this, that they would not for a long time inhabit an unravaged Sparta, if they used in their assemblies advisers like that. (**181**) And at the same time he called forward another of the Spartans, a man not well-favoured at speaking, but conspicuous in war and remarkable for justice and moral endurance, and commanded him to express the same sentiments, as best he could, which the former speaker had expressed, 'so that the Spartans may vote when they have heard a good man making the speech, but do not receive into their ears the voices of those proved to be cowards and evil'. The old man of self-controlled life from boyhood gave this advice to his fellow-citizens. He would readily have allowed Timarchos or the deviant Demosthenes to participate in public life!

(182) But in order that I should not be thought to be courting the favour of the Spartans, I shall mention our own ancestors also. They were so stern towards acts of shame, and took so much concern over the chastity of their children, that one of the citizens, when he discovered his daughter had been corrupted, and that she had not preserved her youthful beauty well until marriage, walled her up inside an empty house with a horse, by which she was certainly going to be killed when shut up together with her. Even now the house-site is standing in your city, and the place is called 'By the horse and the maid'. (183) Solon, the most famous of lawgivers, has written in ancient and solemn fashion about the good order of women. The women with whom a seducer is caught, he does not permit to adorn herself, nor to attend at the public cult ceremonies, in order that she should not mix with the innocent women and corrupt them. But if she does attend, or adorn herself, he tells anyone who meets her to tear off her clothes, strip off her adornment, and beat her (it is forbidden to kill or mutilate her), thereby dishonouring such a woman and making her life not worth living. (184) He also ordains that the procurers, male and female, be indicted, and, if convicted, be punished with death, because when people desire to commit offences, but hesitate and are ashamed to meet one another, the procurers offer their own shamelessness for a fee and bring the affair on to the test and to negotiation.

(185) These then were the decisions made by your ancestors about shameful and honourable acts; are you going to let Timarchos go free, a man responsible for the most shameful practices? The man who has a male body, but who has committed womanish offences? Which of you then will punish a woman if you catch her doing wrong? Or who of you would not appear to be without understanding of our culture, if you get angry at the woman who offends in accordance with nature, but use as a

political adviser the man who committed *hybris* against himself contrary to nature? (**186**) What feeling will each of you have as he goes home from the court? The man on trial is not obscure, but is well known; and the law about the scrutiny of orators is no insignificant law, but a very fine law, and it is easy to assume that the boys and young men will ask their relatives how the trial was decided. (**187**) So what are you going to say, you who have control over the vote, when your sons ask you whether you voted for condemnation or acquittal? In admitting that you voted to acquit Timarchos, will you not at the same time be overturning our common cultural education? What is the benefit in maintaining slave-attendants, or setting athletic trainers or teachers in charge of them, when those who have the laws entrusted to them are bent down to the acts of shame?

(**188**) I am surprised at this too, Athenians, if you hate the brothel-keepers, but let go those who willingly prostitute themselves. It seems also that the same man who would be elected by lot to none of the priesthoods of the gods, since he is not pure in body in accordance with the laws, is to write in our decrees prayers to the solemn Goddesses on behalf of the city? Why are we then surprised at the ineffectiveness of our public life, when orators like this sign our people's motions? Shall we send outside the city as an ambassador the man who has lived shamefully at home? What would he not sell, when he has sold the humiliation of his own body? On whom would he have pity when he has no pity on himself?

(**189**) To which of you is the repulsiveness of Timarchos not known? Just as we recognize those in athletic training, even if we do not visit the *gymnasia*, by looking at their good condition, so we recognize those who have prostituted themselves, even though we are not present at their activities, from their shamelessness, boldness, and practices. For the man who ignored, over the most important things, the laws and moral control has a condition of his soul which becomes revealed as a result of the disorder of his inclination. (**190**) One would find that it is as a result of men like this that very many cities have been overturned, and the men themselves fallen into the greatest disasters. Do not believe, Athenians, that the origins of wrongdoing lie with the gods, rather than with the grossness of men; do not believe that men who have committed impiety are driven and punished, as in the tragedies, by the Furies with blazing torches. (**191**) It is the impetuous pleasures of the body and the inability ever to think one has had enough that fill the robber bands, make men board the pirates' boats, they are the Fury for each man, which urges him to slaughter his fellow-citizens, to act as the tyrants' underlings, and to help in destroying democracy. They take no account of the shame or of what they will suffer later, but are enchanted by the delights they expect if they succeed. So remove from us, Athenians, natures like this, and turn the models for emulation of the young towards virtue.

(**192**) You must realize this—and do please remember well what I am about to say—that if Timarchos pays the penalty for his habits, you will establish the basis for good order in the city; but if he is acquitted, it would be better if the trial had not taken place. Before Timarchos came to trial, the law and the name of the courts provided a deterrent to some men. But if the man first of all in repulsiveness, the best known of all, shall come into court and get off, it will induce many to go wrong, at the end it will not be speeches, but a clear crisis that will arouse your anger. (**193**) Express your rage not on a crowd but on one man, and keep your good watch on the preparations and advocates of these men. I shall not mention any of them by name, so that they do not make that the excuse of speaking, on the grounds that they would not have come forward had someone not mentioned them by name. This is what I shall do; without mentioning their names, but describing their habits, I shall enable their persons to be recognized. Each one of them will be himself responsible, if he takes the stand and shows his shamelessness. (**194**) Advocates for Timarchos who will come forward fall into three groups: those who have destroyed their ancestral estates through daily extravagance; those who did not use their prime of life and their bodies properly and are frightened not for Timarchos but for themselves and their practices, in case they be brought one day to trial; and still others from the self-indulgent and those who have unstintingly used such people, so that they may trust in their support and commit offences the more easily. (**195**) So before you listen to the pleas of the advocates remember their lives, and tell those who have committed offences against their bodies not to go on bothering you, but to stop speaking in public. The law does not investigate those living their private lives, but those engaged in politics. Tell those who have consumed their inheritances to work and acquire a livelihood from some other means. And tell those who are the hunters of such young men as are easily caught to turn themselves to the foreigners and the metics, so that they may not be deprived of their inclination, but you are not harmed.

(196) You have now heard everything that it is right for you to hear from me. I have expounded the laws, and I have examined the life of the defendant. So now it is you who are the judges of my arguments, and soon I am to be the spectator. It is with your verdicts that the case rests. If you wish it, by doing what is both right and to the city's advantage, we shall have the chance to win more honour from you by investigating those who break the laws.

COMMENTARY

STRUCTURE

The plan of the speech may be summarized as follows:

This bald summary reveals a number of significant points about the case and the strategy of the speech (see also Intro., pp. 53–67). First the structure is carefully designed. In particular it displays a concern for 'ring-composition' characteristic of the surviving trial speeches, especially the longer ones; many important themes—especially concerning the laws and the necessity of their implementation, and the relation between 'moral' behaviour and public life—are introduced in the two opening sections and strongly recapitulated in the concluding section. On this feature in general, see Worthington 27–39; however, his argument that such carefully designed composition implies later revision of such public speeches for publication is open to question: see Johnstone (1999: 12 and n. 63). Secondly, the dependence of the case on allegations of Timarchos' offensive and illegal behaviour, largely unsupported by direct evidence, is brought out by the repeated attempts by the prosecutor to insist that all in Athens know the truth, that the goddess 'Report' is the star witness, and those who might have given the fullest evidence are inherently unwilling to testify. Third, it emerges that accusations of the dissipation of Timarchos' inheritance, his treatment of his relatives, and his political corruption, are all of considerable importance to the case, though they seem to yield priority to the allegations of sexual improprieties (see also the analysis of the narrative section on **37–117**). Finally, much of the prosecution is devoted to attacking a number of Timarchos' important friends and supporters as well as Timarchos himself: his most important lover, Hegesandros, with his brother Hegesippos, who are evidently still backing Timarchos, and the two eminent men who are said to be going to speak extensively for him, the anonymous General, and, most important of all, Demosthenes (see also on **117–24** and **166–76**).

SECTION I **1–6** Introduction: The trial and the public good

1–2 Not one of my fellow-citizens . . . have I ever prosecuted. The Athenian legal system depended on individuals to bring prosecutions in cases of public interest as well as in private affairs, and in some cases successful volunteer prosecutors could be rewarded with a share of the fines (e.g. Harrison 1968–1971: II, 211–21; R. G. Osborne 1985b: 44–8; Hunter 1994: 126). But there was a serious danger of being labelled a 'sykophant' for launching a prosecution for the wrong motives, such as money, or serving the aims of other, more influential politicians. This led most prosecutors to emphasize the much more acceptable motives of personal revenge and the punishment of those who were wronging the city: on the complex issues here, see R. G. Osborne (1990a); Harvey (1990); Hansen (1991: 194–6); Hunter

(1994: 125–9); and most fully Christ (1998). Prosecutors also tend, for the same reasons, to assert (at times with great implausibility), their total lack of experience in bringing prosecutions (whereas defendants may claim complete absence from the law courts, e.g. Hyper. *Lyk.* 16–18). So Aeschines here uses all three tactics. He emphasizes mostly the public danger, as the case rests mostly on the damage that the very fact of Timarchos' continuing political activity was doing to Athens' political life and repute in the world. He also claims, correctly as far as we know, that (while he has been an 'orator' and ambassador for two to three years) he has never previously been the prosecutor in a *graphe* or attacked anyone at a scrutiny of an officeholder (*euthyna*). As Christ (1998: 151) points out, this does not exclude some involvement in someone's else's prosecution or scrutiny case (see also Aeschines' claims in the Embassy speech, 2. 184). Demosthenes indeed alleged that he had been involved as supporting speaker (*synegoros*) for Aristophon in a prosecution of Philonikos (19. 290–1), and Aeschines' claim here is no argument against that claim (see Rubinstein, forthcoming, against Harris 1995: 155).

On this basis, he can proceed to make the counter-charge that it is Timarchos, not he, who is the sykophant: in fronting the legal attack on Aeschines for misconduct on the embassy, Timarchos is playing a supporting role to Demosthenes; the verb *sykophantein* is the word used for Timarchos' part in the prosecution against him in **1** and again in **3**. This in turn leads to the third tactic: Timarchos' attack legitimizes Aeschines' action as an act of preemptive retaliation (cf. e.g. Apollodoros' attack on Stephanos at Ps. Dem. 59. 41–3; see also Davidson 1997: 267). This point is especially necessary in this case, in view of the obvious objection, made in Demosthenes' bitter response a few years later (19. 287) and no doubt with much greater force in this trial, that if Timarchos' ineligibility was so obvious he should have been prosecuted many years earlier, when he began his political career. In fact a very high proportion of known politically motivated prosecutions (and defences) were collaborative ventures of two or more friends or political colleagues, see Christ (1998: 126–7) and above all Rubinstein (forthcoming).

1 public action. A *graphe*, literally a written statement, is regularly used in Athenian legal discussions to distinguish a legal action where prosecution is in theory open to all citizens, where there is some form of public interest, or reason to fear that no prosecution may be possible, from those cases (called *dikai*) where prosecution is restricted to the person or persons wronged (or to relatives in the case of homicide). On this distinction, see generally Harrison (1968–71: II, 76–8); Hansen (1991: 192–5); Todd (1993: 99–102). Aeschines has in mind particularly here trials between politicians, where the offence is explicitly against the community as a whole (such as bribery, military desertion, or incompetence, or mismanagement on an embassy, the trial he is currently facing).

examination of office. All who held any form of office or magistracy in the democracy, performed public duties, or were in charge of public funds, had to submit themselves to accounting procedures known as *euthynai*. Various magistrates called account- ants (*logistai*) and assessors (*euthynoi*) conducted the scrutinies, and any other citizen could present their accusation; these investiga- tions might lead on to formal prosecutions before a jury. See in detail Piérart (1971), and briefly Hansen (1991: 222–4), and on **19–20**.

just how I shall reveal. In fact Aeschines says extraordinar- ily little about the political motives for Timarchos' action, about Philip, Demosthenes and the embassy, or about Timarchos' other political activities of the last year (see on **166–9**, where all such arguments are said to be irrelevant, and on **81–4**, and see Intro., pp. 54–6 and Davidson 1997: 260–3).

2 most shameful things for me not to come to the aid of the whole city, the laws, you yourselves, and me. 'Coming to the aid' (literally 'running up at the cry for help', *boethein*) was in the first place a term used for the action Greeks hoped from friends or passers-by seeing people in trouble, as an example of the community's self-help practices (see Hunter 1994, 134–9; Fisher 1998b: 88–9); by extension, litigants in private cases often ask the jury to 'come to their aid' by their verdicts (e.g. Dem. 54. 2). Here, as in other public cases, Aeschines claims, both as a personal victim and as the man choosing to act for the city, that he is under the obligation to 'come to the aid' of the city and the legal system as well as himself (see also Lys. 22. 3; Dem. 22. 1, 24. 8; Christ 1998: 148). Aeschines also claims a highly developed sense of 'shame' (*aischyne*) for the community (and see also on **26**); this is designed to contrast with the total shamelessness shown by Timarchos throughout his career.

clerk of the court. A clerk (*grammateus*) was attached to each court; his duties were to read out the formal indictment at the start of the case, and any relevant laws or testimony or other prepared written material on the invitation of the litigants (see Arist. *Ath. Pol.* 67. 3, and Ar. *Wasps* 894–7). Such *grammateis* were probably citizens, like the *grammateus* charged solely with reading out documents to the assembly and the Council (*Ath. Pol.* 54. 5), and may well have been, as he was, elected by the *demos*. 'Clerk', the conventional translation, masks the fact that a primary duty of these functionaries was to read documents out at public meetings (see Johnstone 1999: 144, n. 1). On Aeschines' career as a *grammateus* see Intro. pp. 12–13.

brought this case of scrutiny. The technical term for this act is used here, *epangellein ten dokimasian* (and at **32, 64, 81**: see Harrison 1968–71: II, 204). See also Intro. pp. 5–6, and on **28–32**.

private enmities do very often correct public affairs. This sentence (and see **3**, and **195**) in effect confirms and defends the conclusion that a politician with a morally murky past would be very likely to escape without attracting a prosecution unless he endangered the career or property of another, who would then allege that he was bringing an action out of a combination of personal enmity and public concern. The generalization thus encapsulates the inextricable connections of the political and the personal in Athenian public life. See also the similar statements on motives for prosecutions at e.g. Dem. 24. 6–10; Ps. Dem. 59. 1, 12–15; Hyper. *Eux.* 13; and see the discussions of R. G. Osborne (1985b); S. C. Todd (1993: 154–63); Hunter (1994: 125–9); Rubinstein (1998: 135–6 and forthcoming); Christ (1998: ch. 4, esp. 155).

3 it is that man there who has brought it on himself. Just after claiming credit for his own initiative in bringing the case, Aeschines strikes a different note, and one which is repeated throughout, and with particular emphasis at the end of the speech (see **190–1**): that it is ultimately Timarchos, with his shameful past, who is responsible for the trial. In view of his record, he could and should have avoided active public life, and so escaped this trial.

4–6 In this second brief section of the introduction, as an appropriate general preamble to the exposition of the laws, Aeschines emphasizes the function of the laws as the fundamental safeguard for a democratic political system. This is another major theme to which he returns at the end of the speech (**177–9**).

4 things which you will clearly have heard from others in the past. By 'others' Aeschines probably calls to mind in the first instance other political and law-court speeches where such moves may be made. This type of debate on the nature of political regimes might also have been heard in public readings from historians such as Herodotus (see esp. 3. 80–3), or in the public lectures of sophists and philosophers, and orators may well be influenced by such more theoretical presentations (see Adkins 1978: 145 and Ober 1998, 369–73).

It is agreed that there are three forms of government. Aeschines uses an identical move, expressed in very similar language, in the introduction to the Crown speech of 330 (3. 6–7). This standard division into three basic types of *politeiai*, constitutions or political systems (the one, the few, or the many), is first clearly expressed in Herodotus (3. 80–2—where the more favourable monarchy, not tyranny, represents one-man rule), and regularly thereafter. Fourth-century philosophical and rhetorical theory developed more complex schemes. For example Plato, in the *Republic*, distinguished one ideal state (rule by one or more philosophical kings), timocracy, oligarchy, democracy, and tyranny; Aristotle employed a sixfold version in the *Politics*, while Isocrates (*Panath.* 131–2) reverted to the simple threefold category (in terms very similar to Aeschines'), but insisted that they could all be 'aristocracy', i.e. excellent, if they allowed the 'most competent people' to have most power. As Lane Fox (1994: 144) observes, Aeschines' generalizations are smugly overconfident, like many such flattering statements designed to ingratiate the speaker with the democratic audience (as often observed by comedy, e.g. Ar. *Ach.* 633–40, and *Knights*, *passim*; see also Ober 1989: 161–5); oligarchies and monarchies could equally pride themselves on rule in accordance with their laws and of being ruled by the best men.

but democratic cities are governed by the established laws. Other contrasts in the orators between life under democratic laws and under oligarchies can be found in Dem. 21. 209–11, 22. 51–2, 24. 24–6, 75–6, and Ps. Dem. 25. 20–1, as well as in drama (see e.g. Eur. *Suppl.* 429–37). Athenians swore to obey and protect the laws in their ephebic oath; see Burckhardt (1996: 57–63), and on **18**.

5 protect the bodies of those living in a democracy and their system of government. Hansen (1989: 74–8, and see also 1996: 97–8) lists other examples of this argument, and suggests that these rhetorical commonplaces or *topoi* all derive their power before the democratic audience from the view that democracy protected the bodies and the interests of the many against the few through the operations of the laws. This is above all the central argument of Demosthenes' *Against Meidias*, which emphasizes the protection offered to the bodies of ordinary citizens by the law of *hybris*, the key term used for the outrages (whether violent or sexual) of those with power against the weaker provided the people apply the laws (see on **15–16**, and Ober (1996: 86–106; 1998: 181–2). But, as Lane Fox points out (1994: 144–5, and see Thomas 1994: 123–5), Aeschines' use of these commonplaces differs from the others, in that it is not concerned essentially with defences of citizens against maltreatment from their leaders, or the rich, but with the imposition on future leaders of a prohibition of immoral lifestyles ('those whose speeches or styles of life are contrary to the laws'). In this way Aeschines subsumes the issue of improper lifestyles under the more general category of anti-democratic illegality and outrage, and thus adapts the *topoi* to the needs of his speech while retaining their power. In this way he also prepares the way for the condemnation of Timarchos' sexual behaviour as in effect constituting *hybris* (see on **15–16**).

Suspicion and armed guards. Cf. Xen. *Hiero* 10, where Simonides advises the tyrant Hiero to diminish unpopularity by using his mercenary army and guards 'positively' by protecting all the citizens, in town and countryside, against criminals and outside enemies.

SECTION II 6–36 Citation and discussion of the laws

The second section, as is common in these speeches, is devoted to citation and discussion of the allegedly relevant laws. Here Aeschines mentions not only the specific procedure of the case, the *dokimasia rhetoron*, but many other laws as well, which could be seen to concern the control of moral behaviour in relation to boys and youths as well as adult citizens: laws which Timarchos has allegedly infringed throughout his life. The purpose is both to build a varied indictment against Timarchos and so blacken his moral character from the beginning, and to implant in the jury a sense that the whole of their moral and educational system and the moral example set by their political leaders is in danger unless they convict (see also Intro. pp. 58–67; Dover 1978: 23–39; Ford (1999: 241–9).

In the Athenian courts litigants themselves had to find the texts of relevant laws and then invite the Clerk to read them out; they may seek to persuade the jury to adopt the interpretation of the laws which suits their case. This procedure often, as here, enables the litigant to mix selective quotations from laws with his own phrases expanding or 'elucidating' the texts. The main sanction against the obvious possibilities of abuse of this freedom appears to be a law (Ps. Dem. 26. 24) punishing with death anyone who cited a law which did not exist. How, if at all, this law was enforced is not clear. There is no evidence that the secretary of the court was permitted to object to a citation, or to inform the presiding judge if he were asked to read out inaccurate or invented phrases; presumably the opponent, if sharp enough to notice, could object. Even if the clerk read out an accurate text, there was still plenty of scope for litigants to be highly selective, and to argue over varied interpretations. See generally Kapparis, *Neaira* 198–9.

6 to obey the laws we have established. For other examples of this argument, that what the jurors must above all consider, if the city is to be in a good state, is the need to *implement* the good laws they have by actually punishing offenders, see Ps. Andoc. 4. 21–2; Dem. 21. 214–19, 223–5, 24. 216–17.

how much concern was shown for moral control (*sophrosyne*). This concept of self-restraint or self-control (*sophrosyne*)—

which is seen in this speech essentially in relation to sexual morals—is central to the whole prosecution, with its intense focus on the supposed threat to the youth of the city of the wrong sorts of relationships. There are twenty-eight instances in this speech, most applied to the control of homosexual desires or behaviour (**7, 9, 11, 20, 22, 25, 48, 121, 122, 133, 137, 140, 151, 159** (two cases), **180, 189**: see also Ford 1999: 242). This emphasis on *sophrosyne* was noted with public distaste by Demosthenes, commenting on the inappropriateness of Aeschines and his family as champions and reformers (*sophronistai*) of the behaviour of the young (19. 285), and was made the centre of Aeschines' counter-boast that he deserved credit for his appeal to the *sophrosyne* of the young (2. 180: see Intro. pp. 53–4). On the concept in general, see North (1966: *passim*); Dover (1974: 119–23); Cairns (1993: esp. 168, 314–21).

by Solon, our ancient lawgiver. The term for 'lawgiver', *nomothetes*, is the term standardly used from the later fifth century for a single legislator; see Ostwald (1986: 92–3). Fourth-century Athenians believed, rightly, that Solon, two hundred or so years earlier, had been appointed a special legislator and had written down (see Solon's own confirmation of this point, fr. 36. 15–16 West) wide-ranging laws, which remained the foundation of their legal system. The traditional date for his archonship is 594, and many scholars place the lawgiving activities in that year too, though there is an argument for dating these to a few years later; consistently with either date, Demosthenes (19. 251) put Solon's epoch about 240 years before the date of that speech (343). It is clear that new laws were passed, in a rather haphazard manner, throughout the rest of the sixth and fifth centuries, but that between 411 and the 390s Athens undertook a complex and contested process of revision and systematization of existing laws. With the re-establishment of the democracy in 403/2, a clearer distinction was made between laws, designed to be permanent and of general application, and decrees which were more specific; and a new, more complicated, procedure was established for making new laws, which took some powers from the assembly and gave them to specially constituted panels of jurors also called 'law-givers' (*nomothetai*) (see e.g. Hansen (1991: 169–75; Thomas 1994: 120).

Despite this, with increasing regularity and emphasis fourth-century orators made often historically absurd ascriptions of almost all their laws to 'Solon' (including, for example, the setting up of the *nomothetai* procedure itself, Dem. 20. 92); further, they made great (and misleading) appeals, as Aeschines does here and throughout the speech, to the authority figure of the wise Solon, the founder both of their democracy and of their moral and cultural traditions, whose 'intentions' seen through the laws are confidently elucidated. As Hansen (1990) and Thomas (1994) have suggested, this persistent appeal to a single authority figure of the past, rather than to the continuing good sense of the people themselves, may present a conservative, deferential, and nostalgic impression of the fourth-century democracy, opposed to thoughts of rational changes in the laws (though such changes of course continued to be made). Similarly, Aeschines later on makes equally 'conservative' appeals to the authority of the Areopagos, to a pre-Solonian Athenian myth and even to Sparta (see notes on **81, 92, 180–4**). But what is most important about the rhetoric of the appeal to the intentions of the lawgiver is to give authority to their own, usually partial, interpretations of the laws relevant to their case: see Johnstone (1999: 25–33).

Drakon and the other lawgivers. No further use is made of these 'lawgivers', added for an immediate effect of venerable antiquity. Drakon was apparently a 'lawgiver' of a generation before Solon; after Solon, the only laws of Drakon still in use were the homicide laws (see Carawan 1998), which were not relevant to this case, and there is no reason to suppose he had any other figures in mind for the 'others' (see Thomas 1994: 123).

7 First of all . . . the moral control (*sophrosyne*) of our boys (*paides*) . . . laid down expressly what habits a free-born boy . . . As the discussion proceeds, it becomes clear that this phrasing indicates a legal concern both for instilling sound habits of self-control in the boys and youths, and also self-restraint in relation to them of their teachers, trainers, and slave attendants. The laws were naturally concerned to protect the boys both against improper sexual abuse from their instructors, or other frequenters of the establishments (for interest in watching boys training, see Fisher 1998a: 93–5), and also from the boys' own experimental misbehaviour.

Aeschines claims to have found in the laws a clear and explicit pattern of moral protection for three distinct age-classes, boys (*paides*), youths (*meirakia*), and adults, reflecting 'Solon's' firm intentions. In fact he adduces rather more of a hotchpotch of laws (see Ford 1999: 242–3) subjected to his own careful glossing, to do with regulations of schools and teachers, and the protection of children from prostitution and sexual assault, before reaching a number of laws, one of which he proclaims to be very recent, concerned solely with those in public life. Wooten (1988) points out that most of these laws could be considered irrelevant to the case, and suggests they are merely an attempt to build up prejudice against Aeschines, and an example of the rhetorical use of enumeration to produce not clarity, but useful obfuscation. It is true that the laws concerned with schools and the protection of boys are not strictly relevant to the specific case against Timarchos, as Aeschines in effect admits at **39**, when he says he will 'pass over' all Timarchos' offences before he came of age; but his citation of them serves a very important purpose for his overall argument and strategy. It creates the context of a deep and ancient legislative concern for the *sophrosyne* of the citizens (see also on **24–6**, **137–40**, **183–4**), against which the need to implement the particular law regulating the politicians is to be seen; it also conveys the sense that Timarchos has been in breach of these rules all his life (see Thomas 1994: 123; Ford 1999: 243–4; Johnstone 1999: 31–2; at 146, n. 51 Johnstone gives a one-sided impression of Aeschines' purpose in discussing the law of the scrutiny of orators, focusing on the danger to the city's political life, though at p. 32 he recognizes the general emphasis on the *sophrosyne* of the whole community). The citation of the laws of *hybris* serve a different purpose again (see below on **15–17**).

not only in the case of private individuals, but also of the *rhetores*. On the opposition in general between individuals (*idiotai*) and *rhetores*, see Hansen (1989: 37–55); Rubinstein (1998). The law in this case is deliberately set up only to apply to the *rhetores* (see the conclusion, **194–5**; Dem. 22. 30, see Intro. pp. 51–3).

8 I would like now to develop my argument. Aeschines claims to be carefully following the pattern clearly laid out in the laws, when he has in fact created this pattern to assist the development of his case against Timarchos.

orderly conduct (*eukosmia*) of your boys. *Kosmos* is an important value-term, with a range of uses stemming from the root sense of 'order': it may be (from the fifth century at least) the world as an orderly, rule-obeying, harmonious system (cf. our scientific sense of the word 'cosmos'); attractive appearance or ornament (cf. our cosmetics); the good order and discipline of a state, or the good, orderly, and decent behaviour of individuals inside a community (see e.g. Cartledge, introduction to Cartledge, Millett, and von Reden 1998). Along with *sophrosyne*, it functions in this speech as a very significant standard for Athenian educational and political culture, against which Timarchos is to be judged; see notes on **22–7, 33, 43, 67, 183.**

not only . . . of the *rhetores*. Some editors (e.g. Bekker in 1823) have suggested that this phrase, repeated from **7**, should be deleted as unnecessary. But it may be that Aeschines is very deliberately and emphatically repeating this vital distinction.

9 school-teachers. As his father Atrometos had been a school-teacher (Dem. 19. 249, 18. 129, see Intro. pp. 9, 12–13) Aeschines had good opportunities for learning about any such laws, and in view of the attacks on their social and moral status which surface in Demosthenes' abuse, he had a special reason for emphasizing the strict controls imposed on their conduct.

These specific laws regulating educational establishments are not attested elsewhere for classical Athens: they may be Solonian laws, as Aeschines claims, laws passed later, for example some time in the fifth century, or bold inventions by Aeschines. The laws cited at **138–40** prohibiting slaves from exercising in *gymnasia* and being the lovers of free-born boys are probably Solonian, as is the law of *hybris* (**15–17**). It is less certain that Solon passed any other laws concerning *gymnasia* or schools (there is no particular reason to suppose that the law of theft which specified penalties for theft from *gymnasia* were Solonian: Dem. 24. 114; see Kyle (1987: 22); D. Cohen (1983: 38–40)). One may argue, however, that the idea is not wholly implausible. If Solon was interested in regu-lating by status access to *gymnasia* and praised 'noble pederasty' in his poems, he might have passed other regulations (see Mactoux 1988: 338–9). Other sixth-century evidence attests homosexual contacts at these settings (see Theognis 1335–6; Plut. *Sol.* 1. 3–4, Athen. 609d, and Paus. 1. 30, on the tradition of an altar to Eros established by the tyrant Peisistratos' supposed lover Charmos at the entrance to the Academy; for the evidence for athletic facilities in sixth-century Athens see Delorme 1960: 36–42; Kyle 1987: 21–2, 64–92). Evidence for schools in Greece begins at the very beginning of the fifth century, but their casual nature and the large numbers of pupils attested in smallish communities (e.g. 60 boys at Astypalaea, Paus. 6. 9. 6–7, 120 at Chios, Hdt. 6. 27) seem to imply they were no innovation then (see W. V. Harris 1989: 56–7, 57–60). Increasing sixth-century evidence for the use of writing and reading by relatively ordinary people, found on pots, on graffiti, and on rock-cut *horoi* (see Lang 1976; Ober 1995; Whitley 1998: 314–17) make it impossible to rule out some early sixth-century schooling regulation. But if there was a Solonian prototype, the more detailed regulations may yet be fifth- or early fourth-century additions, as we know was the requirement that a *choregos* for boys to be at least 40 (see below) (see e.g. Golden 1990: 60–2). For schools in classical Athens and later, see also Morgan (1998: 9–39).

10 gymnastic teachers (*paidotribai*) to open the wrestling-schools (*palaistrai*). A *palaistra* was originally an area for wrestling training or a wrestling 'school', while a *gymnasion* was rather an establishment for all types of athletic training and contests (and might include one or more *palaistrai*); but either term could be used interchangeably for the whole activity: see Delorme (1960); Kyle (1987: 64–9). Similarly, a *paidotribes* (literally a 'polisher of boys'), was originally a trainer of boys for combat sports, whereas a *gymnastes* might be more of an athletic trainer; but it could be, as here, a general term for any athletic trainer (see Kyle 1987: 141–3; S. G. Miller 1991: nos. 123–7).

During the Hellenistic period (*c.* 336–*c.* 146), widespread epigraphic evidence attests that it was normal for a city to inscribe its laws regulating the powers, duties, and behaviour of the gymnasiarch, the annual magistrate in charge of their main *gymnasion*. The *gymnasion* became perhaps the leading cultural and educational institution of the Greek communities throughout the Hellenistic world. The fullest surviving such text, from Beroia in Macedonia, dated not long before the defeat of the Macedonian monarchy by the Romans in 168 BC, opens with the statement that as other cities (namely in Macedonia) have published their law, it is right that Beroia should so likewise, on a *stele* to be set up in the *gymnasion*, with a copy in the state archives: 'so that the young men will feel a greater sense of shame and be more obedient to their leader' (see text and full discussion by Gauthier and Hatzopoulos 1993; translation in Austin 1981: no. 118 and S. G. Miller 1991: no. 126). This law displays detailed concerns about status distinctions, order, and the avoidance of improper sexual contacts very similar to those listed here. It regulates the age of the gymnasiarch (between 30 and 60, A 24–5), opening and closing times (at the gymnasiarch's discretion, B 2–5); those over 30 need explicit permission to strip and exercise (B 1–3); the youths (*neaniskoi*—i.e. those between ephebic status and 30) may not associate with or talk to the boys (B 13–15); those excluded from exercising in the *gymnasion* are slaves, freedmen, their children, those physically unable to exercise (*apalastroi*), those who have committed *hetairesis* (i.e. those who have in effect sold themselves, as is alleged Timarchos had), those who work in the market, and anyone drunk or mad (B 26–39). Though they could not be members, slaves performed duties in the *gymnasia*. At Beroia, the man who sold off the mixture known as *gloios* (oil, sweat, and dust scraped off with the strigil or skimmed off the bath), apparently for medical uses might also hold the office of '*palaistra*-attendant' (*palaistrophylax*), and had to obey the gymnasiarch, on pain of a whipping by the gymnasiarch (B 96–9): on this official in Greece and in Hellenistic Egypt, see K. J. Rigsby, 'Notes sur la Créte hellénistique', *REG* 99 (1986), 350–5. The reference to a '*palaistra*-attendant' in the Hippocratic *Epidemics* (6. 8. 30) who suffered a head-injury wrestling, and also perhaps the reference to 'barbarians boxing' at Dem. 4. 40–1, may suggest that slave-attendants did not only sweep and clean, but also acted as sparring partners to the free men exercising: see Golden (1998: 54), and Golden (2000: 160–1). All this goes some way to support the view that the laws Aeschines cites here are probably at least laws current in his own time, and that over time such laws became standard throughout Greek cities.

slave-attendants (*paidagogoi*). On the function of such slaves to escort and protect boys when out in the city, and the contradictions in Athenian practice and attitudes towards them, see esp. Golden (1984, and 1990: esp. 145–63). They might presumably either be tempted to misbehave themselves or be bribed by others wishing to exploit their charges.

Mouseia. This school event is mentioned also in Theophrastos' sketch of the stingy man (*aneleutheros*—defined as the man who refuses to spend money in order to win renown or civic recognition), who claims his children are ill rather than send them with suitable contributions to their school for the *Mouseia* (Theophr. *Char.* 22. 6). It was probably some sort of annual festival where the pupils performed their party-pieces, e.g. in song or recitation, before assembled parents and friends (and where some men might take too much of an interest in the boys).

Hermaia. Hermes and Herakles were the two primary gods associated with the *gymnasia* (see M. P. Nilsson, *Die Hellenistische Schule* (Munich, 1955), 62; Delorme 1960: 339–52; P. Gauthier, 'Trois Decrets honorant des citoyens bienfaiteurs', *REG* 95 (1982), 226–31; and Kyle 1987: 80). Much evidence exists for this festival, especially in the Hellenistic period. The setting for the discussions in Plato's *Lysis* (206d–e) is a celebration of the *Hermaia* in a recently opened *palaistra*, suitable for their purposes as boys (*paides*) and youths (*neaniskoi*) are all together (hence too a greater than usual need for vigilance). Evidence from many other Hellenistic cities reveals the *Hermaia* as the major annual festival of any self-respecting *gymnasion*; especially notable are the rules laid down for the contestants, stipulating good condition, discipline, and hard-work, for different age-classes, in the gymnasiarchy law from Beroia (Gauthier and Hatzopoulos 1993: esp. 95–123), and see also D. Knoepfler, 'Contribution à l'épigraphie de Chalcis', *BCH* 103 (1979), 165–88 on a similar inscription from Chalcis.

How many *Hermaia* were celebrated in a large city like Athens with a good few *gymnasia* and *palaistrai*, and whether any one had precedence, is not clear. Some Athenian Hellenistic inscriptions record *Hermaia*: in *IG* II² 1227, of 131/0 BC the *demos* of the Salaminians (see on **26**) honours the gymnasiarch, and mentions young male 'basket-carriers' (*kanephoroi*) and contests at a *Hermaia*; in *IG* II² 2980 an ephebe called Eumarides won a torch-race at a *Hermaia*. Significantly different appears to be *IG* II² 2971, in which Demetrios, the grandson of the more famous Demetrios of Phaleron, who was placed in power in Athens after the Chremonidean War by the Macedonians *c.* 260, won a chariot race at 'the *Hermaia*' when hipparch in *c.* 325/4: see S. V. Tracy, *Athenian Democracy in Transition: Attic Letter-Cutters of 340 to 290 B.C.* (Berkeley and Los Angeles, 1995), 43–4, 171–4 and J. D. Mikalson,

Religion in Hellenistic Athens (Berkeley and Los Angeles, 1998), 195. This appears not to be connected to a *gymnasion*, but to Demetrios' role as cavalry-commander for which he is honoured by the cavalry, who exercised by the 'Herms', near the Royal Stoa, in the NW of the Agora (Kyle 1987: 62–4; G. R. Bugh, *The Horsemen of Athens* (Princeton, 1988), 219–20; J. K. Camp 'Excavations in the Athenian Agora: 1993 & 1994', *Hesperia* 65 (1996), 257–9; C. Habicht, 'Ein neues Zeugnis der athenischen Kavallieres', *ZPE* 115 (1997), 121–4); a sign of this Demetrios' luxury, according to the gossipy historian Hegesandros of Delphi, in Athen. 167e, was that he erected a platform by the Herms bigger than them for his Corinthian mistress to watch the events (see also Habicht 1997: 153–4).

regulation of the company the boys may keep. The *scholia* here asserts that there were small shrines (*naiskaria*) in the back rooms of Athenian *palaistrai*, and also a source of water where the boys could drink when thirsty (naturally, after exercising in the hot sun), and to which they tended to repair secretly to 'be depraved', presumably to share juvenile sexual experimentations, perhaps like the energetic youths of the same age pleasing each other on Mount Lykabettos, in Theopompos fr. 30 K–A; as Delorme notes (1960: 347, 349) it is not wholly safe to trust this report, without knowing its source (perhaps also a joke from a comedy). Friendships formed at school, which may have included both such sexual experimentation and more serious 'loves' are likely to have been important, and possibly lasting and formative, for many Athenians (see e.g. Xen. *Symp.* 4. 23–4; Kritoboulos and Kriton; and Foxhall 1998: 58). Aeschines is also envisaging possibly 'shameful' relationships between older youths and the boys which might have lasting effects. Foxhall's further suggestion, that schools were organized by tribes, and that therefore relationships formed there might have political 'overtones' seems to rest on a misinterpretation of Dem. 39. 24–5, where the issue concerns boys' 'cyclical choruses' (see below), which were tribally organized, but has nothing to do with normal schooling.

of the cyclical choruses. Whether the text should be *enkykloi choroi*, as the manuscripts have, or *kykloi choroi* (Franke's emendation, usually accepted), there was probably a shift in sense from the circular dance movements made by singing choruses to the idea of the 'cycle' of recurring choral performances in the city through the year (see also Dem. 20. 21, of the annual liturgy system): see P. J. Wilson (2000: 55–6 and n. 22), and also Morgan (1998: 33–9) on the development of the phrase *enkyklios paideia* to describe the general or complete educational system of the Hellenistic and Roman worlds. Here, these choruses were the boys' choruses in the dithyrambic competitions, organized by the ten tribes, most importantly at the City Dionysia, and also the Panathenaia, Thargelia, perhaps also the Hephaestia and Promethia. See Arist. *Ath. Pol.* 56. 3 (with Rhodes *ad loc.*), *IG* II² 3065–70; and see B. Zimmermann, *Dithyrambos. Geschichte einer Gattung*, (Göttingen 1992); R. G. Osborne (1993). Large numbers of Athenians were involved, for example about 1000 men and boys a year at the City Dionysia, though the dithyrambic poets (unlike most of the tragic and comic poets) were mostly non-Athenians: see P. J. Wilson (1999: 64).

11 choregos. The extra age-limit only for the *choregos* of boys is attested in Arist. *Ath. Pol.* 56. 3. This rule was not in force before the fourth century, as both Alkibiades and the speaker of Lys. 21 (1–5) had so acted when clearly less than forty (see Rhodes *ad loc.*; D. M. MacDowell, 'Athenian Laws about Choruses', *Symposion: Vorträge our griechischen und hellenistiche Rechtsgeschichte* 1982, 65–77, Cologne, 1989). The narrative of the *choregos* of Antiphon 6, accused (possibly sykophantically) because a boy in his chorus had died suddenly, shows the care a late fifth-century *choregos* for boys' dithyramb would take (6. 11–13) to recruit and train boys for a chorus without giving offence or alarm to their parents. Given that *choregoi* were by definition rich, and many of them active politicians, usually with active enemies, care to avoid any suggestion of improper approaches was strongly advisable. See especially P. J. Wilson (2000: 55–7, 75–7, 81–6, 116–20, 148–55).

   nature of a person receives a bad start right from his education (*paideia*). The image of a man's 'nature' here is one that is not completely formed at birth, but one which can be permanently affected by childhood education; thus the importance of moral education for citizens is emphasized (see Dover 1978: 109). Aeschines adopts early in the speech a generally traditional and moralizing attitude to education at a time of much debate, see Intro. pp. 58–62, and Ford (1999: 243). The striking tactic in the last clause, speaking as if the lawgiver's main intention was precisely to prepare a legal system to deal with Timarchos, is one used repeatedly: see on **18**.

Read these laws to the jury. The litigant gives the instruction to the clerk (*grammateus*): see on **2**. The formulae commonly used for this instruction seem to emphasize the impersonality of the office and the authority of the text by not mentioning the title of the reader; either, as here, there is a direct command to him to 'read . . .', with no form of address, or the formula 'he will read the law. . .' is used.

12 Laws. On the undoubted spuriousness of all the laws and testimony included in this speech, see Intro. p. 68. In the case of the laws cited in this paragraph, the many reasons for spuriousness include the following (see Drerup 1898: 305): many points made by Aeschines are not included, e.g. the control of the *paidagogoi*, the cyclic games, the *Mouseia*; some linguistic forms are late; the title 'Law of corruption of the free' is inaccurate; the regulation forbidding any adult to enter schools when boys are there goes beyond what Aeschines says (and does not fit the picture in, say, the early Platonic dialogues); and the *choregoi* were in fact appointed by the tribes, not by the assembly.

13–17 lays down laws. The three laws cited in this section (dealing with hiring-out, procuring, and *hybris*), like those cited in **9–11**, are all expressly described as dealing with treatment of Athenian 'boys', which appears (see **18**) to mean in this context those not yet registered as citizens in their demes. (The *hybris*-law of course could be applied to anyone, boy, man, woman, free or slave, but Aeschines here is focusing on its possible use against Athenian boys.) They have no more relevance to the case against Timarchos, as Aeschines later expressly lets him off all his (alleged) offences as a 'boy' (**19**). As the speech proceeds, however, Aeschines constantly, and illegitimately, tries to refer back to these laws, and to the general value-term *hybris*, to claim that behaviour by Timarchos and some of his lovers might render them open to these penalties (see on **72**, **87**, **98**, **160–3**, and Dover 1978: 26–31, though he does not quite bring out the significance of the restriction of these provisions to sex with boys, see below on **15**). Aeschines seems to be summarizing (or expanding) in his own words the two laws on hiring-out and procuring, and it seems from the text as we have it that the clerk did not actually read these laws out, though he read out the *hybris*-law. Aeschines later (**72**) claims these hiring and procuring laws were read out (see Dover 1978: 28), and proceeds to misinterpret them.

13 to be an escort (*hetairein*). On the terms *hetairein* and *hetairesis*, which suggest a relationship where the lover provides gifts of money, presents, or maintenance, but one which is less explicitly mercenary than that indicated by the terms *pornos* or *porneia*, see Intro. pp. 40–2. The male noun *hetairos* is used instead to mean a male friend, companion or political associate usually with no erotic connotation, though Aeschines does make a play on these two meanings with his use of the adverb *philhetairos* in **110**, and perhaps also with the emphasis on *hetairos* in his misquotation from Homer at **148**.

  does not permit an indictment (*graphe*) against the boy himself, but against the man. The idea of this law would be to prevent a father, other relative, or guardian from exploiting the youthful charms of their charges by making a particular arrangement with a (presumably richer) lover. The procedure would apparently be called a *graphe hetaireseos*; like other offences in relation to dependent members of a family, the public suit, with prosecution open to 'anyone who wishes', makes sense both because the boy himself would be too young, and the offenders his guardians, and because there is an element of public interest, as the boy so hired out might find his rights to speak in the assembly challenged (as Aeschines implies in **14**, see Dover 1978: 28). See also on **15–16** and **19**.

  Aeschines does not specify here what the possible penalties were in such a case, though of the procuring law he claims that the lawgiver 'prescribed the heaviest penalties'. By this he means the death penalty (see **72**, **87**, Dover 1978: 27), and this probably means, though he does not say so explicitly, that like the *hybris*-law, the case was open to *timesis*, and the jury would decide what penalty to impose, which might be death. At **20**, he claims that the *graphe hetaireseos* applied to a politically active citizen carried the most serious penalties, and later, at **72**, **87**, he seems to assert that the *graphe hetaireseos* might make both parties subject to the death penalty (followed by Fisher 1992: 41; Ford 1999: 244); but it is suspicious that he does not here specify the penalty, as he does

with the procuring-law. Further, the subsequent provision allowing the son not to maintain his father implies that the death
penalty could very well not be imposed (Dover 1978: 28). It may
be best to suppose that there was an expectation that juries might
treat those who hired out an Athenian boy to a single client less
severely than one who put him into prostitution; and we have
further grounds for treating Aeschines' use of these laws with
great caution.

support his father. Basic obligations between parents and
children were firmly founded on the notion of strict reciprocity
(see in general Dover 1974: 273–5; Golden 1990: 100–9, and below
on **28**). Parents were under legal and moral obligations to rear
and bring up their children, and leave them a reasonable inheritance, and could legally expect in return maintenance (*tropheia*) in
their old age and burial rites. This was protected by a public suit
for 'maltreatment of parents' (Harrison 1968–71: I, 77–8), as well
as by a provision in the *dokimasia rhetoron*, see on **28**. According to
Plut. *Sol.* 22 failure to teach his son a livelihood also freed him
of the obligation to keep the father in old age; but for necessary
caution in accepting Plutarch's unsupported testimony for
Solonian laws see D. Cohen (1989); S. C. Todd (1993: 230, 238,
262).

perform the customary rites. On the importance of funeral
rites performed by the family (or by state-officials if no family-
members are available) and the problems associated with non-
burial, see e.g. D. Kurtz and J. Boardman, *Greek Burial Customs*
(London, 1971), ch. VII; Parker (1983: ch. 2); Burkert (1985:
190–4).

14 how finely framed. The principle of reciprocity is used with
precision to justify the exact provision of this law; the father
should not receive the normal repayment for upbringing from the
son, in the form of material sustenance or support, as he deprived
the son (in effect) of his full rights to 'free speech' (*parrhesia*) in the
democracy; but he should receive the final 'honours' of full burial
rites, which should be given to all human beings.

is no longer conscious. For the sake of his argument here,
that the father's punishment was very precisely calculated,
Aeschines chooses to assume the view that the dead have no consciousness at all, so that the father would not be aware that he was

receiving the honour of burial in exchange for his bad conduct, but the body at least would receive the treatment on which the gods were thought to insist. This appears to have been the less popular of the available views on consciousness after death: see e.g. Dover (1974: 243).

law against procuring (*proagogeia*). A law concerning procuring of free women is also cited by Plutarch (*Sol.* 23), who claims that Solon fixed the penalty as merely a fine of 20 drachmai, accepted by e.g. Harrison (1968–71: I, 37), who adds that the remarkable increase in penalties available cannot be dated. But see above p. 137, for caution in accepting statements about 'peculiar Solonian laws in Plutarch, though this may be a ground for at least supposing the law to go back to Solon. In fact, despite Harrison (1968–71: II, 81–2), the penalty for both *graphai*, for *hetairesis* and procuring, may not have necessarily been death, but, like the *graphe* of *hybris*, open to *timesis*, assessment. Both laws protecting boys against exploitation by their parents or guardians may perhaps go back to Solon.

15–16 The law against *hybris*. For the meaning of this important value term in general see above all D. M. MacDowell, '*Hybris* in Athens', *G&R* 23 (1976), 14–31; Fisher (1992) and Cairns, '*Hybris*, Dishonour and Thinking Big', *JHS* 106 (1996), 1–51; with reference to Athenian law and sexual offences, especially Dover (1978: 34–9); MacDowell, *Meidias* 18–23; Fisher (1990); Cantarella (1992: 43–4); D. Cohen (1991b; 1995). It is now generally agreed that its essence in legal and social uses is to describe and condemn intentional, serious attacks on the honour of others, which typically (though not inevitably) suggest a mental state of excessive self-importance and self-indulgence (the *hybrizon* enjoys his actions, and cares little or nothing for the shame inflicted on others). I have emphasized the infliction of dishonour and shame—MacDowell and Cairns rather the arrogant mentality. *Hybris* is a broad term (though not a specifically religious one) and was clearly not defined in the law (as Aeschines in effect acknowledges 'takes in all such offences in one summary clause'). The commonest types of activities so characterized in legal contexts are humiliating violence, imprisonment, and sexual assault (see Fisher 1992: 38–53; D. Cohen 1991b, who over-emphasizes the numbers of sexual cases).

The text of the law given in **16** is, like all documents included in this speech, spurious, patently an incompetent invention by a reader, based on a casual reading of the speech and his own ideas. It does not reflect Aeschines' language at all closely, being restricted to sexual abuse against boys, whereas the law of *hybris* was evidently framed in very general terms; and it specifies the guardian of the boy as prosecutor when we know that the *hybris* law allowed 'anyone who wishes' to prosecute under the *graphe* procedure. Aeschines' own words in **15** quote part at least of the law, but as always one must be on one's guard against selective quotation, and insertion in parentheses of the orator's own comments. Another citation of the *hybris*-law, found in many of our manuscript texts of Dem. 21. 47, uses initial phraseology almost identical to the text offered by Aeschines, and most scholars, including the latest editor, MacDowell, *Meidias* 46–7, and 263–5, have argued that there we do have an accurate text (see also Lipsius 1905–15: 421–5; and Fisher 1992: ch. 2). Indeed, it is often taken (e.g. by Carey 1998) as the classic example of the form of an Athenian *graphe*. This view has been trenchantly challenged by E. M. Harris (1992, his review of MacDowell, *Meidias*), who argues, following Drerup (1898: 297–300), that the compiler of the *hybris*-law in 21. 47 used the text of Aeschines, along with his general knowledge of *graphe*-laws, to produce a plausible version, but, importantly, was deceived by Aeschines' habit of intruding his own comments. Harris argues that the expanding phrase 'if he does anything outrageous (*paranomon*) against any one of these persons' was Aeschines' addition. This phrase has caused much debate in discussions of this law because it has appeared either pointlessly tautologous, if *paranomon* means here specifically 'illegal', or hopelessly vague, if it means more broadly (as it clearly can) 'improper, contrary to a social code, or the legal system in general' (for discussions of the development of the term, Ostwald 1986: 111–29, MacDowell, *Meidias* 264–5). Against this argument it should be pointed out (so Lipsius 1905–15: 424–5; Fisher 1992: 54) that the same phrase is also added in the manuscripts' text of another Demosthenic speech, *Against Makartatos* (Ps. Dem. 43. 75), in the law instructing the eponymous archon to protect orphans, heiresses (*epikleroi*), and widows against hybristic abuse. The orator there (76–8) picks up both terms in his elaboration of how his opponent breaches this law (*hybristes* and *paranomotata*, most outrageously). It is perhaps easier to believe that the law offering protection to weaker members of the family took over the existing phrases from an existing *hybris*-law, than that the inventor of an appropriate law for that passage had recourse to the same expansion of the law found in our text of Aeschines' speeches, or to the forged document already in the text of the *Meidias* speech. Hence it may be best to accept the essential genuineness of the quotation of the law in Dem. 21. 47, and also that in Ps. Dem. 43. 75, and suppose that the addition of the *paranomon* clause was probably intended to reinforce the generally anti-social nature of a serious act of *hybris*. The date of the introduction of the law is also debated; for arguments for a Solonian date, see Mactoux (1988); Murray (1990b); Fisher (1992: 76–82).

15 and the man who hires a boy for his own use surely commits *hybris* against him. This phrase (which I have put between dashes) is undoubtedly Aeschines' explanatory addition, designed to make it seem a natural and inevitable interpretation of the law. Dover (1978: 37–8), who pointed this out, then claimed that the addition is totally 'idiosyncratic and illegitimate', because as is clear from elsewhere in the speech, a man who contracts or hires an Athenian youth for sex is not committing a legal offence (indeed, as the case alluded to in **160–4** suggests, it may be a contract recognized by the law, if socially disreputable). But since (see above on **13–17**) Aeschines is still explicitly envisaging hiring of a boy, not yet registered, possibly valid legal scenarios might be imagined. An Athenian boy's father or guardian, learning that a rich youth or man had made a financial arrangement for sexual use of a (foolish) boy without his permission might hold that this was grievously insulting to the boy (and his family); or else an outsider or more distant relative (anyone who wishes) *might* hold that such an arrangement, even if accepted by the boy's guardian, was even so unacceptably dishonouring to boy and family, and even a harmful example to the city (see D. Cohen 1987: 3–5; 1991b: 176; 1995; seeing a form of 'statutory rape' in such a possible use of this law). But, like possible applications of the law to help slave-victims, this is more probably a matter of 'principle' than practice; such cases seem extremely unlikely (see also Intro. pp. 36–9). Further, there is no doubt that later on (**72, 87, 165**) Aeschines builds on this citation, as on those in **13–14**, to suggest illegitimately that the sort of 'hiring' relationships Timarchos was allegedly involved in were not only socially disgraceful but in fact illegal.

whatever the guilty party should suffer or pay. This is the standard formula for the procedure of determining penalties where the jury had to select, after conviction, between a penalty proposed by the prosecutor and one by the defendant: such cases were known as *timetoi*, subject to *timesis*, assessment. See Harrison (1968–71: II, 80–2); S. C. Todd (1993: 133–5).

17 wonder, on suddenly hearing. The assumption that many people might be surprised to discover a feature of a well-known law such as the *hybris*-law is designed to fit the ideological stereotype of the good citizen who avoids litigation (see Dover 1974: 189–90; Christ 1998: 203–8); but it rather contradicts the assumption found in the next paragraph, that citizens are expected to know the laws.

referring to 'slaves' (*douloi*) as victims. The inclusion of slaves, at least in theory, as potential victims of this law offered frequent opportunities for Athenian orators to exploit what might seem a paradox (besides this one, Dem. 21. 47–9, and also two cases merely referred to by Athen. 266e–7a, from Hypereides and Lycurgus), and has puzzled many modern scholars. If the essence of *hybris* can be seen as deliberately damaging the status of others, and the law was particularly concerned to protect the persons and status of citizens, especially from attacks by those richer or more powerful (cf. Dem. 21 *passim*, esp. 180, where it is glossed as treating people as if they were slaves, 54. 1–10, etc.), it is problematic to see what could count as *hybris* against slaves. I have argued elsewhere in more detail (Fisher 1995) that *hybris* against slaves is perhaps conceivable in principle, in that they may have some minimal status and right to be protected against the most degrading abuse. Solon, though concerned (see on **9–11**) to define the boundary between slaves and citizens, may also have thought them as worthy of some respect as basic human beings; and slaves in his day were perhaps not so clearly identified, and disdained as non-Greek barbarians; and some were perhaps highly regarded by their masters (see also Mactoux 1988, Murray 1990b). More likely too Solon will have taken the view Aeschines adopts here (as did Plato, *Laws* 777c), that to signal as fully as possible the unacceptability of *hybris* all forms of it, and hence all possible victims, should be covered in his law. Aeschines' choice of justification was not of course an exercise in historical reconstruction. He concentrates on this line (contrast Demosthenes, 21. 48–9, who added a gross and patronizing flattery of the Athenians, who were prepared to show such gentleness and humanity in treatment of their barbarian slaves) because he will suggest throughout that Timarchos is guilty of serious *hybris* not so much against others, as against himself, in collusion with his lovers, (see on **29, 55, 108, 116, 185, 188**). In addition he supported his most famous 'lover' Hegesandros in committing grievous *hybris* against someone Aeschines calls (perhaps wrongly) a state-slave, the unfortunate Pittalakos (**62**), and committed acts of sexual *hybris* also against the husbands of many women he debauched when governor of Andros (**107–8**). Thus to argue that Solon believed that absolutely every act of *hybris* should be covered by the law fitted his purpose perfectly; this is sharpened by the last phrase that any *hybristes* at all was 'not a fit person to share in the political system' (see esp. Dover 1978: 34–9).

18 anyone is registered in the citizen list (*lexiarchikon grammateion*): each deme maintained a list of its citizens; there was no single central list of citizens held in the city. The list was kept by the demarch, and might get lost, as allegedly happened in Halimous (Dem. 57. 8, 26, 60–2; Whitehead 1986a: 103–9). The 'list' may have been, or been attached to, something more like a minute-book, with honorary decrees and perhaps other information collected as well; see *SEG* 2. 7. 20 with R. G. Osborne (1985a: 72–3). See also on **103** below, and Harpocration s.v., with Hansen (1991: 96). The deme-list was almost certainly introduced at or very soon after the beginnings of the deme-structure with Cleisthenes; for this, and the unresolved debate on when the lowest property-group of Athenians, the *thetes* were first included on it, see e.g. Whitehead (1986a: 35), Raaflaub (1996: 156), Ruzé (1997: 399–401). The argument rests in part of interpretation of the first certain attestation of the *lexiarchikon grammateion*, the decree of the third quarter of the fifth century, *IG* I³ 138, concerned with raising a tax on members of the land forces to maintain the sanctuary and training ground of Apollo Lykeios: see C. Habicht, 'Falsche Urkunden zur Geschichte Athens im Zietalter der Perser

Kriege', *Historia* 89 (1961), 5–6; Rhodes (1972: 173–4), and above all M. H. Jameson, 'Apollo Lykeios in Athens', *Archaiognosia* 1 (1980), 213–35. It seems to me unlikely, for all the ways in which thetes were not given full recognition (see Raaflaub 1996, Cartledge 1998), that thetes were not registered from the start, if the demes were to exercise any sort of control over their members.

knows the laws of the city. This runs slightly counter to the assumption in the last paragraph, that citizens might suddenly hear about the text of a law; yet the system naturally also assumes that citizens have a general knowledge of the laws, in order to obey them, and be punished if they do not (ignorance of the law was certainly no defence). It is not clear what mechanisms existed for instruction. One might think of the *dokimasia* of the youths, and the subsequent two-year *ephebeia* (see Intro. pp. 13, 65–6) and on **49**). The ephebes swore an oath, and our surviving text is certainly an authentic and archaic document; it was prominently republished in the temple of Ares at Acharnae in the Lycurgan period (Tod II 204 = Harding 109; see P. Siewert, 'The ephebic oath in fifth-century Athens', *JHS* 97 (1977), 102–11). In the oath they swore to obey the magistrates and the established laws; but even the detailed account of the ephebes' duties in the elaborated *ephebeia* of the post-Lycurgan period in Arist. *Ath. Pol.* 42, while it mentions a tour of the sanctuaries, has nothing to say of any training in 'civics' or the laws. Famously, the personified Laws in Plato's *Crito* press the claim to Socrates, when he is urged to flee to avoid his execution, that he like all citizens is bound by a form of agreement to obey the laws, which have been responsible for their education and training. They explain that when an individual passes his *dokimasia* and sees the city's affairs and the laws, he has the choice of leaving; if he stays, this constitutes a binding commitment (*Crito* 50a–52d). On balance, the likelihood must be that whatever discussion of the constitution and the laws was offered may have been perfunctory, at best, for most new citizens, who would otherwise find out about laws and constitutional opportunities as and when they needed to.

another person, but the man Timarchos himself. For dramatic effect, the name of Timarchos is substituted for something more like the more abstract 'the young man himself', to give the impression that all the lawgiver's work was somehow designed to deal specifically with Timarchos. (The reading here is confirmed by a papyrus text: see H. Wankel, 'Aeschines 1. 18–20 und der neue Kölner Papyrus', *ZPE* 16 (1975), 69–75.

19–20 In these sections, Aeschines summarizes what appear to be further provisions of the *graphe hetaireseos*, one of the two possible means of taking action against those who may have been involved in *hetairesis* who then engage in active politics. He gives the impression that this law is specifically directed at young men just of age (*meirakia*, **22**), as part of a carefully graduated schema for dealing with Athenians from boyhood to middle age; the actual basis of the case, the *dokimasia rhetoron*, is then presented (**27–32**) as part of the provisions for 'good order' for the conduct of Athenian politics and the assembly. The purpose of thus artificially separating his account of the *graphe hetaireseos* procedure from the *dokimasia*, when in fact they seem both directed at the same issue, is presumably to make Aeschines' choice of the *dokimasia* challenge seem the natural mechanism for dealing with an established politician well in middle age (see also Ford 1999: 244–50). The idea of prosecuting escorts or prostitutes under a *graphe hetaireseos* procedure if they subsequently entered public life seems unlikely to have been introduced as early as the sixth century (see Lane Fox 1994: 150); it was evidently in place at least before 424 (Ar. *Knights* 876–9).

Aeschines' summary of the provisions presents a list of public activities which constitute 'active political life'; once again he has cunningly mingled what are probably accurate quotations with his own carefully loaded additions (marked in the translation by inverted commas and dashes) designed to remind the jury that Timarchos' past has left his body unfit and impure, and to suggest what sort of politician he actually is (i.e. a corrupt and litigious sykophant).

19 those officials wear the sacred wreath. On Timarchos' unclean and disgusting body, see on **26, 160, 164, 188**. On the importance of wearing garlands, and other varied procedures to give a sense of sacredness to the conduct of public meetings as well as sacred rites, see Parker (1983: ch. 5), and also see **183**, with Ps. Dem. 59, 85–7 and Parker (1983: 94–5, 268), on the representation of sexual deviants and corrupt politicians as 'pollutions' and threats to the city's relations with the gods.

become an advocate for the public. The phrase here, 'act as an advocate' (*syndikein*, be a *syndikos*) for the public', is hard to interpret, and the understanding of the phrase in the law may have changed over time as the people called *syndikoi* (and also *synegoroi*), who appeared in the courts changed over time. *Syndikoi* and *synegoroi* may be representatives of an organization (e.g. the *polis*, deme, or phratry; Arist. *Ath. Pol.* 42.1; *IG* II² 1196, 1197), members of a board of prosecutors in cases of the scrutiny (*euthuna*) of outgoing magistrates or a board somehow involved in cases of confiscated properties (e.g. Arist. *Ath. Pol.* 54. 2; Lys. 16. 7, 17. 10). The law (if this phrase is accurately reported by Aeschines) may have originally indicated restrictions on performing such official roles; increasingly the terms were also used of the advocates who shared in the prosecution and defence in many, mostly public, cases, and the law would no doubt have been taken to apply to these as well. There is no reason to infer from this passage that performing such roles was restricted to citizens. On all this see Rubinstein (forthcoming).

21 LAW On the relationship of this wording of the alleged law to Aeschines' text, see Drerup (1898: 306–7); the compiler has mostly followed the text, but rephrased parts, taking some phrases from Aesch. 3. 176.

nor enter upon the publicly funded cults, On this idea of the publicly funded cult (*demoteles*), see on **183** below.

proceed inside the sprinkling bowls of the agora. These phrases seem to be taken from Aesch. 3. 176. The *agora*, the main civic centre of Athens below the Acropolis and the Areopagos, was the central area used alike for public business (council of 500 and most of the law courts were situated there), for business, shopping, and leisure activities; and religious affairs. Its boundaries and its sacred significance were marked both by stone boundary markers (*horoi*: they state simply 'I am the *horos* of the agora') and by lustral bowls from which one might sprinkle oneself in purification (whether every one did on entering the agora is not known). See Wycherley (1957: 218); J. K. Camp, *The Athenian Agora* (London, 1985), 48–52; and Parker (1983: 19).

22–7 Aeschines moves to consider laws or regulations concerned with public business and all the citizens. He continues to give the impression of a coherent set of laws all passed by the lawgiver Solon, concerned to uphold the highest standards of *eukosmia* and *sophrosyne* in public life. In fact he cites a rather more varied collection of regulations to do with running the assembly, not all of which are probably currently operated (see on **23**), then passes to the all-important law concerning the *dokimasia rhetoron*, the basis of the current case, and ends with a very recent law about rowdy behaviour (see Ford 1999: 245–6).

22 'Laws', he says, 'concerning good order (*eukosmia*)'. If the regulations here summarized did have this label, it probably meant essentially the properly and orderly conduct of public business. Aeschines enlarges its scope, and brings it into the closest connection with *sophrosyne*; *eukosmia*—good order, discipline, decent appearance—is used, in ways which are crucial for his purpose, to link together all these aspects, and to unite the issues of private life and control of the body (see especially on **8**, **183**), and public appearance and decorum, and to claim that they are all equally essential to orderly and democratic government

23 When the sacrificial victim has been carried round. Every assembly was treated as a solemn and formal occasion; the territory was ritually circumscribed and purified each time as the boundary of the meeting-space was marked out by the carrying-round of the sacrificial victim, a young pig. This was performed by special, archaic sounding, officials called *peristiarchoi* ('rulers round the hearth'). The custom is first alluded to in Ar. *Ach.* 43–4, and *Eccl.* 128, and details and names are provided above all by the *scholia* here: see also J. Rudhardt, *Notions fondamentales de la pensée réligieuse et actes constitutifs du culte dans la Grèce classique* (2nd edn., Paris, 1992), 163–70; Parker (1983: 21–2); Hansen (1989: 145, 185; 1991: 142); Ruzé (1997: 405–6).

  the ancestral prayers. The approval of the gods was sought by prayers, which were proclaimed by the herald of the Council and assembly, prompted by a clerk, and they included a formal curse directed against the enemies of the state such as those who take bribes to mislead the people (Dein. 2. 14; 16 Dem. 19. 70, and cf. the elaborate parody at the women's assembly in Ar. *Thesm.* 347–51: see also on **188**). The herald of the Council and assembly was one of the most important heralds maintained by the state for making internal announcements and acting as the city's formal representatives (see also below). There is evidence that the post was not only permanent, but also could be virtually inheritable. Eukles, evidently a non-Athenian, was rewarded with this post for his 'manliness and eagerness' in making a notable contribution to the restoration of the democracy in 404/3, and, probably at this same time with the citizenship; his son Philokles held the post from before 358/7, and so, after a gap, did his son, also called Eukles, from 303/2: see *IG* II² 145 with Andoc. 1. 112–14; *IG* II² 678, 848, 914–15, and the account of Osborne (1981–3: 39–41), and also S. Lewis (1996: 52–3).

he commands the presiding officers (*prohedroi*) to take the initial votes (*procheirotonia*). The nine *prohedroi* and their chairman the *epistates* acted as the presiding officers of the assembly since some time between 403/2 and 379/8: see F. X. Ryan, 'The Date of the Introduction of *proedroi*', *JHS* 115 (1995), 167–8, who argues for a lower date between these limits. They were chosen by lot to act for one day from the 450 *bouleutai* not currently serving as the *prytaneis* (Hansen 1991: 140–1). The taking of initial votes (*procheirotonia*) is also mentioned by Dem. 24. 11–12 and Arist. *Ath. Pol.* 43. 6; the lexicographers (e.g. Harpokr. s.v. *procheirotonia*), followed with good arguments by Hansen (1983: 123–30; 1991: 139–40), offer the explanation that when such a vote was taken, routine business, where the *boule* was making uncontroversial proposals, could be passed immediately at the start of the meeting, if no one opposed the proposals and insisted on a debate; another, perhaps less plausible, possibility is that where there were too many items for debate, there was a preliminary vote on which ones to consider, and which to delay (see Rhodes, 529–31, and 1997: 15–16).

to do with ancestral religious matters, dealing with heralds and embassies. See also Arist. *Ath. Pol.* 43. 6, where it is said that these items had to be taken at the third and fourth assemblies of each prytany, and Pollux 8. 96, who assigned heralds and embassies to the third, and religious matters to the fourth assembly: see Rhodes, 528–9. See also **188**, where it is assumed that all politicians are likely at some point to propose motions relating to prayers to the gods.

The leading heralds (*kerykes*) in Greek states usually held permanent appointments, needed loud and effective voices, and the more important of them were regarded as men under the special protection of the gods (see the stories told by Herodotus, 6. 60, 7. 133–7, of the hereditary Spartan heralds, the Talthybiadai). From early in the fourth century, there were heralds' contests at Olympia and other major games, and the winners then made the announcements at the games: see S. G. Miller (1991: nos. 95, 144), and N. G. Crowther, 'The Role of Heralds and Trumpeters at Greek Athletic Festivals', *Nikephoros* 7 (1994), 135–55. There were different categories of heralds maintained in Athens. The *scholia* to **20** identify four types: those concerned with festivals and rituals, including the aristocratic members of the old Athenian family or *genos* called the Heralds (*Kerykes*); those concerned with contests (*agones*); those with processions (*pompai*); and those with the *agora* and areas where goods were sold (this last might include men like the relatively poor father of the speaker of Dem. 44, who earned a living as a herald in the Peiraieus). But this list leaves out the heralds acting as the voices and representatives of the *polis* (cf. the herald of the Council and assembly just discussed); here the heralds reporting to Council and assembly are those who travelled abroad, protected by the staff of Hermes, to make declarations of *polis*-decisions and deliver and return messages to and from other states and their representatives abroad. Ambassadors, on the other hand, were appointed *ad hoc* and largely from the groups of politically active *rhetores*, for specific duties representing their states, which included making formal speeches and negotiating agreements or alliances which they might recommend to the assembly back home (as with Philokrates and his nine companions, whose controversial peace settlement has produced this trial). On the distinction between heralds and envoys, and their activities in general, see D. J. Mosley, *Envoys and Diplomacy in Classical Greece* (Wiesbaden, 1973); S. Lewis (1996: 63–74).

'Who wishes to speak of those above fifty years of age?' Many (e.g. Hansen 1987: 171; 1989: 12; 1991: 142, like the *scholia*) accept this statement, along with the rest in this paragraph, and suppose that the herald did still in 346/5 invite speakers over 50 to speak first, and also accept Aeschines' later claim (3. 4) that the practice 'nowadays', i.e. by 330, had ceased. On the other hand Lane Fox (1994, 148–9) suggests that Aeschines invented the practice here. There are very good grounds for believing in a good deal of Athenian 'invention of tradition' in this period: see

Thomas (1989: 83–94), and J. K. Davies 'Documents and "documents" in fourth-century historiography', in P. Carlier (ed.), *Le IV* *siècle avant J.-C.: approches historiographiques* (Paris, 1996), 29–40. Lane Fox argues that Aeschines modelled this idea on a restriction to those over fifty of *ephetai* in the homicide courts (attested by Suda s.v. *ephetai*), on a similar restriction for trierarchs in the 'Themistocles decree' (ML 23. 22 = Fornara 55), a text which was certainly republished and much quoted in this period, and perhaps in part, or even wholly, invented; and on a restriction which may have applied in some cases of embassies (though not the recent one to Philip, where Demosthenes and Aeschines were under fifty). A third possibility is the most likely: that it was an old Solonian law, but had long lapsed, perhaps as early as the mid-fifth century, but perhaps never formally repealed. In this speech, Aeschines treats it as if it were still valid, but in 330, more accurately, as defunct: see K. Kapparis, 'The Law on the Age of the Speakers in the Athenian Assembly', *RM* 141 (1998), 255–9, and Ford (1999: 245–7). It is remarkable, if the practice was still a live one, that no other source mentions it (see the list of sources at Hansen 1987: 171, n. 581). The lengthy disquisition on the need for respect for age and discipline is a theme which runs through this speech (see esp. on **180–1**), and this explains why Aeschines misleadingly treats it as a current rule.

24 older men are in their prime when it comes to good judgement. This commonplace of the value of the experience and judgement that comes with age can be found in Homer (*Iliad* 9. 53–60) and the principle of giving priority to older men operated among Athenian ambassadors, if no longer in the assembly (Aesch. 2. 25, 47). Similar standard views on the characteristic qualities and deficiencies of young and old and those in their prime (who usually win the palm) are set out in Arist. *Rhet.* II. 12–14. See also Dover (1974: 102–6).

wishing it to be compulsory for them to speak on public affairs. This point is a grotesque exaggeration. Even if the rule giving priority to those over 50 in the assembly were still in force, it can never have been intended to *compel* the old to speak.

25 The older orators. The three great names selected here from the previous century, Pericles, Themistocles, and Aristeides, were all generally acceptable to Athenians' (often highly inaccurate) views of their democratic past (Thomas 1989: 197–213, Rhodes on Arist. *Ath. Pol.* 28. iii). The idea that a significant change in decorum of dress had taken place after the time of Pericles was a fourth-century *topos*, and the usual suspect for beginning the decline was Kleon, who was said to have ranted violently and hitched up his cloak short, in contrast to predecessors who spoke 'decently' (*en kosmoi*); this is noted in the *scholia* to this passage, and found in Arist. *Ath. Pol.* 28. 3; Plut. *Nic.* 8 (arguably based on Theopompos), and then many other writers. See generally Gomme, *HCT* I. 48; Connor (1971: 32–4, 48–9, 132–4); Carey (1994b: 77–9); Ford (1999: 247). It is probable that a somewhat exuberant piece of rhetoric by Timarchos on the military danger (cf. the admissions of Dem. 19, 233, 251, and 286) has been exaggerated and twisted to fit the existing model of a decline in decency among politicians.

One who has a nickname so unlike. On the very important part played by nicknames in the strategy of the speech (Timarchos' and Demosthenes') see Intro. pp. 56–8; as a form of common report or gossip, they are taken to reflect the truth of the individual's character. Aristeides' well-known nickname, 'the just' (*dikaios*) (cf. Plut. *Arist.* 6–7), is mentioned in both Aeschines' other speeches (2. 23, 3. 181—where he makes a similar contrast between Aristeides' nickname and Demosthenes' of '*batalos*', see also **131**). The phrase 'the so-called "just"' found in the manuscripts here is pretty certainly an interpolation, as the contrast is much more effective without it, as Timarchos' nickname is deliberately and teasingly withheld at this stage; hinted at further at **52** and **77–80**; at **130**, and again **157**, it becomes clear that the nickname is simply *ho pornos*, the 'whore'. For a survey of nicknames in general in Athenian life, Grasberger (1883); they were attached especially frequently to those of relatively notorious social lives, such as politicians, parasites, gourmets, and wits, and prostitutes and *hetairai*.

speak holding one's arm outside one's cloak. This emphasis on visual presentation before the gaze of the people, and the assumption of a necessary connection between the physical condition of the body and moral goodness of the individual, ran deeply through Greek culture, and is central to this speech. See

Stewart (1997: 63–85), and Intro. pp. 55–6. On the importance of 'brilliant' visual display for liturgists like the *choregoi* see P. J. Wilson (2000: 136–43, 245–65).

all of you have sailed. The island of Salamis sprawls along very close to the mainland of Attica and Megara, and Athenians might easily visit it for a number of reasons. Aeschines (3. 158) cites a law regulating the safety of passengers on the (presumably very frequent) ferry-boats over to Salamis; a ferryman who overturns a boat is debarred. See Lambert (1997b: 102).

statue of Solon. Realistic portraiture was inconceivable in the early sixth century, so Aeschines' assertion that this statue could authentically reveal Solon's moral character is in principle absurd (Richter 1965: 83–6); nonetheless it had a later use, when the claim that Solon was proud of his bronze statue at Salamis, though he was not given one at Corinth, is made in Favorinus' Corinthian oration (=Ps. Dio Chrysostom, *Orat.* 37. 7) as part of the argument that his own statue at Corinth should be restored to full view, see Gleason (1995: 8–20); S. Swain *Hellenism and Empire* (Oxford, 1996), 44–6. In response Demosthenes convincingly refutes Aeschines' claim, interestingly adducing the oral testimony of those who lived at Salamis that the statue was erected 'less than fifty years ago' (i.e. some time after *c.* 393), and turns the specific explanation of its erection at Salamis, Solon's patriotic elegy urging the Athenians to fight Megara to establish permanent control of the island (fr. 1–3 West) and his supposed contributions to its military recovery (cf. the dubious stories in Plut. *Sol.* 8–10, with M. C. Taylor 1997: 25–40), into an attack on Aeschines' record as a betrayer of Amphipolis (Dem. 19. 251–4). As he implies it is more likely to show Solon reciting a poem (e.g. the Salamis exhortation) than speaking in the assembly (see the *scholia ad loc*, Ford 1999: 247). A dedicatory epigram allegedly to be seen under the statue is quoted by Diogenes Laertius (1. 62), which referred to the belief (see also Diog. Laert. 1. 45–7) that Solon was born in Salamis, as well as to Salamis as the place where the Athenians quashed the Persians' *hybris* in the sea-battle. The epigram may (or may not) have been added after the erection of the statue, but the assertion presumably rests on the desire among the 'demos of the Salaminians' to tie Solon yet more closely to the island, to support an interpretation of the first line of his Salamis poem as a reference to his birthplace, and the idea that he was buried there (see M. C. Taylor 1997: 24). Aeschines does not mention the bronze statue in the Athenian *agora* in front of the *Stoa Poikile*, as do Ps. Dem. *Against Aristogeiton* (26. 23)—probably an authentic speech from 323 (see e.g. Hansen 1976: 141–2; Sealey 1993: 235–7), Pausanias (1. 16. 1) and Aelian (*VH* 8. 16); the reason may be that it was yet to be erected or that it did not have so convenient a pose, see Wycherley (1957: 207, 216). Appropriately enough, the surviving full-length statue-type of Aeschines (Richter 1965: II, p. 213, no. 6, a Roman copy found in the theatre at Herculaneum), has his arms well covered and only part of one hand visible. One might suspect that this statue was voted for Aeschines after his triumph in this case, and showed him appropriately imitating Solon, in his speech defending traditional moral values; but it is as likely in principle that it was designed and put up some time after his death, and the original of the statue is currently dated on stylistic grounds to the 'late fourth century' (R. R. R. Smith, *Hellenistic Sculpture* (London, 1991), 37 and ill. 38). The famous statue of Demosthenes (Richter 1965: II, 216, n. 1, a copy probably found at Tusculum), presents Aeschines' rival as aesthetic and introspective, but also in contrast to the Aeschines statue, shows both arms and half the chest uncovered; this is probably a copy of the famous statue by Polyeuktos erected forty-two years after his death, *c.* 280 (Ps. Plut., *Mor* 847a, see Richter 1965: II, 216).

civic centre (*agora*) of the Salaminians. In the classical period the town of Salamis was on the east side of the island, probably at modern Ambelaki; though few remains have been excavated, see the description of its agora, statues, and public spaces in M. C. Taylor (1997: 105–23). Athens controlled the island from the sixth century onwards, and there appears to have been a significant settlement by klerouchs just after the time of Cleisthenes (*IG* i³ 1 = *ML* 14); but it never became integrated into Cleisthenes' system of demes and tribes. An annual *archon* was appointed, and the settlers seem to have constituted themselves as 'the *demos* of the Salaminians' or 'Atheno-Salaminians', while also in most, perhaps all, cases, being members of mainland demes: see Arist. *Ath. Pol.* 54. 8, with M. C. Taylor (1995; 1997: *passim*), and Lambert (1997b; 1999). The relationship to Salamis and its '*demos*' of the '*genos* of the Salaminioi', to which a number of Timarchos' friends belonged, remains disputed (see on **54–71** below).

26 the other day. Timarchos' over-exuberant gestures, apparently imitating a fighting routine, suggests that the topic probably concerned military dangers to Athens, and was perhaps, as Demosthenes asserts (19. 286), related to an occasion when Timarchos proposed penalties in the Council for any one caught trading arms to Philip; Timarchos, as proposer, would have had also to speak in the assembly, very probably one of the speeches referred to by Aeschines where he spoke of 'repairs of walls' and 'towers' (**80**) (see Davidson 1997: 306). This would be a little earlier than the debate when the Areopagos responded to a proposal of Timarchos concerning the Pnyx (**81–3**), early in the next year, which was the occasion when Aeschines announced his charge. It is quite likely, then, that exuberant self-displays of this type, and a hint of adverse reaction among the assembly-goers, gave Aeschines the idea that a prosecution raking up the old charges might have a chance, once Demosthenes and Timarchos brought their charge against him. It is of course an essential part of Aeschines' strategy to conceal the political issues on which Timarchos was seeking to supply leadership (Intro. pp. 54–5).

did all-in fighting routines (*pankratiazein*) naked in the assembly. Timarchos is alleged, first, to have gone well beyond the 'modern' habit of gesticulating and revealing hands or even arms, in this shameless 'naked' display. One suspects that in fact all that happened was that his *himation* slipped a little, through his energetic gestures, and revealed perhaps undue amounts of chest. While Athenians regularly enjoyed watching men exercise or compete naked in the *gymnasia* and in many events in the games, public nakedness in the political *fora* or in daily life was disgraceful (see e.g. Theophr. *Char.* 11. 2, and R. G. Osborne 1998a); the rhetoric of the passage thus suggests that Timarchos has committed a serious breach of this clothing code, and, what was worse, has done so despite the fact that his body was no longer attractive. Demosthenes' acknowledgements that Timarchos, disregarding possible suspicion, had employed a habit of life that was somewhat 'enthusiastic' (*itamos*) and that his 'headstrong manner' of speaking (*propeteia*) had afforded Aeschines a target for abuse, strongly suggest that something untoward occurred at least once (19. 233, 251). See in general on the dress-code for the *himation*, Plat. *Theat.* 175e; Ar. *Birds* 1567–71; Geddes (1987: 312–13); M. C. Miller (1997: 183).

Aeschines' rhetoric here may have contributed to the similarly vigorous attack by Cicero on Antony's display of his ageing and degenerate body at the *Lupercalia* (*Phil.* 2. 86, 3. 12): 'what remarkable eloquence that was of yours, when you spoke naked at the public meeting'—in fact Antony was wearing a goatskin as a *Lupercus*. Cicero gave a positive evaluation to Aeschines' style and delivery as an orator, which he held second only to Demosthenes, and translated both Aeschines' and Demosthenes' speeches in the Crown trial of 330 (*de opt. gen. orat.* 5.14, see Kingstrand 1982: 25–30). It is very likely that he had the *Timarchos* speech very much in mind when composing the Second *Philippic*; there are clear parallels between the attacks on Timarchos' earlier life and Cicero's assaults on Antony's early career as a 'male prostitute' and as Curio's 'wife', and as a drunk and a gambler (2. 43–6, 64–75). Wooten (1983) explores the relation of Cicero's *Philippics* to their main model, Demosthenes' *Philippics*, but does not contemplate any Aeschinean influence. See also below on **75, 181**.

The fixing of this unpleasant image of an ageing and worn body in the jury's minds at the start was vital, to reinforce the connection between men's bodies and their moral worth. Timarchos was at least 45, and probably the same age as Misgolas and Aeschines, and slightly older than Aeschines claims at **49** (see E. M. Harris 1988, and Intro. pp. 10–12); so much is made of the contrast between Timarchos' youthful fit and attractive body and his present appearance (see also **61**) that probably some serious signs of wear should be assumed.

The gymnastic image chosen is that of the *pankration*. This was a mixture of boxing, wrestling, and kicking, an event at all major Panhellenic and local games, including the Athenian Panathenaia (complete sources in G. Doblhofer and P. Mauritsch, *Pankration: Texte, Ubersetzungen, Kommentar* (Vienna, 1996); some sources in English in S. G. Miller 1991: nos. 30–1). Contestants did not (always) wear leather thongs on their hands, so in some ways it could seem less injury-prone than boxing (Paus. 6. 155); yet finger-bending, kicking, and kneeing, including blows aimed at the genitals, were legal, while biting and gouging were the commonest 'fouls' indulged in; deaths are attested. A close modern equivalent may be the new, unofficial, and dangerous 'sport' of 'total fighting' which is apparently becoming popular in some circles in the UK. It gives an appropriately wild and frenetic picture of Timarchos, as pankratiasts employed the greatest variety of gestures, with hand, feet, and whole body (see also the positive metaphorical use made of pankratiasts being prepared for blows from anywhere, Aul. Gell. 13. 28); hence it gave a powerful impression of extravagant lack of decorum. There is probably also a hint that Timarchos, like an aged, but still shameless, pancratiast, was as ever prepared to do anything.

drink and disgusting behaviour (*bdeluria*). *Bdeluria*, *bdeluros*, is a strong term, but fully acceptable in the normal register of oratory, for behaviour that is revolting and disgusting, and makes people feel sick (see Dickie 1996: 171). It is used thirteen times in this speech, always with reference to Timarchos' behaviour, whether his alone, that shared with his friends, or behaviour of people like him (see **26, 31, 41, 46, 54, 60, 70, 88, 95, 105, 107, 189, 192**, and 3. 246). It covers more than his sexual acts, and may include violence, and as here perhaps excessive consumption of food and drink.

covered their eyes. Though Timarchos was completely shameless, the sensible men in the assembly audience 'veiled themselves' in shame for the city. See Thuc. 4. 27, on the 'sensible' men's reactions to Kleon's wild promises about Pylos. While women veil themselves all the time in public, men do not; but they may veil for specific reasons, above all to display their strong feelings of shame, grief or anger, or because they have caused, or are in the presence of, pollution. Many cases are found in tragedy. Aeschylus was allegedly famous for introducing grief- and shame-struck characters, veiled and silent, such as Achilles and Niobe (Ar. *Frogs* 907–12, see O. Taplin, 'Aeschylean Silences and Silences in Aeschylus', *HSCP* 76 (1972), 57–98); Euripides' Herakles, who has just killed his wife and children, and Orestes, who has killed his mother, veil themselves at the arrival of Theseus, and Tyndareus, respectively (*Her.* 1155–62; *Or.* 467–70). Cases where men veil themselves at the shame caused by another include Sophocles' *Ajax* 245–50, where the chorus of Ajax' sailors suggest they might cover their heads and sneak away, and apparently the name character in Euripides' *First Hippolytus*, which gained the distinguishing title of *Hippolytus Kaluptomenos* ('the Veiled'), presumably because he veiled himself prominently in shame and horror at Phaidra's proposal of an affair (see fr. 436 Nauck[2]). Cases from prose fiction include the joker and food-parasite

Philippos, in Xenophon's *Symposion*, who covers his head in (mock)-shame when his jokes go unappreciated (1. 14–15), Phaedo, who covers his to hide his tears, when Sokrates drank the hemlock (Plat. *Phd.* 117c), and Sokrates, covering his head in shame and embarrassment when delivering the parodic speech of the 'non-lover', outdoing Lysias' effort (Plat. *Phaedr.* 237a and 243b). See above all Cairns (1993: 291–3), and Parker (1983: 313–14). This is a very powerful visual image of the disgrace Timarchos was bringing on the city, carefully inserted into this early passage ostensibly laying out the legal basis of the charge.

27 He does not keep away. This sentence contains a firm statement of egalitarian ideology that low birth or demeaning occupations did not debar citizens from addressing the assembly (see Thuc. 2. 37, 40, and see Hansen (1991: 309); (Raaflaub 1996). In practice, the 'orators' were an identifiable group of regular practitioners, most of whom were wealthy before they entered politics, and many of whom made it their complete careers (see e.g. Hansen 1984; 1991: 266–77); the assumption that active public life will be the preserve of an identifiable group is the basis of the *dokimasia rhetoron* (scrutiny of orators), and permeates the whole speech. Later, challenged himself in 330 with very intermittent political interventions amid periods of 'quietness' (*hesychia*), Aeschines again defends the right of anyone to speak when and as he chooses, while he claims excessive, daily, public speaking is the mark of the professional, doing it for money (3. 220–1). Here the main point is to emphasize by contrast that the concerns of the law of the scrutiny of the orators were the moral fitness, not the backgrounds or sources of income, of those who represented their city.

ancestors who were generals. Behind this clause is, in addition to the basic egalitarian principle of access to public speaking for all, a consciousness of identifiable changes in the backgrounds of *rhetores* over the previous century. The rise to political prominence of those not from wealthy, landed families but with a background mostly in slave-owning or manufacturing, was a major political issue from the 430s and above all the 420s, and focused on so-called 'low-class demagogues' like Kleon (see Connor 1971, and Davies' review, *Gnomon* 47 (1975), 374–8). Furthermore there was a gradual specialization of both political and military roles, so that in the fourth century it was unusual for anyone to combine effective political leadership with the generalship, and the advisability of suitable 'friendships' and co-operation between the two was widely recognized (see e.g. Dem. 2. 29; Aesch. 3. 7). The orator Aeschines and his military brothers may form an example, as may Euboulos' connections with Phokion (and perhaps Aeschines' as well): see esp. Davies (1981: 122–31), and note the reservations, not wholly convincing, in Tritle (1988). A further distinction is that one can identify in the fourth century many more convincing cases of distinguished families whose members held generalships over generations than one can of politicians (Davies 1981: 124–6). The ability to cite 'ancestors who were generals' was evidently of value in elections to the generalship; it is also evident that what was worth mentioning in court about one's ancestors or one's own achievements was military offices, dangers, and deeds, and financial outlays for the city (liturgies, etc.), but not the mere holding of civic offices such as the archonship, or the making of speeches (see Thomas (1989: 108–23; P. J. Wilson 1997).

even any one who works at some trade to support those he has to maintain. The language here is apparently designed to celebrate the absence of prejudice against the poor as potential speakers; it also clearly reveals the obstacles the poor might face, and hence the limitations to Athenian egalitarianism. It is notable that abusing a citizen or citizen women for working in the *agora* (selling goods from a stall) can be grounds for a slander case, and such allegations against the speaker's mother, for selling ribbons, were apparently part of the case that Euxitheos' citizenship was questionable, when the deme Halimous surveyed its citizen-lists under the *diapsephisis* of 346/5 (Dem. 57. 30. 6; see on **77**); and Aeschines had to endure Demosthenes' savage abuse of his family's origins (see Intro. pp. 8–19). His family's rise nonetheless does show that those of hard-working but relatively humble backgrounds could become both leading orators and generals.

28–32 Who then . . . should not be permitted to speak? Those who have lived shamefully (*aischros*). Finally Aeschines reaches the crucial law, while the image of Timarchos' flabby display in the assembly is fresh in the jury's mind. Again he mixes what appear to be quotations from the law with his own additions and explanations; in distinguishing quotation from explication I have followed Dilts' punctuation, but it is possible that some additional clauses in some or all of the instances of shameful living are Aeschines' additions. On this law, for which this speech is the primary evidence, and which apparently provided for a *dokimasia rhetoron* (scrutiny of orators), leading to a case before a jury court, see Harrison (1968–71: II, 204–5); Hansen (1991: 267); and Intro. pp. 5–6, 40. Lane Fox has questioned whether the Athenians needed this procedure in addition to the *graphe hetaireseos*, and has tentatively suggested that Aeschines may be inventing an extra procedure here (1994: 149–51); perhaps all he actually did was claim in the assembly that he would bring a *graphe hetaireseos*, which he then did. I doubt if this sceptical case can stand. As Lane Fox admits, Aeschines did win his case, and had no pressing need to invent this extra procedure which he is supposedly acting under. There are also two other places in the orators where the procedure appears to be referred to. First, Lys. 10. 1, where the process may be seen in action against a man apparently accused of speaking in the Assembly after a conviction for military cowardice; the case is stronger if one accepts Gernet's emendation (in the Budé text) of *epengelle*, 'challenged', the technically correct verb, see on **32**, **81**, for the manuscripts' *eisengelle*, 'indicted' (see S. C. Todd 1993: 116, 258). Second, Harpokration s.v. *dokimastheis* cites Lycurgus' speech 'On his administration' for a distinction between three types of *dokimasiai*, for the archons, for the *rhetores*, and one for the generals (fr. 18 Conomis). Finally, the *dokimasia* concerns those who have 'lived shamefully' in a number of different ways (four main ones are listed by Aeschines, not necessarily an exhaustive list). If the *graphe hetaireseos* was introduced first, targeting both those who hired out boys and also the 'escorts' themselves only if they engaged in politics, the Athenians could well have accepted (at the latest by the end of the fifth century) an extension of that principle of imposing higher standards in many different areas just on the politicians, under a catch-all formulation and a slightly different initial procedure; in some cases the implication would be that they had not been prosecuted for the specific offence (e.g. maltreatment of parents or discarding a shield), and in other cases the examples of 'shameful living', such as prostitution or consumption of one's inheritance, were not in themselves illegal. One could compare the *probole* procedure which introduced, in stages, from the end of the fifth century, an initial hearing to deal with a variety of offences committed at festivals: see MacDowell, *Meidias* 13–17. It seems that the penalty of disenfranchisement (*atimia*) was both expected (**134**) and in fact imposed in this case (Dem. 19. 257, 284), whereas both lesser and greater penalties seem conceivable for the *graphe hetaireseos* (see on **13** and **19**).

Aeschines' selection of offences, if not the complete list, will have selected the most significant headings, most of which he could make relevant to Timarchos' career. Dein. 1. 71 suggests that the laws required 'the orator and the general' to own land in Attica and have produced legitimate children, but this is not quite enough to add these two items to this list, especially since Aeschines emphasizes that poverty or a 'trade' is not a bar (**27**) and his claims that Timarchos has sold his estates (**95–100**) make nothing of a specific requirement to own land. The four types of 'shameful lives' Aeschines details constitute major failings to live up to the fundamental ideals of the city and what it required of its male citizens (see also Fisher 1998b: 68–73): protecting the family, fighting for the city, upholding an independent and non-mercenary sexual identity, and maintaining the family property for his heirs. Not coincidentally, there is overlap with the list of questions asked of potential archons at their *dokimasia* before the Council (see next note), and also with the (possibly incomplete) list we have of those especially shaming allegations, which if made in a public place, may entitle the abused man to bring an action for slander (see Lys. 10 *passim*, with S. C. Todd 1993: 258–62): father- or mother-beater, shield-abandoner, as well as murderer, and disparaging citizen's work in the *agora* (according to Dem. 57. 30). The further elaborations itemize effectively the general arguments always employed in these cases, which emphasize the harmful effects men of bad personal morals may have on public life, the reputation of the city, and their relations with the gods or other states: see Intro. pp. 51–3.

28 'beats his father . . . provide a home for them'. On the obligation to return to parents the good treatment one has received, see above on **13**. There was a public suit (*graphe*) dealing with their maltreatment (see Arist. *Ath. Pol.* 56. 6; Dein. 2. 17–19; and Harrison 1968–71: I, 77–8); and archons were subjected to a special, probably archaic, *dokimasia*, before the council, which asked them *inter alia* where their family tombs were, and whether they treated their parents well (Arist. *Ath. Pol.* 55. 3 with Rhodes *ad loc.*, and cf. Xen. *Mem.* 2. 2. 13). The idea of beating up one's father or mother appears prominently in Aristophanic comedy and elsewhere as a paradigmatic sign of moral decline and the dangerous teachings of the sophists (Ar. *Clouds* 1321–450; *Birds* 755–68, 1337–72; *Frogs* 149–50) and as presenting a major problem for society (Lysias 10. 6–8, 13. 91; Plato, *Laws* 881b; see Parker 1983: 196–7).

29 did not go on those campaigns . . . has thrown away his shield. There were naturally also *graphai* for these military offences, failing to turn up when required for military service, desertion, and abandoning weapons in battle (see e.g. Lys. 14; And. 1. 74; Dem. 21. 103, 24. 103, 119; Aesch. 3. 175–6; and see Pritchett 1974: 233–6 and S. C. Todd 1993: 106, 110, 183).

   'Or any one who has prostituted himself (*porne-uesthai*)', he says, **'or acted as an escort (*hetairein*)'.** If Aeschines is quoting the law as I have punctuated it here, it confirms that the law envisaged the two related but distinguishable forms of 'mercenary' relationships, in the forms of these two verbs.

   who had sold his own body in *hybris* would readily sell the common interests of the city as well. This is the first of six places (cf. **55, 108, 116, 185, 188**) where Aeschines seeks to cash in on the benefits of the analysis of the *hybris*-law (**15–17**) by describing Timarchos' sexual offences in this highly charged way. The idea of dishonour or outrage being self-inflicted is paradoxical, but nonetheless to be taken seriously. Davidson (1997: 113 and n. 335) seeks to reduce *hybris* in sexual contexts to little more than 'use for sex' rather than out of love or affection; this view seems related to his broader position (with which I agree) that selling sex for money is the most important basis for the sexual case against Timarchos (see Intro. pp. 40–2, and on **38**). But it seems clear that serious uses of the term *hybris* in legal contexts all carry a strong charge of the infliction of shame or disgrace on a 'victim', not merely the idea of the careless pleasure of the agent, or of 'bought sex'. Timarchos, then, is presented throughout the speech as having willingly and carelessly subjected his own body to sex acts which in their context are disgraceful and should result in lasting dishonour; it seems to be the combination of certain acts (unspecified, but essentially buggery) and the motives and conditions which constitute the dishonour, and equally the sense that he has brought everything on himself. See Intro. pp. 44–9, and below on **49, 55, 74, 185**.

30 who has consumed his ancestral goods, and whatever else he was heir to. The language here, again if correctly quoted from the law, seems to distinguish between what a man has inherited directly from his father as ancestral goods (*patroia*) and property he may have received as heir (*kleronomos*), in effect from another of his relatives. See Harrison (1968–71: I, 124–30). The term 'consumed' means literally 'eaten up' (*katesthiein*, perfect form *katedekoka*), and is used throughout the speech in this way (see **31, 42, 94, 106, 154, 195**). The idea is used literally in Homer's *Odyssey* of the suitors 'consuming' the estate of Odysseus (e.g. 2. 237), and of an heir eating up his inheritance by dining daily on tuna and its sauces by Hipponax (fr. 26 West), and was very frequent in classical Athens: see Davidson (1997: 206–10).
 who had managed his own household badly would deal with the common affairs of the city in a similar way. It is important to reiterate that most of the arguments constantly used against those with shameful sexual lives being permitted to be active in politics are regularly applied with equal force to those who have betrayed their obligations to their family and their inheritance, and these points may have had particular force with some jurors. Demosthenes and other orators too were happy to cast around allegations connecting together extravagance on food, drink, and other luxuries with political unreliability and a preparedness to betray their country for money: see e.g. Lys. 19. 9–10; Dem. 19. 229, 18. 296; and see Dover (1974: 178–80).
 the same man could be a rotten (*poneros*) man in his private life and a good man in public life. For a similarly elaborated view of the necessary connection between a citizen's behaviour in public and private life, but put the other way round, see Hypereides' defence of Lykophron against the charge of adultery, that his whole life has been blameless, and his behaviour as a cavalry official on Lemnos had been unimpeachable (Hyper.

Lyk. 15–18); see also Lys. 31. 2203; Dem. 24. 201, and Dover (1974: 198–9).

31 The point that bad arguments from a good man are more use to the city than good arguments from a debauched man, recurs with greater emphasis at the end of the speech, in the appeal to an alleged Spartan tradition (**180–1**).

a fine and good man (*kalos kagathos*): The fine-sounding phrase, *kalos kagathos*, for a good all-round man, does not appear to have been, as usually thought, originally a term for the characteristic virtues of Greek aristocrats well-established from the archaic period, but rather a phrase which gained currency as a fashionable and contested term in the last third of the fifth century (first appearing in Herodotus and Aristophanes): see esp. Donlan (1973) and Bourriot (1995). Bourriot's study proposes specific, varied meanings in different contexts: a Spartan sense, those who distinguished themselves in manhood contests or war; in Athens, an attachment, in praise or ironical criticism, to sophistic, Laconophile, young snobs such as Alkibiades, or to moderate oligarchs like Theramenes. But his account seems unduly precise and reductive. The phrase is used twice later, of two of Aeschines' associates (Misgolas **41** and Hegesandros **69**). Here (unnoticed by Bourriot 1995: 435–57) it is evidently used without irony of decent (but not necessarily aristocratic or élite) men who may look fit and attractive, but have lived decently, and not acquired rhetorical skills (that is, the opposite of one of Bourriot's categories, one to which he thinks Aeschines is still alive: see on **41**).

debauched man. On the term *bdelyros*, see on **26**.

consumed his ancestral estate shamefully (*aischros*). The keynote term of shame is sounded once more. See on **2**.

32 makes slanderous attacks (*sykophantein*) and behaves disgustingly (*aselgainein*). These additional phrases clearly do not represent anything which may have been in the *dokimasia* law, which will not have demanded that the politician with the shameful past must also be committing political offences in the present. Rather, they are there to justify Aeschines' decision to bring a prosecution, in revenge for Timarchos 'sykophantic' attack on him, to remind the jury of the allegedly demeaning exhibition in the assembly (**26**), and generally to reinforce the point that one reason for this law is that those who led shameful early lives go on to behave equally disgracefully in public life. *Aselgainein* (adjective *aselges*) is a term of abuse found frequently in comedy and oratory (though not in serious poetry) to indicate seriously offensive, self-indulgent, or insulting and violent behaviour (see MacDowell, *Meidias* 220; the term is used sixteen times in that speech). Aeschines applies it in this speech to the debauchery on which Timarchos and Hegesandros squandered money (**95**), Timarchos' outrages against free men's wives when governor on Andros (**107, 108**), the foul behaviour of the 'shameful' lover (**137**), and men's general 'grossness' (**190**).

Let any one of the Athenians who is entitled proclaim a scrutiny. On the technically correct language here see on **2** and **28–32**

33 you yourselves have added a new law. This allegedly recent law is mentioned also in his speech of 330, 3. 4, where he complains that not even now can laws, the *prytaneis*, the *prohedroi*, or the presiding tribe control the disorder (*akosmia*) of the *rhetores*. It may be doubted whether this new law was really specifically brought in because of Timarchos' boxing routine; but it was presumably a very recent measure passed under the procedure of the *nomothetai*, and reflected a view that assembly-meetings were getting excessively rowdy, perhaps because of excessive shouting or inappropriate behaviour from the politically active, the *rhetores* and their supporters; see Ps. Dem. 59. 43, where Apollodoros alleges that when Stephanos had not yet been a *rhetor*, he was 'a sykophant, one of those who shout by the platform'. But if Timarchos' uninhibited display was adduced in the debate on this issue, this might also have helped Aeschines to conclude that the time was right for this sort of prosecution on the issues of *sophrosyne* and *eukosmia* in public life. If it really was further the case (as claimed in **34**) that Timarchos had joined with others in opposing this bill with an indictment for passing an inappropriate law (*graphe nomon me epitedeion theinai*) it will have further encouraged Aeschines to represent it as in effect directed at him (see Ford 1999: 248). On the possible details of the measure, see Hansen 1987: 71–2; 1989b: 161–2, 178; 1991: 137 ('Athens passed a law . . . perhaps to prevent hecklers'); and alternative views in G. R. Stanton and P. J. Bicknell, 'Voting in Tribal Groups in the

Athenian Assembly', *GRBS* 28 (1987), 63–4, and E. M. Harris, 'How Often Did the Athenian Assembly Meet?', *CQ* 36 (1986), 364. The *graphe nomon me epitedeion theinai*, the specific procedure for challenging a new law, was introduced as a consequence of the introduction of a sharper distinction between laws and decrees formalized in 403; see H.-J. Wolff, *'Normenkontrolle' und Gesetzes-begriffe in der attische Demokratie* (Heidelberg, 1970); Hansen (1991: 175).

34 We must break them of their habits ... their aim is to enable themselves to go on living and speaking as they please. Again, the issue of condemning Timarchos is put in the broader context of cleaning up Athenian public life and the over-all behaviour of the politicians, in public as well as in their private activities.

35 Laws. Arist. *Ath. Pol.* 44. 3 confirms that the *prohedroi* had charge of *eukosmia*, good order, in the assembly. But the detailed provisions here, which are not on this occasion expansions of the speech itself, are also no doubt later inventions, betrayed by places where we have nonsense (e.g. referring a case to the 'first assembly'), and by further instances of later language (see Drerup 1898: 307–8). They cannot be used to supplement what Aeschines says about this recently introduced law about heckling, with which they are not concerned; they may, however, include some accurate information about other laws designed to discipline speakers in the Council and assembly: see Rhodes (1972: 146–7).

praktores. On the role of these officials in recording fines and debts owed to the state, see Dem. 43. 71, 25. 28, with Hansen (1991: 261).

secret ballot. On secret ballot-votes in the disciplining of individuals, see on **112**, and Rhodes (1972: 38–9); Johnstone (1999: 105–6).

36 You have heard. A quietly effective conclusion to the 'laws' section, leaving the jury with an apparently simple and obvious choice. Some more laws relating to slaves are cited in **138–9**, and the theme that the laws must be clearly upheld recurs with emphasis in the conclusion (see **177–90**).

SECTION III 37–116 Narrative of Timarchos' career

This central section is broadly comparable to the 'narrative' in most law-court speeches, and more closely akin to the account (say) of Demosthenes' career in the invectives against him by Aeschines (3). It contains the factual case against Timarchos (such as it was). It is important to remember (see Intro. p. 54) that it is concerned to demonstrate more than Timarchos' sexual depravity; he is held to be liable to the *dokimasia* under one other heading, the destruction of his ancestral estate (and the two are seen as closely related by his own nature), and of illegalities and appalling acts in areas more or less related to the other two (treatment of parents, and performance of military duties to the state) as well (see Hunter 1994: 104). Nonetheless, more time is devoted to the sexual charges than the rest, they carry by far the greatest rhetorical weight, and it is the issue of the achievement of control and good order (*sophrosyne* and *eukosmia*) in the area of sexual relations which is the focus of attention in the more general concluding arguments.

The structure of this middle part of the speech may be analysed in detail as follows

a) **39–70:** First charge: the narrative of Timarchos' sexual career. Aeschines gives a detailed account under the first major charge, the allegation that Timarchos lived with a succession of lovers, and at times in effect behaved as a prostitute: lovers singled out for special treatment are Euthydikos, Misgolas, Pittalakos, and the · most important one, Hegesandros; others are mentioned in passing.

b) **71–93:** Discussion of the absence of witnesses. This, the major problem for the prosecution, is faced, and a variety of arguments are adduced to persuade the jury that Timarchos' career was so well known to all, and so often alluded to in public, that its truth can be taken as certain.

c) **94–105:** Second charge: narrative of Timarchos' dissipation of his inheritance. Aeschines first responds to an anticipated claim by the defence that one cannot simultaneously earn as a prostitute and dissipate an inheritance; and offers a list of properties and assets which Timarchos has sold off. This section also includes allegations of Timarchos' shameful treatment of his mother and his uncle, and so comes close to claiming that he is liable under the third charge of failing to support one's parents.

d) **106–115:** Final charge: corruption and other illegalities in Timarchos' political career as a councillor, and an official in Athens and in the Aegean. Here Aeschines in the first place comes as close as he can to charging Timarchos under the heading of military cowardice. But this emphasis on political corruptions has two other advantages. It counters the obvious defence argument that whatever Timarchos' early life and character may have been, he is now an honest and useful orator and politician; and it reinforces the central argument for the application of the law, in that Timarchos' political career demonstrates the correctness of the *dokimasia rhetoron* and confirms that it must be applied, as Timarchos has been continuing to show in political life the same vices of total shamelessness in pursuit of money and pleasures and the same contempt for the community and the laws, as he had in his private life.

37 practices which are ignoble by nature. *Epitedeuma* (practice) is one of the commonest words for an important aspect of a person's behaviour, often an objectionable or anti-social type or trait (e.g. Thuc. 6. 15 where it refers to Alkibiades' behaviour in his private life which caused resentment among the democratically minded mass). It is used a further twelve times in this speech (see **44, 67, 79, 123, 138, 153, 154, 157, 185, 189, 193, 194**), in all cases for the improper and shameful homosexual relationships Timarchos was involved with; but the term does not clearly distinguish between sexual acts and the terms of the relationship. The mood is set at the start for the ensuing narrative by the claim that such 'practices' are not right (*kala*) by nature. On the use of 'nature', see also on **185** below.

38 It would not be just for you to criticize me, if I use plain language. The polite conventions of speech in the official public discourse of assembly and law courts were held to preclude the sorts of explicit words relating to sex or excretion found for example in comedy, in certain cults, and on graffiti (see Dover 1978: 22–3; for the areas of permitted obscenity, Henderson 1991; Halliwell 1991: 289; Carey 1994: 174–5). M. Biraud, 'La décence ou l'absence du corps: La répresentation sociale du corps dans les plaidoyers des orateurs attiques', *LEC* 59 (1991), 335–43, offers a brief statistical survey of words for body, parts of the body, and its conditions, which are mentioned in the orators, which reveals the absence of explicit terms. The idea that an orator might, for a special effect, come close to breaching this convention is interestingly posed by some suggestions in later rhetorical writers. They claim that Lysias and Apollodoros, when denigrating a *hetaira* (Antiope and Neaira, respectively), each employed the abusive and slightly more explicit phrase 'made her living from two (or in Neaira's case, three) holes', but that such phrases were subsequently removed from the speech ('obelized') because they were thought vulgar or cheap: so Tzetzes, *Histories* 6. 35–7 = Dion. Hal. fr. 23, on Lysias' use, and Hermogenes, *On Types of Style* (p. 325 Rabe) and also Dion. Hal. *Dem.* 57, on Apollodoros' use. Carey (*Neaira*, 141–2 and 1994: 175) suggests that it is 'extremely difficult to imagine so graphic a phrase' being used in this otherwise so evasive speech; Kapparis, *Neaira* 402–4 argues plausibly that the external evidence for the existence of the phrase somewhere in the speech is too strong to evade, and that Apollodoros, at the risk of giving offence, chose in that way to express his apparently overwhelming sense of outrage, at a climactic passage such as Ps. Dem. 59. 108.

Aeschines, however, decided not to risk such an expression. His very heavy emphasis on all aspects of good order and decorum as central to the case made it rhetorically more effective for him to make a great point of adhering to such rules; hence his elaborate apology here, and the great fuss he makes before uttering in his own person the term *pornos* which he has already used in citing the law (see also on **52**, and Intro. pp. 56–7). This reticence in no way excludes the repeated use of enjoyably titillating phrases, which can be euphemistic or ambiguous, and so encourage the jury to imagine the worst (e.g. at **41**, **51–2**, **55**, **70**, **131**, **185**, and esp. perhaps **187**: and see Carey 1994: 175). It might have helped the modern debate on the importance (or not) of anal sex and phallic penetration in the judgement of good and bad erotic practices if he had chosen to hint a little less vaguely (though see the note on 'bend down' at **187**); but one may at least conclude from his maintenance of reserve in that specific area, that proof specifically that a youth had accepted (e.g.) anal sex was not believed to be fundamental to a charge of *hetairesis* or *porneia* under the law, whereas accepting the sexual choices of others for money or other rewards was (see Intro. pp. 42–5, and Davidson 1997: 253–6; Calame 1999: 139–40).

39–70 *Timarchos' lovers and his willing self-*hetairesis

39 how reasonably I am going to deal with Timarchos . . . I shall pass over. An excellent example of the orator's tactic called *paraleipsis* or *praeteritio*, where facts allegedly damaging to the opponent are in fact mentioned while the orator claims credit for not going into detail over them, and avoids having to make them plausible (let alone provide any evidence). Cicero uses the *topos* in a very similar (if more elaborate) way against Verres (2. 1. 32–4), ostentatiously forbearing to mention all the wicked deeds of his boyhood and youth, and proclaiming his own modesty of language. The *Timarchos* may again be among Cicero's models.

boy . . . young man. On this distinction between boys (*paides*) and youths (*meirakia*), see on **7, 19–20**.

like the acts committed in the time of the Thirty or before the archon year of Eukleides, or acts before any other similar date imposing a statute of limitations. Aeschines alludes to the famous 'amnesty' provisions of the settlement at time of the restoration of the democracy in 403/2 after the brief but brutal rule of the Thirty (Arist. *Ath. Pol.* 39–41; Xen. *Hell.* 2. 3–4; Andoc. 1 *passim*); the ringleaders (the Thirty and others who served on crucial boards under them) could be prosecuted, but no others, whether for offences committed during the period of the Thirty's rule, or earlier. See generally T. C. Loening, *The Reconciliation Agreement of 403/402 B.C. in Athens: Content and Application* (Stuttgart, 1987). These provisions and their implementation, rightly or wrongly, won wide praise for generosity and for achieving a lasting reconciliation, and Aeschines thus compliments the jury as Athenians, and gratuitously, and perhaps half-humorously, associates his forbearance in 'letting Timarchos off' his early offences with 'their' generosity. Second, a number of cases in Athenian law recognized a period of years (e.g. five years for cases of wrongdoing to wards) after which no prosecution for an offence could be brought; this is called the 'law of the fixed time' (*prothesmia*) at Dem. 36. 25, see also *IG* I³ 41, 95; Dem. 38. 17; Ps. Dem. 43. 16; Harrison (1968–71: II, 120).

40 he settled in the Peiraieus at the surgery of Euthydikos. Euthydikos the doctor (*LGPN* 8; *PA* 5551; *PAA* 432495) also appears as providing vital testimony in Mantitheos' second speech against his half-brother Boiotos (also called Mantitheos). Allegedly, to incriminate Mantitheos, Boiotos had asked the doctor to fake a head-wound, but the doctor gave evidence of the deceit to the Areopagos (Dem. 40. 33). The date of speech was probably *c.* 347/6, and the alleged fight a few years earlier: see S. C. Humphreys, 'Family Quarrels: Dem. 39–40', *JHS* 109 (1989), 182–5, and also Humphreys (1985b: 327) on doctors as witnesses. Euthydikos appears to have been a fairly well-known doctor, probably a citizen, who found himself often involved in the fights and disputes of litigious Athenians. Another shady doctor in the Peiraieus was, apparently, one Eryxias (*LGPN* 3), probably a metic, who connived with others in a deception against the speaker of Demosthenes 33 (Dem. 33. 18, of 325). There is no sign that these or the other doctors mentioned in law-court speeches, e.g. those mentioned in Dem. 47. 62 or 54.10–12, were among those whom some states publicly recognized as qualified (*demosieuontes*), and to whom they paid retainers, which seems in any case unlikely to have involved any commitment to free treatment: cf. Cohn-Haft (1956).

Aeschines says little explicitly against him, but allows the clear implication that he was happy to let Timarchos act as a prostitute in his house/surgery, had wide contacts, and presumably was in fact acting as pimp as well as lover. How much truth in this, if any, cannot be known (no testimony seems to have been provided, below on **50**; in all probability he had no clients' names to offer). The rhetorical purpose is to establish at the start a picture of Timarchos' preparedness to offer his body to anyone for money, from among the raffish population of those of varied statuses in the Peiraieus, which no doubt provided plenty of work both for doctors and for prostitutes and pimps. Aeschines here, and also at **43**, **158**, is not interested in distinguished transient foreigners, *xenoi* from metics, and only mentions the metics, contemptuously, at **195**, cf. Whitehead (1977: 52). Thus it was a wholly appropriate setting for the beginning of Timarchos' alleged career of debauchery: see R. Garland, *The Peiraeus from the Fifth to the First Century BC* (London, 1987), 69–70; Davidson (1997: 80–2); von Reden (1995 and 1998); and Roy (1998). Nonetheless, it is perhaps hard to believe that Aeschines picked on Euthydikos totally at random. Either he may have had other reasons for wishing gratuitously to insult Euthydikos in court, or we might suppose at least that Timarchos initially did consider a medical career, and spent some time as an apprentice there (see Cohn-Haft 1956: 17–19). It is conceivable also that Timarchos thought that he might make useful social or political contacts there, but that some gossip stuck, as gossip of homosexual relations between skilled men and their apprentices or pupils tended to (cf. Aeschines' later allegations against Demosthenes and his rhetorical pupils, **131**, **170–6**).

Earning fees for that very thing which the law forbids one to perform. See on **41** below.

41 There is one Misgolas. Misgolas, son of Naukrates of Kollytos (*LGPN* 1; *PA* 10225; Develin, *AO* no. 2006): no Athenians of this name are known other than the two mentioned in this note. He appears on two inscriptions elsewhere; in *IG* II ^{2} 2825, 2 (mid-fourth century) he appears second in a list of ten men in regulation tribal order, with a secretary (*grammateus*) and under-secretary (*hypogrammateus*) listed at the bottom, apparently a college of ten responsible for a votive dedication to Artemis (see Develin, *AO* p. 352); and in *IG* II² 1554 (*SEG* 18, 36, 335, 339) Misgolas and his brother Naukles manumitted two slaves under the curious *phiale*-dedication procedure in 330s (see D. M. Lewis 1959, 1968). A likely ancestor has been identified in the Misgolas of Kollytos who appears as a secretary to the three treasurers of the sacred moneys of Athena and the other gods in 403/2 (*IG* II² 1370, 1371, and 1384 = *SEG* 23. 81. 5; Develin, *AO* no. 2005).

man in all other respects fine and good (*kalos kagathos*), and one would not in any way find fault with him. Aeschines handles Misgolas very carefully. He praises him in general as a man of status and merit, but with a 'phenomenal' passion for youths (see note below). This is probably related to the fact that he has tried to persuade him to agree to a delicately phrased form of testimony agreeing that Timarchos had lived in his house for a time. Presumably Aeschines wished, for whatever political and/or personal reasons, to maintain tolerable relations with Misgolas and/or some of his friends (cf. Dover 1978: 25–6, comparing Demosthenes' careful treatment of Euboulos in 21. 206–7). Misgolas' description as in general a *kalos kagathos* has been variously interpreted. (For the term, see on **31**.) Ober (1989: 257) suggests that here it 'can be read' as 'rather heavy-handed sarcasm', building on the jury's prejudice against the pederastic predilections of aristocrats; Bourriot (1995: 440–1) claims that the tone is that of the defenders of traditional education, directing a sarcastic nuance, as Bourriot believes was the case in Aristophanes' early plays, at young Athenians sunk in luxury and debauchery. Like Dover (1978: 25–6), however, I am not convinced that there is necessarily any sarcasm or hostility in the use of the term here; it is notable, however, that at the end of the speech (**195**) Aeschines gives strong advice to those with such tastes to avoid citizen youths. Nor, given what we know of Misgolas, does the term 'aristocrat' seem appropriate. Perhaps the phrase *kalos kagathos* rather suggests that Misgolas (probably, like Aeschines, a man of relatively new wealth) had some claim to be a decent and cultivated citizen who played some part in civic life (but see also on the more hostile use of the term applied to Hegesandros at **69**).

phenomenally devoted to this pursuit. The adverb used for 'phenomenally' is *daimonios*, implying that this passion has been given him by some god or *daimon*; this view contrasts with the line which Aeschines chooses to adopt in the conclusion, where the view that evil men may have been driven to commit mad crimes by the Furies, as in tragedy, is firmly rejected (**190–1**). The word for 'devoted' (*spoudazein*) is the word used by Plato for Alkibiades' supposition of the erotic interest Socrates may have in him (Plat. *Symp.* 217a).

always to have singers to the lyre and lyre-players around him. The *kithara* was the large box-lyre, used in many public and private performances; players often had somewhat higher status than *aulos*-players (see West 1992: 51–6, P. J. Wilson 1999). Misgolas' particular penchant for these musicians seems to suggest a physical preference for the slenderer, less athletic type (see Dover 1978: 73–5, comparing the debate between the two mythical brothers, the *kithara*-player Amphion and the tough fighter Zethos, Eur. *Antiope*, frr. 184–7), and perhaps also a taste for more musical and cultivated boys. Misgolas' passion for smooth musicians was also the subject of jokes in at least three comedies, all quoted by Athenaeus at 338e–9c. Antiphanes fr. 27K/A, from his *Woman Going Fishing*, has a character setting out a fish-stall and matching fish (seen, characteristically, as sex-objects, see Davidson 1997: 10–12, and on **42**) with well-known gourmand fish-lovers and *hetairai*: Misgolas will not fancy the conger-eel with its thick spiny back:

> But this *kitharos* ('lyre-fish') here,
> if he sees it, won't be able to keep his hands off it.
> I tell you, it's really amazing, how with all the lyre-players,
> he sneaks his way in really close to them. (ll. 15–18)

Alexis fr. 3 K/A, from his *Agonis*, has a son begging his mother not to threaten him with Misgolas (as with a bogey-figure: the line parodies Euripides' *Orestes* 255–6), because he is not a lyre-singer; and similarly in Timocles' *Sappho* (fr. 32K/A) someone, probably a youth, is told that 'Misgolas doesn't seem to make approaches to you, though he is fired up by young men in bloom'. All these passages confirm that Misgolas was popularly believed to pursue, importunately, all who were, or had the physique of, kithara-musicians, and the Alexis fragment interestingly suggests the possibility that mothers might warn attractive sons against notorious pederasts like him, while the joke may be how well informed as to his tastes the son is (cf. Arnott, *Alexis, ad loc*). Unfortunately, we cannot date any of these plays precisely, and cannot decide therefore whether Misgolas' predilections were well known to theatre audiences and hence many jurymen before the trial, or whether the comic poets fed off famous trials and accompanying gossip about them for their next topical jokes (see on **44**, and also on **157**, where there is a reference to a recent comedy in relation to Timarchos the 'whore').

   a good body, was young and disgusting. *Eusarkos* (literally 'of good flesh') is not a very common word of praise, but see Xen. *Lak. Pol.* 5. 8. and Dover (1978: 69). It suggests well-conditioned and trained flesh, not flabby (as the jury will 'remember' Timarchos' prolonged self-indulgence have now rendered his flesh, **26**). Elsewhere Aeschines emphasizes Timarchos' exceptional good looks (**75**, and cf. **126**—Demosthenes will be unable to deny it, and does in fact admit it, 19. 233) The implication that he especially appealed to Misgolas may be designed to suggest that, while not, it seems, a musician, he was nevertheless slim and not exaggeratedly athletic; more important is the assertion that he was disgusting, *bdelyros*, prepared for any sexual acts.

the act which he had made it his choice to perform and Timarchos his to endure. The phrasing is carefully chosen, and raises an important, and contested, issue. *Prohaireisthai* is a serious word of careful, reflective decision about matters important to one's life—in Aristotle's moral philosophy it pays a major part as the process of making character-forming decisions. Here, used of Misgolas, it indicates a settled policy of pursuing his 'enthusiasm' (*spoude*) for his type of attractive young men; for Timarchos, it is selling his body. It is very important that Aeschines does not claim anywhere that Timarchos physically enjoyed whatever sexual acts he is hinting at here, or that he became the sort of depraved individual considered by Aristotle (*EN* 1148b15–19) and Ps. Aristotle (*Problems* 4. 26) who, by nature or childhood habituation, comes actually to crave 'passive' sexual acts, in Ps. Aristotle's case, explicitly anal intercourse (see Dover 1978: 168–70, Intro. pp. 46–7). What Aeschines chooses to argue is that Timarchos did not merely consent, but was fully prepared (see also **42**, 'did not hesitate; he submitted to it all') as a deliberate life-choice to accept such shameless behaviour, so that he becomes simultaneously the agent and the willing victim of *hybris*; cf. Omitowoju (1997: 5–6), who demonstrates that issues of status and shame, rather than of 'consent', determined the laws and discourses of sexual behaviour, homosexual and heterosexual.

This section raises clearly the question of what exactly is 'the act', and why Aeschines found it so important to emphasize this point, yet not to use direct language to name it. It is something that involves accepting or enduring (*paschein*), not activity or mutual pleasure, and appears to be something shameful for a male in addition to the fact that it is done for the money, which Timarchos wants to spend on his own pleasures. Aeschines repeatedly used phrases indicating that the 'act' itself is morally significant: 'the very thing which the law forbids one to do' (**40**), 'the name of the act which he used to do' (**45**), 'this [act]' (**52**), 'the deed' (**75**), and cf. also 'women's *hamartemata*' (**185**); and he makes a great fuss at not naming an act more clearly. It seems hard to avoid the conclusion that penetrative sex, essentially buggery, is presented in these phrases as shameful in part because it involves accepting, not acting, and adopting in that sense the part of a woman. See Intro. pp. 42–4, and on **185**.

42 His father left him. Here we have an anticipation of the other plank of the case, the wilful dissipation of the ancestral property. The chronological relation, however, between his dissipation of his own wealth, which involved selling off a number of estates and slave-enterprises, and his living off these men to fund his own desires, is left deliberately vague. Here he seems in need of extra money for his luxuries while he is still living in a relationship of *hetairesis*; at **95–6**, he sold major portions of his estate at or towards the end of this *hetairesis*-stage, when Hegesandros' estate which had come with his wife was also exhausted. As becomes clear (**94–7**) there was a difficulty here that Demosthenes was ready to exploit, and Aeschines does not fully get round: can Timarchos have been simultaneously living off his lovers *and* beginning to run through his own inherited wealth through luxurious expenditure?

    which he has himself consumed. On the importance of these persistent metaphors of eating and drinking the inheritance, found in comedy as well as oratory, see on **30** and **95–6**.

    slave to the most shameful pleasures. The use of slavery-language here reflects a prevailing element in Greek morality, that it was an important element in being a free, male citizen that one not only avoided enslavement to others but also was *sophron*, in control of one's desires, not weaker than or enslaved to them (see Dover 1974: 179–80, 208–9; Golden 1984)

    fish-eating (*opsophagia*), extravagant dining. *Opson* initially indicates any form of tastier, if more expensive, food eaten with a cereal staple (such as bread) (see esp. Pl. *Rep.* 372c–373a). But fish came to be the most distinctive type of taste-provider in classical Athens at midday and evening meals (apart from the freshly sacrificed meat only provided at festivals, or off-cuts sold for feasts, etc.); it came either in the cheaper forms of salted or pickled fish, or small fry, or the much more expensive forms of fresh fish. Hence *opson* (or the diminutive *opsarion*) came to mean 'fish' (as still in mod. Greek *psari*), and, as here, *opsophagia* means '(expensive) fish-eating' and *opsophagos* a luxury-lover who relished monopolizing the available large fresh fish. As fish-eating was the most distinctive type of gluttonous pleasure, the price of fish became a significant political issue, and those who were constantly buying up the contents of the fresh-fish stalls were often suspected of being criminals: see above all Davidson (1993, and 1997: 3–35, 186–90, 234–6, 278–301), also on possible variations in price, and wider availability at times, Fisher (2000: 368–9).

girl-pipers (*auletrides*) and escort-girls (*hetairai*). The *aulos* was a double-reeded and usually double-piped instrument (much more like an oboe than a flute). It was taught in schools as well as the lyre, and played in various contexts in Athens by both males and females (notably the male musician accompanying choral and dramatic performances). See for the musical details West (1992: 81–107), and for the social significance of male and female *aulos*-players, P. J. Wilson (1999). Female pipers were a constant feature of entertainments at *symposia* and subsequent revels (*komoi*) in the streets, and a good many of them at least were expected to act as prostitutes as well, at the parties, or subsequently (and some of these, perhaps, were not actually expected to be very expert musicians); a maximum price for hiring such female 'musicians' and singers for a night was regulated by the city-magistrates (*astynomoi*; Arist. *Ath. Pol.* 50.2), probably both to restrain violent arguments and fights in the streets between those planning or engaged in parties, and also to keep the prices affordable (see Davidson 1997: 80–3; P. J. Wilson 1999: 83–4; Fisher 2000: 367–8).

dicing On the importance of dicing (*kubeia*), see on **53** and the Appendix.

who was neither a family friend nor a man of his own age. It is very important (see below on **49**) that the jury believes Misgolas to be an older man, and not a family connection, and therefore necessarily a richer lover, not merely a 'age-mate' *helikiotes*, of about the same age, with whom Timarchos hung around. On the term see Foxhall (1998: 58–9).

43 one in particular. This episode is supposed to have taken place when Timarchos was still very much a youth, a *meirakion*, presumably then not much over 20, and hence relatively early in the 360s, when the other two were also in their 20s.

It was the procession of the City Dionysia. Most festivals involved an important community procession (*pompē*); see the general surveys in M. P. Nilsson, 'Die Prozessiontypen im

Griechischen Kult', *JDAI* 31 (1916), 309–39 = *Opuscula Selecta* (Lund, 1951), I. 166–214, 1916, J. Kohler, *Pompai: Untersuchungen zur hellenistichen Festkultur* (Frankfurt, 1996). Processions in Dionysiac festivals were especially spectacular, and likely to become particularly riotous, with much drunkenness and licensed personal abuse surrounding the carrying of large phalloi on wagons, were regular features (see Plat. *Laws* 637b, and H. Fluck, *Skurrile Riten in griechishen Kulte* (Endigen, 1931), 34–46; Halliwell 1991: 291, 294–6; Cole 1993; Csapo 1997). On the other hand these were official events, stated officials were charged with organizing them and leading the processions, and the city was on display in the presence of many foreigners: the possibility that regrettable incidents might occur was in principle not small, and the Athenians established the *probole* procedure to try to deal swiftly with cases of 'wrongdoing concerning the festival' (see esp. MacDowell, *Meidias* 13–18, and E. M. Harris 1992); and the archon, helped by tribally elected *epimeletai*, regulated the 'good order' (*eukosmia*) of the festival (Arist. *Ath. Pol.* 56. 4 with Rhodes *ad loc.*, *IG* II² 354, 15–19 and Theophrastus *Char.* 26. 2). Before the actual performance of the plays at the City Dionysia, on 10th Elaphebolion, the statue of Dionysos Eleuthereus, (which had been removed the day before to a temple near the Academy, in the suburbs on the road to Eleutherae, on the Boeotian border, and brought back again to the city) was escorted in ceremonial procession to the theatre; after a huge sacrifice of oxen and a banquet, a more disorderly procession or revel, the *komos* took place (see Pickard-Cambridge 1968: ch. II).

Phaidros, the son of Kallias of the deme of Sphettos. This member of a family prominent in public life over many generations (and from the same deme as Timarchos) was born by at least 390. He was general in 347/6 (*IG* II² 213.8 = Tod II 168 = Harding no. 83), again *c.* 334/3 and in 323/2 (see Davies 1971: 524–6). Phaidros also appears in the list of twenty-three Athenians, who guaranteed money for triremes to be lent to Chalcis in 340 (*IG* II² 1623 l. 174–5) see on **64**. He was the grandfather of two major Hellenistic figures, Kallias and Phaidros, on whom see T. Leslie Shear Jr., *Kallias of Sphettos and the Revolt of Athens in 286 BC. Hesperia* Suppl. 17 (Princeton, 1978); his son was Thymochares, a firm associate of the Lycurgan group, and *hieropoios* at the Amphiareion in 329/8, later a frequent general (and probably a supporter of Demetrios of Phaleron); probably in the late 340s, he bought some land sold by his deme Sphettos (Lambert 1997a, F6B41–2 and p. 162, pp. 213–17 on the date). Phaidros was evidently better known to the jurors than was Misgolas, though less so than Hegesandros, and probably closer at this time to Aeschines. He, apparently, was prepared to provide some testimony (**50**), unlike Misgolas, but it is not quite clear what he assented to: conceivably he admitted the trick pulled on the 'foreigners' (as a boyish prank), and that Timarchos was living in *hetairesis* with Misgolas, or perhaps he owned up to no more than that they were all social acquaintances at the time.

were to process together. It is not clear exactly what roles Phaidros and Misgolas (with their hanger-on Timarchos), on the one hand, and the 'foreigners' on the other, were supposed to be playing at the Dionysia, nor what their respective 'preparations' were. The mention of 'lunch' (*ariston*) makes it likely that we are concerned with the main procession, not the later *komos*, which probably took place in the evening, after the feast of the sacrificed oxen. Conceivably, Phaidros and Misgolas (or one of them) held official positions, for example as *choregoi*, and had to wear elaborately coloured robes and crowns (see Dem. 21. 33–5, 53–7, with MacDowell, *Meidias* 252 and P. J. Wilson 2000: 96–8; Davies (1971: 525) thinks this 'likely enough' but not certain; Goldhill (1994: 361), that they were probably, but not certainly, acting 'in an unofficial capacity'). Since any official post would have greatly increased the irresponsibility of their behaviour, Aeschines' failure to specify it is an argument against the assumption. Many other Athenians, and metics, had representative roles in the processions, carrying bread loaves, water-jars, wineskins, dancing round the phallos-poles, and no doubt wore appropriately festive costumes, and probably the three Athenians had one of these roles; 'preparations' might be their costumes, and perhaps extra refreshments and wine as well.

Misbehaviour at the *komos* was probably more frequent; interestingly Demosthenes (19. 287) accused Aeschines' brother-in-law Epikrates, the so-called Kyrebion (on whom see Intro. pp. 17–18), of having disgraced himself and his family by 'performing in the *komos* in the processions without a mask', a charge rebutted earnestly by Aeschines at 2. 151. This suggests that some Athenians took a flamboyant part in the Dionysiac *komoi* dressed up and masked, perhaps as satyrs; they probably engaged—in a generally inebriated atmosphere (cf. Plato, *Laws* 637b)—in dancing round the phallos-poles and floats, and in jesting and personal abuse (*gephyrismos*): see Ar. *Frogs* 417–34; *scholia* to Dem. 19. 287; and to Dem. 21. 180). The wearing of the mask was thought to give comic license and immunity to abuse without offence, since masking meant being taken over by another personality: see F. Frontisi-Ducroux, 'Un scandale à Athènes: faire le *comos* sans masque', *DHA* 18. 1 (1992), 245–56; and P. J. Wilson (2000: 97 and nn. 213 and 214), who is perhaps over-sceptical of the probability of licensed abuse at his *komos*; Csapo (1997). Occasionally cases of violence or disorder at festivals, most famously Meidias' punch on Demosthenes, led to a *probole* and (perhaps) a court case; more often, one suspects, allegations of inappropriately drunken and insulting behaviour were flung around with abandon, but taken no further.

There were probably official delegations of foreigners in these processions. As in the fifth-century empire, Athenian 'colonists' abroad, and arguably some at least of their allies, members of the 'Second Athenian Confederacy', were encouraged to attend and bring offerings to Athens' two greatest festivals. An inscription of the late 370s recording a settlement with the Parians gives them the right to bring a cow and panoply to the Panathenaia and a phallos to the Dionysia as an *aristeion*, since they are colonists of the Athenian people (*SEG* 31. 67, 2–6, see Cargill 1981: 163; P. Krentz, 'Athens' allies and the *phallophoria*', *AHB* 7 (1993), 12–16; Dreher 1995: 113, 128–30; Parker 1996: 221, suggesting this amounted to little). If these foreigners, however, were official delegates with their offerings, again one suspects Aeschines would have made even more of the affair (though they might perhaps have been friends attached to the leading delegates). Most probably, Phaidros and/or Misgolas had some relatively minor role in the procession, while Timarchos met up with some foreigners among the crowds coming to Athens hoping to enjoy the festivities and if possible make sexual contacts.

tenement-house (*synoikia*). On such houses of multiple-dwellings or uses, see below on **123–5**. The implication here is that this particular dwelling was an inn or wineshop, where they were all drinking and eating snacks, and probably that it served as a brothel as well, or at least might hire out rooms for sexual purposes.

made threats at the foreigners, and told them to accompany them to the prison, because they had corrupted a free young man. This appears to be presented as a sudden decision to try to cheat the foreigners, not a well-formulated plan. The threatened legal action seems a bluff. 'Corrupted a free young man' seems easier to understand as illicit sex (Dover 1978: 34) than preventing him from fulfilling his festival duty (canvassed by Scafuro 1997: 82, n. 42). But even for foreigners, it is in fact unlikely that it was illegal to persuade or buy an Athenian youth for sex (he is described as a *meirakion*, not a boy); but already Aeschines is beginning to assume, what his citation of the laws did not in fact demonstrate, that those who entered a relationship of *hetairesis* or *porneia* with free Athenian youths were liable to serious charges (see Dover 1978: 26–7, and on **45, 72, 87, 163**). It would probably not have been appropriate either to use the swift, summary procedure of *ephegesis* of common criminals to the Eleven, labelling them as *kakourgoi* (see Hansen 1976; D. Cohen, 1983). But in fact the story is probably meant to imply that Phaidros and Misgolas were relying on the foreigners' ignorance of the law (see Dover 1978: 34–5; Scafuro 1997: 82), reasonable fear of influential Athenians, and anyway a desire to avoid an embarrassing incident on their day out at a major Athenian festival; so they are said naturally to have made a swift exit. The episode is presumably designed to display Timarchos' promiscuity and flightiness; the contemptuous lack of hospitality towards foreign visitors at a festival of his older, but still youthful, companions; the obsessive and jealous nature of Misgolas' passion; his and Phaidros' preparedness to risk missing their part in the procession in order to recover Timarchos; and their collective irresponsible willingness, when they find the foreigners, to play a quick trick, frighten them off, and cheat them out of their 'preparations'.

44 a person not unknown to you, and that your knowledge of him concerns that very same practice. In **41** Aeschines introduces Misgolas carefully, as if he was not well known to the jury; now he appears to believe he will have reminded some at least of them of an episode in which his strong feelings for Timarchos produced a scandal. It is noticeable that he does not refer to jokes at his expense in any comedy though he may well be hoping that the audience do remember such comic references: see on **41**.

On matters that are not known to a jury . . . remind one's hearers of what they know. A bold, but necessary, assertion, given that Aeschines has very little, if any, evidence to support his claims of Timarchos' misdeeds. Other cases where prosecutors appeal to what 'you all know' include Deinarchus 1. 41–7, 2. 8–11, 3. 15–16; at times litigants appeal to what is known not just in Athens but throughout Greece (e.g. Lyc. 1. 14–15).

45–8 I have written out a testimony. Athenian procedures for trying to get hostile witnesses into court and to give testimony were very different from more modern legal systems (cf. Harrison 1968–71: II, 138–47). There seems in fact no procedure for compelling a possible witness to attend court comparable to the modern *subpoena* (S. C. Todd 1990b: 24–5). In the cases in this speech, as in e.g. Isaeus 9. 18; Lyc. 1. 20; Dem. 19. 176; Dem. 58. 35; Ps. Dem. 59. 28, the litigant who has not already got a testimony-statement from individuals who are likely to be present, but might well be reluctant or hostile, may offer them a prepared statement. Faced with it, they have only three choices (which Aeschines runs through): to agree to the testimony, to deny its truth on oath (an *exomosia*), or to refuse to say anything, in which case they faced, apparently, a procedure of 'summonsing' (*kleteusis*) and a possible fine of 1000 drachmai. It was not possible, it seems, to substitute one's own testimony, but one had to line up firmly either with the litigant offering the challenge, or against him. This is in conformity with many aspects of the laws relating to testimony in the Athenian courts, which indicate that a major purpose was to line people up and enable the jury to assess the quality of the supporters and friends on each side, as well as to arrive at a precise account of what might have happened through evidence and cross-examination. See on all this Humphreys (1985b); S. C. Todd (1990b: 19–39); C. Carey, 'The Witness's *Exomosia* in the Athenian Courts', *CQ* 45 (1995), 114–19; and Carey (1994: 183–4).

not uncultured . . . no danger and no shame. The noun *apaideusia* (lack of education or culture), and the adjective *apaideutos* occur in a number of important contexts in this speech (see on

132, 137, 166, 185); it indicates the failure to conform to, or to understand, the traditional ideal of 'noble' or 'cultivated' pederastic love. So presumably the language of this proposed testimony was designed to give the impression of a relationship between the two which was compatible with this ideal, and was not necessarily based on mercenary exploitation, naming no specific act or anything else which might, according to Aeschines' misleading claims about the law, produce 'danger' as well as 'shame' for those admitting a relationship. Presumably he wished Misgolas to admit at least to having associated with Timarchos at that time, perhaps that he had spent time living in his house, and then leave the jury to draw their conclusions.

47 as a demonstration to the others of his type that he knows well enough how to keep secret. Aeschines cunningly suggests a general conspiracy of those involved in these shameful practices (see also **193–5**). In fact, whatever the nature of their relationships (on which hard information would be difficult to come by), many would refuse to testify against their former, and often no doubt still current, friends. What Aeschines could have done with was a former lover or close friend who had become Timarchos' enemy, but as far as one can see he did not find one (see Foxhall 1998: 58–60; Fisher 1998a: 103).

    embarking on a difficult task. Aeschines seems to believe here, and perhaps the confident command to the clerk in **50** confirms it, that at least some of the (less close) friends of Misgolas and Timarchos may give evidence, at least to confirm that they did live together. How many gave testimony is not clear.

48 moral man. The term for 'moral' here is once more *sophron*: cf. on **6**; and the term for 'pure' (*katharos*) suggests a life free from any religious or moral stain (see Parker 1983: 323). Thus the requirement for the avoidance of trouble is placed ludicrously high, and the generalization makes explicit the assumption on which the speech depends, that widespread rumours of disgraceful living must have some basis in fact. This assumption ignores the facts (which are recognized elsewhere in the speech: see e.g. **2, 108, 110, 155–8**) that gossip flourished in Athenian society, and all those active in politics were likely to acquire enemies: see Hunter (1990); Dover (1978: 39–41).

49 fellow-*ephebos*. This passage (Aesch. 2. 167; Xen. *Poroi* 4. 51–2; and *IG* II^2 1250) constitutes the primary evidence for some formal military and gymnastic training for the ephebes, the youths of *c.* 18–19 on the threshold of becoming full citizens, in the fourth century down to the major ephebic reform of 335/4 in the Lycurgan era: see Gauthier on Xen. *Poroi* 4. 51–2; Sekunda (1990); and Burckhardt (1996: esp. 29–33). It remains uncertain to what extent the poorest Athenians (sons of *thetes*) were expected or permitted to participate (see e.g Rhodes on Arist. *Ath. Pol.* 42; Winkler 1990b: 25–33; Hansen 1991: 108–9). On the military roles of patrols and garrisons, including the ephebes, in the first half of the fourth century, see the somewhat divergent views of Ober (1985); Munn (1993); V. D. Hanson, *Warfare and Agriculture in Classical Greece*^{2} (California, 1998), 91–2; on the possibility of other roles, closer to countryside 'policing', see Hunter (1994: 151–3), Fisher (1999: 80).

and we are both now in our forty-fifth year. On the probability of a very significant distortion here, underestimating Timarchos' age to make him younger than Misgolas, see E. M. Harris (1988), and Intro. pp. 10–12.

Herakles To invoke Herakles is in comedy (and probably in ordinary conversation) a frequent response to a shock, surprise or fright (e.g. Ar. *Ach.* 284; *Clouds* 184; *Birds* 93); in speeches, it may give emphasis to a sudden thought or new idea (as here and Aesch. 3. 21) or (real or faked) indignation (Dem. 21. 66, 19. 308; Dein. 1. 7). See also **52, 55, 73**.

50 call now for me. It appears that Phaidros and at least a few of their other acquaintances have supplied some testimony; perhaps a version of the story which admits that Misgolas and Timarchos were going about together; whether Phaidros admitted anything of the Dionysia incident is uncertain.

read the testimony of Phaidros. Those, like (presumably) Misgolas and Hegesandros, who took the oath of denial, did so in person. Those who agreed that their testimony could be presented originally used to appear in court, make their statements orally, address the court for as long as they wished, and might be subjected to cross-examination (see e.g. Andoc. 1. 69, 1. 14; Lys. 17. 2); but at some point relatively early in the fourth century, this practice was replaced with one whereby witnesses agreed in advance a written form of testimony which was read out by the clerk, and might merely be confirmed as correct by the witness (see Dem. 45. 44, and MacDowell 1978: 242–3). In part this change reflects the growing use of written documents in many areas of Athenian public and business life (see Thomas 1989: 43; W. V. Harris 1989: 71–2, and on **160–4**, **171**); it may suggest that the careful scrutiny of witnesses was not seen as an indispensable element of a trial (see S. C. Todd 1990b: 27–31). The change was probably also motivated by the desire to prevent witness statements and subsequent discussions taking up too much of the time allocated to the case, and preventing the litigant who spoke second from having equal time: see Rubinstein (forthcoming).

just in case he is prepared . . . to give evidence of the truth. The inventors of alleged testimony in our manuscripts provided a statement for Misgolas, but nothing for Phaidros and the others; but as this is spurious, we cannot determine whether in fact Misgolas did in fact assent to whatever civilized statement was offered him. One can only suspect, however, in view of the careful preparation Aeschines offers for a likely refusal ('in case after all . . .'), that he did indeed refuse, as Hegesandros certainly did (**69**); if he had given evidence, contrary to expectations, one would expect explicit acknowledgement. If it is indeed the case that Aeschines deliberately lied in his claim that Misgolas was older than Timarchos, he had a good reason for refusing to assent to whatever Aeschines wrote for him, apart from the fact that he might seem to be assenting to the insinuations of the speech as well as to the actual words supplied.

51–2 This is an important transitional section. First, it eases, first, the move from the Misgolas narrative to the more important and extended narrative above all to do with Hegesandros (**53–73**), second, it emphasizes the point, based on the number of lovers, that Timarchos may properly be considered to have been not merely involved in *hetairesis*, but actually a *pornos*.

52 passing over those wild men *(agrioi)*. Another effective use of the tactic of *praeteritio*: see also **39**, **109**, **131**, **170**. Aeschines throws in a gratuitous mention of some notoriously plausible pederasts without making the slightest effort to offer details, let alone testimony, to support the allegations that Timarchos had had affairs with these men.

Agrios as a term designating excessive sexual habits is found in comedy (e.g. of Hieronymos son of Xenophantos, Ar. *Clouds* 347–9); the picture is of long-haired, shaggy, and centaur-like men, given to uninhibited and indiscriminate sexual pursuit of women or boys: see Dover (1978: 37–8), and Henderson (1991: 252). Nothing is known of Kedonides or Thersandros, but Autokleides (*LGPN* 2; *PA* 2079; *PAA* 2387885) was probably the target of the *Orestautokleides* of the comic poet Timocles. The first of the two fragments (27 and 28 K–A) displays eleven *hetairai* as old hags sleeping near and haunting an unfortunate man (hence perhaps the title figure, Orestautocleides), like the Furies at the start of Aeschylus' *Eumenides* (see Athen. 567e); the second mentioned the law court known as the *parabuston* where the Eleven tried *kakourgoi* (Boegehold 1995: 6–8, 11–15, and *testimonia* no. 156). 'Orestes', the son of Agamemnon, the hero who committed matricide, was driven mad by the Furies, and came for trial to Athens as a polluted outsider, appears in Athens as a nickname for a variety of wild men, violent muggers, or unscrupulous rogues (see Dunbar, *Birds* 451–4, 691–3; Fisher 1999: 71–2). This play, then, may well have portrayed a complex comic persona built on the shaggy pursuer of boys and women and a wild or criminal type being harried by a chorus of the most famous of Athens' *hetairai* acting both perhaps as Furies (chasing the son of Agamemnon) and as Areopagites and/or the Eleven, pursuing a criminal: see T. B. L. Webster, *Studies in Later Greek Comedy* (Manchester, 1970), 59; Webster's argument for dating the play some time later than Aeschines' speech, that the *hetairai* are presented as old hags, fails to consider the effect of the transformation into Furies. Whether Autokleides is also being satirized through the title-character of Alexis' *Asklepiokleides*, cannot be determined, see Arnott, *Alexis, ad loc.* On the possible reuse of some of this material in Aristogeiton's prosecution of Timarchos, see Intro. pp. 22–3.

and by Dionysos. This appears to be the only case in the Attic orators of an oath sworn by Dionysos: Zeus, with or without 'the other gods', or another god such as Apollo, is very frequent. Perhaps this is felt appropriate because Aeschines is claiming a licence to utter a rude or explicit word as if at a comedy or Dionysiac festival where *parrhesia* is allowed; when later (**55**) he refuses to state what exactly Pittalakos did to Timarchos, a more solemn 'by Olympian Zeus' is employed. This sentence, already long and drawn out, has its climax delayed and suspense further built up by the insertion of this oath.

wrapping it up. *periplekein*, weaving around, used of covering cloths or veils, close-woven nets, as well, as here, for euphemistic or over-elaborate, or deceitful, play with words (Eur. *Phoen.* 494–6; Antiphanes 75. 1 K/A; Straton 35. 1K/A; Goldhill 1998: 118, n. 38.)

to have prostituted himself. It might seem an anticlimax that the only word he comes out with after such a long apologetic warning is a form of the verb *porneuesthai*, to prostitute oneself (a word apparently used by the law he has in fact already cited at **29**). But this partly humorous build-up aids the crucial clarification of the issues in the case, and enables the production of the dangerous, and in fact completely unprovable, allegation that Timarchos was (virtually) a prostitute, a *pornos*, to come out with a flourish (see also on **119**). Further, (see Intro. pp. 56–8), he is playing with the jury over the gradual revelation that *pornos* has long in fact been Timarchos' nickname; this word, as it is finally produced, should have produced a good laugh.

performs this act indiscriminately Willingness to do the 'deed', presumably anal sex, is meant to be part of what makes a *pornos*, but this passage overall supports the view that what is above all crucial to the applicability of the charge is the question of the conditions and terms of the sex. The distinction between the two charges of *hetairesis* and *porneia* is relatively fluid, but focuses on the number of clients, the lack of any exercise of choice over whom to sleep with, and the explicit provision of cash, see also Intro. pp. 40–2. Apollodoros' prosecution of Neaira displays a comparable and equally convenient oscillation between treating Neaira as a classy and expensive *hetaira* and as a common prostitute (*porne*): see Carey, *Neaira* 140–1; Kapparis, *Neaira* 408–9.

53 wearied of the expense and sent him away. Obviously this is Aeschines' gloss on the ending of the relationship (if it ever existed), suiting the character of Timarchos, ever desperate to satisfy his own luxurious desires. As the *scholia* say, it reminds them of the other charge, of dissipation of his estate. The verb translated 'wearied', *apeipein*, can mean 'give up through exhaustion'; but it can also, with a direct object, mean 'renounce', 'reject', as a father may officially reject his son, or a husband his wife, and perhaps this nuance may be heard as a subtext.

Antikles the son of Kallias of the deme Euonymon. (*LGPN* 21; *PA* 1065; *PAA* 133345): his father Kallias (*LGPN* 21; *PA* 7864; Develin, *AO* no. 1508) was a member of the board of *hellenotamiai*, financial officials concerned with the Athenian Empire, in 410/9 (*IG* I³ 375. 26); it was a common name in Attica.

away in Samos with the klerouchs. The island of Samos had been Athens' most loyal ally in the last years of the Peloponnesian War, and right at its close in 405 the Samians were honoured by the offer of a form of Athenian citizenship (ML 94 = Fornara no. 166). After Athens' defeat, the Spartans established a strong oligarchy on the island; subsequently it fell under the control of a Persian garrison. The Athenians, under Timotheos, besieged and regained control of the island around 366/5 (Dem. 15. 9; Isocr. 15. 108–11), and in 365 (so Diod. 18. 18. 9) or (less probably) a little later in 361 (so the *scholia* here) established a first group of Athenian settlers there, known as klerouchs; a second foundation came in 352/1 (Philochoros, *FGH* 328 F 154 = Dion. Hal. *Dein.* 13). For these events, their dates, and the debate on whether these interventions were 'aggressive' in intent, and constituted *de facto* breaches of the undertakings of the Second Athenian Confederacy, or rather merely a legitimate re-establishment of the close link with the democratic elements of the island forged some forty years earlier, see Griffith 'Athens in the Fourth Century', in P. D. A. Garnesy and C. R. Whittaker (eds.), *Imperialism in the Ancient World* (Cambridge, 1978), 137–41; G. Shipley, *History of Samos 800–188 BC* (Oxford, 1987), 138–43, 155–8; Cargill (1995: 17–21); App. B no. 105. Aeschines says merely that Antikles is currently away on the klerouchy on Samos, and gives no information on when he went (presumably the alleged relationship with Timarchos would have ended at the latest in the mid-360s). Someone very probably his brother (. . . os son of Kallias) appears on a fourth-century list of klerouchs (*IG* II² 1952. 5), who may have been heading for Samos (see Cargill 1995: 112, nos. 105, 728). Aeschines' ostensible reason for not discussing this case any further is that Antikles cannot testify (and therefore neither can Aeschines try to make capital from a refusal to testify). It is more likely that there was never any more than the tiniest piece of gossip, if even that, linking them, and thus another name, safely out of Athens, could be added to the long list of lovers.

he did not admonish himself or take to better pursuits. Another reminder that Timarchos was constantly making deliberate choices to stay with this mode of life.

the gaming-house, where the dicing-table is set up, and men set the cocks fighting. After 'set the cocks fighting', the manuscripts add 'and play the dice', rightly deleted by editors as a later explanatory addition.

Dicing was a popular pastime throughout the ancient world and indulged in by those of all classes. It could be played on six-sided dice (*kuboi*), or on four-sided knucklebones (*astragaloi*: see on **58**). Frequent allusions to it focus on it as among the typical debauched and expensive activities of the degenerate young, both invective in law court speeches (e.g. Lys. 14. 27, 16. 11; Isocr. *Antid.* 15. 287), and jokes in comedy (e.g. Ar. *Wasps* 74–6; Eupolis 99. 85). 'Dicers' is the title of a good many Middle Comedy plays (see Arnott on Alexis' *Kubeutai*). On the settings and organization of gambling establishments see below on **57** and the Appendix. How realistic is the assumption here that the jury know 'the place', or at least have heard of it, is hard to say, nor is it clear whether the phrasing is supposed to indicate that there was one main place, or that many of them would have heard of the particular site where Timarchos and Pittalakos had been known to hang out (on gambling-places, see the Appendix).

dicing-table. The word used here, *telia*, refers to a variety of large, round, flattish objects: e.g. a chimney cover (Ar. *Wasps* 147) or a sieve for flour (Ar. *Wealth* 1037); here it is either the tray on which dice can be thrown, or, less likely, a larger bounded arena within which the birds fought (so *scholia* to Ar. *Wealth* 1037 which is apparently offering an interpretation of this passage of Aeschines, but not necessarily a correct one). See also Pritchett (1956: 315) ('a gaming board for cock-fighting').

cocks fighting. Cock-fighting and quail-fighting were also very popular sports in Athens; obviously, they offered exciting opportunities for competition and betting, and ideologically they afforded demonstrations of masculine courage and virility which find reflections in many aspects of Athenian cultural life. See below on **55, 57,** and H. Hoffman (1974); O. Taplin, 'Phallology,

Phlyakes, Iconography and Aristophanes', *PCPS* 30 (1987), 92–104; Fowler (1988), and above all Csapo (1993).

54–71 Timarchos, Pittalakos, and Hegesandros. This is the most substantial and detailed narrative, and it features as its leading character a currently prominent politician and opponent of Aeschines, Hegesandros son of Hegesias, of Sounion (*LGPN* 11; *PA* 6307; Develin, *AO* no. 1350; Hansen, *Inventory* 47). The narrative gives an indication of the date when they first became involved, and the dramatic events with Pittalakos took place: it was soon after Hegesandros returned from the Hellespont, after serving as treasurer to Timomachos; this seems to have taken place in 361/0 or perhaps a little earlier (see on **56**). In **109** it is alleged that Timarchos was on the *boule* in the archonship of Nikophemos, also in 361/0, and the allegations of Hegesandros' and Timarchos' misconduct in Athens in that year (see on **110–12**) include adverse gossip current at that time concerning their sexual relationship. Aeschines seems to hope that the jury will not manage to remember exactly how many years ago this archonship was, so that they will not conclude that Timarchos was at least thirty in that year, and at least forty-five at the time of the trial (see also Intro. pp. 10–12, and on **49** and **95**).

Hegesandros, and his more famous and powerful brother Hegesippos (*LGPN* 17; *PA* 6351; Develin, *AO* no. 1360; Hansen, *Inventory* 47: on the family, also Davies, *APF* 209–10 and Kroll, in *RE*), and probably other people in the story as well, were members of the *genos* of the Salaminioi, which had charge of a number of important cults in Attica, for example in Phaleron, at the temple of Athena Skiras, in Sounion, at a sanctuary of Herakles, and in the city, at the Eurysakion. The affairs and conflicts of the *genos*, split between those at Sounion, and those from the 'Seven Tribes', are known above all from two large and informative inscriptions published by Ferguson (1938), though the *genos* is not mentioned in our speech or any other literary source. On the *genos* and the greatly disputed issue of its origins and its relation to the island of Salamis, see Ferguson (1938), M. Guarducci, 'L'Origine e le vicende del *genos* attico dei Salaminioi', *RFIC* 26 (1948), 223–43; R. G. Osborne (1994); Humphreys (1990); M. C. Taylor (1995; 1997: 47–63); Parker (1996: 308–16); Lambert (1997b) (with new texts of the inscriptions), and (1999). Their name, and cults associated with Skiras, Skiros, and Eurysakos the son of Ajax, all suggest close connection with Salamis, while the members of the *genos* all have Athenian demotics. Various accounts have been proposed: that they were native Salaminians who moved into Attica, either in the Dark Ages, or as Salamis became Athenian at the end of the sixth century (e.g. M. P. Nilsson, 'The New Inscription of the Salaminioi', *AJP* 59 [1938], 385–93; Humphreys 1990; R. G. Osborne 1994b), that they were Athenians who settled in Salamis but were later expelled (Guarducci), or Athenians who claimed a connection with Salamis as part of the Athenian claim to the island (Ferguson 1938; M. C. Taylor 1997: 59–63), or that they, like the *demos* of the Salaminians (see on **25**), took part in the late sixth-century settlement on the island, but maintained lands and homes in Attica, and were able to maintain or developed cult-privileges, some of which emphasized the connection between Attica and Salamis (Lambert 1997b; 1999). None of these theories is without difficulties. See further the Appendix.

54 One of those from that place of leisure is one Pittalakos, a public slave-fellow, a servant of the city. This character plays a prominent role in this part of the speech (and is, rather curiously, singled out for special mention in both the hypothesis to Dem. 19, and Tzetzes, *Chil.* 6. 56); the lurid story, and the involvement of a slave (or ex-slave) in Timarchos' affairs, apparently made a big impact on later scholars and perhaps on contemporaries. Initially the treatment of Pittalakos is slanted to emphasize the degradation involved in Timarchos, a free young Athenian, submitting to the unspeakable desires of a state-slave, as well as spending much of his time and money in the gambling den. With the introduction of Hegesandros, however, increasingly Pittalakos becomes a victim, for whom the jury seem to be invited to feel some (albeit patronizing) sympathy, as he is savagely whipped, and ruthlessly frustrated in his attempts to get legal revenge. One may compare the attitudes Apollodoros seems to attempt to evoke towards the *hetaira*-'prostitute' ex-slave Neaira in Ps. Dem. 59. Generally that speech is full of brutal contempt for her career living off successive men, but occasionally a slight tinge of sympathy, perhaps, creeps in; the main case is the party at Chabrias' house, where everyone present, including the slaves who waited at the table, slept with her while her lover Phrynion was asleep (59. 33–5). Omitowoju (1997: 8–12), seeks to limit the subjective interest in Neaira's feelings, pointing out that Apollodoros only uses the term *hybris* when reporting her account of the insult to Stephanos (59. 37); there seems to be more sympathy for her than Omitowoju allows in the terms he does use in his own voice, especially at 59. 35: 'she was wantonly humiliated' (*aselgos proupelakizeto*): on *aselges* see on **32**, and *propelakizein*, literally 'to trample in the mud', is a strong term often associated with treating people with *hybris* (see Dem. 21. 7, 72–3, and Fisher 1992: 48, 53, 107). Aeschines' switch towards sympathy for Pittalakos is markedly more pronounced, as the main purpose of his account turn to the condemnation of Hegesandros' and Timarchos' brutal revenge and manipulation of the legal procedures.

public slave-fellow. This translates *anthropos demosios*, where *anthropos*, literally meaning (mere) human being, is commonly a contemptuous way of referring to someone of inferior status: often a slave (so throughout this passage), in some cases a freedman or woman (e.g. Isaeus 6. 20, of Dion a freedman who had children by the prostitute Alke), or a metic (Hyper. *Athen.* 3, of a 'speech-writer, a businessman and most important, an Egyptian'); and *demosios* 'public' indicates a state-owned slave. Pittalakos' exact status is a problem. The blunt labelling of him here as 'a public slave, a servant of the city', gives the greatest force to the denunciation of Timarchos' degradation. Athens maintained a fairly large number of publicly owned slaves (Jacob 1928; D. M. Lewis 1990: 254–8). They included the low-grade 'police' who assisted the Eleven, known, until the early fourth century, as the Scythian archers, officials of the courts and the administration, in the dockyards, the mint, the prison, road-workers, building-repairers, and so on, amounting to a thousand or more. Some of these had fairly high-grade, skilled, and responsible jobs—especially one might mention the duties of the coin-testers in the Agora and the Peiraieus enumerated in the document of 375/4 (Stroud 1974 = *SEG* 26 72 = Harding no. 45), or, if he was in fact ever a slave, Nikomachos, the man involved for many years in the revisions of the laws between 411 and *c.* 399, see S. C. Todd 1996. It is not stated what post Pittalakos held or had held.

As the narrative proceeds, the picture of Pittalakos changes somewhat. Aeschines ascribes to him surprising wealth, with his own gambling business and his own house; he shows him able to take advantage of remarkable sexual opportunities, living as the lover of Timarchos. If he is a slave, this is contrary to the laws cited at **139**, but Aeschines does not here say the acts are illegal, as well as degrading, though in many other places he falsely asserts that Timarchos' clients or lovers, even though Athenian, were breaking laws; and he ascribes to him surprising legal rights (he begins an action against his assailants and the destroyers of his property, though he has to give it up). His defender Glaukon resists the claim of Hegesandros that he is his personal slave by the process known as 'taking away to freedom', not by asserting he belongs to the city (see on **62**). There is thus a strong probability if not a certainty (Jacob 1928: 147–76, 187–9; S. C. Todd 1993: 192–4; Hunter 1994: 231), that Pittalakos is, now at least, a freed-man, conceivably as a result of having been able to accumulate some wealth as a public slave (cf. the case of the trader Lampis, able to give evidence in court, in Demosthenes. 34, yet described there as a slave). Aeschines seems to treat Pittalakos' status in the same contradictory way that he does his role in the story—*qua* lover of Timarchos he is a slave, and his treatment of him further degraded Timarchos, but *qua* victim of Hegesandros' violence and contempt, he seems more like a free man of low status; hence freed status is the most likely. It is also intriguing that Hegesandros claimed he had belonged to him (see also Appendix).

from that place of leisure. *Diatribe* (see also on **132**) prob-ably means here 'place for a specific leisure activity' (and see also **175**), though the meaning may perhaps be 'one of those who lives for that pursuit'.

At the time of these events (*c.* 361/0) Pittalakos may have been running or helping to run an establishment which provided the gambling entertainment of bird-fights and dicing, and was very fond of this activity and his birds. He is called the 'bird-dealer' (*ton ornithian*) by the *Hypoth. to Dem.* 19 and Tzetzes (*Histories* 6. 56). This may have a side-line to whatever jobs he had done as a state-slave, or a career he had taken up after manumission; but perhaps it had always been an activity he had been involved in. There are several puzzling features in this picture of Pittalakos' status and activities, and his and the others' interests in gambling and bird-fights: see the Appendix.

that polluted wretch. The rhetoric of denunciation is fierce and very pompous in tone here (on the register of *miaros*, 'polluted', as an insult see Parker 1983: 3–5; Dickie 1996: 167). The passage is full of words indicating shame and degradation, and Aeschines brings in his own contrasting moral seriousness and respect for the jury's sensibilities with another use of the rhetorical *topos* that the deeds perpetrated by Pittalakos the slave on the body of Timarchos the young citizen were so degrading and in effect hybristic (though voluntarily 'endured' by him) that he could not mention them.

financial sponsor (*choregos*) for his foul debauchery (*bdeluria*). The state-appointed sponsors (*choregoi*) performed their 'liturgies' by contributing their time and money sponsoring a chorus for competitions at community festivals. Some may have been forced by the legal requirements or yielded to social pressures; but it was hoped that many contributed from the desire to participate in a mutually beneficial system of exchange with the community, in which the community gave 'honour' in various forms in return (the good form of *philotimia*): see most recently P. J. Wilson (1997 and 2000: esp. 171–97). Timarchos, it will later appear, allegedly avoided this system, by spending all his available wealth on his own pleasures. Here he is said to have voluntarily entered on a vile perversion of it, himself seeking a sponsor for his degraded pleasures (*bdeluria* again, see on **26**); when it should have been the city treating him as the 'sponsor' for its legitimate activities in honour of the gods. Worse, he cared nothing that the sponsor (*choregos*) of his 'most shameful' desires was not a rich citizen, but a slave. For a similar point made against Demosthenes, see Aesch. 3. 240; and P. J. Wilson (2000: 176–8).

55 offences. For the wrongs which Timarchos committed willingly against his own body, Aeschines uses here the general term *hamartema*: an error or an act of wrongdoing which may be more or less deliberate. It recurs in a crucial passage of denunciation of Timarchos' 'womanish offences' at **185.**

by Olympian Zeus. When Aeschines did bring out, with a flourish, the word 'prostituted', he swore by Dionysos (above, **49**); here, as he refuses to state the acts performed, he uses an oath by the most powerful god of all, Olympian Zeus. He has chosen to apply a particularly strong version of this 'I couldn't possible mention . . .' rhetorical ploy, because of the status dissonance of the relationship: slaves were normally unable (and rightly, in slave-owners' ideology) to prevent owners inflicting physical punishment or sexual assault on their bodies, and rigorously prevented from asserting any form of physical dominance over, or even equality with, the free (see Golden 1984, and on the laws cited at **138–9**). One might suppose also that Aeschines wants the jury to think that these unmentionable acts were at least anal and perhaps also oral sex, and anything else they could imagine which they found particularly distasteful.

a man came sailing back from the Hellespont. The word order carefully delays for effect the introduction of the subject of the sentence. The two brothers Hegesandros and Hegesippos were politically and socially the most important of Timarchos' old acquaintances, and it was naturally very important to Aeschines to discredit them as far as he could.

56 Timomachos of Acharnae: Timomachos (*LGPN* 4; *PA* 13797; Develin, *AO* no. 3097; Hansen, *Inventory* 60) a general and a relation by marriage (*kedestes*) of the very powerful politician Kallistratos of Aphidna (*LGPN* 50; *PA* 8157; Develin, *AO* no. 1564; Hansen, *Inventory* 50–1). For the relationship, see Ps. Dem. 50. 48; Timomachos was probably Kallistratos' son-in-law (so Davies, *APF* 280). Timomachos seems to be a descendant of a Timomachos (*LGPN* 3; *PA* 13796) who worked as a carpenter on the Erechtheion (J. M. Paton (ed.), *The Erechtheum* (Cambridge Mass., 1928), 340 no. XI, col. iii, l. 20 = *IG* I³ 475, 245), in which case the family achieved a notable mobility which enabled him to marry into the family of the leading politician and to be elected general. One can compare the rise of Aeschines' own family, and an even closer example, Iasos of Kollytos, a sculptor on the Erechtheion in 408–6 and a man of the same name and deme, probably the same person, who acted as a *choregos* for a comedy in 387/6 (see Davies, *APF* 242).

Timomachos was general in 367/6, when in joint command of two forces with the Spartan Naukles, he failed to prevent Epaminondas from crossing Mt Oneion, near Corinth, on his way to encourage the Achaeans to join the Boeotian-Peloponnesian confederation (Xen. *Hell.* 7. 1. 41; Buckler 1980: 187–8). He was general again in 361/0, and apparently helped to cause Apollodoros, serving as trierarch, much trouble, enumerated in his speech against Polykles (Ps. Dem. 50). He was sent to Thrace and the Hellespont, where he was apparently to support if possible the rebel Thracian king Miltokythes against Kotys I the more powerful Odrysian King, to protect Athens' friends in the Hellespont and the grain (Ps. Dem. 50. 5–22: for a recent narrative of these campaigns, see Heskel 1997: esp. 146–53). Timomachos kept using Apollodoros and his lavishly equipped trireme months after he should have been released from his trierarchy of the previous year (e.g. 39–40), and in particular tried, without success, to get him to convey on his ship Timomachos' in-law Kallistratos, recently exiled (43–52: Hansen 1975: no. 87, trial in 361). Apollodoros followed up his indictment of Autokles, general of 362/1, for failure adequately to support Miltokythes—whether as a proposer of a decree (Dem. 23. 104) in Athens, or on the ground in Thrace, or both (see Hansen 1975: no. 90), and his personal prosecution of his supposed trierarchic successor Polykles (Ps. Dem. 50) for forcing him to stay with his ship and incur much additional expense with a series of further indictments (Dem. 36. 53), of Autokles' successor Menon, of Timomachos, and of Kallippos (Hansen 1975: nos. 95, 91, 92). The prosecution of Timomachos (whether by Apollodoros alone, or with assistance, as Hypereides seems to have assisted the prosecution of Autokles, Hyper. fr. 55 Jensen; Trevett 1992: 133–4) would have focused on his failure to prevent Kotys from seizing fortified sites in the Chersonese which the Athenians felt were theirs (Dem. 23. 115, 19. 180; Schol. Aesch. 1. 56; Hyper. *Eux.* 1), and his attempt to transport Kallistratos to Thasos (and to plan for his recall), for his part in which Kallippos also faced his indictment. Aeschines' contribution to attacks on these failures is naturally to claim that Hegesandros, serving as treasurer (*tamias*) with Timomachos, expropriated a large sum, and hence was 'in some way, not the least responsible' for his downfall (a remarkably small claim, in fact). Timomachos chose, like many a general, not to return to Athens to face the trial and was sentenced to death (see also Roberts 1982: 210, n. 97; Heskel 1997: 149).

Later in the speech it appears that Hegesandros was a *tamias* of Athena in 361/0 (**110–11** with *scholia*); he can hardly have combined that post based in Athens with a post acting as treasurer to one or more of the generals in Thrace (Develin 1989: 267). Possibly he held the Athena post the previous year and there was, or might be thought to have been, some slight overlap in practice;

or perhaps he had the post with Timomachos in a previous year (so Schaefer 1885–8: II, 331, n. 6, followed by Davies, *APF* 209), and Aeschines is falsely, if vaguely and without any evident testimony, implicating Hegesandros in the case against Timomachos, and also asserting another instance of his venality.

57 was pleased with the sight, desired him . . . his nature was very close in kind to his own. The implications of this narrative for Hegesandros' character are presumably that he fancied Timarchos instantly, purely on the basis of his physical charms, and that he recognized, and liked, Timarchos' shamelessness and delight in a wide range of pleasures.

quickly persuaded him . . . wickedness and infidelity. This provides an assessment of Timarchos' faults, to balance those of Hegesandros: his extreme readiness to go off with Hegesandros suggests he had no scruples in deserting one lover for another who seemed richer, more influential, and more fun. The emphasis on the lack of fidelity towards Pittalakos is designed to contrast with the proper trust and affection expected in the more 'cultivated' relationships; Aeschines is clearly not here treating Timarchos seriously as a prostitute.

58 was very upset. The language of this paragraph in particular seems to present Pittalakos with some sympathy, as a wronged and jealous lover, prepared to pursue his interest to the point of being a 'nuisance' (a word from the same root is applied by the defence to Aeschines' own behaviour as a lover at the *gymnasia*, at **135**). Though he has just been called a slave, this idea seems to have dropped somewhat from view, in order to emphasize the brutality and contempt of his treatment; but some ambivalence no doubt remains.

59 shaking knucklebones. Throwing knucklebones (*astralogoi*), normally sheep or goat bones, afforded other games of chance and opportunities for betting. It seems to have been especially associated with children's games, and with sanctuaries (sacrifices would be likely to be the source of the bones), and knucklebones were often buried with the dead (see also on **149**). Kurke (1999: 283–95) tries to establish a consistent 'discursive pattern; of rigorous differentiation between the more 'positively valued' knucklebones, associated with innocent children, and aristocratic settings such as the *palaistrai* and the *gymnasia*, and negatively valued, lower-class, gambling with *kuboi*; the distinction may be too sharp even for the archaic period, but it is hard to maintain that it was as dominant in classical Athens. This passage (as Kurke recognizes at p. 283; but she seems not to pursue its implications) suggests that a gambling haunt operated both *astragaloi* and *kuboi*; and many passages suggest that dicing with *kuboi* took place at religious sites (see Appendix). As in other instances, the distinctions between élitist and democratic leisure pastimes had probably become considerably subverted and confused by Aeschines' time.

The word 'shaking' (*diaseistos*) may allude to the fact that, as now, dice or bones would be vigorously shaken before being rolled: see Harpokration s.v. *diaseistos*, who claims this helps to satisfy players that the dice are not 'harmed' (*akakourgetoi*)—which might possibly include being deliberately 'loaded'. It may also be relevant that some knucklebones found on sanctuaries have been planed smooth, or reinforced with lead or other metals (Kurke 1999: 288). Harpokration quotes the same phrase from a play of Menander's (319 K/A), and it is also mentioned with no explanation in Pollux 7. 203 s.v. *kubeia*.

the quails and cocks, of whom that thrice-miserable man had been very fond, they killed. The term *triskakodaimon* (found also in comedy, e.g. Ar. *Ach.* 1024, *Fr.* 19), like the simple form *kakodaimon*, is used of a man plagued by evil power or terrible luck, can be an insult or an expression of pity; here perhaps a rather patronizing sympathy (see Dickie 1996: 168; W. S. Barrett, Euripides, *Hippolytus* (Oxford, 1964) on l. 1362). His fondness for his birds, and the cruelty of his enemies' killing them, may also evoke some sympathy for him, and hostility towards Hegesandros and Timarchos though probably not as much as it would in a British jury, notoriously more sympathetic to pets: for routine cruelty to edible birds, see Ar. *Birds* 523–38, 1072–87, 1579–91, with Dunbar, *Birds* 360–9, 719–20.

Quails. Quails were used both for fighting, like cocks, and for the betting game of 'quail-tapping', at which one contestant placed his bird on a board, and the other sought to drive it off the board by flicking it with his finger, or pulling its feathers. See Ar. *Birds* 1297–9 with Dunbar *Birds* 643–4, and Pollux 9. 102, 109.

finally they tied Pittalakos himself to a pillar and gave

him the worst beating imaginable in the world. The emphasis is on the ruthless violence, taking place at night and heightened by drink; the impression given is of a gang bent on destruction and humiliation. The most striking feature, tying the man to the pillar and administering a savage beating, is clearly designed to indicate their treatment of him as their disobedient slave. A closely comparable case is the revenge whipping of Teisis, a case described in detail in a fragment of Lysias (fr. 17). According to the dramatic narrative which is all that Dionysius of Halicarnassus quotes from that speech (Dion. Hal. *Dem.* 11), Archippos, having been involved in an altercation at a *gymnasion* with Teisis, and, in all probability his guardian and lover Pytheas as well, was inveigled into Teisis' house for an after-dinner drink, was tied to a pillar and savagely whipped; even worse, the next morning he was again tied to the pillar and whipped, this time by Teisis' slaves. (Teisis' alternative view, naturally, was that Archippos had broken into his house at night, drunk and insulting his and his womenfolk, cf. the similar tale at Lys. 3. 7). On that occasion, one may suspect that the slavery motif was introduced by Archippos' insults, directed perhaps at Teisis' voluntary sexual 'enslavement' to his lover/guardian; in our case, there are clear signs that Hegesandros and Timarchos claimed Pittalakos actually was a slave, asserting illegally some citizen rights. See Hunter (1994: 182–3); D. Cohen (1995: 137–9); Fisher (1998b: 78; 1999: 67).

even the neighbours. Though the neighbours, allegedly, could hear the cries, Aeschines does not (or could not) claim that they did not take any action; contrast the cases mentioned below on **60**. Whether any of them contributed to the testimonies mentioned at **66** is not clear.

60 came unclothed . . . the altar of the Mother of the Gods. The altar to the Mother of the Gods (*Meter*), evidently in the open air where a crowd would naturally gather, was located in the heart of the civic centre, in the middle of the East side of the Agora. It stood just in front of the large building called the *Metroon*, which from the last decade of the fifth century contained a shrine to the Goddess with a statue by Pheidias (Pausanias 1. 3. 5; Arrian *Periplous* 9) or his pupil Agorakritos (Pliny *NH* 36.17), and also was the official storage place for the decrees and other records. It had been established as such as part of the major

revisions of laws, law-making procedures and record-keeping
between 411 and *c*. 400 (see e.g. Aesch. 3. 187 and *scholia*;
Boegehold 1972; Thomas 1989: 38–40; testimonia in Wycherley
1957: 150–60). It is debated whether, as has traditionally been held
by the American excavators of the Agora, the Metroon replaced
the so-called 'Old Bouleuterion', where the Council used to meet;
or whether there had long been a shrine to the Mother, while the
Council had previously met nearby, perhaps in the open air,
before the new building was built also at the end of the fifth
century: see S. G. Miller (1995), and Shear's response (1995), and
the earlier discussion of the site in Thompson and Wycherley
(1972: 29–38). On the remarkable incorporation of the cult of
the Phrygian Mother Kybele into the heart of the city and its
business, and her possible connections with earlier more indige-
nous goddesses, see Parker (1996: 188–94). This is the only case we
hear of for the use of this altar as a place of refuge. Slaves, and
others, were more often said to resort to the Theseion, or to the
shrine of the Semnai: see testimonia in Wycherley (1957: 114–19).
Perhaps Pittalakos, asserting that he was not a slave (whether one
belonging to the state or to Hegesandros), deliberately chose a
different, but very central and public, altar; and he appeared
'unclothed' (*gymnos*)—which probably implies here not that he was
completely naked, but that he revealed enough flesh to display his
weals.

A crowd came running up, as always happens. Other
narratives of gratuitous violence and *hybris* often present bystanders as acquaintances of the parties playing important roles in
remonstrating or expressing preparedness to testify; see especially
Humphreys (1985b); Hunter (1994: 138–9); Fisher (1998b: 88–9;
1999: 66–8). Here the version is that the threat of such community
action so alarmed Hegesandros and his friends that they spared
no effort to mollify Pittalakos.

some of their dicing-companions. This detail is meant to
increase the impression of the perpetrators as a co-ordinated gang
of dissolute characters; but if there is anything in it, it could
support the view that a gambling dispute was an important part of
the affair.

61 the whole affair was a drunken brawl (*paroinia*). That
the Greeks had words meaning something like 'be offensively

drunk' (*paroinein*)', 'drunken misbehaviour' (*paroinia*) and that it nearly always indicates drunken fighting, suggests a ready acknowledgement of the pervasiveness of the phenomenon. For the common defence tactic in cases of alleged assault of claiming such brawling was often not serious, see Lys. 3. 43, 4. 19, fr. 17; Dem. 54. 13–22, with Carey & Reid *ad loc.*; D. Cohen (1995: 126–7, 134, 137–8); Fisher (1998b: 75–7), Kapparis, *Neaira* 264.

not yet as unpleasant to look at as he is now. See on **26**, **49** above. This detail both helps the plausibility of the Pittalakos story—that he would fall for this deceit and give up his sanctuary—and serves to keep before the jury the idea that Timarchos really had been remarkably attractive and could turn on the charm when he wished.

touching the fellow on the chin. The gesture of touching the chin may be performed as part of courtship or as indicating affection (see Dover 1978: 93–4), or as part of the formal act of supplication: see Gould (1973), and for such gestures in Greek art, G. Neumann, *Gesten und Gebärden in der griechischen Kunst* (Berlin, 1965), 67–75; here it is likely to be taken as both affectionate, reminding Pittalakos of previous intimacies, and as an act of supplication. Pittalakos is allegedly engaged in an act of supplication by clasping the altar of the goddess, and Timarchos persuades him to give that up by a personal supplication, accompanied by a promise of good treatment.

do anything that might satisfy Pittalakos. Presumably the jury is intended to hear not just the general plea to treat him well, but a sexual offer, to renew his preparedness to accede to any sexual demand (see **54**).

62 The fellow took their *hybris* against him very badly, and brought an action (*dike*). What action did he start? On Aeschines' account he might in some sense have very good grounds for an action of *hybris* (see on **15**), having been savagely whipped as if he were a slave, and having had his livelihood destroyed; even if a public slave, he could be, as Aeschines has emphasized at **17**, considered a victim of legally actionable *hybris*. But, whether he was a (still) public slave, or was now freed and of metic status, he would apparently not have the status to bring a *graphe hybreos* himself (if the text of the law at Dem. 21. 47 is sound, see above on **16**; see MacDowell, *Meidias* 265; Harrison 1968–71:

I, 195, n. 1); this point seems to be missed by Hunter (1994: 242–3). In any case he would certainly not have the public confidence to bring such a serious case against men of political significance. Hence he appears to have started not the public action of the *graphe hybreos*, but a private action, a *dike*, probably for battery (*dike aikeias*), but conceivably for the damage done (*dike blabes*) or forceful acts (*dike biaion*).

Glaukon of Cholargos. (*LGPN* 18; *PA* 3035; *PAA* 277135). Nothing else known of this allegedly decent man; one can of course have no confidence that the name Timaios given for his father is correct.

he sought to bring Pittalakos back into freedom. The procedure used here, called *aphairesis eis eleutherian*, was the remedy to deal with those who, like Hegesandros, claimed an individual was their slave and took him or her forcibly back into ownership; naturally it has to be performed by a third party who challenged the legitimacy of the ownership by himself operating on the principle of self-help and removing the alleged slave 'into freedom'. In most cases, no doubt, the alleged owner resisted and legal process ensued (the rescuer had to provide sureties for the later appearance of the slave). The matter might then be settled at arbitration (or, as here, dropped), or be heard before a jury: the person whose status was under dispute either reverted to slavery, or retained freedom, and if the 'rescuer' were in the wrong he would have to pay a penalty. See also Lys. 23. 9–11; Dem. 58. 19; Harrison (1968–71: I, 178–80); Scafuro (1997: 400–1).

63 handed the matter over for arbitration to Diopeithes of Sounion, a fellow-demesman of Hegesandros. The most famous member of a Sounion family, Diopeithes son of Diphilos of Sounion (*LGPN* 48; *PA* 4327; *PAA* 363675; Hansen, *Inventory* 44, and also Davies, *APF* 167–9), was a member of the Salaminian *genos* who was archon for the branch based at Sounion in 363/3 (Lambert 1997b: Text no. 1, lines 69–70). He was later general in 343/2 to 341/0 continuously, took klerouchs to the Chersonese, and was engaged in anti-Philip activity (see above all Dem. 8). This may well be the man (Schaefer II² 340, n. 5 even surmised that he might also be the 'general' who would speak for Timarchos, see **132–40**). Alternatively (see Lambert 1999: 110–11) the arbitrator and friend of Hegesandros may be another

Diopeithes son of Phasurkides of Sounion (*LGPN* 57; *PAA* 363670, also a member of the Salaminian *genos*, for whom he took an oath in 362/2 (Lambert 1997b: Text no. 1, lines 70–1).

Parties to any dispute might before reaching court try to settle by agreeing to put the matter to one or more private arbitrators; a settlement proposed in private arbitration has been thought to be legally binding on both parties (e.g. Lipsius 1905–15: 220–6; Harrison 1968–71: II, 64–66), but Scafuro has given reasons for questioning this belief, at least for the fourth century (1997: 119–27, see also 393–9). In certain private cases, heard before the Forty, recourse to a non-binding hearing before public arbitrators (who were citizens aged 60) was required before a case came to court: see Arist. *Ath. Pol.* 53, and Rhodes *ad loc.*, Hunter (1994: 55–67); Ferguson (1938: 48–9); Scafuro (1997: 383–92); and Allen (2000: 317). The language here strongly suggests that this was a case of private arbitration, agreed to by both parties; contrast the language of a public arbitration at Dem. 21. 83, where the official term *diaitetes* is used; further, if this Diopeithes is the man who was an active general of the late 340s, he can scarcely have been 60 in about 360. The question then arises, if there is any truth in this account, why Pittalakos should be supposed to have agreed to an arbitrator who was a fellow demesman, and alleged former lover, of Hegesandros (and a member of the same *genos*). The jury may be supposed to imagine both that Pittalakos was extremely naïve, and perhaps also that Diopeithes was known to him as a fellow gambler. Parties seem to have been expected to select as private arbitrators those known and friendly to both sides (see Humphreys 1985b; Hunter 1994: 59–60; Scafuro 1997: 131–5). If in fact, the activities of the *genos* of the Salaminioi were somehow involved in the affair (see the Appendix), it may make more sense that they agreed on another member of the *genos*, whether it was the Diopeithes the son of Diphilos or the son of Phrasurkides. For the arbitration for the whole affairs of the *genos* recorded in the Salaminioi inscription, they apparently avoided arbitrators from the *genos* (Lambert 1999: 115–16); but for a more personal dispute they may have preferred to keep it within the *genos*.

but kept putting it off time after time, to do a favour to these men. Delays and manipulations of these procedures are alleged in other arbitrations; for overall assessments of the successes and failures of private arbitration in the Athenian system, cf. Hunter (1994: 55–61); Scafuro (1997: 393–9). Whether Diopeithes did in fact simply put things off, or perhaps even found for Hegesandros, may be questioned.

64 his war with Aristophon of Azenia Aristophon (*LGPN* 19; *PA* 2108; *PAA* 176170; Hansen, *Inventory* 37–8; and also Davies, *APF* 65) was a senior and experienced politician (cf. the comments of Dem. 19. 297; Hyper. *Eux.* 28; Aesch. 3. 138–9, 194). He was born in the 430s, and his career began with his opposition to the Thirty, for which he was awarded immunity from festival liturgies (Dem. 20. 148), and continued until his death, at nearly 100, between 340/39 and 330 (*scholia* to this passage). No specific activity is in fact attested between *c.* 403/2 and the mid-360s, but see Whitehead (1986b), for a justified corrective to the assumption (found e.g. in Oost 1977), that Aristophon's career was dormant between these years. He was a general in 363/2, and perhaps earlier, an ambassador to Thebes (Aesch. 3. 139), see Trevett (1999: 188), and was especially active in proposing measures (see the list in Hansen 1984: 161–2) and in political trials; Aeschines' claim that he boasted of having defended himself successfully in seventy-five cases of having proposed illegal measures (the *graphe paranomon*) is no doubt a gross exaggeration (see Oost 1977; Whitehead 1986b; Worthington 264), but it does at the least attest to exceptional activity in making proposals, and a reputation for effective defences of his views. As well as the threatened prosecution of Hegesandros alleged here, he is said to have brought impeachments (*eisangeliai*) against four or five other politicians and been a defendant in at least one (Hyper. *Eux.* 28, *fr.* 17 Jensen, and see Hansen 1984: 161–2). Some time before 348 he apparently expressed opposition to Euboulos over the issues of making peace with Philip, and may have been initially prosecuted by him for the failure to produce the crowns he had undertaken to produce (Dem. 21. 218 and *scholia*). The evidence demonstrates that by 361/0, probably earlier, and certainly over the next few decades, he was among the most influential and successful of politicians.

His mention here makes two points. First, it emphasizes Hegesandros' and Hegesippos' political importance, that they were engaged in a major political conflict with this man, and thus helps to explain Pittalakos' decision to give up his fight. It also enables him to bring in a further piece of old gossip, which may have produced at least a threat in the courts from a fairly respected politician, that Aristophon had alleged the same form of unacceptable relationship existed between Hegesandros and Leodamas as between Timarchos and his lovers (see also **111** below, and on Aristophon, his later mention at **165** below).

the same formal pronouncement in the assembly (*epangelia*). On the formal language of laying this charge, see on **2**. On the evidence of such threats, see on **135** below.

his brother Hair-bun (*Krobylos*). Hegesippos (see also on **54–71**), the more important brother, and at the time of the trial and subsequently a strong and vigorous ally of Demosthenes in the attempt to undermine the Peace of Philokrates, is referred to in this speech only by his nickname. This seems to derive from the adoption of a style of keeping his hair long and tying it in a bun at the back with an elaborate clasp. As the *scholia* note, this type of male adornment was designated by Thucydides an archaic fashion characteristic of the luxury of the old Athenian nobility (1. 6). On the one hand, Hegesippos may have been trying to present an image of an old-fashioned dignity, perhaps appropriate to a leading member of the Salaminian *genos* (cf. Lambert 1999: 111). On the other, his opponents who relished using the nickname were presumably conveying rather the ideas of an old-fashioned élitism and contempt for ordinary people, combined with ostentatious luxury and decadence. The fact that Aeschines clearly felt it useful to refer to Timarchos' old friend, and one of his current major political opponents, only in this way suggests strongly that the hair-style could carry powerful negative associations. The *scholia* on **71** suggest that Hegesippos was the subject of jokes in comedy for being 'shameful in appearance' (possibly a reference to the hairstyle, but perhaps a suggestion that his body was flabby and debauched like that of Timarchos); and also because he had made errors in relation to the Phokians. His political career, passionately anti-Macedonian and long associated with Demosthenes, is attested both in inscriptions and in the literary texts. In particular he proposed in the 340s a decree concerned with Euboia (*IG* II² 125 = Tod II 154 = Harding no. 66, see on **113** below), and in 337, one offering honours for loyal Akarnanians (*IG* II² 237 = Tod II 178). He also appears in the list of twenty-three Athenians (inscribed on naval accounts of 334/3, *IG* II² 1623 l. 185–6) who guaranteed in spring 340 to undertake responsibility for triremes which were to be lent to Chalkis, Athens' recent ally and organizer of an anti-Philip alliance (see Aesch. 3. 91–4; Philochorus, *FGH* 328 F 159–61, [Plut.] *Mor* 849f.). The money was recovered from fifteen of these guarantors or their heirs in 325/4, including Hegesippos, *IG* II² 1629, l. 543: see F.W Mitchel, 'Derkylos of Hagnous and the Date of *IG* II², 1187', *Hesperia* 33 (1964), 337–41; Brunt (1969: 255–65), Hammond and Griffith (1979: 545–54); L. Migeotte, 'Souscriptions athéniennes de la période classique, *Historia* 32 (1983), 142–4 and *L'Emprunt public dans les Cités grecques* (Québec/Paris, 1984), no. 69; Gabrielsen (1994: 203–6). Other well-known Athenians who contributed included Demosthenes, Demades, Proxenos the son of Harmodios (and descendant of the tyrannicide), Phaidros, son of Kallias of Sphettos (see on **43**), and Kriton (see on **157**). We probably have a speech written by Hegesippos, as the Demosthenic speech 7 (*On Halonnesos*) was almost certainly his work: it gives a good impression of a vigorous and belligerent style in support of a very strong anti-Philip line; there also survives a smart quip of his, quoted in Plutarch's *Life of Demosthenes* 17.

65 Which of you has ever gone to the fish-stalls (*to opson*) and not witnessed the expenditures of these men? For the social and political importance of rich men monopolizing the supplies of fresh fish and arrogantly displaying their conspicuous wealth, see on **41** and **42**.

Which of you, chancing on their street-revels (*komoi*) and fights, did not feel outraged? On the prevalence of drunken fighting in Athens, especially over *hetairai*, girl-pipers or boys, see on **61** and **134–5**. Aeschines here asserts that the fights the brothers and Timarchos got into were serious and extremely offensive, and hopes that the jury will accept that this was common knowledge; at **134–6** he will naturally claim that his erotic fights were not serious, whereas those of Timarchos were.

66 Testimonies. Most of the material here is taken from the speech, and there can be no confidence in the details which do not appear there, such as the name of Glaukon's father, and the alleged additional witness, Amphisthenes. The last words of this notice 'and the rest' suggest the compiler is becoming a little bored with his invention; it may not be coincidence that the next testimony is the last document preserved in our manuscripts of the texts of Aeschines (see Intro. p. 68)

67 testimony that is more decent than fits him, but is a little more explicit than the one I wrote for Misgolas. The word for 'decent', *kosmios* recalls the *kosmos*, the 'good order' that is a major motif of the speech: see on **8**; the testimony written presumably mentioned relationships of *hetairesis*, but preserved the decorum of language normally preserved in the courts (see on **38**).

I am not unaware. Aeschines no doubt knew very well that Hegesandros would be present, along with his brother, and would deny any testimony put to him. The political links between Timarchos, Demosthenes, and the two brothers were close, united in their attempts to undermine the peace. Hegesippos is probably included among those of Demosthenes' partners whom Aeschines accused of resisting sending a force to help Philip immediately after the peace was made (2. 137; cf. Dem. 19. 72–3, with *scholia*: Schaefer 1885–7[2]: II, 276–7), and his subsequent role is well known (see esp. his own speech *On Halonnesos*, Ps. Dem. 7). It is equally likely that Timarchos and the brothers retained a close friendship and shared social interests, whether or not they had ever shared sexual relations (see Davidson 1997: 268–77). It is therefore important to Aeschines' case to blacken in advance the reputation of both the brothers, to prevent Hegesippos, the more influential figure, from being able to aid Timarchos by his support. Since Aeschines could be confident that Hegesandros would deny any statement put to him, he could include more precise indications of the sexual relationships. When Hegesandros then felt forced to deny on oath such assertions of relationship between him and Timarchos, as well as the previous relationships with Leodamas and Diopeithes, his general credibility would be diminished among those of the jury who were tempted not to believe the denial; thus, Aeschines hoped, the brothers' support for Timarchos would be tainted. Later, much more of the speech of course will be devoted to undermining Demosthenes' credibility.

men who despise the gods, have contempt for the laws. Aeschines thus suggests that those jurors who do not believe Hegesandros' denial on oath of the truth of testimony offered him will conclude that he exhibits the same shamelessness and contempt for the gods, the laws, and the democratic system which has already been asserted for Timarchos, and that this contempt is related to their habituation to sexual relationships which equally outrage decent Athenians.

68 Testimony An alleged document in which, again, the compiler makes a bizarre mistake, giving an incorrect name for the father of Hegesandros, Diphilos, not Hegesias. It is odd, but probably not significant, that the name Diphilos is that of the father and of the son of Diopeithes the arbitrator, and allegedly friend and ex-lover of Hegesandros (see on **63**); this seems more likely to be a guess, rather than a confused memory of the connection between the two (though see Lambert 1999: 111, n. 8). It does nothing to increase confidence in the information here that while there are variant readings in the manuscripts for Hegesandros' demotic (*steirious/speirieus/peirieus*), the manuscript reading is much more likely to have been Steirieus, or even Peiraieus, than Hegesandros' actual demotic, Sounieus, from Sounion.

Leodamas. Again Aeschines relies heavily on existing gossip linking Leodamas' and Hegesandros' names together. Leodamas, son of Erasistratos of Acharnai (*LGPN* 3; *PA* 9077; Develin *AO* no. 1781; Hansen, *Inventory* 53) was a substantial rhetor and politician, presumably, like Diopeithes, a little older than Hegesandros. His name (relatively rare in Athens) and deme Acharnai suggest plausible links with a number of other prominent men (see Davies, *APF* 521–4). One is Phaiax of Acharnae (*LGPN* 1; *PA* 13921; Develin, *AO* no. 2297: his deme is provided by three of his surviving *ostraka*—Lang 1990: nos. 653–6); of noble descent (Plut. *Alk.* 13. 1) in about 416 he was a candidate for the last ever ostracism, of Hyperbolos (see, e.g. Rhodes 1994); another was a Leodamas who was denied an archonship in 382 on grounds of involvement with the Thirty (Lys. 26. 13; cf. Arist. *Rhet.* 1400a30–2; Sealey 1993: 17), as he may have been distantly related to Erasistratos, one of the Thirty (Xen. *Hell.* 2. 3. 2). The Leodamas cited here was allegedly a pupil of Isocrates (Ps. Plut. *Mor.* 837 d), a frequent ambassador to Thebes (Aesch. 3. 138–9; see Trevett 1999: 186–7), and a determined opponent of the general Chabrias. He opposed the proposal to honour Chabrias after the battle of Naxos in 376, and again spoke against his son Ktesippos in the prosecution of Leptines' law *c.* 355 (Dem. 20. 146). In 366 or 365 he, with

Aristophon of Azenia (though he was to be 'at war' with Hegesandros a little later, **64**) led the prosecution of Chabrias and Kallistratos over the loss of Oropos (Diog. Laert. 3. 23–4; Ar. *Rhet.* 1364a19–23; MacDowell, *Meidias* 284–5; Roberts 1982: 70–3; Sealey 1993: 72–3, 87). According to Diogenes Laertius, Hegesippos (referred to as 'Krobylos the sycophant') was involved behind the scenes too, as he had tried unsuccessfully to dissuade Plato from speaking for Chabrias, threatening him with the same hemlock Sokrates had drunk; this anecdote thus portrays Hegesippos working in a supporting role to Leodamas and Aristophon, and also as something of an aggressive bully. Lambert (1999: 112) suggests an existing association between Plato and the family, pointing to a Hegias listed among the executors of Plato's will, Diog. Laert. 3. 42; but the anecdote seems to imply more of a hostile approach.

Leodamas' brother Euaion, it seems, exercised a violent streak, when he killed his friend Boiotos (probably the uncle of the other Boiotos, see on **40**) in retaliation in a fight at a party *c.* 348 and was convicted by just one vote (Dem. 21. 71–2; see on this Carawan 1998: 308–10). There is a possibility that Leodamas too was a member of the *genos* of the Salaminians; the main reason (but not a decisive one) is that the name Phaiax recurs in the family (Leodamas' son was also a Phaiax) and the mythical hero Phaiax was offered cult by the *genos* (Lambert 1997: Text 1, line 91); subsidiary arguments are drawn from Leodamas' associations with other members of the *genos*: see Lambert (1999: 118).

69 as a fine and good man (*kalos kagathos*) and a man who hates the bad. We have here probably rather ambiguous language. *Kalos kagathos* might be used by Hegesandros of himself, to mean an upstanding and decent gentleman, with a hint of the idea of a traditional member of Athens' élite (perhaps appropriate for a member of the Salaminioi); but the term can have a critical edge in a law court speech, and does so here (unlike, I suspect, the other uses of the term *kalos kagathos*, see on **32**, **41**, **134**): see E. M. Burke, 'The looting of the Estate of Demosthenes the Elder', *C&M* 49 (1997), 58, citing also Lys. 12. 86; Andoc. 1. 133; Dem. 19. 110, 22. 32, 47, 24. 92; and also Bourriot (1995: 441–2). The other term, 'hates the bad' (*misoponeros*) might mean, favourably, hating both bad actions and evil men, or more sinisterly perhaps, 'despising those he considers bad', i.e. showing contempt for one's social inferiors (cf. also Dem. 21. 204, 209–12).

who Leodamas is, the man at whose name you gave a shout when the testimony was being read out. The self-righteous defence of his innocence which Aeschines imagines Hegesandros might put up deliberately reaches absurdity with the idea that he might claim not to know Leodamas at all. Aeschines claims support from an instantly hostile audience reaction; one cannot know whether he really achieved some form of response, or if so how far it was orchestrated by his support among the observers; see generally Bers (1985).

70 more explicitly than my own nature inclines me. As ever, Aeschines prefers to insinuate 'unspeakable' depravities, rather than name practices unambiguously—the repeated use of the 'prostitute' words (*porneuesthai* and *pornos*) and the same words again for disgusting and violently drunken misbehaviour (*bdeluria* and *paroinia*) seem to be the excuse for this claim. His rhetoric becomes more intense (appeals to gods, indignant questions to the jury); and his attacks calculatedly put Hegesandros on the same level. Hegesandros is alleged have been a *pornos* too, though all that has been asserted (with no witnesses) is two relationships of *hetairesis*. The jingle 'prostituted himself with the prostitute' emphasizes their moral equivalence; and in this sentence the outrage is directly more decisively on the nature of the acts a *pornos* must commit rather than the numbers of partners he may have. Further, the jury is asked to use their imagination, to envisage 'excesses of repulsiveness' of the two together, drunk and alone. This of course might reveal, to any who stopped to think, the basic problem with the whole process, the fact that no one else knows what two people get up to on their own (see Intro. pp. 43–4, 49–51). Two incompatible ways of conceiving Hegesandros' mentality seem involved here. On the one hand, like Timarchos, he is totally lacking any shame, and is prepared to do anything; on the other he retains a sense of having been humiliated by what Leodamas made him do, and determined (like an ex-slave who has become a slave-owner, cf. Dem. 24. 124) to do even worse to his paid boy.

71–93 *The absence of direct witnesses*

71–2 the man himself and his brother Hair-Bun energetically and rhetorically come leaping up onto the stand. The language gives the impression of the vigour and aggression of the brothers' style, which the narrative has emphasized (the 'force' with which they treated Pittalakos), and is also to some extent reinforced by our other evidence at least for Hegesippos (see on **64**); it may also recall Timarchos' energetic self-display (**26**). On issues of the moral construction of deportment and gesture, see Bremmer (1991), Hall (1995: 53).

71 they will demand of me. This, one might suppose, was a reasonable set of requests. In order to discredit it, Aeschines has carefully introduced it just after a ferocious denunciation of the repulsive shared sexual practices of the pair. He then responds with a wholly misleading claim that a hire-agreement for such a purpose between Athenian adults was in itself illegal and could entail the death penalty, and that it would not be expected, therefore, that Hegesandros would admit to anything. He appeals to laws cited earlier (**13–17**), but see notes there, Intro. pp. 36–7, and Dover 1978: 26–7.

72 I do not, after all, suppose that you are so forgetful. It is quite frequent for orators to suppose that deceitful opponents might think the Athenians in the assembly or on a jury to be astonishingly forgetful, but that this is not in fact the case (e.g. Lys. 12. 87, 26. 1; Aesch. 3. 221; Ps. Dem. = Hegesippos 7. 19). This is a more forceful, almost bullying, version, in the form of a direct address to the jury—'You surely are not so forgetful as to have forgotten that . . .' The reason is presumably that Aeschines is engaged in an especially shameless and important deception, and spares no effort in persuading the jury not to question his illicit statement of what was illegal. This false claim will be repeated: see on **87, 98, 160–3**.

or if any one hires himself out. i.e. Timarchos; but he would only be liable to charges if he went into active politics (**19–20**)

What man is so foolhardy. The adjective *talaiporos* usually means 'distressed', 'full of cares or hardships'; here it seems to indicate a man who is prepared to bring extra hardships down on himself.

73 the man who endured the acts to admit what happened. It would be equally unlikely for Timarchos to admit to anything, as that would be to admit his guilt in this very trial. Aeschines is in effect compelled to admit that he expects a conviction without having any one prepared to bear witness to the nature of the relationships which involved Timarchos; so he attempts to mask the admission by an appeal to a different god, Poseidon this time, and, as he does repeatedly, by an appeal to the common knowledge of the Athenians, and by a claim of the threat to the whole idea of the city's government. This seems in fact to be the only instance of an oath by Poseidon in the orators, though 'by Poseidon' is found very frequently in Attic comedy. It is difficult to see either why it is generally not found in the courts, or why it is used here. Conceivably Poseidon, who competed with Athena for the title of chief protector of Athens, and had a prominent share in the Erechtheion, the second temple on the Acropolis, seemed appropriate for an appeal to the principles of the city's management. For other oaths by Herakles, Dionysos, and Zeus, see on **49, 52,** and **55**

74 those men over there, sitting in those little huts (*oikemata*). Presumably Aeschines pointed to some houses visible from the court, known to be places where male prostitutes plied their trade. Where exactly in the *agora* this case would have been heard is not certain (see recently Hansen 1991: 191, Boegehold 1995: *passim*). Possible locations for the so-called Heliaia, where many important trials with large juries were held (testimonia collected in Boegehold 1995: nos. 96–138), include the large rectangular building (currently labelled Heliaia) towards the SW corner of the agora next to the fountain house (but see Stroud 1999: 85 who with the aid of a new inscription identifies this building as the *Aiakeion*, the shrine of Aiakos, where grain was stored, to be sold nearby in the *agora*); the largest of various buildings 'Building A', where dikastic equipment has been found, now submerged under the Stoa of Attalos on the NE side of the *agora*; or the stone benches on the West side, under the Hephaisteion. Housing has been excavated along the south slopes of the

Areopagos running down to the *agora*, along the road and drain leading to the SW away from the rectangular building, and (most notoriously perhaps, and easy to point at from the benches) the Kerameikos area, past the Dipylon and Sacred Gates to the NW. This was a known prostitutes' haunt, and is the site of the most plausible female brothel so far excavated (building Z[c] of the Kerameikos excavations: see Knigge 1991: 88–95, and below on **124**).

sitting in their little huts (*oikemata*). The word *oikema* can mean 'dwelling house' (like the more usual *oikia*) but it can also designate a magistrates' office, a prison building, or a hut, stall, or room; but the use here, for a small house or room used for prostitution, male and female, is frequent (cf. e.g Dein. 1. 23; Hdt. 2. 121, 126). The overall impression here, which fits such other literary evidence as we have for male prostitution, is of small individual huts or cubicles; see Davidson (1997: 90–1) and on **124**. On 'sitting' as the term often applied to prostitutes who work in a brothel or hut, as opposed to those who walk the streets, see on **124**, Ps. Dem. 59. 67 and Kapparis, *Neaira* 312; Isaeus 6. 19; Dein. 1. 23.

brought by necessity to this. The implication is that 'normal' (e.g. tax-paying, see **119**) male prostitutes work solely from economic necessity, and are ashamed of their profession, but everyone knows what they are doing. Male prostitution was no doubt a common activity, involving both slaves and the free poor. In most ancient Greek societies, where, for all the extensive local variations, probably a very high proportion of free males had some form of homosexual sex in their youth, it seems likely that occasional recourse to a male (boy or youth) prostitute remained a not uncommon option for many in later life, whether or not they pursued free youths in the *gymnasia* (cf. Halperin 1990: 91–2, Intro. pp. 34–6). Aeschines' gesticulation towards the images of those operating at the cheaper end of the market both degrades Timarchos by association of his acts with theirs and effectively contrasts their performance of the acts of shame, covered by what little decency they can muster, with Timarchos' voluntary and shameless behaviour.

75 when a youth, still quite young. Here, describing Timarchos at the start of his sexual career when responsible for his actions, Aeschines qualifies the usual 'youth' (*meirakion*) with another word for 'young' (*neos*), to emphasize his boldness, at the very start of his manhood, in settling in with his lovers and spending all the time in their houses.

spends his nights in other men's houses . . . enjoys expensive dinners without making any contribution to them. This doubtful parallel between confessed prostitutes in their cubicles and Timarchos' lifestyle is here extended, in a crucial argument from 'probability'. Aeschines was not alone in arguing in this way. Athenaeus (572c–d) quotes two passages from comedy describing the behaviour of certain boys with their lovers at dinner, from the perspective of other diners (Athenaeus uses an apparent coinage of his own for such a character, *philosopho-meirakiskos*, a lad fond of learning, or of philosophers, and the counterpart of the orderly or apparently decent *hetaira*). The first (Alexis, *Sleep* 244 K–A—also attributed to Antiphanes) suggests that such a 'rent-boy' (*pornos*) would avoid eating leeks when dining 'with us', to avoid offending his lover when kissing him. The second (Ephippos, 20 K–A) leads Athenaeus to comment that Aeschines 'says the same thing in his Timarchos speech'. The Ephippos passage, from his *Sappho*, is indeed close:

> When a young man,
> going out, learns to eat another man's fish (*opson*),
> and puts a hand to the food that pays no share (*asymbolon*),
> you must believe he pays his reckoning in the night.

The text of the second line is corrupt. One change, as translated above, is to emend 'going in' to 'going out'. A more radical emendation (by Kaibel, accepted in the Loeb edition), which might seem to bring the wording closer to Aeschines', would read 'going in to another's house without being seen'. But the reference to 'escorts' consumption of expensive fish (*opson*) is also highly appropriate and has its counterpart elsewhere in Aeschines' denunciation (see on **42**) and many other comic passages (cf. Davidson 1993: 62–5), and may well be right. Both passages also insist that the young men 'pay no contribution': *symbola* in the contexts of commensality are the equal contributions all guests should make to shared dinners (*deipnoi apo symbolon*), and those who never paid their share, in this form, or by reciprocating hospitality in their own houses, were held to be supplying other, more shameful services, either as toadies or parasites, or as sexual objects. See generally Nesselrath (1990: 309–17); Arnott, *Alexis* 22–3, 336–45; Davidson (1997: 270–3).

The wording and ideas are close enough for the possibility of direct influence of one to the other to be suspected; including a reticence in the last line which even in Middle Comedy was not absolutely necessary, though it is much less routinely or joyously obscene than Old Comedy. Our dates for Ephippos' plays easily allow this to be written before or after the trial in 346/5 (he appears on the catalogue of comic victors, *IG* II² 2325 line 145, sixth in a list which begins *c.* 378/7, and some plays can be dated to the 360s or later (Koerte in *RE* V 2; Nesselrath 1990: 196–7)), but he could equally well be still composing immediately after this speech, and taking a line from it (see on 41, on comic references to Misgolas). On the other hand, suspicion of boys often seen dining with their lovers was no doubt common (see Intro. pp. 50–1), as Aeschines was relying on, and the similarity of wording may simply reflect this common pattern of gossip. A very similar argument is reported by Aulus Gellius from Scipio Aemilianus' invective against Publius Sulpicius Gallus, from a speech of 142 BC (6. 12. 5), see Corbeill (1997: 109–10), and Williams (1999: 23, 129). Romans engaged in the intense second-century debates over the 'Hellenization' and possible corruption of Roman social and political life will have read the Attic orators and some Middle and New Comedy, as well as watched the Roman adaptations of the latter on their stages.

76 *some* pleasures. Aeschines is here playing with the jury, tantalizing, but deliberately not satisfying their interest in whether he is going to be more specific. One imagines there was a heavy emphasis on the **some** (*tinas*).

by Olympian Zeus, to know in what other more euphemistic way. We find again here the unusually solemn oath, used to indicate the effort needed to keep his words reasonably pure in this setting, and to justify his refusal actually to be explicit: see on **55**.

77 scrutiny on the citizen lists. A general revision of the lists of citizens, called a *diapsephisis*, might be decreed by the people on special occasions. The revision was held in each deme (the *lexi-archikon grammateion*, see above on **19**) and was ordered by the people in 346/5, on the proposal of Demophilos; the archon date was also given by Harpokration s.v. *diapsephisis*, quoting Androtion (*FGH* 324F52) and Philochoros (*FGH* 328F52). Demophilos the proposer (*LGPN* 14; *PA* 3664; *PAA* 320855; Develin, *AO* no. 775; Hansen, *Inventory* 43) is not obviously to be identified with any of the many other men called Demophilos in this period. To judge from his other activity (see **87**) this Demophilos liked to appear as a rigorous defender of democratic procedures against corruption. It may be another indication of a changing public mood that these tough 'clean-up' measures are proposed and implemented: see Intro. p. 62. On the time these procedures took and the implications for the date of the trial, see Intro. pp. 6–8.

Now whenever I am present in the court and I hear the disputants pleading. Courts were regularly surrounded by a circle of spectators (the larger in the more public or famous trials), and one may well suspect that politicians, legal and rhetoric experts, and friends or enemies of the litigants were especially well represented (see on **117**, **175** below, Lys. 27. 7, Plut. *Dem.* 5. 2; Lanni 1997: 187). Aeschines will no doubt have taken care to increase the impact of his arguments that 'all Athenians' knew of Timarchos' reputation and nickname by planting supporters among the onlookers to create a 'hubbub' (*thorubos*) at the right moments (see also on **69**, **159**, Bers 1985; Hall 1995).

the same argument carries weight with you. This is a particularly disreputable argument, even by the standards of this speech. One of the obvious dangers of Demophilos' procedure of revision of the deme lists was that, in cases where it was argued that people had been admitted onto lists because of bribery or political partiality with influential members of a deme (cf. the alleged goings-on at Halimous described in Dem. 57), they might either be confirmed by the influence of the same members, or rejected, rightly or wrongly, by a different, hostile, group achieving a vote through numbers, intimidation, or manipulation of procedure at the deme-assembly meeting that went through the list. The safeguard against this second result was the appeal to a jury-court. But if the court is going to accept the word of the deme-prosecutor, unsupported by any witnesses (as Aeschines claims he saw happen regularly, and approves) the safeguard evaporates. Aeschines' later allegation of serious malpractice in Kydathenaion which was aided by Timarchos (**114–15**) makes his use of this argument here all the worse.

79 if, as on the issue of birth, so on the issue of this style of life. Again, Aeschines applies his dubious parallel, to appeal to the supposed general knowledge of Timarchos' career, and so to reach a verdict in effect by relying on existing prejudice and gossip, bypassing any need to provide further evidence. This time the appeal is to an alleged recent occasion when the assembly could not prevent itself laughing at Timarchos' known reputation as a 'prostitute'.

   The hollow ballot . . . This is the earliest evidence for the sophisticated system of balloting in the law courts, which is fully described in Arist. *Ath. Pol.* 68–9. Each juror was assigned two bronze ballots, one of which was pierced through its middle, and the other solid; the pierced one indicated a vote for the prosecutor, and the solid one for the defence. Each juror, when called to vote, placed the vote he wished to count in a large bronze jar and the invalid one into a wooden jar, keeping it secret from observers which ballot was which. On the surviving ballots, see Boegehold (1995: 82–6), and for all the literary testimony, *id.* (209–22).

80 mounted the rostrum in the Assembly. The manuscripts include the words 'the Council (*boule*)' before 'when he was on the Council', which is not grammatical. The easiest correction of the sentence is, as suggested by Baiter and Sauppe, and accepted by Dilts, to delete the words 'the *boule*'. The sentence will then refer to speeches made by Timarchos in the assembly, in his position as a member of the *boule* in the year 347/6; Aeschines here, as often in law-court speeches, treats the responses of the assembly to his speeches to be the settled verdict of 'you' on Timarchos' character, thus identifying for practical purposes any Athenian jury with the Athenians present in any assembly, as both adequately representing the people as a whole. See below, **173**, where the jury is identified with a jury of fifty years earlier. On the other hand the alternative decision, to distinguish assembly from jury, is taken only a very little later; see on **85**, where the assembly as a possible witness is distinguished from the jury. At all events it is not likely (as Davidson 1997: 79, 262 seems to suppose) that Aeschines is alluding to Timarchos' 'lecturing the Committee' or 'making speeches in the Council'.

Timarchos was presumably discussing issues of defence (*walls, towers*, etc.), perhaps with a view to a possible war with Philip, possibly also recommending arrests of suspected traitors (cf. Dem. 19. 285–6, and see Intro. p. 21 and on **26**). According to Aeschines, all the assembly could attend to was the sexual innuendo. The double entendres here focus on the tendency for cheap prostitutes to hang around the more deserted areas near the walls or towers on the outskirts of the city, as they did around cemeteries, and on the idea of people being 'taken off somewhere' for sexual purposes. The assumption was that Timarchos knew too much about such places and activities. Athen. 604d–e records an anec- dote of how the tragedian Sophocles had a quick sexual encounter with a pretty boy under cover of his cloak, by the city wall, but the boy made off with the cloak: see also Halperin (1990: 91–2; Davidson 1997: 79, 307–8). The strategy, conceivably an effective one, was to suggest that that the people have already given a decisive verdict against Timarchos by their natural tendency to see unintended double entendres in Timarchos' mouth, or in those of others mentioning him. There is also the clear implica- tion that because of his past (and regardless of his actual record as a politician) it is impossible for him to be taken seriously as a politician. His voice, trying to discuss vital issues of policy, was drowned out by the laughter. On this effect of 'silencing' Timarchos, see Davidson (1997: 262–3, 306–7).

when he was on the council last year. In 347/6. See Intro. pp. 4, 21.

81 in the very assembly-meeting at which I proclaimed this legal process against Timarchos (*epangelia*). On the timing of this meeting and of the laying of the charge, see Intro. pp. 5–6 and on **26** and **32**. It was probably right at the end of the conciliar year 347/6, towards the end of the last month, Skirophorion, when Demosthenes and Timarchos had just launched the prosecution against Aeschines; the Areopagos was presumably responding to a proposal which Timarchos had fostered when still on the Council.

When the Council of the Areopagos. The Areopagos, which had lost most of its early wide-ranging political powers in the democratic reforms of 462–450, was from the middle of the fourth century onwards becoming increasingly involved in a variety of contemporary issues, investigating cases with religious or moral implications, or expressing its concern at the rise of Philip's powers in Greece. On the complex issues involved here, see Ostwald (1955); Wallace (1985: 108–21, 174–84); de Bruyn (1995: 111–64); and Intro. pp. 64–5.

the decree . . . about the dwelling-houses on the Pnyx. On this passage see Wallace (1985: 120), also de Bruyn (1995: 147–8). Wallace denies, probably rightly, that the Areopagos had a specific role concerned with building regulations (rather the province of the *astynomoi*—Arist. *Ath. Pol.* 50. 2). Timarchos, as a member of the *boule*, had apparently made a proposal in the assembly in a debate on buildings and space in the Pnyx area; the Areopagites were consulted, and then sent representatives to explain their opposition to it. Aeschines, unfortunately, is not interested in reminding or informing the jury of the actual proposal and the issues of disagreement between the *boule* (represented by Timarchos) and the Areopagos (represented by the dignified, if faintly absurd, Autolykos); he only wishes to remind them of the alleged amusement at the double entendres which allegedly convulsed the assembly at the association of Timarchos and the lonely places on the Pnyx. So, from his account, we can glean only that specific proposals concerned areas around the Pnyx itself: unbuilt-up, secluded areas (*eremiai*), deserted house-sites, cisterns, all places of inactivity or seclusion. In fact some reasonably substantial houses have been excavated both near the entrances to the Pnyx, and between the Pnyx and the Hill of the Nymphs: see H. Lauter-Bufe and H. Lauter, 'Wohnhaüser und Stadtsviertel des klassischen Athen', *Ath. Mitt.* 85 (1971), 109–24, and Ellis Jones (1975: 63–136). The area under discussion may have been not exactly where the excavations took place, or conceivably parts of those areas may have become less fashionable and rather disreputable by the 340s. It may then be that this was a relatively small-scale tidying-up programme of what may have appeared unsatisfactorily neglected or even shady and disreputable areas close to the heart of the city's decision-making processes; in which case the involvement of the Areopagos is a little hard to understand (see Wallace 1985: 120, 194 and n. 48, who suggests they get involved perhaps because they saw it as a 'moral matter').

But the proposals may well have been more radical. It is now certain that the major rebuilding that produced the considerably enlarged Pnyx of Phase III is best placed in the later fourth century, probably in the 330s (see S. I. Rotroff and J. K. Camp, 'The date of the Third Period of the Pnyx', *Hesperia* 65 (1996), 263–94, and also Hansen 1996b: 23–33). H. A. Thompson (1982: 145, n. 40) had already suggested that the debate recalled by Aeschines might be concerned with the initial stages of what was to become this major programme, perhaps concerned with the buying up of private properties and sites which in any case needed attention, and that the original plan for a new Pnyx came from Euboulos rather than Lycurgus. Hansen modified that picture to the extent that the evidence of the fourth-century pottery found in the fill suggested the actual building was after all Lycurgan; but it would not be surprising if a proposal first under discussion towards the end of 347/6 was seriously delayed in the next few years, and only completed in the 330s, along with so much else in the rebuilding and reinventing of Athens. Major thinking about the reorganization of the Pnyx may then have begun at this period. If so, it is especially noteworthy that the Areopagos evidently chose to express its opposition to one precise proposal, and presumably claimed to view it as a matter of general concern to the 'constitution' or the 'image' of the city. Hence it may be a further example of a changing atmosphere in Athens towards the city's identity and its sense of its past (see also Intro. p. 64). The only other clue to Timarchos' proposal is the double entendre of 'little expense', which suggests Timarchos' proposal was for only moderate rebuilding on this enterprise.

dwelling-houses (*oikeseis*). This is explained by the *scholia* as indicating that there were some deserted and fallen-down dwellings on the Pnyx. Davidson (1997: 306–7) suggests this variant on the many words for house or building is a revealing term in this context, as he suggests it often carries associations of temporary or pre-urban types of settlement, of shabby or of primitive dwellings, but this conclusion seems unsafe. Elsewhere in this speech (**123–4**), in Isocrates (*Areop.* 52), and many times in Aristotle's *Politics* (e.g. 1330b1–1331b14), it appears as a general term for dwellings or buildings of all types including large town houses, dwellings for the gods, and workshops

member of the Areopagos . . . Autolykos. Ironically, this is very likely to be the same Autolykos the Areopagite of Thorikos (*LGPN* 2; *PA* 2746; *PAA* 239810; Develin, *AO* no. 520; Hansen, *Inventory*, 39) who was prosecuted after Chaeronea by Lycurgus, and condemned, probably to death, on a charge of 'cowardice', because he sent his wife and children away (he did not apparently flee himself, as Ostwald 1955: 127), probably by the *eisangelia* procedure (Lyc. 1. 53; Ps. Plut. *Mor.* 843d; Harpokr. s.v. *Autolykos*; Hansen 1975: 104; de Bruyn 1995: 152–3). He could well have been the Autolykos (*LGPN* 3; *PAA* 239805) who in 368/7 proposed an amendment to a decree honouring Mytilenaeans and the Athenian ambassadors to Lesbos, naming himself and two colleagues as the honorands (*IG* II² 107). The Areopagite is not likely to be the Autolykos of Thorikos (*LGPN* 11; *PAA* 239830; Develin, *AO* no. 521) who was honoured for his *philotimia* as *kosmetes* of the ephebes in 334/3 (*SEG* 23. 78; Reinmuth 1971: no. 1—for the demonstration of the date of the decree, and the plausible suggestion that this man was the grandson of Autolykos the son of Lykon, see, against Reinmuth, F. W. Mitchel, *ZPE* 19 (1975), 233–43). To make the identification of the two Autolykoi one would have to suppose that Lycurgus did not prosecute the 'coward' until after his year in office and crowning, and that his reputation was not already sufficiently tainted; but one would imagine that the most important post in one of the earliest years of the new 'Lycurgan' *ephebeia* would have to be filled by a man of unquestioned integrity.

by Olympian Zeus and Apollo. The oldest manuscript *f* omits 'Olympian', which may well be right; where Aeschines invokes Olympian Zeus elsewhere (**55**, **76**, 3. 255), he does not attach Apollo or another god to him.

82 'Timarchos is more experienced . . .' The impression created of Autolykos is of a rather pompous and humourless man, standing very much on the dignity of the Areopagos, surprised at the people's continued uncontrollable laughter, and unable to deal with it (but conceivably he was playing the audience, well aware of the effects he was achieving, see Winkler 1990a: 52). If he was the man prosecuted later by Lycurgus, and had children too young to fight in 338, however, he is perhaps likely to have been no more than in early middle-age in 346/5. Presumably Autolykos meant by his remark that Timarchos as an orator and current member of the *boule* was well acquainted with the Pnyx, whereas some at least of the audience immediately decided to take it as a reference to his former career as a *pornos*.

83–4 quietness . . . little expense . . . building sites (*oikopeda*) . . . cisterns . . . (*lakkoi*). The double entendres can be unravelled. What Autolykos meant was presumably that as the area by the Pnyx under discussion was not overcrowded with existing buildings, though there were some foundations, or old wells or water-tanks, whatever redevelopment was planned would not be too expensive. *Oikopeda* were building-plots, or uncompleted, or partially ruined or abandoned, buildings on a site: see also **182**. The texts recording the public auctions of the properties of those condemned over the affairs of the Herms and the Mysteries in 415–413 (the 'Attic Stelai'), mention, among the properties of one Pherekles of Themakos, an *oikopedon* by the Pythion—see Pritchett (1956: 265–6). For other examples, see also Plat. *Laws* 741c; Thuc. 4.90; *IG* II² 1672.25; and see Lambert (1997a: 227, 237). For the audience, 'quietness', 'little expense', and 'building site' all suggested cheap prostitutes taking clients to deserted plots for 'quickies'; and cistern (*lakkos*) or 'cistern-arse' (*lakkoproctos*) applied to a prostitute or excessively lustful woman or man, implied a large, or expandable, orifice, never capable of being filled, as well as other forms of insatiability. See Halperin (1990: 90–2); Davidson (1977: 79, 175–6, 210). For another hillside with a similar reputation, see Theopompos fr. 30 KA, where the personified hill Lykabettos grumbles that 'on my sides over-active youths (*meirakia*) pleasure themselves with their age-mates' (on which see Dover 1978: 87, n. 48). The effect is to distance Timarchos from the daytime crowded Pnyx where public, serious debates took place, and locate him among lonely wastelands at night, shabby, neglected, or half-completed houses and brothels: see Davidson (1997: 306–8). The mention of 'cisterns' in particular brings Aeschines a little closer to making the sort of explicit sexual references he claims to be so carefully avoiding, though it is not as unambiguously crude as the reference to the 'three holes' which *may* have appeared in Apollodoros' speech against Neaira (see on

38); but he is also protected by the fact that he is only reporting double entendres.

84 but still the truth is so strong that it overcomes all men's calculations. This passage suggests the power of laughter even in formal occasions such as political meetings and trials, and the tension between the audience's enjoyment of wit and theatrical display, its taste for insulting abuse, and its sense of proprieties: see Halliwell (1991: 292–4); S. Goldhill, *Foucault's Virginity: Ancient Erotic Fiction and the History of Sexuality* (Cambridge 1995), 14–16. F. R. Wüst (*Philipp II von Makedonien und Griechenland*, Munich, 1938, 47–9), claimed that Aeschines' tone here was sarcastic and critical of the Areopagos; but this view is insufficiently subtle. While there is some cruel humour directed at Timarchos, and some gentle but well-intentioned mockery of the apparently unworldy Autolykos, the main tone is one of general praise for the serious concerns of the Areopagos (and see also **92**); there is hence no need to date (as Wüst wished) the Antiphon affair and Aeschines' rebuff by the Areopagos before the trial of Timarchos (Dem. 18. 132–4; Plut. *Dem.* 14. 4; cf. Sealey 1967: 184; E. M. Harris 1995: appendix 8.)

Pyrrhandros. A man evidently well known to the jury, and no doubt the elderly politician of Anaphlystos (*LGPN* 5; *PA* 12496; Develin, *AO* 2649; Hansen, *Inventory* 58), mentioned in Aesch. 3. 138–9, in a list of those who over a long period had favoured friendly relations with Thebes (see Trevett 1999: 186–9), and was still alive (presumably very old) in 330. Our other evidence for him shows him, suitably enough, as active at the time of the establishment of the Second Athenian Confederacy and the alliance with Thebes, in 378/7, going on embassies to Byzantion and Thebes and proposing the admission of Chalkis to the alliance (*IG* II^2 41. 20, 43. 76–7, 44. 7, = Tod II 121, 123, 124 = Harding nos. 34, 35, 38; Develin 1989: 223, 224, 322). As a known and presumably respected elder statesman, if never a leading figure, he was well placed to administer a good-humoured and dignified rebuke to the assembly.

The general point of the retelling and embellishment of this occasion is of course to reinforce the views, first, that Timarchos is already condemned as guilty by the people in assembly, and second that he is indelibly tainted by his disgraceful past, so that comic ridicule necessarily accompanies him, and makes serious debate on an (apparently) important issue impossible.

85 it would not be proper to convict the people of false testimony. Aeschines risks here a fairly blatant attempt to equate the alleged preparedness of members of the assembly to laugh at double entendres which implied acknowledgement of the rumours concerning his activities with formal witness statements to his guilt. This will be outdone in bold exaggeration at **130**, where the goddess Report herself is introduced as a witness whom it would be impious not to believe. Litigants who had lost a case might challenge the evidence during the trial, and follow this up with a prosecution of one or more witnesses for false testimony; this was a fairly common means of continuing a dispute: see on the procedures, Harrison 1968–71: II, 192–3; MacDowell 1978: 244–5; and on its importance in litigation, Cohen 1995: 90–3, 107–12 (with comments on this passage), 167–72; and Christ 1998: 28–31. But the people in the assembly would not be subject to such a legal action. It is also striking that, whereas in the previous sentence, and in the next sentence, Aeschines has, as is common, identified those present at that assembly with this jury, in this sentence he seems to distinguish between 'the people' who have 'testified', and 'you', the recipients of the testimony.

86 another illustration on these matters. Aeschines cites other alleged recent cases, where Demophilos, and then a Nikostratos (*LGPN* 11; *PA* 11008: it was a very common name in Athens) made accusations of bribery against assemblymen and jurors. The public actions (*graphai*) specifically dealing with bribery of the assembly or jury are discussed by Dem. 46.26; a special word—*dekazein*—was developed for this, allegedly after the first instance in 410 when the perpetrator was Anytos. See generally D. M. MacDowell, 'Athenian laws about bribery', *RIDA* 30 (1983), 57–78, and *Meidias* 337, and also Harvey (1985: 88–9). In general, serious bribery of enough assemblymen to swing a vote is implausible, but one could conceive that attempts were made to win over a few who would then indicate their views. Sometime around 340, it seems, new and extremely elaborate procedures to minimize any possibility of bribery in the courts were introduced, perhaps a consequence of these investigations, see Boegehold (1995: 36–41, 110–13), and Intro. p. 63.

87 an absolute necessity. This is scarcely a compelling argument, or parallel, since jurymen who had been offered, but refused, bribes might give evidence, as might those who witnessed it, or there might be other circumstantial evidence, more persuasive than any Aeschines offers on the *hetairesis* charge.

hires an Athenian for *hybris* . . . for the shame (*aischyne*) of his own body. Aeschines uses again here, as he had at **72**, and will again at **90**, the fallacious argument that any who hired out an Athenian adult, or an adult who agreed to be hired out, for *hybris* or for shame, was liable to a capital charge: see on **72.** The close conceptual connection between *hybris* and the imposition of shame is clear here, as in a great many cases.

88 by Herakles . . . by Zeus and Apollo. Double emphasis is added to this penal severity imposed on poor citizens whose offences were far more venial than those of Timarchos by the doubling of oaths, by Herakles and by Zeus and Apollo (see on **49** and **81**).

they were condemned to death. See Dem. 21. 182, 24. 123, for the readiness of Athenian laws and juries to impose death penalties on poor citizens who similarly, out of poverty, sought to gain the pay for assembly or jury service, or took illicit payments; see Dover (1974: 109–10); S. C. Todd (1990a: 152).

disgusting behaviour. *Bdeluria* once more, as the most telling word to encapsulate his generally disgusting behaviour, see on **26.**

89–91 Aeschines presses as hard as he can this fundamental point, that he can and should get a conviction even though he has no witnesses, simply because all Athenians 'know' the truth, and could even be considered themselves as good witnesses (see on **85;** later the goddess Report herself will be metaphorically called as a star witness). The argument neatly reveals the singularity of the whole legal procedure, calling people to account for episodes in their private lives of many years earlier, where the crucial acts, as acknowledged here, normally take place between consenting men in private.

89 were taking place in an appellate city. Aeschines pursues the rhetorical conceit that the Athenians are all reliable witnesses of Timarchos' guilt by invoking the idea of a trial in which a city other than Athens were to provide the court of appeal, so that the Athenian people as a whole could appear before it as the chief witness. The phrase 'appellate city' (*ekkletos polis*) is defined in lexicographic sources as a 'city which one asks to judge a case' (e.g. *Etym. Magn.* s.v.); it occurs not infrequently in fourth-century and Hellenistic inscriptions. Various Athenian documents are known. Some which regulate legal disputes between Athens and members of her fourth-century Confederacy seem to impose Athens as the appelate city. An inscription of 363/2 dealing (*inter alia*) with possible disputes between the cities on the island of Keos and the Athenians (after the Keans have returned to membership of the Second Athenian Confederacy) stipulates that cases be heard, according to oaths and agreements, in Keos and in 'the appellate city at Athens' (*IG* II² 111, lines 45–9 = Tod II 142 = Harding no. 55); probably in the 350s there is a second similar provision for cases involving Keans (*IG* II² 440, lines 16–20) and a comparable case concerning cases between Athenians and Naxians (*IG* II² 179, lines 15–18). See Wade-Gery (1958: 189–91); Cargill (1981: 134–40). In the Hellenistic period, two cities may, by a permanent agreement (*symbolon*) designate a third as the appellate city (e.g. *IG* II² 778, 789, Athens and the Boeotian League, with Lamia as the appellate city), and in a good many Hellenistic interstate arbitration agreements the phrase designates the other city which the parties agree may act as the arbitrator, or may receive fines in case of a breach of the agreement: see S. Ager, *Interstate Arbitrations in the Greek World, 337–90 BC* (California, 1996), e.g. nos. 13, 47, 48, 71.

90 in lonely places and in private houses. The somewhat prurient phrasing recalls the double entendres of the Pnyx debate (**81–5**), and continues the invitation to the jury to imagine Timarchos engaged in sexual acts on the dark hills and building sites of Athens.

91 What clothes-snatchers. As is not uncommon in prosecution speeches, Aeschines argues that an acquittal would have very wide implications and lead to many other cases where criminals would escape justice (cf. e.g. Lys. 1. 36). His arguments are, as usual, misleading, and expressed in a somewhat compressed way. This has in fact contributed to modern confusion on some complex issues of Athenian law. He combines two of the categories of thieves who were certainly subjected to the summary procedure of *apagoge*, that is the more specialized clothes-snatchers (*lopodutai*) and the more general term for thieves (*kleptai*), along with two other types of 'very serious criminals', seducers (*moichoi*, see on **183**) and homicides. In all these types of cases, Aeschines suggests, there might either be summary procedures allowing immediate execution, or alternatively jury trials, if the accused are not caught 'in manifest guilt' (*ep'autophoroi*), or if they deny their guilt, when the jury has to decide 'on the basis of probabilities'. Hansen (1976: 44–5), followed by D. Cohen (1984: 156–7; 1991: 111–12) and others, suggest that Aeschines is describing, in all these cases of theft, adultery, and homicide, the possible operation of the *apagoge* procedure, in which 'malefactors' (*kakourgoi*) might be arrested by the victim and carried off to the Eleven, who were empowered to execute them if they confessed their guilt. This passage is thus the major piece of evidence for the view that *moichoi* and homicides might be considered *kakourgoi* under this procedure and dragged off to the Eleven. But, as M. Gagarin ('The Prosecution of Homicide in Athens', *GRBS* 20 (1979), 317–22) and especially E. M. Harris (1990: 376–7; 1994: 180) have convincingly argued, it is unsafe to suppose that the summary procedures Aeschines alludes to all necessarily fall under the same general heading, the one described by Arist. *Ath. Pol.* 52. 1, of the *apagoge* procedure to deal with *kakourgoi*: neither term is actually used in the passage (see also Carey 1995: 411–12; Kapparis, *Neaira* 304–5). Aeschines is rather alluding, first, to the *apagoge* procedure against thieves, and, second, to the summary powers given to husbands or other *kyrioi* to kill those men they find 'manifestly' engaged in sexual intercourse with wives or daughters, and third, perhaps to the separate procedure used against homicides who were found frequenting sacred places or the *agora* (see Harrison 1968–71: II, 226–8; Hansen 1976: 36–44; on the case of the homicide prosecution of Herodes, who complained that the *apagoge* procedure was wrongly used against him, see also Carawan 1998: 333–40). On the meaning of the phrase *ep'autophoroi* see above all E. M. Harris (1994), who argues persuasively that it means in the fourth century 'manifestly', and implies either 'caught in the act' or 'found patently in possession of the stolen goods', and see also Carawan (1998: 316–17, 351–4).

Aeschines' argument, then, is that all serious criminals who are *not* found in unambiguous guilt or with good witnesses to their committing the crime, will not be convicted in any subsequent jury trial, if the demand that witnesses be produced for Timarchos' acts is upheld. What is thus being excluded is conviction solely on the basis of any form of argument apart from eyewitness observation or testimony, and this is described by the general heading of 'the probabilities' (*ta eikota*). This term was central in the formalized teaching of Greek rhetoric from the second half of the fifth century for the use of what came to be called 'technical' proofs (*entechnoi pisteis*), that is those derived from the speaker's skills (as opposed to 'non-technical', 'pre-existing' proofs, such as testimony freely offered, slave evidence offered after torture, and documents. Technical proofs characteristically offered arguments from the circumstances involved and the characters of the agents (for example, the argument of **75** that Timarchos, a youth often enjoying dinners beyond his means in the company of older men, must have been repaying with sexual favours; such arguments were of course absolutely central to this case). On the importance of such arguments in Greek rhetorical theory and law-court practice, from Corax, Gorgias, and Antiphon onwards, and the controversial nature of excessive reliance on them, see Plat. *Phaedr.* 267a: Arist. *Rhet.* 1357a30–625, and see e.g. G. A. Kennedy, *The Art of Persuasion in Greece* (London, 1963), 26–51; M. Gagarin, *Antiphon, The Speeches* (Cambridge, 1997), 13–21; Carawan (1998: 20–8, 184–91, 316–21).

92 the most scrupulous legal body in the city. Such praise of the Areopagos and its decisions is found frequently in law-court speeches, especially in the 340s and 330s (see also Intro. pp. 64–5), and reflects both the respect felt due to this most traditional element of the Athenian system and a recognition that its members, all of whom had been archons for a year, and then served as Areopagites for life, might be more experienced, and had more opportunities to maintain a consistency of decisions, than the ordinary *dikasteria*. See also Aesch. 3. 20; Dem. 23. 66; Lys. 5. 14; Lyc. 1. 12; Wallace (1985: 126–7).

Aeschines uses the term *synhedrion* for 'legal body', a term for a formal meeting or place of meeting which is elsewhere used to refer to the meetings of the Areopagos: cf. its use in Eukrates' 337/6 law about the dangers of tyranny and treason: see Meritt (1952: 355 esp. lines 1–16), and Lyc. 1. 12, with Wycherley (1957: 126–7), and Boegehold (1995: 46).

but also on the basis of their own knowledge and of their own investigations. The argument from alleged cases heard by the Areopagos is, as often, vague and unsubstantiated. As this passage suggests, however, another sign of the respect given to this legal body was that it alone was, it seems, able to investigate on its own initiative both cases referred to it and those in which it took an interest; see Intro. pp. 64–5, and Wallace (1985: 121–2).

93 what you yourselves know. Aeschines makes two appeals to the jury here: first, that they pay attention as he 'reminds' them of 'public knowledge' of Timarchos' current political behaviour, characterized by greed, corruption and shamelessness; and second, that they be encouraged to trust long-standing gossip as a provider of 'knowledge' of past behaviour.

94–105 *The dissipation of Timarchos' estate*

94 a certain speechwriter . . . devising the defence speech. The delicate transition from the narrative and arguments about Timarchos' career as a '*pornos*' to the second major charge, is managed through another riposte to a likely objection from the defence. This is itself introduced through a pre-emptive sneer at Demosthenes, labelling him first a 'speechwriter' (*logographos*). This and the sneering tone of 'devising' appeals to the general prejudice against acting as a *logographos*, see on **117** and **119**, and hits both at Demosthenes' pride in his rhetorical skill and Timarchos' inability to compose his own defence. See also Dover (1968: 155–6); Christ (1998: 36–9); Rubinstein (forthcoming). On Demosthenes' contribution to the defence, see Intro. pp. 23–4.

the act of a boy . . . the act of a man. There are two assumptions behind Demosthenes' supposed argument of self-contradiction. One is that most or all male 'prostitutes' are youths (*paides*) who have not entered into property-ownership, whereas dissipating a property can only be done by those who have entered the citizen lists and into control of their inheritance; so the two alleged offences are chronologically distinct. The other, which Aeschines only hints at rather than spelling it out, is that prostitutes or 'escorts' demand fees or upkeep because they need the money, whereas those with properties have no need to. Probably the defence took the line that Timarchos and Hegesandros were always just friends who may have contributed jointly to their expenses, and that at no time did Timarchos live off Hegesandros, or off anyone else, or have any need to. Aeschines' response is that Timarchos continued to participate in his mercenary relationships for long after the 'usual' time, and took advantage of his lovers' wealth; the string of lovers enumerated, beginning with Euthydikos, began when he became a citizen and a young man (*meirakion*), and presumably lasted for some years. But it was allegedly only when he and Hegesandros had run through the latter's available moneys, and Timarchos was no longer so attractive, that Timarchos started seriously dipping into, and selling, his own estate. This issue certainly was a problem for Aeschines, comparable to those of the relationships with Phaidros and Misgolas (see on **42, 43**, and **49** above). It is not explained why Timarchos needed to live off Pittalakos or Hegesandros when he was still in control of his sizeable inheritance. Aeschines fails to provide dates for the alleged sales of Timarchos' properties, but on the indications of the speech, they should have occurred after Timarchos had already served on the *boule* in 361/0

On the other hand, the rhetoric of this passage establishes neatly a set of appropriate connections between Timarchos' behaviour as an 'escort' and his sales of properties, in that both were performed to satisfy his own insatiable and shameless appetites for his own pleasures, of gambling, food, drink, and sex with expensive *hetairai*: on this see especially Davidson (1997: 209–10).

goes around the *agora*. As the main civic centre, where the *boule* and most of the courts sat, and very close to the Pnyx, the *agora* was naturally where one would find the greatest crowds of the politically interested. See e.g. Millett (1998: 222–4).

95 heiress (*epikleros*) whom Hegesandros had married. A daughter whose father died without sons became an *epikleros*, and her male relatives, in strict order of precedence, were under the obligation to marry her and take over the property, on the understanding that it would eventually pass to their sons as the primary heirs; in many cases (as here, allegedly) this might be a financial advantage, and might lead to the disruption of existing marriages. See on these laws, the frequency of such marriages, and resulting familial conflicts, Harrison (1968–71: I, 132–8); Schaps (1979: 25–47); Hunter (1994: 14–25); Cox (1998: esp. 94–9); Scafuro (1997: 281–305).

money lasted which Hegesandros had . . . journey with Timomachos. The jury is reminded of the political corruption alleged earlier against Hegesandros (see **56**).

past his youthful bloom, and no one, reasonably, would give him anything. The term for 'past his bloom' (*exoros* = past one's *hora*) reinforces the persistent assumption that standard homosexual activity involved an older man who desired the attractions of a boyish or youthful physique. One important criterion of being 'past one's bloom' was the growth of a full beard (see e.g. Theognis, book II, 1299–1304, 1305–10, 1327–34; and Dover 1978: 84–7). Aeschines expects the jury to find it plausible ('reasonably') that a young man past his bloom would be unable to find lovers to maintain him (or even clients to pay for sex with him); see also Williams (1999: 83–6), on an apparent contrast in this respect between Greek and Roman culture, where there was a more recognized market for older male prostitutes (*exoleti*). The comment here is also a useful reminder both of Timarchos' earlier attractiveness, and of his current bloated and unappealing body.

but this man's revolting and unholy nature still longed for the same pleasures. In view of the pleasures listed at **42**, and the fact that to satisfy these insatiable lusts, Timarchos turned to consume his own estate, this statement cannot, I think, be taken to mean that Timarchos actually enjoyed being penetrated, and went out to pay people to do this to him: that view is taken by Williams (1999: 85). His 'revolting (*bdelyros*) and unholy nature', the 'same pleasures', and his 'excess of insatiability' are rather, as throughout the denunciation, all concerned with the activities listed in **42**, that is gambling, food, drink, and sex with *hetairai*; those are presumably the 'daily habits' to which he returned. This passage does not then suggest, nor does any other passage in the speech, that Timarchos is presented as a *kinaidos*, as a man who positively enjoyed, rather than merely accepted, the 'woman's part' of being penetrated (see Intro. pp. 48–9 and on **185**).

95–6 gobbled up . . . eat it up . . . drank it down. The climactic metaphors in this very heavy denunciation of his excessive debauchery are carefully chosen. Timarchos is seen to be consuming his estates immediately and fervently, as he consumes all his pleasures, in the form of gorging on food and guzzling down wines; the language of 'eating up' one's estate, which was apparently used in the law, and has already been repeatedly used by Aeschines (see on **30**) is intensified here; first the more vivid and rare verb *katopsophagein* ('gulp down fish') denoted the rapid, greedy, consumption of *opson*, expensive fish, eaten when hot, then more 'eating' words, and finally 'drank down' (*katepinein*). It all suggests that Timarchos had no time to seek a good buyer for the estates, so quickly had the wealth to travel down the gullet. Isaeus 10. 25 uses an equally rare verb to attack the client's money-grabbing opponent, who has allegedly already consumed one household property on pederasty (*katapaiderastein*). In general, see the material and discussion in Davidson (1997: 206–10). Latin uses *ebibo* in the same way (e.g. Plaut. *Trin.* 250). Cato the Elder's witticism against the man who had sold his ancestral coastal estate appears in Plutarch's Greek version ('what the sea washed away with difficulty, he drank down easily') with the same verb that Aeschines uses repeatedly (*katapinein*); see Corbeill (1997: 202), who does not, however, acknowledge Cato's, or Plutarch's, debts to Greek political and comic invective in these cases.

96 could not wait . . . sold it for what it fetched on the spot. This piece of invective adds an extra point to the general argument that selling one's landed properties for ready cash (rather, say, than leasing it out) was thought economically, socially, and politically damaging, and was one of the grounds for the *dokimasia rhetoron*. Aeschines insists on Timarchos' desperation to sell immediately, no matter what price the properties reached. The implications of this are that there might be temporary fluctuations in the property market, and hasty sellers might agree to sell at a bad time; and also that possible purchasers might find it difficult to raise large sums in a hurry. Arist. *Ath. Pol.* 47. 3 reveals that the state allowed purchasers of confiscated properties five years in the case of houses, and ten years in the case of landed properties, to pay the full price bid at the auctions of the 'sellers' (*poletai*). See above all Millett (1991: 79–84).

97 his father . . . would even have been able to perform liturgies. For nuanced attempts to analyse the evidence and quantify the implications of phrases of this type, and so fix the level of wealth at which individuals were expected to perform liturgical duties (festival-financing or the trierarchy) for the community, see Davies (1971: xxiii–iv; 1981: 21–34), and Gabrielsen (1994: 43–53). It emerges that there were no fixed limits. Those with estates worth two talents (or even perhaps at times less) might not be totally exempt, or might even volunteer to perform a liturgy, while those worth at least four talents would find a liturgy very difficult to avoid. The jury is invited to imagine Arizelos' property as substantial, which should have been more than enough to induce Arizelos and Timarchos to perform at least some liturgies; perhaps then they would have assumed that it amounted to at least about 3–4 talents, and perhaps rather more than that before Arizelos sold two properties and the silver-mining workshop (**101**).

There was a house . . . This is one of the most detailed enumerations of property holdings of well-to-do Athenians preserved in our speeches, and it therefore features prominently in analyses of fourth-century wealth creation and management. Arizelos' wealth was split into a set of mixed holdings (varied properties in town and country, slave workshops, mining interests, money lent out, and goods); other evidence suggests that such a pattern had become the norm for well-off members of Athenian society in the fourth century. See generally Davies (1981: ch. IV); R. G. Osborne (1991); Millett (1991: 163–71).

house behind the Acropolis. The Greek has 'behind the polis': for this use of *polis* for Acropolis cf. Thuc. 2. 15, and see Gomme in *HCT ad loc*. This rather vague description of a location perhaps suggests the other side of the Acropolis from the Agora, to the south; Timarchos (**98**) sold this house to a comic poet (Nausikrates), who then sold it to a chorus-trainer (Kleainetos), which also fits this suggested location, as the house would be on the same side of the Acropolis as the theatre of Dionysos. It is a possible further inference from this location and the purchaser that Timarchos himself, like many politicians, liked to associate with theatre people (see Hall 1995: 45). On our evidence for town houses in the centre of the city, see Pritchett (1956: 270–5); Graham (1974); Jones (1975).

a piece of marginal land (*eschatia*) at Sphettos. The term *eschatia* designates an outlying estate, near the sea, a boundary, or (often in Athenian texts) up in hilly country (so in essence the *scholia* here, and see the discussions of D. M. Lewis (1973: 221–3) and Lambert (1997a: 225–33). Sphettos, Timarchos' own deme, was a medium-sized deme of the Akamantis tribe, in the inland *trittys* of the tribe, on the SE slopes of Mt Hymettos (on the complexities of Kleisthenes' structure of deme, *trittyes* or ridings, and tribes, see Arist. *Ath. Pol.* 21 and e.g. Hansen 1991: 46–9); Sphettos had five representatives on the Council (see the lists in Whitehead 1986a: appendix 2). It is noticeable that Aeschines does not treat this as *the* ancestral piece of property in the family's home deme, but rather as a large, unworked estate allowed to run wild (perhaps by the father as well as by the son). The land-holdings that Arizelos had acquired do not seem to have any focus either in terms of locality or type of land (see R. G. Osborne 1985a: 49–50). The documents of sales of properties owned by demes and other corporate groups in the Lycurgan period (the so-called *rationes centesimarum*: see now Lambert 1997a) included a large number of properties designated *eschatiai*, much of it probably hitherto treated as 'public land', but little used, though the seven properties sold by the deme Sphettos are in fact all designated as landed properties (*choria*) (see Lambert 1997a: 121–2, 186–7).

another landed property (*chorion*) at Alopeke. Alopeke, a large deme in the city *trittys* of the tribe Antiochis (with ten representatives on the Council), immediately south of the city on the way to Phaleron, as Aeschines puts it (**99**), 11 or 12 stades (about a mile and a half) from the city wall. Lambert (1999: 112) notes this house in Alopeke in connection with his arguments suggesting overlapping memberships and hence social connec-tions between members of the *genos* of the Salaminians and the members of what are probably *thiasoi* of Herakles, based in Alopeke (*IG* II^2 2345).

some slaves. Many craft-working slaves in Athens worked essentially independently; in small workshops/houses or on their own (sometimes known as *choris oikountes*, those living separately); they contributed greatly to the impression, popular especially among critics of the democracy, that slaves at Athens were hard to tell from free men, and hence were excessively 'free' (Ps. Xen. *Ath. Pol.* 1. 10–12; Plato, *Rep.* 563b). See E. Perotti, 'Esclaves *choris oikountes*,' *Actes du colloque 1972 sur l'esclavage* (Besançon, 1974), 47–56; Y. Garlan, *Slavery in Classical Greece* (Ithaca and London, 1988). On the importance of such activities in the Athenian economy and the economic choices of the rich, see also Davies (1981: 41–9); R. G. Osborne (1991). It is notable, here and elsewhere, that slaves are mentioned when craft-workshops are enumerated, but not in relation to country estates; this does not necessarily imply anything much about the extent of use of slaves in farming rather than in craft businesses. There the slaves effectively were the capital assets of the business, whereas the land itself was the primary asset, and the slaves, perhaps less specialized, might be sold separately or turned to other activities. See Fisher (1993: 43).

each one of whom brought in a rent of two obols a day. The term used here, *apophora*, is the standard word used for this form of regular payment such slaves would pay to their masters: see e.g. Ps. Xen. *Ath. Pol.* 1. 10–12; Andoc. 1. 38.

woman skilled in *amorgina*-cloth. This term (*amorgina*) refers to expensive, delicate, garments which were thought to have some connection with the small Aegean island of Amorgos. In comedy, the term refers particularly to fine, even diaphanous, linen clothes worn by women (see e.g. Ar. *Lys.* 150: 735–7). Ancient commentators suggest that these were fine textiles woven from *amorgis*, a plant apparently similar to (or a variant of) flax. See generally on linen-working, especially in Egypt, Barber (1994: 189–206). However, G. M. A. Richter, 'Silk in Greece', *AJA* 33 (1929), 27–33, suggested the term may rather indicate silken garments, woven, perhaps typically on Amorgos, from wild silk (from the tusser silkworm, imported from the East). The discovery in a rich grave in the Kerameikos from the late fifth century of six fragments of Oriental silk gives the idea support: see Barber (1991: 32, 204), and M. C. Miller (1997: 76–9), and in general her discussion of varied forms of Eastern luxury which reached Athens from the mid-fifth century. Conceivably, Amorgos (and other islands, like Cos, later famous for its diaphanous clothes) was a centre for both types of delicate weaving (see also R. J. Hopper,

Trade and Industry in Classical Greece (London, 1979), 63). Many of the women's garments (usually called *chitons* or *chitoniskia*) listed on the Acropolis inventories of objects dedicated to Artemis Brauronia are described as *amorgina*: see T. Linders, *Studies in the Treasure Records of Artemis Brauronia Found in Athens* (Stockholm, 1972), esp. pp. 20, 45, 62; and Cole (1998: 36–42).

man skilled in pattern-weaving. The term here (*poikiltes*) suggests the working of varied colours into cloth, and is more likely to indicate the weaving of complex patterns or images rather than needle-embroidery. Items so made may be expensive, best-quality clothing, or decorated hangings (*peripetasmata*); one of the sales listed in the Attic Stelai (I. 173), mention *peripetasma poikilon*, a multi-coloured woven hanging: see Pritchett (1956: 248–50). Religious occasions and dramatic festivals also called for patterned woven clothes. See generally Geddes (1987: 313–15); M. C. Miller (1997: 76–7). Wool-working of all types was considered essentially women's work (see in general Barber 1991: 283–98), and in many cases in Greece the women of the household and their female slaves made cloth for the market as well as for domestic needs: see e.g. Hdt. 2. 35, who assumes that for most peoples, including evidently Greeks, weavers were usually female, whereas in Egypt they were male, and generally Pomeroy, *Xenophon, Oikonomikos: A Social and Historical Commentary* (Oxford, 1994), 61–5. But some male slaves employed these skills as well. In addition to this passage, one may cite Plato's elaborate discussion of weaving in his *Statesman*, which often assumes male craftsmen. On the manumissions inscriptions from Athens of the 330s (D. M. Lewis 1959; 1968) wool-workers (*talasiourgoi*) form the largest category of those whose occupations are given (50); most of them appear female from their names, though in some cases the names might denote male or female.

men who owed him money. Loans made by or taken out by Athenian citizens can be divided broadly into three types. First, many Athenians still followed the traditional model of mutually supportive, reciprocal loans, which often did not carry interest, in which family members, friends, neighbours, or members of religious and social associations gave assistance to those in difficulties; where such a loan was organized on a collective basis, it might be labelled the relatively formalized '*eranos*-loan'. Second, Athenians (or non-Athenians) might make interest-bearing loans, when they were not especially connected to the borrowers, and wished some of their spare cash to earn income; the so-called 'bottomry' loans, helping to finance overseas trade by loaning money to shipowners or traders to purchase cargoes, constituted a significant part of this category. Finally, loans, often at higher rates of interest, might be made by more 'professional' bankers or small-scale (and naturally unpopular) moneylenders or usurers. See generally Millett (1991), who emphasizes the prevalence of reciprocal rather than money-making motives, and in contrast the more 'modernizing' picture of E. E. Cohen (1992). Aeschines gives very little detail here, but probably implies that Arizelos had some, perhaps a small amount, of his spare cash invested in interest-bearing loans of the second type (see also **105**, and Millett 1991: 163–71); whether the loans were made to acquaintances or strangers is not stated.

and some personal effects. Furniture (such as couches and chairs) and generally personal possessions which are neither land, cash, nor slaves, often appear, labelled, as here, *epipla*, as assets in inventories of properties such as this: see e.g. Lys. 32. 4–5; Isocr. 21. 2; Isaeus 7. 35, 11. 42–3; Dem. 27. 9–11. See generally Harrison (1968–71: I, 228–30), and the relatively small amounts for which furniture and fittings are sold on the 'Attic Stelai', the lists of confiscated properties of those condemned in 415–413, Pritchett (1956: 210–11); Geddes (1987: 328–9); Millett (1991: 79–80). The *scholia* say that *epipla* are what 'we now call *oikoskeua*', that is household equipment.

98 there is no risk, as there was previously, and no shame as well. See above on **45**; a further admission that there were no useful witnesses to Timarchos' sexual activities.

The house in the city he sold. The main point made about Timarchos' treatment of his inheritance is the speed, ruthlessness, and desperation with which he sold off the real estate. The prices Timarchos accepted for these properties ought therefore to be presented as rock-bottom, but this is impossible to test in the absence of any detailed information of their sizes, or the quality of the furnishings or of the land. Information on property prices is found in other law-court speeches and in the accounts of the magistrates called the *poletai* such as the 'Attic Stelai' and documents of sales of properties owned by demes and other corporate groups in the Lycurgan period (the so-called *rationes centesimarum*). See for assessments Pritchett (1956: 269–76); Davies (1981: 50–2); Lambert (1997a: 229–33); Kapparis, *Neaira* 247. As far as one can tell, 2000 drachmai seems an average sort of price for a town house; Aeschines clearly wishes us to suppose that Timarchos let it go for considerably less than Kleainetos gave to Nausikrates, but his failure to state the price Timarchos received reduces the effectiveness of the point. It is conceivable (but unlikely) that Nausikrates' testimony (**100**) gave the missing figure. There were other reasons why politically active Athenians needed ready cash, such as sudden demands for liturgies (see R. G. Osborne 1991); but if Timarchos was unable to adduce many liturgies performed, as Aeschines suggests, or rebut the allegations of having failed to maintain his obligations to his family (and Dem. 19. 283–7 does not explicitly contradict this, though he does mention Timarchos' mother and children), the charge of wilful property-dispersal may have done some damage to his case to be considered a useful citizen and valuable politician.

Nausikrates the comic poet. The manuscripts are divided between comic *poet* and comic *actor*; he was in fact both, as were many (*LGPN* 23; Ghiron-Bistagne 1976: 344; Stefanis 1988: no. 1773). He appears as both in the records of victors at the Lenaia (*IG* II² 2325, col. iii, 148 and 196, from the mid-fourth century; we have three fragments from his plays (*PCG* VII, 33–5).

Kleainetos the chorus-master. The name is frequently found among fourth-century Athenians, for example we know of Kleainetoi in Alopeke, Ikaria, and Melite, as well as a member of a famous family, a descendant of the fifth-century politician Kleon, son of Kleainetos, of Kudaithenaion. But this person is almost certainly the man who was also a tragic poet (*TGF* I Snell, no. 84; *LGPN* 17). He was said to be among a group of poor poets who were worse than Euripides by the first-century BC Epicurean philosopher Philodemos (*On Poems*, p. 37 Gomperz); he won the third prize with a *Hypsipyle* in 363 (*SEG* 26. 203. 12), and is mentioned in an unnamed comedy of Alexis as one 'accommodating' enough to eat boiled lupins complete with their husks (266 K/A, see Arnott *ad loc.*).

Mnesitheos of Myrrhinous. This man (*LGPN* 42, *PA* 10297) is attested as the son of Tachyboulos of Myrrhinous, who served as a syntrierarch in 341/0 (*IG* II² 1623, 24–5): see Davies, *APF* 393.

No prices are offered for the sale of this *eschatia* at Sphettos, Timarchos' own deme.

99 his mother supplicated and begged him to let alone, as I have heard . . . for her to be buried in. Probably his mother is to be supposed to have begged for this piece of land to be saved from the enforced sales, because it came with her as part of her dowry: see R. G. Osborne (1985: 50). The third offence for which a *dokimasia rhetoron* might lie, 'beating a parent, failing to support them, or failing to provide a home for them', is not directly adduced, but Aeschines' refusal to maintain his mother's ancestral plot for her to be buried in comes close (see Hunter 1994: 105; and also Cox 1998: 99–103 on the norm of a close bond between mothers and sons). Demosthenes' version of his speech of 343 claims that Aeschines has asked the jury not to have any pity for Timarchos' mother, children, or anyone else (19. 283), which pleas do not occur in Aeschines' published version; instead we have an attempt to excite pity for his mother, in her pleas to her son, and no mention of any children. We cannot know whether a passage has been excluded from Aeschines' published version, or whether Demosthenes is misrepresenting what he said.

Aeschines represents Timarchos' mother as employing for maximum effect the formalized supplication (*hiketeia*) procedure, which in its full form involves the suppliant completing symbolically significant acts of self-abasement and reaching out to the chin and/or knees of the person supplicated, who should then feel under a very strong obligation, backed by Zeus *Hikesios*, to respond with the appropriate restrain (*aidos*) and grant a favour (see generally Gould 1973). The extent to which the binding force of these ritual actions remained fully active in the lives of ordinary citizen families is uncertain, but the rhetorical effect of the picture of a mother pleading for her burial plot is undoubtedly intended to be greatly strengthened by the use of the language of supplication; in general on 'supplication' as a rhetorical ritual in these speeches see Johnstone (1999: 114–25). The addition of 'as I have heard' suggests, as one would expect, that no actual testimony for this scene was forthcoming, and the source was perhaps to be supposed to be a leak from Timarchos' household (cf. Hunter 1994: 99–105).

100 Metagenes of Sphettos. This man (*LGPN* 11; *PA* 10090) is likely to be the Metagenes who is mentioned by Aesch. 2. 134 as an envoy sent to the Phocians by the Athenian general Proxenos. He is also mentioned, along with his daughter, on a mid-fourth-century funerary monument found at the modern village Koropi, the site of Sphettos (*IG* II² 7523). Thus both the purchasers of these properties who seem prepared to testify for Aeschines may have been men of substance and/or involved in public service. But Aeschines seems to have found only one of Arizelos' supposed debtors to attest that Timarchos had achieved a complete repayment, and this for only a small proportion of the original loan.

101 Fearing he would be liable to liturgies, his father sold the properties. Arizelos died when Timarchos was still a boy (**103**); if Timarchos was thirty in 361/0, and born no later than *c.* 391/0, Arizelos must have died some years before 371/0 (though Davies 1981: 54 puts him in ownership of his properties in the 360s). The tactics of deliberately selling off land, and keeping one's wealth less open to scrutiny, to avoid responsibilities and moral obligations to the community, was evidently not uncommon: see generally M. R. Christ. 'Liturgy-Avoidance and *Antidosis* in Classical Athens', *TAPA* 120 (1990), 147–69; E. E. Cohen (1992: 191–8); and R. G. Osborne (1991: 138–9), who compares the case of Demosthenes' father (on whom see also Davies, *APF* 127–33); Osborne does not distinguish Arizelos' alleged motive of liturgy-avoidance from his son's craving for extravagant gratification.

　　piece of land (*chorion*) in Kephisia. This was a medium-sized deme (it had six representatives on the Council), in the inland *trittys* of the tribe Erechtheis, NW of the city towards the northern slopes of Pentelikon. It boasted a *palaistra* (*Arch. Delt.* 24A (1969) 6; R. G. Osborne 1985a: 74 n. 24).

　　another in Amphitrope. The manuscripts have 'another *agron* (piece of land)', but the word *agron* was plausibly deleted by Cobet as an explanatory addition by a later editor. Amphitrope was a very small deme (it had two representatives on the Council), in the coastal *trittys* of Antiochis, in the middle of the mining area of southern Attika, probably at or near the modern village of Metropisi (Eliot 1962: Ch. IX, see now *Arch. Delt.* 49 (1994) 64–6).

　　two workshops in the silver-mining areas, one in

Aulon, the other near Thrasymos. Both these places are mentioned quite frequently in our fourth-century records of mining leases (collected and discussed by Crosby 1950), and in the second case these enable us to correct the manuscripts reading and speculations in the *scholia*. Aulon seems to have been a small village or region, in the hills in the Sounion deme, near which mines are cited and roads to it mentioned (Crosby 1950: nos. 2, 8, and 10). The manuscripts here give 'Thrasyllos' as the name of the second place, and Demosthenes' manuscripts at 37. 25 also give 'Thrasyllos' as a mining area in the text of a legal complaint; Harpokration s.v., and the *scholia* here, claim there was a monument to a dead man or hero called Thrasyllos. But the mining leases consistently place mines 'near Thrasymos', or mention roads going 'towards Thrasymos' (*IG* II² 1582 = Crosby 1950, no. 16, and other references in Crosby's index, 309, and see also *Hesperia* 26 (1957) 3 no. S2 line 12); these references make it certain that this is the right reading for both passages, as was proposed first by G. P. Oikonomos, 'Eine neue Bergwerksurkunde aus Athen', *AM* 35 (1910), 298–300, and accepted by Crosby (1950: 213); Hopper (1953: 217); Eliot (1962: 91); Carey & Reid, 135–6; and R. G. Osborne (1985a: 113); it has apparently not been spotted by any editors of Aeschines including the latest, Dilts. The ancient commentators' mention of a 'monument' is evidently their free invention based on an already corrupt text. Thrasymos then was the name of a village in the mining region, also within the deme of Sounion, probably near the modern village of Kamareza (Eliot 1962: 90–2). On excavations of workshops with their ore-smelting ovens and washeries in the mining regions, see J. Ellis Jones, 'Laurion: Agrileza 1977–83', *Archaeological Reports for 1984–85* (1985), 106–23, and on the silver mines operations more generally see Hopper (1953; 1968); Lauffer (1979); J. Ellis Jones, 'The Laurion Silver Mines: A Review of Recent Researches and Results', *G&R* 29 (1982), 169–83; R. G. Osborne (1985a: ch. 6).

102 Eupolemos the gymnastic-trainer (*paidotribes*). Nothing else is known of this man (*LGPN* 24; *PA* 5392; *PAA* 442460). For the duties of the *paidotribes* see on **10**. One may suspect that Timarchos benefited from his uncle's occupation to make an early and impressive show at the *gymnasia*; but Aeschines avoids making the connection with Timarchos as an athlete or gymnastic beauty, probably because (see Intro. p. 20) this would suggest a more respectable setting for his associations with older men. It is probably implied at **155–8** that he did attract admiration at the *gymnasia*; and see Dem. 19. 233. Aeschines prefers to invite the jury to imagine the youthful Timarchos not in the *gymnasia* but among the seedy tenement-houses of the Peiraieus and the desolate areas round the Pnyx.

Arignotos, who is still living, an old man who has lost his sight. No more is known of Arignotos either (*LGPN* 5; *PA* 1614; *PAA* 162010). In this case too Aeschines approaches the third category of named offences, wronging one's parents. Arignotos' blindness and helplessness are milked extensively, not so much to excite sympathy for him as to blacken Timarchos the more for his callous neglect once he took control of his property (see also Cox 1998: 112).

103 when he was still a boy. Aeschines chooses not to emphasize the fact that Timarchos' father died when he was young, nor the idea that this may have removed a restraining influence on his choice of friends and his extravagance; similarly he had not mentioned his father's death when describing how Timarchos had settled in with Euthydikos on leaving boyhood (**40**). Part of the reason is that Aeschines wishes to cast Arizelos also in a bad light, as a wealthy but unpatriotic citizen who preferred to sell properties rather than perform liturgies.

citizen list (*lexiarchikon grammateion*). See on **18**.

accepting the payment given to the disabled. Among the scrutinies administered by the Council (Arist. *Ath. Pol.* 49) were those of the 'disabled' (*adunatoi*): in the early fourth century, when Lysias wrote a speech (24) for a claimant whose right was being challenged, it awarded one obol a day; by the time of the *Ath. Pol.* it had risen to two obols a day. The requirements stated in the *Ath. Pol.* were that claimants had to be worth less than three mnai, and sufficiently disabled that they could not do any work; the defendant in the Lysias case argued that though he could still earn small amounts, he was still entitled to collect, and how much he actually earned was one of the areas of dispute: see C. Carey, 'Structure and Strategy in Lysias XXIV', *Greece and Rome* 37 (1990), 44–51, and Dillon (1995). The implication of the phrase 'lose the prytany payment' in **104** is probably that at the time of Arignotos' appeal

(361/0, see **109**) the Council paid out every prytany, that is ten times a year: on this point see the convincing arguments of Dillon (1995: 41), against the doubts of Rhodes (1972: 175–6) and id. *Ath. Pol.* 570. Dillon observes that such regular payments would be more humane for the allegedly needy recipients, and that *IG* II² 222, lines 37–48 provide a good parallel for monthly payments, made to Peisitheides an Athenian benefactor, exiled from Delos, to whom Athens is offering protection and sustenance.

104 suppliant bough. Under this procedure (as explained in the *scholia*) citizens or foreigners could petition for a personal hearing before the Council or the assembly by laying an olive-branch wrapped in wool in supplication (*Ath. Pol.* 43.6, with Rhodes *ad loc.*; Gould 1973: 101; Gauthier 1985: 187–9; Johnstone 1999: 116–17). Orators inform us of a number of cases, like this one, where citizens sought help or the righting of a wrong (Andoc. 1. 110–6; Dem. 18. 107, 24. 12, 52, 18. 107; Aesch. 2. 15); and some fourth-century inscriptions, cited by Gould and Rhodes, record petitions by non-citizens, the point of which was that the petitioner, admitting to be to some extent in a weak position or in the wrong, begged a favour from the community, backed by the power of the gods. In this case, by supplicating, Arignotos in effect admitted an error in failing to attend the hearing, and begged for sympathy, but his case allegedly won no support.

Timarchos . . . did not think it right to speak up for him. Aeschines' complaints point to an interesting contradiction. On the one hand Timarchos allegedly allowed his uncle's wealth to fall below the limit, and gave him no support, so that he had to claim the allowance; but when the claim was challenged as Arignotos failed to attend the scrutiny, Timarchos failed to speak in favour of his case even though he was one of the presiding magistrates (*prohedroi*) of the Council on the day. On the other hand, as Rubinstein (1998: 137–8) observes, Aeschines' argument assumes that magistrates might legitimately feel under an obligation to help their relations or friends in difficulties, where we would expect them to 'declare an interest' and withdraw, and she adduces other evidence revealing conflicting attitudes to such questions, not least in Aeschines himself. If the argument was that Timarchos, as (still) a reasonably wealthy man of about 30, should have been maintaining his uncle, his reluctance to say anything in defence of his uncle's claim is readily understandable, as he would be agreeing that he was either too poor or too mean to support the blind old man (see Dillon 1995: 40). If anything like this took place on the Council in 361/0 (and allegedly Arignotos himself gave written testimony, though how much of this he confirmed is not clear), Timarchos might in fact have sought to avoid the embarrassment of a commitment either to support Arignotos himself or to advocate restoration of the grant, by a 'principled' refusal to intervene. Whether he was in fact now supporting his uncle is unclear.

105 But someone might perhaps say. No witnesses are apparently cited for this bold claim that Timarchos has now no resources left, whether of land, slaves, or interest-bearing loans, unless (which is unlikely) Arignotos' testimony supported this view. Timarchos must surely in fact have had some cash resources both for his political career and his social life; Aeschines gives the impression that he kept any money he had liquid, ran through it instantly, and then resorted to various corrupt means to gain more.

criminals (*kakourgoi*). As seen already, this is the standard all-embracing term for those thieves, robbers, and kidnappers open to summary processes such as *apagoge* (see on **91**, **113**, and above all Hansen 1976; Hunter 1994: 134–79), or it may be a more general term for any wrongdoer.

All that is left to him. By a bold rhetorical device (a form of personification: cf. a positive version of the same idea in Oscar Wilde's famous declaration to the US customs—'I have nothing to declare but my Genius'), Aeschines claims, summarizing this section of his speech, that all Timarchos has left as his inherited family assets are his vices. The list, in effect, offers a useful summary of how Timarchos has systematically undermined all that is expected of a good citizen, as envisaged by the *dokimasia* law: first, his shameless preparedness to do disgusting things (*bdeluria*, i.e. his alleged sexual offences); second, his luxury (*tryphe*)—hence his dissipation of property and refusal to protect his relatives; third, his cowardice (his failure as a citizen-soldier); and lastly his *sykophantia*, which led to illegal money-making and political corruption: see also Patterson (1998: 162–3).

106–116 *Timarchos' public career*

106 consumed . . . Aeschines makes the transition from Timarchos' handling of his family inheritance to his political life by a neat and effective repetition of the vivid language of greedy consumption, see on **96**.

Timarchos has the age (*helikia*) which you see for yourselves. Aeschines may be making several points here. First, he seems to suggest that Timarchos (in fact at least 45, but Aeschines had suggested he was younger, see on **49**) is still relatively young to have held so many offices, and the further allegation follows that he sees them largely as a source of profit. Earlier, however, (**26**, see also **49**) the point made about his appearance was that, though young, his body looked raddled (and he was in fact younger than the well-preserved Misgolas). So here the further inference may be that 'he has (had) the youthful lifestyle (whose effects) you see', and yet has also held (and made money out of) many offices', even holding offices while still engaged in his shameful relationships (see **109–12**). *Helikia* often means 'prime of life' or 'lifestyle' as well as 'age'; see **120**, **155**, **162**; at **182** it is a girl's 'youthful prime', in effect her virginity

bought his way into them all. No evidence or further argument is offered for this allegation. On such allegations of bribery, constant in our speeches, and often with very little evidence supplied, see Wankel (1982), who argues that all allegations of bribery which were not made the subject of specific legal charges should be taken to be false, and Harvey (1985), who suggests that some, at least, might be well founded, especially if witnesses or documents were apparently produced (see on **114**).

107 auditor (*logistes*).. Ten annual auditors (appointed by lot) examined the accounts of magistrates who had handled public moneys at the end of each year, assisted by 'advocates' (*synegoroi*) who prosecuted if cases came to court (Arist. *Ath. Pol.* 54. 2 with Rhodes *ad loc.*; Piérart 1971: 526–73; Roberts 1982: 17–18; Rubinstein forthcoming). On allegations of corrupt behaviour among such magistrates, see also Christ (1998: 135).

did a very great deal of damage. This statement fits the usual pattern of allegations against corrupt officials or sykophants, that they took bribes from the guilty to cover up their crimes, and blackmailed the innocent. Absence even of any names, let alone any witnesses, does not give confidence: see Wankel (1982: 40–1).

an office (*arche*) in Andros. The date of this (as of the previous post) is uncertain. Aeschines enumerates the following political activities: auditor, official on the confederate island of Andros, member of the *boule* in the archonship of Nikophemos (361/0), inspector of the mercenary troops in Eretria (348), and finally an aborted prosecution in the *diapsephisis* of 346/5. This list may be in chronological order, and hence the posts as *logistes* and *archon* on Andros occurred before 361/0 (so e.g. G. L. Cawkwell, 'Notes on the Failure of the Second Athenian Confederacy', *JHS* 101 (1981), 51–2 and n. 47, followed by Develin, *AO* p. 262, tentatively placing the *logistes* post in 364/3, and the office in Andros 363/2); it would follow that the garrison of Andros was introduced before the end of the 360s, with important implications for the history of Athens' relations with her allies in the Second Confederacy. But Aeschines seems to be operating with a different classification of posts, two allotted posts where Timarchos could operate on his own (*logistes*, the office on Andros), the allotted but collegiate place on the council of 500, and an elective post as inspector of the troops. So the inference that the office on Andros predates 361/0 is possible, but not certain. It is certain that a garrison and an official called the *archon* with a generally supervisory role were in place on Andros by 356, as an Athenian inscription dated to the eighth prytany of Agathokles' archonship, i.e. *c.* May 356 (*IG* II² 123 = Tod II 156 = Harding no. 69), records the successful motion of Hegesandros, by which one of the existing generals is charged with ensuring the 'safety' of the island of Andros, a member of the Athenian Second Confederacy since 373, and the payment of money for the garrison already present (see Cargill 1981: 155–7), and an Archedemos is also to collect money owed from the islands and give it to the *archon* on Andros, to pay the troops. But it is not quite certain whether the office attributed to Timarchos is the same as that envisaged in the inscription. On the problems of identifying where *archontes* were placed and what they did in these allied cities, see Cargill (1981: 151–60; 1995: 145–52). It is intriguing to observe Timarchos' close friend Hegesandros involved with the problems of financing the garrison on Andros and conveying money to the *archon*; but as Aeschines does not on this occasion allege, as he will *à propos* of the affairs of 361/0, a case of joint corruption by the pair, there need be no connection between that interest and his friend's office (whenever that took place).

bought for thirty mnai, borrowing the money at nine obols for the mna. Presumably it is alleged that Timarchos borrowed this money from one or more of his friends, to bribe some one somehow to tamper with the allotment process, or buy off any alternative candidates (see Hansen 1989: 232–3); the rate of interest, 1½ drachmai per 100 drachmai per month, works out as 18 per cent per annum, and is cited as indicating a high rate (though higher rates are attested: see the list at Davies 1981: 63–4). This is intended to reveal Timarchos' eagerness to worm his way into a lucrative and enjoyable post, that would enable him to live his preferred luxurious life on Andros as well as to pay off the loan; the story is also designed to suggest Timarchos' own lack of ready cash. See generally G. E. M. de Ste Croix, *The Class Struggle in the Ancient Greek World* (London, 1981), 604–5, who cites this allegation, and also the decree of Arkesine on Amorgos, which honours Androtion (on whom see also **165**) for his support when governor there also during the Social War period (357–5); it praises him for not wronging any citizen or foreigner and for lending the city money free of interest, apparently ways in which Athenian élite individuals, generals, governors, and other officials, may have made money out of the Confederacy (as also from the fifth-century Empire). Millett (1991: 278) questions whether Aeschines is alleging here financial corruption as well as opportunity for his sexual outrages, and adds reasonably that Timarchos will also have been looking for the prestige of the office. But the point of mentioning the loan taken out to buy the office certainly includes the imputation to Timarchos and his friends and creditors of the expectation of being able to pay back the loan with interest, and also, probably, of ending up with a surplus to spend on further debaucheries back in Athens.

made your allies the source of supplies. The Athenians established their second league with many promises that the allies' council (*synedrion*) would be respected, and the objectionable practices of the fifth-century Empire would be avoided (see *IG* II² 43, and Cargill 1981: 131–45). From the early 350s onwards, they were aware of the instability of many of the alliances, especially under pressure from Mausolos of Caria and faced the revolt of many allies in the 'Social War': see Cargill (1981: 161–88); S. Horn-blower, *Mausolus* (Oxford, 1982), ch. vii. Andros seems to have remained loyal and friendly, despite the possibly oppressive presence of garrison and officials, at least until *c.* 348/7 (*IG* II² 1441, lines 12–13, and see Tod II 166–7). Hence Aeschines can attack Timarchos for his allegedly gratuitous and tyrannical assaults on one of Athens' most loyal allies; but the allegation should not readily be believed.

debauchery . . . wantonness in relation to the wives of free men. The strong terms *bdeluria* and *aselgeia* are again used here (see on **26** and **32**) for Timarchos' grossly offensive behaviour. Allegations of the abuse of power by the sexual exploitation of adultery assimilates Timarchos' behaviour to that of the standard tyrant, who was seen as deriving pleasure not only from the sex but also, perhaps more, from the infliction of dishonour or *hybris* on the free male householders whose women he abused: see Fisher (1992: 30–1, 128–9) and especially Omitowoju (1997: 4–6) on the primary focus in these descriptions on the dishonour to free males, not on the lack of consent by the direct victims. On the portrayal of Timarchos here as a tyrant, see also Meulder (1989: 319); Davidson (1997: 282).

on which he has chosen to keep silent. In this case, the probability that these allegations are total inventions explains the lack of witnesses, which Aeschines here has to acknowledge. But he has chosen to make this admission in relation to the allegations of sexual abuse of wives, rather than the allegations of bribery or sycophancy, because it was plausible that Andrian husbands would be reluctant or even unable to give testimony in an Athenian court at least two decades later about their family's shame at the hands of an Athenian magistrate. See analogously Arist. *Rhet.* 1373a35, with D. Cohen (1991: 129–32; 1995: 148, 155); Foxhall (1991; 1994: 142–3), on the likelihood that many Athenian men may have been prepared to hush up cases of extramarital sex with their wives or daughters to avoid public ridicule.

108 a *hybristes* not only against other people but also against his own body. Once more, as Timarchos' acts of sexual *hybris* against non-Athenian householders are described, the jury is reminded of the 'indivisibility' of *hybris* as a force driving individuals to shameful deeds, and hence the necessary connection between a youth who offended against his own body and masculinity and an adult, tyrannical, *hybristes*. See Dover (1978: 38).

where laws exist, where you are watching him, where enemies are set against him. This dramatic phrasing offers a vivid (if perhaps one-sided) picture of the sense that members of the politically active élite in Athens faced both the constant, intrigued and possibly hostile gaze of the *demos*, and the active hostility of their personal enemies. See generally Winkler (1990a: 59).

no one appeared as a buyer of the city of Andros. The final effective hyperbole again presents Timarchos as the tyrant and indeed as the virtual owner of Athens' loyal ally, prepared to sell it, as he sold himself and all his own property, to any buyer. See Davidson (1997: 257, 261–2).

109 To recount all the wrongs. Once more Aeschines resorts to the device of *praeteritio*, asserting there are many more scandals, which he will forbear to mention, thus enabling him to throw out vague allegations without giving the slightest detail. See also on **39, 131, 170.**

was a member of the Council in the archonship of Nikophemos (361/0). This is the most important indication of a date for any of Timarchos' earlier offices. On its implications, see Intro. pp. 11–12, 21, and on **42, 43, 49, 54–71, 95.**

110 Hegesandros. Timarchos' old friend appears again in closest collaboration. He was apparently one of the ten treasurers (*tamiai*) of Athena in the same year (but see on **55** above). On the history of the *tamiai*, the primary disbursers of some of Athens' public moneys, see generally W. S. Ferguson, *The Treasurers of Athena* (Cambridge, Mass., 1932), and especially ch. XII on *tamiai* in this period and 138, n.1 on this episode. Other evidence suggests regular scrutiny by the *boule* of the treasurers' financial handling (Arist. *Ath. Pol.* 47. 1 with Rhodes *ad loc.*, and e.g. IG II² 120). It was perhaps a plausible accusation that a member of the *boule* might help cover up expropriation by a treasurer (Rhodes 1972: 110); this time the reported malicious accusation from Pamphilos gives a somewhat greater sense of authenticity.

very amicably The adverb used here meaning 'amicably',

philetairos, is cunningly designed to suggest two distinct types of inappropriate relationship. The primary meaning of the term applied to male co-operation would suggest the loyalty of *hetairoi* which may be admirable or excessive; the contested nature of the term is pointed out in Thuc. 3. 82. 4, where among the altered valuations of terms in conditions of *stasis* irrational daring is called *philetairos andreia*, that is courage in showing loyalty to the politically motivated group of friends, or Theoph. *Char.* 29. 4 where the man who likes to associate with villains praises one of them for being a 'loyal friend'. A group of close friends and political associates is often called a *hetaireia*. See also e.g. Dem. 21. 20 and 149 (on Meidias' crooked supporters, prepared to give false witness), and Dem. 54, 14 and 56 (similarly of Konon's band of unruly and arrogant revellers), with G. M. Calhoun, *Athenian Clubs in Politics and Litigation* (Austin, 1913), and MacDowell, *Meidias* 356–7. Here then the word suggests that Hegesandros and Timarchos are part of, or constitute, a tightly-knit political association to deceive the people. The other implication, which becomes more evident as we hear Pamphilos' allegation, is to suggest that Timarchos' relation to Hegesandros is still one of *hetairesis*. See the play on 'be a *hetairos*' and be involved in self-*hetairesis* at Andoc. 1. 100–1 and also below on **173**.

Pamphilos of Acherdous. (*LGPN* 33; *PA* 11540; Hansen, *Inventory* 56). Many Athenians of that name are recorded, but no one else from this deme.

he ran up against Timarchos. In what way is not made clear, but the implication (see **2**) is that a reasonable man would not attack another for political offences in the assembly or the courts unless first provoked, so that revenge and defence of *polis* interests worked together.

they are stealing from you, a man and a woman together. The procedure Pamphilos used appears to be the public indictment, *eisangelia*, to the Council, leading to its investigation, and the possibility of a jury trial. See Hansen (1975: esp. p. 119, no. 143). Pamphilos' formal charge may conceivably have included *hetairesis* with Hegesandros (so apparently Hansen), as well as embezzlement; more likely, these were merely insulting and attention-grabbing remarks against both Hegesandros and Timarchos (if they were uttered at all), and were not included in the formal indictment.

Pamphilos' insult assimilated Leodamas' and Hegesandros' relationship, and now that of Hegesandros with Timarchos, to that between a man and a woman (see also Ar. *Eccl.* 102–4). What exactly this was meant to imply is disputed. Most (e.g. Cantarella 1989: 159; D. Cohen (1991a: 188–9) see it as the representation of their sexual relationship as the 'unnatural' subservience of the junior partner adopting the passive, 'woman's' role, i.e. submitting to penetration. Davidson, however, as part of his extended argument against the 'penetration people', suggests that any specifically sexual reference in these allegations is less prominent than a more general presentation of the younger man's social and political dependence, accepting meals and favours from the older man as a 'flatterer' or 'parasite', and in return supporting him in crooked political activities as a sykophant (1997: 270–7). There seems little doubt, however, what Aeschines means to imply, by repeating (as he claims) these insults. In the light of **70, 75–6**, and **185**, the important move, made over and over again, is to argue from the evidence of close association and social and financial dependence between a pair to the conclusion that they perform, in secret, shameful and 'unmentionable' acts of sexual depravity, involving the younger partner selling his body, committing *hybris* against himself, and playing the woman, and Aeschines is surely here enlisting Pamphilos and those who heard his remarks as further 'witnesses' to what Athenians 'all knew' about these relationships. It is probable that, if Pamphilos did actually make such remarks, he meant to suggest all those aspects of dependence which Davidson elucidates; but it is impossible to avoid concluding that a major point of such an offensive labelling of a political and social relationship as 'man and woman' (or 'man and wife') is strongly to imply a deficiency in his sexual masculinity. Such abuse would in all or almost all cases be picking up on existing sexual gossip, and summoning up at least the possibility of a prosecution under these laws aimed at the politically active.

111–12 leaf-votes. This is the prime passage for this procedure of internal self-discipline for members of the *boule* (see Rhodes 1972: 38–9, 144–7; Hansen 1991: 258). In such a case, the Council took a preliminary secret vote, using, for some unexplained reason, olive-leaves, and if there was a majority against the councillor, they took another secret vote (perhaps after more investigation and a longer hearing) with the more usual pebbles (*psephoi*) and could then pass the case on to a court, or perhaps merely expel him from the Council. It is conceivable that this method of voting, like ostracism, was modelled on ancient scape-goating rituals: see Ogden (1997: 143). Another case appears to have been mentioned in a speech by Deinarchos written for some-one in a legal action against Polyeuktos, who had apparently been convicted under the leaf-vote procedure: whether this Polyeuktos was one of the several prominent men of that name in the third quarter of the fourth century is not clear (see *PA* 11928 and Dein. ed. Conomis, pp. 74–6).

What may have happened in this instance cannot be deter-mined. It is perhaps likely that Pamphilos made some accusations against Timarchos and Hegesandros, and also that the Council was denied its crown that year; but these two events may not have been causally connected, nor need the accusation of collaboration in peculation have been justified; no doubt Timarchos claimed that Pamphilos was an enemy peddling sycophantic lies, and that he was fully exonerated by the Council's second vote.

113 But which of you does not know of his notorious con-viction for embezzlement? It is perhaps surprising that nothing is made of Timarchos' cowardice, nor of the apparent absence of a military career (see Burckhardt 1996: 238, n. 302). This is the nearest to that, but his part in the campaign in Euboia was as an inspector of the numbers of mercenary troops, and the emphasis lies on the corruption, not on any cowardice (contrast the sneers at Demosthenes and others who evaded service by such posts at 2. 148, 151, 177). But it is Demosthenes, not Timarchos, who is presented as effeminate and a *kinaidos* (Burckhardt seems to confuse **113** and **131**, to suggest that general allegations of cowardice, *kinaideia*, and woman's clothes are made against Timarchos). One may suspect that in fact Timarchos could cite solid instances of military service, though perhaps no particular deeds of glory (or else Demosthenes might have reminded the jury of them e.g. at 19. 283–7).

Such a conviction as alleged here, if true, constitutes a far more serious charge than any of the previous allegations about Timarchos' career. In 348 Athens responded to the appeal from the alleged 'tyrant' of Eretria, Ploutarchos, by sending select troops (*epilektoi*) and perhaps other soldiers (on these troops see Tritle 1988: 76–80; Munn 1993: 189–90) in support of his mercenary army, against internal Eretrian opponents, and other Euboians. On these events see G. L Cawkwell, 'The Defence of Olynthus', *CQ* 12 (1962), 127–30; Brunt (1969: 248–51); J. M. Carter (1971: 418–29); Knoepfler (1981; 1984: 152–6; 1995: 338–46), Dreher (1995: 155–97) and Burckhardt (1996: 122). Athenian troops, under Phokion, and with Aeschines playing a prominent role (see Intro. pp. 13–14, 16–17), won a victory at Tamynai in difficult circumstances, but Ploutarchos proved incompetent and unreliable, and Phokion decided to eject him from the island. The result overall was to weaken Athenian interests and led to many recriminations (Aesch. 2. 169–70, 3. 86–8; Plut. *Phok.* 12–13). Timarchos and his fellow *exetastai* (inspectors), who had probably been appointed in the year 348/7 (Develin *AO* p. 317) had been charged with assessing and scrutinizing the payments to the mercenary troops whom Athens agreed to maintain; in the circumstances this will not have been an easy task.

You sent him as an inspector (*exetastes*) of the mercenary troops. *Exetastai* are listed by Aristotle (*Pol.* 1322b10) with other accounting officials, while late lexicographical notes state more helpfully that they 'are those officials sent out to assess in advance the number of the foreign troops, so that pay may be sent for them' (*Lex Seguer.*, ed I. Bekker, *Anecdota Graeca*, I. 252), and add 'this is because the generals used to tell lies, when hiring troops in foreign lands' (*Etymologicum Graecum*, p. 386, 10). Aeschines' criticisms of contemporary venal politicians (2. 177) includes the allegation that they never see danger themselves, but acquire comfortable jobs as *exetastai* and naval commissioners (*apostoleis*).

The *exetastai* who appear on Athenian documents for a brief period at the start of the third century constitute a later development. Between 301/0 and 295/4, while the rule of the tyrant Lachares in Athens relied heavily on mercenary troops, an *exetastes* was given special financial powers to disburse moneys: see *IG* II² 641, 646, 1270, and *Hesperia* 11 (1942) 278 and M. J. Osborne (1981–3: II, 144–53); Rhodes (1997: 45).

he, alone of the board of inspectors, admitted that he had accepted money. The argument was, presumably, that Timarchos and his fellow-inspectors (on their own, or perhaps in collusion with one or more of the generals involved—for whom see Tritle 1988: 79–80), exaggerated the numbers of mercenaries, or in some other way, appropriated illicit funds: see Parke (1933: 149); Burckhardt (1996: 148–9). This seems damning, and the allegation of corruption by the *exetastai* is usually believed (e.g. by Parke). It is, however, alarming that no witnesses seem to have been cited for what was allegedly a recent offence, confession, and fine, nor is it stated whether the fine was paid, or was still outstanding. Further, enough remains from this murky affair to suspect a complex network of political and personal disagreements and counter-charges among the politicians and soldiers involved in the campaign.

An intriguing Athenian decree may be relevant. Hegesippos *Krobylos* proposed a decree (*IG* II² 125 = Tod II 154 = Harding no. 66) commanding the *boule* to arrange for the punishment of those who had broken laws in relation to a campaign against the territory of the Eretrians, and to ensure that similar offences were not committed in any subsequent campaign there. Knoepfler (1984; 1995: 338–46) has shown that it makes more sense to relate this decree to this campaign of 348, rather than, as previously, to the more successful campaign of 357 (to which *IG* II² 124 = Tod II 153 relates), and that the offenders in the campaign were on the side of the Athenians and their allies. He suggests that Hegesippos may have proposed this some years later, around the time of the Embassy trial in 343, when his and Demosthenes' political positions were stronger. I doubt, however, that one should exclude the possibility that Hegesippos got this motion passed in the more immediate aftermath of the campaign, when mutual personal recriminations were flying around, especially between Meidias who had backed the campaign and Demosthenes who had opposed it (and who left it, arguably early, to perform his role as *choregos*: see also Dreher 1995: 167–73). When Meidias—also, of course, in pursuit of their long-standing personal feud—punched Demosthenes at the City Dionysia of 348, many legal actions ensued (see on **170–2**; Dem. 21. 103–4 for charges against Demosthenes, Dem. 21. esp. 131–5, 162–7, for Demosthenes' accusations against Meidias, with MacDowell, *Meidias* 325–31, 349–54, 380–7; and Knoepfler 1981; Dem. 5. 5, and 9. 57–8). Conceivably, Hegesippos' charges were intended to support a general case against those he and Demosthenes held responsible for the disaster, including Meidias, and perhaps also Euboulos, to whom perhaps Aeschines was already attaching himself. On the other side, the description of the campaign in Plutarch (*Phok.* 12–14. 1, however, exaggerated to present Phokion in a splendid light, and see Dem. 21. 110) presents a picture of widespread treachery and bribery in the island, and ill-discipline and back-biting in the army; it describes the apparent flight of Ploutarchos and his mercenaries, the ejection of Ploutarchos from the island by Phokion, the eventual capitulation of one other general, Molossos, to 'the enemy', the condemnation of another general, Hegesileos, Euboulos' cousin, for collusion with Ploutarchos (Dem. 19. 290 with *scholia*), and ends with the report that Ploutarchos, lacking pay, handed to them Athenian captives who had then to be ransomed at a cost of 50 talents (Dem. 5. 5 and *scholion*). All this allows abundant scope for a group looking for scapegoats, and perhaps also opposed to Demosthenes and his friends, to bring counter-charges against Timarchos and his fellow-inspectors for profiteering or holding on to moneys destined for the mercenaries (see also the accounts in J. M. Carter 1971; Tritle 1988: 81–9).

immediately supplicated concerning the penalty. On such supplications for sympathy, see on **99**; they were naturally frequent in the stage of trials when convicted defendants pleaded for a lesser penalty: see Johnstone (1999: 117–19). Timarchos' admission and grovelling request for mercy allegedly got his fine reduced by a half. If true, it is puzzling why Timarchos alone of the inspectors embarked on this form of plea-bargaining. There is likely to be no little evasion and distortion in this account.

the laws prescribe that thieves who admit guilt are to be punished with death, while those who deny it are to be put on trial. This is a particularly specious argument (though not much is made of it). It attempts to assimilate a political embezzler who confessed his offence in the hope of getting a reduced fine to a common thief, i.e. a *kakourgos* caught in the act or in clearly incriminating circumstances, who might be dragged off to the Eleven and summarily executed (see above on **91**, Hansen 1976; E. M. Harris 1990; 1994).

114 he went straight on to grab two thousand drachmai. There are various problems with this case as well. One is that Timarchos, a member of the deme Sphettos, appears to be taking the leading part in expelling Philotades from the list of the deme

Kydathenaion; nothing else is known of Philotades (*LGPN* 6; *PA* 14924), or his in-law Leukonides (*LGPN* 1; *PA* 9070). One might have thought that Timarchos' only proper role in the case can have been as a witness both at the deme hearing and the subsequent appeal before the jury, and members of Kydathenaion ought to have presented the case; for the appointment of five official accusers, *kategoroi*, from the deme in such cases, see Arist. *Ath. Pol.* 42.1, with Rhodes *ad loc*. Conceivably what lies beneath the potentially misleading phrase 'took charge of the prosecution' is precisely that Timarchos was brought in from outside as a witness to provide the main argument and weight to the prosecution. Secondly, one possible view is that the money offered by Leukonides through Philemon was the original bribe to support the expulsion, so that there was at the centre of the case an unsavoury dispute between close relatives (so Whitehead 1986a: 295–6); another, perhaps more plausible, view is that the 20 mnai was rather the money put together by relatives to save Philotades by persuading Timarchos to drop, or to arrange to lose, the case. For the first of these alternatives, see Davidson (1997: 234), suggesting the scenario where one member of a family seemed poor, and vulnerable to the accusation of having been a slave, while a brother-in-law managed to get together the cash to deal with the problem; for the second, that the deal was done by presenting the prosecution case deliberately badly, see Rubinstein forthcoming. Assuming some truth in this story, the family may have worked together, to decide tactics and deploy contacts, after the initial shock of the adverse vote in the deme, and eventually decided on paying the powerful Timarchos. It is less than clear whether they—or some of them—always intended to follow this up by informing against Timarchos—through Philemon the actor—or whether this came about in some other way. Aeschines does at least in this case appear to have two prime witnesses and copies of the agreement to be read to the jury: see Harvey (1985: 92).

he took the sacred offerings. Timarchos is shown, first, to have been fully prepared to perform the complete ritual of the solemn oath, making the essential physical contact with the sacred objects of the sacrifice; and second, apparently, to have immediately been convicted of perjury: see Burkert (1985: 252).

gods of oaths. For the importance of taking the oath in these deme procedures, see Dem. 57. 8, 63; Arist. *Ath. Pol.* 42. 1 and Whitehead (1986a: 93). Zeus *Horkios* ('of oaths') is generally the main deity the Greeks swore to ask to attend to those who attest by oath, and hence to ensure the punishment of perjurers. Later sources, that is *scholia* on this passage, who cite also Deinarchos fr. 29 (Conomis), and *Schol. B Iliad* 15. 36 (who refers to a law of Drakon's) identify Zeus, Apollo Patroios, and Demeter as the gods by whom the Athenians especially swore such solemn oaths. Evidence for this triad (collected by A. Cook, *Zeus: A Study in Ancient Religion* (Cambridge, 1914–40), II, 729–30) includes both epigraphic instances: the 'heliastic oath' sworn by the jurors on the Ardettos hill according to Pollux 8. 122 and other lexicographical sources, though a document included in Dem. 24. 151 names Zeus, Poseidon, and Demeter: see Boegehold (1995: 186–7) (on this oath, see also on **154**); two state treaties (*IG* I³ 15, II² 97); and a deme decree from Hagnous or Myrrhinous concerned with bribery and irregularities (*IG* II² 1183; see J. Traill, *Demos and Trittys: Epigraphic and Topographical Studies in the Organization of Attica* (Toronto, 1986), 132); and literary references, e.g. Ar. *Kn.* 941, and Dem. 52. 9. Other combinations were also used. Burkert (1985: 251) explains the choice of these three in terms of Zeus (*Horkios*) as the god for oaths, and a balance between Apollo (*Patroios*) as the patriarchal god of the phratries and Demeter of the *Thesmophoria*, the 'light and the dark'. In the context of demes and citizenship disputes one might think especially of Apollo *Patroios'* responsibility for men's membership of the *polis* through the phratry and the scrutiny of citizens (see Arist. *Ath. Pol.* 55. 3, with C. Hedrick, 'The Temple and Cult of Apollo Patroos', *AJA* 92 (1988), 185–210; Lambert 1993: 211–17), and Demeter as the goddess of those festivals (especially the *Thesmophoria*) which recognized and re-inforced citizen women's membership of the community.

115 Philemon. A successful comic actor (*LGPN* 80) who appears on the list of victorious comic actors at the Lenaia (*IG* ii² 2325 fr. i, c. 370; see also *IG* XII Suppl. 400), and was cited in Aristotle's *Rhetoric* 1413b25 for his skill at varying the tone when repeating the same words, with examples from Anaxandrides' comedy *Old Man's Madness* and the prologue of *The Pious Ones*. See Ghiron Bistagne (1976: 155); Stefanis (1988: 2485).

twenty mnai . . . spent in a short time on Philoxene the

escort (*hetaira*). As a *hetaira*, she can be named in a public speech, unlike respectable daughters or wives of citizens: see Schaps, (1977: 323–30). Women of that name are found on two Attic gravestones at *IG* i³ 1333, *IG* II² 6300 (a relief of a seated woman stretching a hand to her husband, named as Stratippos). For the twenty mnai allegedly spent on his pleasures with this woman, see Loomis (1998: 172). Such a figure would be envisaged to include gifts, maintenance for a period, expenditure on parties and the like, not merely cash payments to the woman, and in any case is likely to be exaggerated, if not simply an extravagant guess.

116 Well then . . . In this transitional paragraph, Aeschines sums up the 'narrative' section dealing with Timarchos' career in reverse order: political career, treatment of relatives, dissipation of property, and sexual career. This enables him to conclude the summary with the repeated, but powerful, phrase 'accepted . . . the *hybris* against his own body', and then to hide the serious lack of evidence by the repeated assertion that they only needed reminding of what they all knew anyway. This point may have been aided by the fact that while most of the events alleged took place decades earlier, he ended his detailed account with two relatively recent events, the Euboian episode and the *diapsephisis*, where some of the jury may well have had a memory of some scandal attached to Timarchos' name.

Two subjects remain. Aeschines has divided the remainder of his speech into the rebuttal of alleged arguments of the defence (**117–76**) and a moral protreptic to the young (**177–96**).

I pray to all the gods and goddesses. The solemnity of the transition is marked again by this invocation of the divinities. See Aesch. 2. 180, 3. 1, and the many occasions in this speech where he has appealed to the gods.

SECTION IV 117–76 Anticipation of opponents' arguments

A common tactic in Athenian law-court speeches is to rebut in advance what litigants claim to have heard will be their opponents' most dangerous arguments. Given the amount of gossip in political circles, then as now, accurate reports of one's opponent's probable arguments may well often have been available, and in any case speculation was also easy; and if the opposition turned out not to use the argument, one could always claim, or let it be thought, that the rebuttal had scared them off. Alternatively such passages could be inserted later into the published speech, to combat arguments which were used.

Here it is evidently central to Aeschines' strategy to get his retaliation in first to counter the arguments expected from the defence, and, equally, if not more important, to undermine Demosthenes' status as his leading opponent by presenting him as an unscrupulous rhetorical manipulator, as no athlete, and as a *kinaidos* whose pose as a teacher and lover of youths was undermined by deficiencies alike of masculinity and loyalty. See in general Dover (1968: 167–70, and on this section, 1978: 40–1).

117–124 *The argument over prostitutes' tax*

117 the man who makes promises. Demosthenes is alluded to here, and named immediately afterwards (119). This first snide reference throws out insinuations, which will be taken up later (131, 170–5, 181), concerning his relations with his rhetorical pupils, and his promises and programmes offered to them. For comparable attempts to represent opponents as excessively clever, and rhetorically manipulative, see Dover (1968: 155–8; 1974: 25–6; 1978: 25); Hesk (1999: 208–18).

exhortation of the citizens towards moral goodness (*arete*). This theme focuses the final section of the speech firmly on the wider context, the future moral well-being of Athens and her young citizens; on the possible success of this exhortation in gaining the condemnation, see Intro. pp. 53–67. This is the first of the six uses in this speech of the term *arete*, the most general and perhaps most highly charged term for moral goodness: see also **140, 146, 151, 180, 191.**

are present in the court. On the regularly assumed presence at the trial of spectators, both Athenians and foreigners, see above on **77**, below on **173**, and Intro. pp. 56–8; on the appeal to a wider non-Athenian interest, and hence the sense that Athens' public reputation is at stake, see. Andoc. 1. 140; Lysias 14. 12–13; Lyc. 1. 14; and Lanni (1997: 186–7).

118 know how to make good laws. This sentence repeats the emphasis in the introduction, and further expatiated on in the conclusion (see on **6**, and **185–7**, **192**), that implementing the laws is as important as having them on the books.

119 over-clever orator. This phrase (*perittos en tois logois*) is applied again to Demosthenes by Aeschines in a slightly extended form at 2. 114; see Dover (1978: 25, 40).

the Council farms out the prostitutes' tax (*pornikon telos*). Demosthenes' first point is going to be that if Timarchos really was a *pornos* (as is alleged both by Aeschines' prosecution and, apparently, by his supposed 'nickname'), proof should be forthcoming in terms of the tax collected, and (as he says in **120**) of specific buildings where he sat plying his trade.

The function of the *poletai* (sellers), in managing in the presence of the *boule*, the farming out of such indirect taxes is attested by Arist. *Ath. Pol.* 47. 2; on the farming process, Andoc. 1. 73, 133–6, the (incomplete) lists of taxes in Ar. *Wasps* 657–9, and the new inscription establishing the farming of a grain-tax on the islands of Lemnos, Imbros, and Skyros of 374/3: see Stroud (1999), and esp. his useful list of known taxes on goods and their rates, 27–30. Farmers of the prostitutes-tax (*pornotelonai*) are mentioned also in Pollux 7. 202, 9. 29, both times quoting from Philonides' *Kothornoi*, where in a list of people 'wholly cursed by birth, whore-tax-farmers, frightful Megarians, parricides' are said to collect the 2 per cent tax. De Ste Croix (1972: 271–2, 398) argues that *pornotelonai* here is more likely to be taken as an abusive term for all tax-collectors, but in favour of a more specific attack it seems perfectly reasonable to suppose that tax-farmers who had to collect from whores and their pimps came in for extra opprobrium.

A more honest response from Aeschines to this challenge might be that he is alleging that Timarchos was 'virtually' a prostitute, but not actually that he ever sat in a patent brothel or cubicle to take cash for sex as his main source of income; rather (see esp. **52**) that he lived with and off a succession of men, and perhaps slept with other men there or in their own houses, and was regularly supplied with food and drink, presents, and perhaps money from some of these 'lovers' (see Dover 1978: 107). Hence he could say that to expect records of tax-collections or evidence of sojourns in specific brothels would be unreasonable. But the idea of

'Timarchos the *pornos*' is too valuable to be undermined by such an admission. Instead, he offers (**121–2**) rhetorical flummery that Timarchos should, if innocent, simply offer stout denial and trust to the jury's knowledge of the decency of his life, together with the sophistic argument that as brothels, like other 'workshops' were fluid buildings, Timarchos in effect converted the houses of the men he lived with into brothels by his activities.

120 prepared to serve on embassies. Presumably Timarchos has served on at least two embassies as well as his other posts: see Hansen, *Inventory* 60; Develin, *AO* p. 351. Serving on embassies was taken to be one of the leading activities of the *rhetores* (see also on **32**). Ambassadors, who had to make effective formal speeches when abroad, and defend their actions when they returned, often in a subsequent law-court action as well as in the assembly, were naturally selected from those who spoke and proposed motions in the assembly: see e.g. Dem. 18. 219, Hansen (1984: 155–7). The argument that it is especially shameful for the city that a man like Timarchos represents it on embassies recurs with much greater vehemence at the end (see on **188**).

121 which is honourable and just . . . unless you are conscious of something shameful. The emphasis throughout the speech on the shamefulness of the whole of Timarchos' life will have enabled Aeschines to impart a knowing and amusing sarcasm to these words.

    have the courage to look straight at the jurymen. See also **161–2**, Dem. 18. 283, on the importance of firm eye-contact with the jury as a sign of manliness and absence of shame, with Bremmer (1991: 22–3); Hall (1995: 51).

    self–controlled (*sophron*) in matters concerning his prime of life (*helikia*). On the term *helikia* as applied to males, see on **106**. Here the reference is clearly to the issue of the sexual relationships of boys and young men.

122 I should think my life to be not worth living. This is a phrase commonly used in law-court speeches, which may operate with differing levels of seriousness. A close parallel to this case, of an individual's own sense of shame if certain accusations against him are believed, is provided at Aesch. 2. 4; Aeschines adopts there the same tactic which he recommends (ironically) for Timarchos here, asserting that his life would not be worth living if the charges of *hybris* and drunken violence against the Olynthian captive woman were believed. An equally serious use comes with the claim at **183** that the purpose of the law imposing humiliations on women convicted of sexual offences was to make their lives not worth living (and cf. Lyc. fr. 10; Dem. 24. 141). Alternatively, one may claim that one's enemy does not think life worth living unless he continues to commit some abuse or crime (Aesch. 3. 149; Dem. 21. 131).

offer up my punishment as the defence for the city to make to the rest of the Greeks. Aeschines deliberately pitches the imagined plea very high, seeming to make the imaginary decent Timarchos admit that if he were guilty, he would deserve a serious punishment, and that the city would need to be seen thereby to clear its name before the rest of the Greeks.

I have not come here to plead for mercy. The word used here—*paraiteisthai*—is commonly employed for the requests for leniency or forgiveness by defendants in trials, whether for a lighter verdict at the stage following conviction where the jury made its choice (*timesis*) between the two alternatives proposed to it (Aesch. 3. 198; Dem. 21.5; cf. also the negative adjective, *aparaitetos*, of Justice, juries, or penalties not amenable to such pleading, Dem. 25. 11; Lyc. 1. 2; Dein. 1. 3); or more generally for a fair hearing (Dem. 18. 246).

123 house at which you were sitting. For this phrase of prostitution, see Ps. Dem. 59. 6 (where it appears to be a phrase used in a law of Solon's, see Kapparis, *Neaira* 311–12), Isaeus 6. 19, and the slave-prostitute Alke in the brothels in Peiraieus and Kerameikos; Plat. *Charm.*163b (*ep'oikematos kathemenai*). See also on **74.**

124 we call it a multiple-dwelling. *Synoikiai*, multipledwellings, here conveniently defined and distinguished from family houses, were naturally extremely common in Attica, especially in the Athens-Peiraieus complex (on the term *synoikia*, see Pritchett 1956: 268; Cox 1998: 135–6). Because Athenians did not allow foreigners settling in their country (metics) to own either land or house (unless they were given that specific right in a grant, or full citizenship, see J. Peçírka, *The Formula for the Grant of Enktesis in Attic Inscriptions* (Prague, 1966); Whitehead 1977: 69–72, 117; M. J. Osborne 1981–3), many Athenians were enabled to earn income by renting out houses, which in many cases might be multiple dwellings (see e.g. Ps. Xen. *Ath. Pol.* 1. 17; Isaeus 2. 27; with Davies 1981: 51–2).

The elaborate reconstruction of the planned city of the Peiraieus proposed by W. Hoepfner and E. L. Schwandner, *Haus und Stadt im klassichen Griechenland* (2nd edn., Munich, 1994), based on a few rescue excavations, but involving the division of virtually every block into similar-sized family-houses, seems to leave insufficient scope either for larger houses owned by rich men (e.g. Lysias' house raided by Eratosthenes on behalf of the Thirty, Lys. 12. 1–12) or for *synoikiai*, many of which were no doubt in the Peiraieus (cf. the discussions in W. Schüller, W. Hoepfner, and E. L. Schwandner (eds.), *Demokratie und Architektur: Die hippodamische Stadtebau und die Entstehung der Demokratie*, Konstanzer Symposion 17 (Munich, 1989), 11–16, 32–5, 39–42). Another area well known for multiple-dwellings, some of which served as inns, wine-shops, and brothels, was the Kerameikos. Isaeus 6 describes the elderly Euktemon's establishment 'in the Kerameikos by the small gate', where he had set up Alke to work and spent much time 'visiting' her; other girls worked there, and wine was sold. A comparable picture is provided by an excavated house, 'House Z (c)', in very much the same area, by the Sacred Gate through which the Sacred Way passed from the Kerameikos towards the *agora*. In this phase of this building the excavators have uncovered a great many small rooms, evidence of much wool-working, three cisterns (and a pitched roof to catch the water), a room with a mosaic floor and a large courtyard, a great amount of sympotic and dining ware, and a good many statuettes and amulets of female god- desses: all this suggests a combined inn and brothel, where the slave-girls worked at their looms in the intervals of serving the clients (Knigge 1991: 88–95; Davidson 1997: 85–90). The natural but unnecessary attempt (Lind 1988) to argue that House Z (c) actually is Euktemon's *synoikia* currently founders on the excava- tors' evidence that this site was unoccupied in the first half of the fourth century, and the dating of the Isaeus speech to 364; there is no problem in assuming that this area knew many such dwellings (cf. also Halperin 1990: 91–2).

The present passage appears to give a general disquisition on how any multiple-dwelling can easily change its use, and hence its designation, when a new owner and business move in; the first example is a doctor's, and the final example is of course a prostitute-manager and female prostitutes, thus creating a brothel. The list may be more subtly composed, as Davidson (1997: 113–15) suggests, to invite the audience to pick up the parallel with the progression described of Timarchos' sexual career through the five houses of his main lovers, and a similar progression from a doctor's—Euthydikos—via Misgolas, Antikles, and Pittalakos, to a politician's who was widely rumoured to have been the '*pornos*' of another, Hegesandros. Aeschines may even, as Davidson also suggests more speculatively, be suggesting a parallel between the house and Timarchos' body, which has also been entered by a succession of men; the impression is that while Timarchos may not have lived in a specific brothel, he has in effect turned the houses he has lived in, and also his own body, into such places.

125–131 *The argument over 'Report' (Pheme)*

125 Another argument . . . composed by the same sophist. A new term of abuse—'sophist'—is now applied to Demosthenes. It alludes both to his advanced rhetorical skills, which may be used to deceive Athenians in assemblies or courts and to his acceptance of 'pupils' in rhetoric and politics; the speech will return to this point with much deadlier effect towards the end (**170–6**). Attitudes to teachers of rhetoric and other experts remained as complex and ambivalent in the fourth century as they had been in the fifth, and calling those of whom one disapproved 'sophists' remained a popular tactic. Prominent examples are the attack on a variety of intellectuals concerned to practice and teach rhetoric as 'sophists' in Isocrates' *Against the Sophists* and his extended distancing of his own practices from such sophists in the *Antidosis* (see Y. L. Too, *The Rhetoric of Identity in Isocrates* (Cambridge, 1995), ch. 5; Ober 1998: 260–8); see also the concluding remarks of the Xenophontic treatise *On Hunting*, arguing that traditional, militarily orientated, practices such as hunting are of much greater use to the young than the useless and convoluted sophistic training and books (Xen. *Kunegetikos* 13; for defences of Xenophontic authorship see J. K. Anderson, *Hunting in the Ancient World* (Berkeley & Los Angeles, 1985). ch. 3 and V. J. Gray, 'Xenophon's *Cynegeticus*', *Hermes* 113 (1985), 156–72). Demosthenes was equally prepared himself to attack sophists. As Aeschines reported (2. 112) he included in his flattery of Philip the claim that others' praise of Philip's memory was more appropriate for a professional sophist than a king; and naturally he retaliated to Aeschines' charge of being a sophist and *logographos* by claiming that Aeschines' own misuse of quotations from tragedy laid him open to the same charge: see 19. 245–50, with the analysis of Hesk (1999: 211–18).

nothing is more unjust than Report. See generally Ober (1989: 148–50); Hunter (1990; 1994: ch. 4, esp. 104–6 on this speech), and S. Lewis (1995: 10–13), on the prevalence of gossip and its general role in Athens as a form of social control. The present objection gets to the heart of the weakness of the case, the lack of virtually any evidence, and reliance on assertions of 'public knowledge', nicknames, and gossip. Aeschines offers in response a lengthy and elaborate disquisition which is as disreputable a line of argument as any to be found in this speech (see Dover 1978: 39–40). Aeschines begins the section by giving some indications of the inaccuracy of 'Report' which Demosthenes is supposed to be going to adduce.

the multiple-dwelling in Kolonos which is called Demon's house. Various men called Demon are known in the fourth century. Two were relatives of Demosthenes: his uncle Demon son of Demomeles of Paiania (*LGPN* 10; *PA* 3735; *PAA* 322715; Davies, *APF* 115–16), and his first cousin, or first cousin once removed, of the same name (*LGPN* 12; *PA* 3736; *PAA* 322730; Develin, *AO* no. 768; Davies, *APF* 117–18; Hansen, *Inventory* 43). This man was involved in a shipping fraud *c.* 340 (Dem. 32 *passim*) and later in the Harpalos Affair (Athen. 341–2 = Timocles 4 K–A, also Plut. *Dem.* 23, 27). Interestingly, he dedicated to Asklepios a house of his and its garden, so that the state cult of Asklepios could benefit from the income. The return for Demon was the grant of a priesthood in exchange, in accordance with a Delphic oracle: see *IG* II² 4969, a mid-fourth-century dedication, with R. Schlaifer, 'Demon of Paiania, Priest of Asclepius', *CP* 38 (1943), 39–43; Parker (1996: 179); and especially Davies, *APF* 117 for a convincing argument that the date cannot be fixed precisely, and may belong either to the 350s or the 330s. It is tempting to suppose that this dedication is the basis of the allusion here, as was argued by Schlaifer and W. Judeich, *Die Topographie von Athen*[2] (Munich, 1931), 460; if the dedication occurred a few years earlier, it may have been still familiar, and the alternative designation of the house would naturally also be in use, and the whole matter was one on which Demosthenes as a relative might claim to be an authority. Davies argued against this that the second example of Andokides' herm (late fifth century: see next note) points to the view that this too was not a contemporary case, and the phrase Aeschines attributes to Demosthenes—i.e. 'it is not Demon's house' instead of the clearer 'it is no longer Demon's house' makes this identification unlikely. But one might argue that this precise choice of language makes Demosthenes' alleged point appear all the more a silly and pedantic correction; further, if the point was that Demon's house had become dedicated to Asklepios, the point of similarity between the two cases becomes the confusion over whether the property was described as belonging to an individual, or to a collective sacral body, not a matter of chronological proximity. An allusion to Demosthenes' relative is, I think, probable. A further alternative has been suggested by Lambert (1999: 107), namely the Demon son of Demaretos of Agryle (*LGPN* 8; *PA* 3734; *PAA* 322660 and 322675) who appears as a member of the *genos* of the Salaminians, and is also listed on the document of those who may, as Lambert suggests, be members of *thiasoi* of Herakles; this is part of his argument linking Timarchos and many of his 'lovers' with members of the *genos* and these *thiasoi* (see on **54–71, 68**). But it seems more likely that Demosthenes would be represented as raising as an example a house of one of his relations, rather than one with which Timarchos' friends might be associated.

Herm of Andokides is not Andokides', but a monument of the tribe Aigeis. Andocides' claimed, in his defence speech of 400 or 399, that he was in fact innocent of actual involvement in the mutilation of the Herms in 415. He asserted that he had opposed the idea when it was mooted at the drinking party of the politically motivated group (*hetaireia*); subsequently, when Andokides was in any case rendered incapable of acting by a riding accident, one of the leaders of the group, Euphiletos, put it about that Andocides had agreed to mutilate the large and well-known 'Herm by the Phorbas-shrine', which had been dedicated by the tribe Aigeis, and was near his family house (Andoc. 1. 62–3). Plutarch twice observes (*Nik.* 13. 2; *Alk.* 21. 3) that, hardly surprisingly, this Herm, famous for being allegedly the only one to escape damage in 415 (Andoc. 1. 62; Philochoros, *FGH* 328 F 133; Plut. *Nik.* 13. 2; Nepos *Alc.* 3. 2; or one of the few, Thuc. 6. 27. 1), was known even in his day as 'Andokides' Herm'. On the appropriateness of targeting tribal herms, as an attack on the Athenians' citizen identity mediated through Cleisthenes' tribal system, see J. F. McGlew, 'Politics on the Margins: the Athenian *Hetaireiai* in 415 B.C.', *Historia* 48 (1999), 18–19. In this case too, the fact that most people probably had an idea why a tribal herm was known as Andokides' makes Demosthenes' point seem trivial and petty. In both cases 'Report', if technically wrong, had a perfectly reasonable point.

126 He brings himself forward by way of a joke. Demosthenes cultivated an austere manner; he was alleged to drink water himself, be distressed by exuberant drinkers, and to abuse the young as 'neat-wine tankards' (*akratokothones*). We have examples of such remarks from his own speeches (6. 30, 19. 46), a retort about such jibes in Hypereides' speech at the time of the Harpalos trials (Priscian 18. 235; Athen. 424d, inserted into Hyper. *Dem.* col. 19 in the Budé edition); and the witticism of the parasite Eukrates 'the Lark', also at the time of the Harpalos trials, apparently retold by Lynceus of Samos (Athen. 245f–246a), that Demosthenes, the man who used to call other people neat-wine tankards had drained the biggest himself. See also Davidson (1997: 67–8, 151, 155–6). Aeschines hence relishes the chance to mock and destroy, in advance, another supposed attempt at self-deprecatory wit from his opponent. The ambiguous language here seems to suggest not only that Demosthenes is going to make a clumsy attempt at ingratiation by inviting a joke at his own expense, but also that the result may be that he is thought to be just a joke.

'Batalos, as I got that nickname from my nurse as a term of endearment.' There seems no doubt that Demosthenes had somehow acquired the nickname *batalos* or *battalos*, and that it was open to varied interpretations (focusing either on the mouth or the bottom). The term in general implies some form of deformity or deficiency, and often implies verbal difficulties, such as stammering. Hence the interpretation favoured by Demosthenes himself, here, and see also Dem. 18. 180 and by his biographer Plutarch (*Dem.* 2–6) is that it was a friendly childhood nickname built on his stammer and his lisp; see Grasberger (1883: 42–6); Holst (1926); Wankel on Dem. 18. 180. Alternatively, it may have been supposed to be a Nurse's term for the baby's bottom (Dover 1978: 75; Lambin 1982: 260). It is noticeable that the one occasion where Demosthenes defends his nickname comes in the Crown speech, when he contrasts his early speech defects, which he has triumphantly overcome, with Aeschines' bad acting, in relation to his retelling of his own courageous and decisive speech made when the news of the taking of Elatea reached Athens (Dem. 18. 169–79).

But words of this form also indicated, as Aeschines notes with relish, deficiencies in masculinity or sexual deviance, whether physical castration, hermaphroditism, or effeminacy and *kinaideia*: see the material collected by Masson (1990: 111–15, 269–73) and most fully by Lambin (1982) (and on Battos the legendary deformed founder of Kyrene, see also Ogden 1997: 56–8). In Athenian invective, the most relevant parallels are Eupolis 92KA, who, according to Harpokration s.v. and the *scholia* to this passage, used *batalos* as a slang word for 'arse' or 'anus', and Antiphanes' *Auletes*, allegedly directed at a pipes-player from Ephesos called (or nicknamed) Batalos, a person of notorious effeminacy (Plut. *Dem.* 4). For the low status of pipes-players (the males were mostly non-Athenians; the females mostly slaves and held mostly to be sexually available, especially for *fellatio*) see also on **42** and P. J. Wilson (1999: 74–5, 83–5). Hence in this speech (**131**, see **164**) Aeschines uses Demosthenes' nickname to indicate his 'softness and *kinaideia*', a little more explicitly at 2. 99–100 he includes snide allegations of *fellatio*: see Dover (1978: 75). Lambin (1982: 262) further adduces evidence that *batalizein* carried associations of violent shakings of the hind quarters and the legs, as with horses suffering from nephritis, and that this type of *batalos*, like the *kinaidos*, was supposed to move his bottom too vigorously in enjoyment (see in general Davidson 1997: 176–8). But the references cited may perhaps be too late to be applicable to classical Athens (*Hippiatrica* 30. 1, 30. 12). On the supposed features of the *kinaidos/cinaidus*, including shaking of the loins, in

Hellenistic and Roman physiognomy, see Gleason (1995: 62–70); Corbeill (1997: 112–23); Williams (1999: 188–93).

So if, he argues, Timarchos was beautiful. In the embassy speech Demosthenes does in fact in a similar way acknowledge that Timarchos did not 'anticipate the suspicion which would arise from his looks at that time', and 'lived his life after that rather more energetically' and so incurred this allegedly unjustified accusation of having prostituted himself (19. 325). See Intro. pp. 53–4, on the importance of this admission; and, for the expectation that the young were reckless and headstrong, and should be disciplined by older, more experienced men, see Hyper. *Dem.* 21–2.

127 in the case of monuments. The first two examples are now explicitly argued to be pedantic and irrelevant to the case, because the 'reports' about monuments and houses which cause their ascriptions to be changed are not of moral significance in themselves. It is rumours about people which matter, and here Aeschines moves into his most important, and dubious, justification for using the alleged widespread gossip about Timarchos as reliable evidence. The careful elaboration of *pheme*, as a power spreading unerringly and automatically throughout the city, revealing details of private lives and even predicting the future, cunningly legitimizes gossip about private lives by implying (before making this explicit) that 'Report' is a divine being, a deified personification, and it is therefore right to attend to her. More commonly in Greek and Roman poetry the picture of Report flying spontaneously and with amazing speed through a community is presented rather as a monster, an 'evil more rapid than any other', and as likely to spread lies or uncertainties as truth (see Hesiod, *Works and Days*, 759–64, in part cited by Aeschines at **129**, and Virgil, *Aeneid* 173–88, and further passages listed in A. S. Pease, *P. Vergili Maronis Aeneidos Liber Quartus* (Cambridge, Mass., 1935), *ad loc.*).

128 established an altar to Report (*Pheme*). The *scholia* here state that the Athenians first set up an altar to *Pheme* in the early 460s, when it was believed that it had been learnt spontaneously at Athens of Kimon's double victory over the Persian army and fleet at Eurymedon before any official message got there. This may well be correct, though it should be noted that Procopius of Gaza (*Ep.* 40: 4th–5th century AD) seems rather to associate the altar with the amazing spread among the Greeks at Mykale of the rumour of the victory at Plataea, on which see Hdt. 9. 100; S. Lewis (1996: 13); Parker (1996: 233–5); Stafford (2000: 10–11). While Greeks recognized previously (cf. Hesiod, *Works and Days*, 763–4) that the power of rumour to spread news (with good or harmful effects) was in a sense divine, it may have taken a spectacularly beneficial and glorious example to persuade a city to institute a form of cult. The site of the altar is not known. Pausanias (1.17.1) follows his discussion of the altar of Pity, which he places in the *agora*, with a mention of other instances of Athenian altars to personifications: *Aidos*, *Pheme*, and *Horme*. Voigt's suggestion of a site on the Acropolis (*RE* s.v. *Pheme*) rests simply on Pausanias' conjunction with the altar to *Aidos*, which clearly is of little value; a site in the agora itself is just as likely, and perhaps more appropriate to the goddess' activity.

You will find Homer often in the *Iliad* saying. Nowhere, in fact, in our texts of Homer does this phrase appear. *Pheme* does not appear in the *Iliad*, and in the *Odyssey* is used rather to mean 'significant utterance' (e.g. *Od.* 2. 35, 20. 100, 105). *Phemis* is used for 'popular speech, rumour' (*Il.* 10. 207; *Od.* 6. 273, 15. 468, 16. 75, 19. 527, 24. 201), which is usually seen as damaging, especially to women. Aeschines' 'quotation' is bogus and misleading. The closest phrase to it seems to be Zeus' instruction to Athena (*Il.* 4. 70, cf. 24. 112) 'Come now, go to the army (*aipsa mal' es straton elthe* for Aeschines' *Pheme d'es straton elthe*); other phrases, such as *kata* or *ana straton*, more commonly express the idea of 'throughout the army'. B. Marzullo, 'Aeschines In Tim. 128', *Maia* 6 (1953), 68–75, adduced a phrase in Sappho's poem on the marriage of Hektor and Andromache (fr. 44. 10): *phama d'elthe kata ptolin* ('report came to the city'), and also Hdt. 9. 100 ('*pheme* flew to the camp'), and argued that our half-line had occurred often in the epic cycle, if not in the *Iliad*. He concluded that when Aeschines said the *Iliad*, he may have meant the whole cycle, or even, to save Aeschines' credit even more, that the word 'little' had fallen out of the text after *Iliad*, and that Aeschines was referring to the poem in the cycle known as the *Little Iliad* which dealt with events which led up to the sack of Troy. This half-line has often been inserted in editions of the fragments of the epic cycle (e.g. *Poetae Epici Graeci*, ed. Bernabé, I (Stuttgart and Leipzig, 1988), *Iliades Parvae* fr. 27; it is marked as doubtful in M. Davies, *Epicorum Graecorum Fragmenta* I (Oxford, 1988), 105). Such ideas are not impossible, though the addition of 'Little' to Aeschines' text seems to me extremely implausible and unnecessary. It is much more plausible to suppose that Aeschines created the half line, on a vague memory of some similar phrases in poetry (so E. M. Harris 1995: 105; Ford 1999: 249–50). If so, it is striking and revealing that he preferred to make up a half-line with *pheme* in it, and claim it occurred 'often' in the *Iliad* and referred to events which then did take place (i.e. that 'Pheme' was true), than to read Homeric texts carefully and make his points more accurately. Had he done so, he might have made use of various passages where an alternative Homeric noun for utterance or report is found, namely '*ossa*' [word]. He could have, for example, made a reference to the '*ossa* of Zeus' (*Il.* 2. 93; *Od.* 1. 282, 2. 216), or even more appropriately quoted *Od.* 24. 413—'and Report [*ossa*] the messenger went swiftly everywhere through the city / reporting on the dismal death and fate of the suitors'.

Euripides reveals. Fr. 865 Nauck[2], also quoted by the Suda s.v, with no more context, and probably taken by the Suda from this passage. Distortion of the text by Aeschines cannot be ruled out, especially as the idea seems very appropriate, that what is said about a person over the longer term (and especially after death) comes to be seen as the truth.

129 Hesiod. Here Aeschines does quote undeniably genuine lines, *Works and Days*, 763–4. He has carefully omitted, however, the previous three lines, which advise the reader:

> to avoid the harmful report of men;
> for report is an evil thing, light and easy to start up
> but hard to bear, hard to cast off.

For Hesiod, *Pheme* is a goddess because of her power suddenly and maliciously to damage people's reputations, not because she beneficially tells the truth (cf. also fr. 176. 2 Merkelbach-West, from the *Catalogue of Women*, where Aphrodite in annoyance threw Tyndareus' daughters into 'evil *pheme*'). One fifth-century poet, Bacchylides, does give the goddess *Pheme* a more positive evaluation as a power (see 2. 1–3, 10. 1–3, and above all 5. 191–4, which refers to Hesiod); it is because she spreads good news abroad about athletic victories (cf. the Mykale and Eurymedon stories), rather than circulate true reports of people's offences.

All men who are ambitious for public honour (*demosiai philotimoi*). He concludes this point with a generalization which might seem at first too obvious to be worth saying; one might suppose that all Greeks would claim to admire the poems of Homer, Hesiod, and Euripides, and to respect all deities. The point, however, is that not all men have cause to respect this particular goddess, or these particular extracts from the poets; men of shameful lives fear them instead. The purpose of this argument is to bring in at this point a distinction concerned with the very important concept of *philotimia* ('love of honour'), one which is central to the speech as a whole. Politicians who show the proper form *philotimia* in relation to the people, that is, those who work to be honoured in return for their good services to the community, also take care to avoid rumours of improper behaviour, and therefore honour, and do not fear, the goddess responsible for rumours. But those who have had a shameful lifestyle, if they choose not to avoid seeking honours from the people, by avoiding the political life, but on the contrary seek public honour where disclosure may bring ruin, fear her. See **160**, and the very end of the speech (**194–6**) where Aeschines closes with a reaffirmation of this theme of the centrality of a controlled private morality to the 'proper *philotimia*' of the élite and their rewards from the community. On the ideas in general, see Davies, *APF* xvii–xviii, and Whitehead (1983; 1993).

130 'Which Timarchos? The whore (*pornos*)?' A crucial moment, one suspects, in the speech (see Intro. pp. 56–7, and on **26, 52**). It is now made crystal clear what nickname Aeschines wishes the jury to believe (rightly or wrongly) has been regularly attached to Timarchos for years; the implication of the revelation here is that the nickname 'the whore' comes stamped with the divine approval of the goddess, and its truth is guaranteed. At another climactic moment, **158**, he will invite jury and bystanders to shout out 'the whores' (*pornoi*) as the category to which Timarchos belongs.

it is not proper (*themis*). The calculated presentation of

Pheme as a truthful goddess reaches its rhetorical climax in this ludicrously bold claim: the fact that there is no good human testimony to Timarchos' youthful offences, but only Report, is not only a reason for believing them to have occurred but even grounds for asserting it to be religious impropriety to doubt it, since that would be accusing a goddess of giving false evidence. *Themis* indicates religious law, or law with a divine stamp behind it; and was herself also a personified deity, apparently with a long-standing cult, along with *Nemesis* at Ramnous, on the east coast of Attica. The rhetorical figure is a form of *prosopopoiia* or personification, summoning a dead or abstract figure to impress the audience. On all this see Stafford (2000: chs. 1–3). The language used here plays on religious associations: *themis* is the term for religious law or propriety rather than secular law, while the verb for denounce, *episkeptesthai*, is both the technically accurate term for laying a charge for false witness (e.g. Harrison 1968–71: II, 192–7) and also a verb often used in its active form, *episkeptein*, in poetry and oratory for solemn commands or injunctions, especially of a dying man for vengeance (e.g. Ant. 1. 1, 29–30).

In the embassy speech of 343 Demosthenes made a spirited response to this apparently successful appeal to the truth of community gossip and the quotation from Hesiod (19. 243–4), with the counter that the argument could be applied with much greater validity to Aeschines' own corrupt role on the embassy, known to vast numbers of people all over Greece, whereas Timarchos was not well known even to his neighbours. Aeschines' response (2. 144–5) was to apply the distinction between 'true *pheme*', which arises 'spontaneously' among the mass of the people, and is recognized as a divine power, from malicious lies and *sykophantia* put about by one's enemy in public meetings. The distinction, if not so sharply put elsewhere, is based on the two alternative modes of expression: the assertion of what all the city hears, and believes (e.g. Dem. 21. 80, 49. 14; Hunter 1994: 99), and what an individual claims as a slanderer, bad-mouther or sykophant: see the many instances assembled by Hunter (1994: 101–2). Once again, Aeschines' case against Timarchos is seen to rest on the prior existence of widespread discussion of Timarchos' *porneia*.

131 Similarly, in the case of Demosthenes' nickname.

Aeschines brings attention back to this demeaning nickname, to reinforce the point about the reliability of *pheme* and further amusingly to undermine the credibility of the defendant's main supporter and speechwriter. He argues naturally that the less innocent interpretation of *bat(t)alos* ('arse') is correct in this case (see on **126**), and it refers correctly to Demosthenes' softness and effeminate sexuality; in 2. 99–100 he claimed that the nickname was first given to Demosthenes 'among the boys' for his shameful deeds and *kinaidia*, and that the fellow-ambassadors were reminded of it when they saw he had large sacks of bedding, one of which he claimed contained a talent of silver—the implication being that Demosthenes was characterized both by softness and by preparedness to sell himself.

effeminacy (*anandria*) and his deviance (*kinaidiai*). This is a consistent strand in Aeschines' mockery of Demosthenes: see **181**, and also Aesch. 2. 23, 88, 99, 151. *Anandria* (the negation of *andreia*) is the general term for a lack of manliness and especially of courage, while the terms *kinaidos/kinaideia* essentially denote a lack of masculinity in appearance, dress, and above all sexual behaviour; *kinaidos* overlapped with, and in part succeeded to, the equally abusive term *katapugon* (see Intro. pp. 42–4). Thus inappropriately soft or womanish behaviour is certainly involved; but whereas many scholars (e.g. Dover 1978: 75; Foucault 1985: 63–77; Winkler 1990a: 46–54; Thornton 1997: 98–110) put much emphasis on males who, by permitting penetration assimilate themselves to women and thereby accept emasculation and powerlessness, Davidson (1997: 167–82) demonstrates that many texts place the moral concern rather on the males' insatiable desires to be 'filled' with sexual pleasures (like women), which are located essentially in the anus (esp. Plat. *Gorg.* 494; Arist. *EN* 1148b15–49a20; Arist. *Probl.* 4. 26: see Intro. pp. 45–8).

Here it may seem at first that Aeschines is not necessarily making any specific assertion about Demosthenes' sexual tastes, but merely casting doubt on his general masculinity and courage by claiming that he liked, in private, to wear soft, luxurious, and effeminate clothes. But at **170–6** his boasting before his 'pupils', and his maltreatment of the unfortunate young man Aristarchos whose lover he 'pretended' to be, are pilloried. Three years later Aeschines accused Demosthenes of selling all parts of his body, and of impurity of mouth, i.e. of practising *fellatio* (2. 23, 88);

Douris of Samos (*FGH* 76 F 8) reported that a similar allegation, that he was not to be permitted to blow out the sacred flame, was made against Demosthenes by Pytheas, presumably *c.* 323–322, as was alleged also against Demosthenes' nephew Demochares according to Timaios (*FGH* 566 F 35), both quoted in the Suda. Also in the embassy speech, Aeschines (2. 149) alleges, when defending his own relations against Demosthenes' smears, that Demosthenes' improper goings-on with another youthful protégé, Knosion (*LGPN* 1; *PA* 8687), extended to putting him to bed with his own wife (for Knosion's later political activity as a Demosthenic supporter, Hyper. *Dem.* 13; another version of the gossip had it that Demosthenes' wife slept with the boy out of jealousy, Athen. 593a). Yet another attractive youth, Aristion son of Aristoboulos, of Plataiai or of Samos is mentioned in Aeschines' Crown speech. He had allegedly lived for a long time in Demosthenes' house (ostensibly, one supposes, as a rhetorical pupil), but by 331 he was close to Hephaestion, and negotiated through him a deal with Alexander on Demosthenes' part: see Aesch. 3. 162, and also Harpokration s.v., referring to Diyllos, *FGH* 73 F 2, who held him to be from Samos, and Marsyas of Pella, *FGH* 135 F 23. Full references are given in H. Berve, *Die Alexanderreich auf prosopographischer Grundlage* (Munich, 1928), II, no. 120). Conceivably Aristion ended up in Athens, if we may relate to him the Attic gravestone of the second half of the fourth century showing an elderly man, of indeterminate status, a woman and a girl, and bearing the names of Aristion son of Aristoboulos, and Soteris (the wife?): see Clairmont (1993: II, 920), and *LGPN* 71; *PAA* 166460. Aeschines alludes there too to Demosthenes' failed masculinity in his relations with youths: 'what he [sc. Aristion] was having done to him, or doing, the accusation may be disputed, and it is not at all a proper matter for me to discuss' (see on **38** for speakers' proclaimed reticence of language in reference to sexual acts). In the light of all these allegations, some deviant sexual practices (though not necessarily anal sex) are presumably to be assumed here too; such was evidently understood by Aulus Gellius (5. 1), who comments on the general picture of Demosthenes' epicene, clothing, and presumed sexual depravities ('no man, and with polluted mouth'), quoting *ta kompsa chlaniskia* and *malakoi chitoniskoi* (see next note) from the present passage.

fancy little cloaks and those delicate little tunics . . .

uncertain . . . the clothes of a man or a woman. Both words (*chlaniskia* and *chitoniskoi*) are applied to garments which may be worn by either sex, but Aeschines uses diminutives as well the adjectives *kompsos* (elaborate, expensive) and *malakos* (soft) to indicate effeminacy and luxury. The overall impression is of an indeterminate, norm-breaking, sexuality; the effeminate clothes worn by the adult sophist and orator suggest that even as a lover of boys he is an ambiguous failure (see **171** and 2. 166).

writing your speeches against your friends. Demothenes is here accused that in accusing his fellow-ambassadors of bribery and treason he is undermining the bonds of friendship and 'salt-fellowship' cf. also Dem. 19. 188–91; Aesch. 2. 23–4; there may also be an allusion to the allegation that he betrayed his client Phormion by colluding with his opponent Apollodoros (see Aesch. 2. 166).

132–140 *The debate on the place of noble love in Athenian culture*

132 one of the generals: speculation on the supposed identity of this figure is not profitable, as a good many 'anti-Macedonian' generals who might be prepared to speak for Timarchos could be mentioned, and in any case Aeschines may conceivably have made this figure up. If he was real, Schaefer's speculative nominee, Diopeithes of Sounion, has the merit of being both a current general politically active on Demosthenes' side and very likely an old friend of Hegesandros and Hegesippos, and a fellow-Salaminian of theirs, see above on **63**. The attribution of these views of a man 'well versed in the *palaistrai*', i.e. the athletes' training grounds, to an unnamed 'general' rather than to Demosthenes further has the effect of reminding the jury that Demosthenes himself was no athlete or habitué of the *gymnasia* or *palaistrai*, but an effeminate who pursued his amours indoors; similarly at 3. 255–6 Aeschines suggests that Demosthenes will be unable to appeal to any former friends with whom he shared hunting or gymnastic activities, because as a young man he preferred to pursue and hunt wealthy young men, as also in **170–2**; and Plut. *Dem.* 4 with Golden 2000: 169–73. On the practice of magistrates and other prominent men appearing as supporters (*synegoroi*) of those facing political trials, and the criticisms this might incur, see generally Rubinstein (1998: 138 and n. 49, and forthcoming).

a laid-back manner, and a self-conscious air. The word I have translated 'laid-back' is *hyptiazein*, a verb which literally means to lean backwards, and probably here denotes a physical style, of a man leaning back languidly and arrogantly. Later, for example in Hermogenes, *On Types of Style*, 2. 1 (late second cent. AD) the term is used of a rhetorical style, indicating a slack or relaxed composition, the opposite of 'rapidity' (*gorgotes*); there may well be a hint of a slow and arrogant voice here as well. 'The general' is presented as an arrogant, self-confident, snobbish, and rather absurd character, concerned to show off his power and influence; one may compare the presentation of Hegesippos as *Krobylos*, the Hair-bun, on **64** and the more solemn attack on generals supporting the younger Alkibiades in Lys. 14, 21, and see Rubinstein (forthcoming). This presentation makes it easier for Aeschines to side with the ordinary jury, in resenting the patronizing cultural attitudes of the other side, while also himself engaging in his defence of 'noble *eros*' and some subtle exegesis of poetry in its support (see Ford 1999: 251–4).

palaistrai **and their discussions (***diatribai***).** *Diatribe*, originally passage/passing of time, is used to denote leisure generally (e.g. Alexis 222K/A 3–6), or specific leisure activities or places, often combined with another noun giving the more precise area of amusement (e.g. **175** below, of humour at court; Dem. 21. 71 and Alexis 190 K/A, of drinking parties). It can also denote more systematic forms of conversation or study (Ar. *Frogs* 1498; Plat. *Apol.* 37c, of Sokratic conversations), or a serious occupation (Ar. *Plut.* 923). Here (and see **54** and **159**) perhaps the phrase conveys 'wrestling grounds and their associated leisure activities', including the various forms of formal and less formal discourse, from casual conversations to philosophical or educational discussions. Plato locates many Sokratic discussions in *gymnasia* and *palaistrai*, and his own school at the Academy, Aristotle's school at the Lyceum, and many other similar institutions, were all attached to such notable athletic centres (e.g. Wycherley 1978: ch. IX; J. P. Lynch, *Aristotle's School: A Study of a Greek Educational Institution* (Berkeley, 1972), and on the new excavations of what is almost certainly the Lyceum, see D. J. Blackman, *Archaeological Reports* 1996/7, 8–10). For a fully adult man to be 'versed in *palaistrai* and *diatribai*' implies he has considerable leisure time, and spends it in such places, perhaps training, watching the training, engaging in erotic pursuits and gossip, impromptu poetic or musical performances, and also varied discussions or formal debates or seminars, for example on politics, rhetoric, or philosophy.

the whole basis of the legal contest. The word for 'basis', *enstasis*, is used again by Aeschines of the origin or basis of 'all the troubles' over the embassy (2. 20). It can also mean a rhetorical or philosophical objection (e.g. Arist. *Rhet.* 1402a31)

created not so much a trial. The implication here seems to be, first, that this trial is a new invention, i.e. that such a process had not been used at least for a very long time. It is true that we have no reason to believe that the law was used with any frequency; for the other actual case we hear of, brought by Kleon against Gryttos (*Knights* 876–9), and the threats to bring such prosecutions, see Intro. p. 53, and on **64**.

denial of our cultural education (*apaideusia*). The noun *apaideusia* is literally an absence of *paideia* (Isocr. *ad Dem.* 33. 2), and so can indicate a lack of education (e.g. Plat. *Rep.* 514a), or a lack of culture or taste (e.g. Thuc. 3. 42). Such lack of taste may show itself in crude personal abuse. Hypereides (fr. 211 Jensen) asserts that 'personal abuse is the most uncultivated thing', whereas clever and amusing jokes, even at another's expense, show one's cultivation: so Aristotle (*Rhet.* 1389b10–12) calls wit 'cultivated *hybris*'. Aeschines uses the word on three other occasions to criticize Demosthenes or his friends: to criticize Demosthenes' tactless and tasteless flattery of Philip (2. 113), and his false and tasteless accusations that Aeschines had committed drunken sexual outrages on a captive Olynthian woman (2. 153), and third to characterize the bad taste involved in the very idea of Ktesiphon, at his trial, calling on Demosthenes to help his defence by praising himself (3. 241). Here the point is that the General will allege that Aeschines' prosecution of Timarchos is in effect an uneducated attack on the place of legitimate homosexual love affairs in Athenian education and culture (see also Intro. pp. 58–60).

'The General' is said to be intending to assault Aeschines as a gross parvenu who corrupts gymnastic life as a participant and yet is posing as a moral reformer, and to that extent purporting, falsely, to defend gymnastic culture. To some extent he is made to seem élitist and snobbish in his rejection of Aeschines, and in his patronizing contempt towards the jury's understanding of poetry (**141**) But it is vital to emphasize (as was first brought out effectively by Dover 1978: 40–2) that the General is not presented as such an old-fashioned or élitist character that he believes that the noble pederasty of the *gymnasia* should be restricted to the sons of the wealthy; his appeal to the democratic ideal of Harmodios and Aristogeiton and to the prayers of ordinary parents (**133–4**) that their sons may win a place among the most admired boys indicate that he is supposed to share with Aeschines and the jury the ideal of a 'restrained' and 'democratic' love and to favour wide access to it. Those (e.g. Ober 1989: 257; S. C. Todd 1990a: 166) who suppose that Aeschines is exploiting popular hostility to traditional forms of 'élite pederasty' ignore these crucial areas of agreement between 'the General' and Aeschines; others (Hubbard 1998: 66–8 and Sissa 1999: 155–7) observe the problem, but resort, in my view, to special pleading, involving 'dual audiences' and internal contradictions in the speech, or a recasting of the arguments in the written version to appeal to a more educated public (see Intro. pp. 58–60).

Harmodios and Aristogeiton. These two were honoured as the founding fathers of the democracy, and their descendants given the right of free meals in the Prytaneion, because their assassination of Hipparchos, the younger of the ruling sons of Peisistratos, was popularly regarded as contributing importantly to the end of the tyranny (e.g. Hyper. *Fun. Sp.* 39–40). They were believed to have acted out of their shared passion and seeking revenge on Hipparchos for his grievous insults on Harmodios and his sister, following the rejection of his advances (see, above all, Thucydides' famous 'excursus' on the end of the tyranny, 6. 54–9). The pair, who were seen, as Thucydides pointedly puts it, as a partnership of a noble (Harmodios, who was *lampros*, eminent) and a 'middling citizen' (Aristogeiton, a *mesos polites*), formed a founding model for this ideal of a legitimate, democratic, *eros* to which all citizens in principle could at least aspire. Visually, in the austere, hard, and heroic pose of the official statue by Kritios and Nesiotes after the Persian Wars and its imitations (see e.g. M. W. Taylor 1991: ch. II; Stewart 1997: 70–5: 'it became . . . the fetish of a generation'), and equally in the popular songs of the *skolia* celebrating how together the tyrannicides had made Athens free and equal, these representations imprint a 'noble love' at the heart of the city's democratic ideology; and they seem to invite the 'moderate and middling citizen' to identify with Aristogeiton in his sexual and political attitudes. The actions of the mutilators of the Herms in 415 (see also on **125**), attacking the civic and sexual assertiveness of the citizens by chopping at the faces and phalloi of the statues, as well as the handling of the episode by Thucydides, deconstructing in a sceptical historian's way the democratic appeal in 415 to the Harmodios and Aristogeiton model, can be seen as offering diverse challenges to this model with its linking of democratic action and noble *eros*; see the subtle analysis of Wohl (1999). But 'the General' and Aeschines agree in continuing to make a bland appeal to the power of the myth.

a benefit for the city. This appears to accept at least a part of the traditional populist case that the killing of Hipparchos by the pair had somehow made a major contribution to the end of the tyranny, despite the fact that the people apparently also knew that eventually it had been achieved above all by the Spartans, and despite Thucydides' insistence, itself consistent with Herodotus' narrative (5. 62–5), that the actual assassination only made the tyranny harsher. On the complexities of the competing traditions, and the reasons why democrats of differing traditions continued to honour the tyrannicides, see Thomas (1989: 239–61).

133 sing hymns . . . eulogize beauty, as though it had not long been celebrated. There is an insistent repetition here of verbs of panegyric; again the point is that ordinary democratic citizens already know all about, and have a stake in the praise of, youthful beauty and noble and *sophron* love, and that Aeschines too is as concerned to defend it as is 'the General' .

the poetry of Homer . . . Patroklos and Achilles. Aeschines will attempt to outdo 'the General' with his own elaborate and subtle disquisition on Homer's presentation of this relationship: see on **141–50**, and Ford (1999: 251–2).

through erotic love. *Eros*, the general term for sexual or erotic desire or love, plays a prominent part in this section, and both his opponent and Aeschines agree it is often, and properly, pederastic in form, and can be a noble emotion that inspires men to heroic, selfless, and brave actions. See Dover (1978: 39–54).

as though it had not long been celebrated. Aeschines later quotes and discusses, with varying degrees of appropriateness, passages from Homer and Euripides. Here he may be expecting the jury to think also of earlier poetry that celebrated love of boys (e.g. Solon fr. 24, 25 West, many poems in the Theognid corpus, especially what we have as book II, and some lyric poems by Ibycus, Anakreon, or Pindar); and also probably the sorts of formalized prose eulogies of the nature of such love of which we find examples in the literary *symposia* of Plato and Xenophon, and which were no doubt found in many other forms, oral and written. On the genres of poetry appropriate for proper love, see Dover (1978: 57–9); Foxhall (1998: 60–1).

bodily attractiveness . . . you . . . all pray. Here the important emphasis on the admiration of the whole community for the physical beauty of young men, and on the agreed assumption that 'you all', i.e, all typical Athenian parents, desire their sons to win repute for this attribute, is especially patent and revealing (see Intro. pp. 59–60, Winkler 1990a: 62–3; Stewart 1997: 63–85).

134 fair and noble in appearance. Another use of the catch-phrase (*kalos kagathos*) here (see on **31, 41, 69**). Here it seems a bland ideal that all Athenians might wish for their children, focused primarily on physical beauty and attractiveness; its use here, attributed to the slightly snobbish 'General', but put in the imaginary minds of ordinary Athenian fathers, is a further indication of the general acceptability of the idea that it was good for youths to attract attention for their physical charms among a good many citizens. Bourriot (1995: 445–6) accepts such a view for this use, applied to boys, who can be generally admired if they do not abuse their 'beauty' by accepting the wrong sort of love, but maintains that for Aeschines adults called *kaloi kagathoi* were likely to be stigmatized as 'decadent snobs', but such a sharp disjunction seems implausible.

become the objects of fights because of erotic passion. This addition subtly slips in an apparent admission from the defence that Timarchos had aroused intense competition and fights among several lovers; even if they did admit this, their view of course would be that he had not overstepped the bounds of '*sophron eros*'. The defence then accuses Aeschines (**135–6**) of himself being an obnoxious lover, and will produce witnesses for 'quarrels and blows' in which he has been involved. These he does not deny, whether because he could not plausibly do so, or because he calculates also that it would not necessarily do his reputation any harm (see Intro. pp. 18–19, 34–6, for the implications for Aeschines' own lifestyle, and for the ages at which men still regularly pursued boys at the *gymnasia*).

This pair of admissions also constitute among the more striking of a good many statements which suggest the routine and acceptable levels of relatively low-level violence in Athenian leisure activities, especially arising from sexual rivalries over boys and *hetairai* (see also Lys. 3. 43; Athen. 555a; Winkler 1990a: 49; D. Cohen 1995: 127–8, 134–5; Fisher 1998b: 73–8). What mattered was the distinction, on which juries in *hybris* and assault cases might have to adjudicate, between acceptable fights where little lasting damage was done, and cases where one party showed excessive aggression in starting it or excessive desire to humiliate and inflict dishonour, or else inflicted unduly savage injuries. Decisions on whether the limits of acceptable violence had been breached might be no easier to make than those concerned to apply the distinction between noble and improper sexual relationships.

135 a raid on me. A *katadrome* is a sudden raid (e.g. Thuc. 1. 142, 5. 56, 7. 27, of various raids during the Peloponnesian War), and by an easy metaphor, a sharp attack on someone's argument (cf. Pl. *Rep.* 472a) or methodology (e.g. Polyb. 12. 23. 1, of Timaios' assaults on Ephoros). The military term perhaps suits this character known only as 'the General'.

a nuisance in the *gymnasia*. The adjective *ochleros* indicates a man whose behaviour causes offence or irritation for various reasons (e.g. Eur. *Alc.* 540; Ar. *Ach.* 460, 472; Dem. 39. 18). The accusations here against Aeschines are that his own competitive, violent, and coarse pursuit of boys at the *gymnasia* is of the 'wrong' sort and that as a result he cannot comprehend that others (including Timarchos) might be more 'noble' and 'controlled'; and finally that his prosecution of Timarchos is not only grossly hypocritical, but worse, it also risks bringing the whole splendid institution into disrepute.

136 I do not criticize erotic love (*eros*) that is just. Here and throughout this section Aeschines emphasizes the common ground between his opponents and himself, namely the maintenance of this tradition of approved homosexual relationships as a valued part of Athenian culture, and he makes it clear that in fact the crucial issue is the actual nature of the relationships in which Timarchos was involved.

engaged in erotic passion (*erotikos*). Foxhall (1998: 58) suggests this usage 'involved in erotic passion' is vaguer than the more certainly dominant *erastes* (lover), and suggestive rather of more egalitarian, friendly relationships with an erotic element; but the admissions that he is still regularly involved in rivalries and fights and composes erotic poetry, and his defence of the tradition of 'noble love', are strong indications that the jury was meant to imagine Aeschines, even as a middle-aged man, competing vigorously to be accepted as a legitimate and noble 'lover' of much younger youths, rather than still engaged in affectionate, still sexually active, relationships with old friends. We may yet think both scenarios equally plausible.

I acknowledge they are mine. Aeschines apparently believed that it would not seriously damage his own reputation to acknowledge not only that he is still occasionally involved in vigorous, yet decorous, pursuit of youths at the *gymnasia*, but also that he composes poems in which (presumably) he praises their beauty and declares his own *eros*. The calculations may have been first, that the poems did exist in the hands of his opponents, along with those who would testify to gymnastic quarrels, but were not unambiguously obscene or crude, though they might contain euphemistic and metaphorical allusions to sexual acts and emotions: see Dover (1978: 57–9), well comparing the conventions in the homosexual poetry we have, especially those of book II of the Theognid corpus, and also Ford (1999: 251). Second, that their existence and nature supported his claim not to be an uneducated and uncultured buffoon whose activities in the *gymnasia* were embarrassingly crude; and third that some involvement in erotic poetry as well as erotic pursuits did not exclude his claiming, in **141**, still to be associated culturally with the mass of the jurors, who had (or liked to be thought to have) picked up sufficient culture to resent being patronized by the likes of 'the General'. This also may have given authority to Aeschines' lengthy elucidation of selected quotations from the poetic classics (**141–54**), in which he will apply techniques of interpretation in deploying classical texts in support of his argument, as he fears 'the General' will also do in 'coarsening' his own efforts.

137 I make this distinction. On the importance of this clear statement of the distinction, both to our understanding of Greek values, and to the strategy of Aeschines' case, Dover (1978: 40–2), and Intro. pp. 58–60.

condition of a generous (*philanthropos*) and sympathetic soul. The adjective 'generous' (*philanthropos*), and the noun (*philanthropia*), basically denotes 'goodwill towards human beings', and was often used of the humanity, sympathy, or generous financial support which might be displayed by those exercising power, whether kings, aristocrats, or democratic juries (see generally Dover 1974: 201–3; J. de Romilly, *Le douceur dans la pensée grecque*, Paris, 1979). In this context it implies perhaps an openness and affection shown especially towards a junior or socially inferior member of a relationship; see Dover (1978: 46–7) and also the note on **171**.

behave grossly (*aselgainein*) . . . non-corrupting (*adiaphoros*). The language designed to mark out acceptable and non-acceptable forms of responses by the 'boyfriend' to the lover remains heavily moralizing, but inexplicit. 'Gross behaviour' (see on **32**) implies nothing more explicit than 'seriously shameful' for the youth, and the use of the term 'non-corrupting' conveys essentially the suggestion that what mattered was the mercenary element, which gave the 'payer' the right to set the terms (see Dover 1978: 48) On what forms of sexual expression might be regarded as acceptable in the respectable relationships, see Intro. pp. 42–5; the refusal to be explicit in the law courts explains why such coy language is used of the positive relationship, and so probably supports the view that some forms of sexual climax at least were (tacitly) permitted or even encouraged.

***hybristes* and an uneducated man (*apaideutos*).** The crucial value-term *hybristes* is repeated in this crucial definitional sentence, with its misleading hint that hirers of adult Athenian youths were liable to the *graphe hybreos*, an insinuation which is asserted with varying degrees of certainty elsewhere (see on **15–16, 29, 72, 87, 90, 162**). The current concern with *sophron eros* as an important element in Athenian culture is brought out by the idea that such a hirer lacks the education and cultivation to understand it.

138 Our ancestors, when they were making laws.

Aeschines returns briefly to the topic of the laws dealing with the regulation of *gymnasia* and *palaistrai* (see **9–11**), to argue, using the fundamental dichotomy between slave and free, that, properly interpreted, 'ancient' laws positively encourage free citizens to engage in homosexual pursuits of boys and youths.

men's practices (*epitedeumata*) and the necessities of nature (*phusis*). For *epitedeumata*, see on **37**. The phrase 'necessities of nature' leaves no doubt, as indeed does this whole section, that Aeschines believes, with most Greeks, that homosexual desire and some homosexual acts were entirely natural for men, but equally that the laws of a community needed to regulate them in certain specific ways. See Dover (1978: 60–8), and Intro. pp. 25–6 and on **188** below. The addition of the words 'goods and evils' after 'necessary things' is usually, and rightly, deleted as an explanatory, but in fact unhelpful, addition to the text; see Dover (1978: 60–1); he adduces Ar. *Clouds* 1075–82 and other passages for appeal to 'compulsions of nature' to excuse or explain those who acted under the influence of strong sexual desires.

prohibited slaves from engaging. The two laws excerpted here, which concern prohibiting slaves from training and competing on equal terms with free men in the athletic grounds, and from pursuing free boys as lovers, should very probably be considered part of Solon's legislation. The argument is cumulative. First, their gist is mentioned also in Plutarch (*Sol.* 1. 3–4; *Mor.* 152d, 751b). Second, in the first law, Aeschines' version includes, for 'rub dry with oil' a rare and arguably archaic verb (*xeraloiphein*), which suggests authenticity. Finally, there are good reasons for believing that such a concern for preservation of status-distinctions may already have existed in the primarily aristocratic athletic training grounds of the early sixth century (see Golden 1984; Kyle 1984; Mactoux 1988; Murray 1990b: 145; Fisher 1992: 80; 1995: 64). Plutarch also echoes Aeschines' argument that the laws in effect recommend these activities for free men; he puts the point (probably appropriately for Solon) in a slightly more élitist way, namely that by forbidding these activities for slaves Solon was assigning them to the sphere of the 'fine and elevated' men, or of the 'worthy'. In general Aeschines' argument has some force, though he overstates the inferences to be drawn when he claims that free men 'ought' so to act, and that the lawgivers 'exhorted' free men to it.

In general in the classical period Athenians, especially élite Athenians, were much exercised by the question of how to distinguish slaves from free citizens in everyday conditions under democracy (see above all Ps. Xen. *Ath. Pol.* 1. 10–12; Plato, *Rep.* 563b–c). A similarly ideological argument which is more relevant to the present passage comes from Xenophon's *Symposion* (2. 4). Sokrates argues that the guests at the party do not need perfumes: the pleasantest male smell, he claims, comes from olive oil applied to the natural body after exercise, provided that the body is free, not slave; if men apply perfume, free and slave smell the same, whereas smells need bodies in good training over a long time, if they are to be pleasant and worthy of the free. See S. Lewis, 'Slaves as viewers and users of Athenian pottery', *Hephaistos* 16/17 (1998/99), 71–90, esp. 80–1.

139 fifty lashes with the public whip. Slaves had standardly to endure punishment in the form of physical torture and whipping, both at the hands of private masters and the state (see on **58**). This penalty of fifty lashes for slave offenders is found in many inscriptions (e.g. *IG* II^2 333, 13–16, 380, 40–2, the text in Stroud 1974, lines 5–6), and in some cases seems to match the corresponding financial penalty of fifty drachmai for free offenders. See generally Hunter (1994: 155–8).

while the boy is not his own master and incapable of judging. This idea that the lawgiver somehow encouraged those who were interested in boys below the age of enrolment in their deme (see **18**) to watch after them, but not (yet) to pursue them actively and make proposals to them, has something in common with the customs (*nomoi*) and practices described and recommended by the enthusiast for legitimate homosexual *eros*, Pausanias, in Plato's *Symposion* (Plat. *Symp.* 181d–f). Weil (1955) argued that Aeschines had specifically this passage in mind, but the idea of expressing the distinction between chaste and improper *eros* in this way may well have had a wider distribution. Aeschines does not quote a new law here, but is presumably continuing his dubious interpretation (notice 'I think') of the law forbidding slaves to 'be a lover . . . or pursue' (see Dover 1978: 48, 55–6). This argument gives no support for an explicit law setting out an age below which any sexual acts were regarded as without consent (see on **15–17** above), but it confirms a set of attitudes advocating a proper caution in approaching younger youths; see also Intro. pp. 36–9.

140 whether one should call it erotic love (*eros*) or whatever one should call it. I have translated here, following Dilts and many editors, Baiter/Sauppe's emendation adding 'whatever' before *tropon* to mean 'in whatever way'; the manuscripts' text would translate as 'whether love (*eros*) is what one should call it', or 'inclination' (*tropos*). *Tropos*, generally a word meaning way or manner, is used by Xenophon as a polite term for the extraordinary desire for beautiful youths shown by a certain Episthenes of Olynthos (*Anab.* 7. 4. 7), comparable to Misgolas' enthusiasm for musicians (see Dover 1978: 52; Hindley 1999: 75). One reason for accepting the emendation is that Aeschines is in agreement with 'the General' in holding Harmodios and Aristogeiton up as the ideal examples of chaste and democratic *eros* which led to their early and glorious deaths at the hands of the cruel tyrants; he would not be likely to wonder if the right term to use of their emotional commitment was one applied in this context more to an unusually lasting predilection of the older lover (see, however, Dover 1978: 63).

it educated them to be of such a kind. This section ends powerfully with the statement of the educative power of a noble love, spurring the tyrannicide couple to heroic deeds worthy of everlasting memory and praise, reinforcing their position as erotic models for all citizens. The statement that no praise of these heroes can match their achievements recalls insistently and appropriately the commonplaces of praise poetry of athletic victors such as Pindar's (e.g. *Pyth.* 1. 81–5), and even more clearly and relevantly prose *enkomia* such as the annual Athenian Funeral Speeches for their war dead (see e.g Thuc. 2. 35; Lys. 2. 1; Dem. 60. 1; and Loraux 1986: 230–8); the last surviving example of the Funeral Speech, Hypereides' of 322, itself includes the tyrannicides and their 'mutual friendship' in the roll-call of Athens' glorious heroes who will welcome Leosthenes in the underworld (*Fun. Sp.* 35–40).

141–154 *Arguments from earlier poetry*

141 Since you are mentioning Achilles. In order not to be thought to be showing off his knowledge of literature and its interpretation, Aeschines suggests that it is because his opponents were planning to appeal to Homer as the basis of *their* conception of the educational system that he is led to this extensive section of quotations from the *Iliad* and more briefly from two of Euripides' plays (Homer, *Iliad* 18. 324–9, 18. 333–5, 23. 77–91, 18. 95–100; Eur. *Stheneboea* fr. 672 Nauck²; and Eur. *Phoinix* fr. 812 Nauck²). Initially he uses the citations and his interpretations to defend the notion of a pure form of male love, and the importance of distinguishing it from the bad form; by the end, however, he achieves a sufficient distortion of Euripides' texts to enable him to use them, and especially the second one from the *Phoinix*, as convenient pegs on which to hang a summary restatement of the case against Timarchos (**153–4**).

This is the most extended exegesis of poetry in Aeschines' surviving speeches, and is produced above all by the nature of the case, and the need to anticipate his opponents' tactics, as well as (perhaps to a lesser extent) his own natural desire to display his cultural knowledge, powers of interpretation, and recitation skills: see Dorjahn (1927); North (1952: 25–7); Perlman (1964: 156, 166–7); Kindstrand (1982: 22); Ober (1989: 179–80); and Ford (1999: 251–2.). Demosthenes was stung, in the Embassy speech, into unusually extended quotations of his own, from tragedy, in response to Aeschines' quotations and distortions (19. 243–55); he repeats and reapplies against him Aeschines' quotations from Hesiod and Euripides' *Phoinix*, and adds long quotations from Sophocles' *Antigone* and Solon; later, in the Crown speech (18. 265–7) a few very brief tragic verses are again used against Aeschines. In his other two speeches, Aeschines restricted himself to briefer quotations from Hesiod and some epigrams; at 2. 144, he rejoins the debate on the use of the Hesiod passage about Report, and at 2. 158 he finds another brief Hesiodic quotation to use against Demosthenes, which he expanded on in 3. 134–6. The only speech which matches this speech in extended use of poetic quotations is Lycurgus' *Against Leocrates*, where again the citations serve primarily a number of major rhetorical strategies: the denigration of the defendant Leokrates (*LGPN* 3; *PA* 9083), a man who had evaded service for the Chaeronea campaign, as a traitor to the whole Athenian political, educational, and cultural system; and the self-presentation of Lycurgus himself as its distinguished defender (see Humphreys 1985a; P. J. Wilson 1996: 316). The extremely heavy moralizing tone is matched by supporting 'witnesses' of the poets Homer, Tyrtaeus, Euripides, and others, as well as the ephebic oath, the oath allegedly sworn at Plataiai, and other alleged documents. On all these uses of quotations, see Perlman (1964: 162, 167–8); North (1952: 24–7); Hall (1995: 45–6); and Ford (1999: 249–56).

were quite ignorant of culture . . . we too have heard and learned something. The language used here makes it clear that the ordinary Athenians' access to the poetry and drama of their cultural traditions is imagined as essentially oral, not acquired through reading: The word for 'ignorant' means literally 'had not heard', and the verb from the same route is then used again. Many 'ordinary' Athenians, then, with whom Aeschines identifies himself, may have listened to, and learnt, some Homer and other poetry at school (depending how much schooling they had), and continued to listen to (and in some cases perform themselves in) performances and recitations of a wide range of poetry, drama, dithyramb, songs, and other music, both at public festivals and contests, and at private *symposia* and other feastings (not all of which were completely restricted to the élites, see Fisher 2000). Nearly all such Athenians would have listened of course to political and legal speeches, and some would have attended the public lectures and 'readings' of historians, philosophers, and other intellectuals and teachers (see Ober 1989: 158–9; Thomas 1992: 101–27; Goldhill 1999, and many other papers in Goldhill and R. G. Osborne (eds.) 1999). Aeschines thus makes an effective point in presenting his opponents as élitist snobs. On the other hand, as usual, his self-identification with the 'ordinary' is in part ambivalent and deceitful (see on 1; and the comparable case of Demosthenes' self-identification with the poor citizen victims of the rich and violent Meidias, on which see P. J. Wilson 1991 and 2000: 156–67, but also Ober 1994). Aeschines' own background as schoolmaster's son, clerk, and actor, and his own more recent access to the social and intellectual life of the political élite (the *palaistrai* and their *diatribai*), will have given him a much greater acquaintance with poetic texts and the intellectual discussions on their interpretations than most members of a chorus or theatre audience will have had, as his use of the texts here reveals (see especially Ford 1999: 252–6); but many may have been flattered as well as entertained by being included in this extended demonstration of apparently serious literary discussions.

142 keeps their erotic love (*eros*) hidden and the proper name of their friendship, thinking that the exceptional extent of their affection (*eunoia*) made things clear to the educated members of his audience. As Aeschines admits, the *Iliad* and *Odyssey* do not explicitly present or allude unambiguously to homoerotic passion, let alone homosexual behaviour, and it is debated whether one should conclude that it was not yet institutionalized as an acceptable practice in Greece, or that it was one of the areas of contemporary life which the epic poems chose not to represent unambiguously. For many (e.g. Dover 1978: 196–9; 1988: II, 115–34) this silence in Homer, and also the apparent silences in Hesiod and Archilochus, are the best evidence for the belief that overt reference to homosexual behaviour was not yet acceptable in the Greek world, and that the celebration of pederasty (above all in sympotic contexts) apparent from the sixth century did not have its origins in earlier practices in male initiation rituals. On the other hand, Clarke (1978), Poole (1990), and Ogden (1996b,) argue, in part along Aeschines' lines, that Homer and Hesiod may in places allude knowingly, if inexplicitly, to homoerotic desire and acts (see also Intro. pp. 27–31). The allusion to the gods' capture of Ganymede, 'the most beautiful of mortals', to be Zeus' cupbearer (*Iliad* 20. 231–5) is most plausibly explained in terms of Zeus' sexual desire (despite 'Sokrates' opinion in Xen. *Symp.* 8. 31, and Dover 1978: 196–7; 1988: 130). It is notable that the Homeric *Hymn to Aphrodite* (202–6) and Ibycus fr. 289 place this story in very close connection with two other stories of unambiguously sexual relations between gods and mortals, Aphrodite's affair with Anchises, and Dawn's with Tithonos, which makes the sexual reference unavoidable in the Ganymede case as well. The *hymn* is to be dated perhaps not very much later than the *Iliad*, late seventh/early sixth century (see R. Janko, *Homer, Hesiod and the Hymns* (Cambridge, 1982), 151–69, who is inclined to believe that it is imitated by Hesiod's *Works and Days*, and so is very close to the *Iliad* in date), while Ibycus is to be dated to the later sixth century. It is uncertain whether Nestor's repeatedly encouraging his guest Telemachos to sleep under a portico next to his youngest son Peisistratos (*Od.* 3. 397–403, 4. 302–5) is intended to hint at a sexual relationship; and greatly debated whether the emphasis in Thetis' advice to the grieving Achilles to think of sex ('it is a good thing to lie in love with a woman') is on the general idea of having sex again, or having it with a woman rather than with a man (as Clarke 1978: 381–3, 386–7).

The main issue, though, for Aeschines, and for modern interpretations of the *Iliad*, and one unlikely to be ever resolved, is whether the emotional relationship between Achilles and Patroklos, which is certainly of a fierce and obsessive intensity unparalleled elsewhere in the epics, is intended subtly to suggest a homoerotic love, or whether (see e.g. Halperin 1990: 75–87) it is a quite exceptional and passionate friendship. There was an intense ancient debate on this, in fifth- and fourth-century Athens, and later (for how the debate affected Hellenistic editors of Homer as seen in the Homeric *scholia*, see Clarke 1978: 384–6). In classical Athens, only Xenophon's Sokrates (*Symp.* 8. 31) claimed they were no more than friends and companions, but Aeschylus (frr. 288, 289), like Aeschines, made Achilles the dominant figure, the 'lover', the nobler and the one responsible for his welfare, whereas Phaidros in Plato's *Symposion* (179e) claims that Achilles, the more beautiful, and the younger, is clearly the 'beloved'. Weil (1955) sees this as a further case (see on **138**) where Aeschines shows his knowledge of Plato's text, but again it is as likely that he has participated in many oral debates on these topics. This debate itself suggests that Homer was not describing a relationship similar to what became the standard version of a noble, educative, love (and see also below on **144**); but Aeschines' general argument that some form of erotic love is involved cannot be shown to be incorrect.

143 Achilles says somewhere. The studied casualness of this mode of reference is notable; Aeschines affects an acquaintance based perhaps on performance, but avoids the impression of being too learned, or having looked the passage up in a text. The ploy is repeated at **151**; see P. J. Wilson (1996: 314); Ford (1999: 252).

Aeschines takes care to bring out .in his discourse not only reasons for supposing that the depth and the purity of the emotion felt by Achilles implies a noble, and homoerotic, love, but also evidence that the obsessiveness of Achilles' drive for revenge after Patroklos' death was at the certain cost of his own life. This element of Achilles' character, which (for modern readers) is often felt to be presented in a darker or more ambiguous way, in view of the brutality and excesses of the revenge when it is carried out on innumerable Trojans, and on Hector's body, is perhaps highlighted by Aeschines to suggest two ideas to the jury: first, the parallel between this couple and the Athenian pederastic role-models Harmodios and Aristogeiton, equally united in their glorious, early, deaths (see Ford 1999: 254–5), and second, the legitimacy of Aeschines' own seeking a lesser form of revenge, through the courts, over Timarchos.

it was because of erotic love (*eros*) that he undertook the charge of Patroklos. The inference from Achilles' sorrow at the memory of how Patroklos had been entrusted to his care and protection to the conclusion that Achilles was his 'lover' is not at first sight obvious (see Dover 1978: 53); the argument must be based on current assumptions that a father would only entrust a son to another man to watch over and return home from an adventure if they were engaged in a 'noble' love between those of unequal age and/or status. See Ford (1999: 253), who also suggests plausibly that Aeschines has subtly strengthened this point by interpreting Achilles' promise to 'bring Patroklos back' in the more precise sense in classical Greek of 'return an object of trust deposited with one' .

144 Ah me . . . Homer, *Iliad* 18. 324–9.

145 With such nobility of soul. This paraphrasing of Achilles' words and actions is heavily idealizing, to make the hero another model of noble self-sacrifice. The brutality of the acts and expressions of revenge, the prolongation of the maltreatment of Hector's body, and the recriminations directed at Achilles by Thetis, following representations from most of the gods, are all omitted; instead the elements of Achilles' obsessive and all-embracing grief and guilt, and his longing to join Patroklos in death, those elements which do indeed suggest that they shared a strangely powerful love, are carefully emphasized.

146 feel envious at their virtue (*arete*) and their friendship (*philia*). The emphasis which Aeschines puts on the exceptional *philia* of this pair in the *Iliad* has been echoed, and justified in detail, in a number of recent treatments of this important aspect of the poem: see e.g. D. S. Sinos, *Achilles, Patroklos and the Meaning of Philos* (Innsbruck, 1980); S. L. Schein, *The Mortal Hero: An introduction to Homer's Iliad* (California, 1984); G. Zanker, *The Heart of Achilles: Characterisation and Personal Ethics in the Iliad* (Michigan, 1994).

147 'Nevermore . . .' . . . faithfulness and affection. Here Aeschines switches from his general paraphrasing of the elements of the narrative he is selecting, to paraphrase the opening lines of the ghost of Patroklos' speech, the proper text of which will shortly be read out by the clerk; he thus highlights the fine picture of the pair, in close friendship and complete isolation from all their other, lesser, friends, engaged in 'deliberation'. This emphasizes the mutual exclusiveness of their close affection, the fidelity and the seriousness of their discussions, further to justify this as an exemplary type of noble love for Athenian citizens to aim at.

So that you may hear these sentiments of the poet in the verse form itself, the clerk will read for you the verses on this theme that Homer composed. So far, with his quotations from Hesiod and the first one from Homer, Aeschines has recited them himself; for the next three, the second of which is much longer than the rest, he asks the clerk to read them out. One reason for the switch, despite the chance for Aeschines to declaim in his emotionally powerful voice, may be that having extracts read out by the clerk makes it clear that Homer, and then Euripides, are being treated, like citations of the laws, or witness statements, as authoritative 'evidence', hence also the initial emphasis on their 'wisdom' (**141, 151**); Demosthenes later complained of his reliance on the poets as witnesses, in the absence of any proper one, 19. 243. See Perlman (1964: 167); Ford (1999: 252). The introduction of the clerk has apparently not made the quotations completely accurate; presumably he read out a text given him by Aeschines, and some of the variations from our texts of Homer seem to reflect deliberate sharpening of his points by the orator (see notes below).

148 dear comrade. Our texts of this passage (Homer, *Iliad* 18. 333–5) have a simple vocative, 'Patroklos', and Aeschines has evidently substituted the more emotional 'dear comrade' (*phil' hetaire*) to emphasize the theme of the depth of the emotion. While this is not of course false to the emotion of Achilles' speech, it is a significant alteration to suit Aeschines' argument. In particular, the use of the word *hetairos* for comrade here and also (correctly quoted) in the next two extracts from the Iliad (23. 77 and 18. 98) may all suggest a contrast between the noble and heroic relationship between the *hetairoi* in the epic poem and the debased relationship of male *hetairesis*, whose participants are never called *hetairoi*, but are modelled rather on the female *hetaira*, and also the male *hetairoi* who may form a subversive political or legal group of supporters. On the use of *hetairos* of contemporary figures in the speech, see on **110** and **173**.

149 No longer. Homer, *Iliad* 23. 77–91. In line 77, 'no longer' is an unimportant Aeschinean alteration for 'not'. There are more significant variations, though, in lines 81–4: some lines in the speech are added ('fighting with the enemy for the sake of lovely-haired Helen, and but so that the same earth may cover you and me | in the golden urn which your mother has provided'—this last line is very similar to our line 92, but has been moved up). These changes may, however, conceivably reflect alternative versions around at this time, rather than systematic changing by Aeschines.

when angered over knucklebones. Knucklebones, though included in gambling dens such as the one operated by Pittalakos, were still very much seen as a game played by children and youths (see Kurke 1999: 283–95, and on **59**). In the passage of the *Iliad* the reminder of a childhood knucklebones game, which led to a homicide, may connect eerily with Patroklos' insistence that his and Achilles' bones should be mingled together after their deaths, and perhaps also hint that it is the gods who play games with the lives, and hence the bones, of mortals (see Kurke 1999: 292). It is possible further that Aeschines, in including these lines in his extended quotation on the deep affection of the heroic pair, would also welcome an awareness of the contrast between the more innocent and heroic games and the more shameful and sordid gambling and violence of Timarchos, Pittalakos, and Hegesandros.

150 'swift-footed godlike Achilles' . . . 'who was far the dearest to me'. The last selection from Achilles' conversation with Thetis in book 18 (Homer, *Iliad* 18. 95–100), focuses on Achilles' undoubting acceptance of early death, since he had failed to protect his 'friend'. There are two changes from our standard text; in place of the line 'to her replied, much aggrieved, swift-footed Achilles' there is the blander 'replied swift-footed godlike Achilles' (the replacement is a formula found twenty-one times in the poem, and the whole line is almost the same as 24. 668, the only difference being 'to him' at the start, as it is Achilles' last reply to Priam); the point may be to emphasize Achilles' nobility and calm acceptance of death. The last phrase—'who was far the dearest to me'—is a change, and the new half-line is built up out of a number, especially perhaps 17. 584, 18. 118, and 20. 410. Again, it is of course not false to the whole picture, but the change enables Aeschines, very suitably, to round off the Homeric section with words which emphasize the depth of the affection between the two.

151 Euripides. Aeschines now turns to quote Euripides, the most popular of the three classic fifth-century tragedians. He does not seem to quote Sophocles anywhere, though Demosthenes claims (19. 24) that he acted regularly in both Euripides' and Sophocles' plays (see Intro. pp. 14–16). One might wonder why he did not cite other still more apposite passages, especially perhaps a line from Aeschylus' *Agamemnon* 938; 'Yet Rumour spread by the people has great power'; but Aeschylus, perhaps now felt to be the least relevant or easily intelligible of the three great fifth-century classics, is not quoted in any fourth-century speech or in Aristotle's *Rhetoric*. See P. J. Wilson (1996: 315).

The love that leads . . . Euripides, *Sthenoboea* 672 Nauck[2]. This passage is placed in context for us by a Byzantine commentator called Ioannes Logothetes, commenting on the rhetorician Hermogenes' *peri methodou deinotetos* 30; the text of Ioannes was edited by H. Rabe, 'Aus Rhetoren-Handschriften', *RM* 63 (1908), 127–51, esp. 146–8. The discussion is concerned with this and similar rhetorical examples of how to quote poetry; Ioannes quotes thirty-one lines in all from the prologue of the *Sthenoboea*, of which these two are lines 24–5. See the text and translation in C. Collard et al. (eds.), *Euripides, Selected Fragmentary Plays* (Warminster, 1995), 79–97. The play was first performed probably in the early 420s, and parodied in Aristophanes' *Wasps* (1074) of 422. Bellerophon of Corinth delivered the 'moralizing' prologue, describing how, while he was a suppliant and guest at the court of Proitos king of Tiryns, who had purified him of the pollution incurred for a homicide committed in Corinth, Proitos' wife Stheneboea tried persistently to seduce him, aided by her nurse:

I would not agree to accept her talk,
nor to outrage (*hybrisai*) the house that was sick, when a guest,
as I hate that terrible *eros* which destroys mortals.
For there are two types of *eros* bred on earth:
the one which is most hateful and which leads to death,
and the *eros* that leads to self-control and to virtue,
and is pursued as enviable by men of whom I would be one. (lines 19–25)

Euripides thus makes very much the same distinction as Aeschines, in the context of heterosexual love inside and outside marriage, between noble and chaste love, and adulterous love; the latter involves *hybris* against the house (and its master) and can destroy it. One might have thought it would strengthen Aeschines' case to quote a little more of this passage, especially given its use of the term *hybrizein* to indicate the damage done by the wrong *eros* (see especially **141**). Perhaps, however, Aeschines wished to avoid making it evident that the context concerns the adulterous desires of a 'bad woman', not love for boys; perhaps for that reason, because it was one of the famous Euripidean plays criticized for presenting evil women in the grip of love (see Ar. *Frogs* 1043–5), he also suppresses the name of the play (see also P. J. Wilson 1996: 314–15).

152 In his *Phoinix*. Aeschines here does give the source, and quotes considerably more, because he was able to apply the sentiments even more appropriately—though once more he does not make it explicit that the slander brought against Phoinix was of having had illicit heterosexual intercourse. In Euripides' version (slightly different from that in the *Iliad* 9. 447–84) Phoinix' father

Amyntas was induced by his concubine Phthia to believe that Phoinix had slept with her, when he had himself (again) refused her advances; not believed, he was blinded and banished (becoming one of Euripides' unfortunate ragged heroes, see Ar. *Ach.* 421–2; hence the play is earlier than 425). Demosthenes (19. 245) quotes the last three of these lines back at Aeschines, damning him by his association with Philokrates, who had by then, by running away, arguably admitted taking Philip's money, and thus again sneering at Aeschines' use of poetry and reclaiming its power for himself (see P. J. Wilson 1996: 315). Demosthenes adds some more digs at Aeschines' presence among the incompetent acting troupes of Theodoros and Aristodemos, and claims that they, and therefore Aeschines, never actually performed the *Phoinix*; since the point of that is to make the link to the quotation from the *Antigone*, on the grounds that Aeschines had taken the part of Kreon in that, there is no particular reason to believe either claim. These lines are also quoted by a good many later authors such as Stobaeus (see references in Nauck² 812 *ad loc.*).

153 sentiments that the poet sets out. As is usual with the orators' quotations from the poets, the assumption is that the extracts they have ripped from their dramatic contexts give the moral sentiments endorsed by the poet himself; another classic example of this is Demosthenes' response (19. 247), the lengthy citation from Sophocles' *Antigone* containing fine sentiments on the duties of a statesman, regardless of the sort of king and ruler Kreon in fact turned out to be in that play (cf. Bowie 1997: 44; P. J. Wilson 1996: 312). Here Aeschines deliberately effaces any sense of the context of Phoinix defending himself on a charge of immorality, and openly identifies Euripides the poet, speaking as one with long experience of judging disputes and character, with the jury asked to judge the character of Timarchos. Further he brings into his exegesis of the text a good many extra considerations only appropriate to the jury's duty in relation to Timarchos, above all the idea that how a man behaves in private life and with respect of his household will determine how he behaves as a politician managing the affairs of the *polis*: see Ford (1999: 25).

It is right then for you. The authority of the poet's words, thus extracted and interpreted, then provide the orator's justification for giving another summing up (see **116**) of the main points of the case. It is again to be noted how the emphasis is squarely on both Timarchos' 'eating up' of his inheritance and on the selling of his body and associations with the likes of Hegesandros; repeated in reverse order at the end of the paragraph, that he has made himself a *pornos* and eaten his ancestral estate. Further, and also perhaps tellingly, he repeats the allegation that Timarchos is currently taking bribes from his public offices; this is not exactly part of the formal charge, but serves as evidence that the rationale behind the offence is correct, that those who committed such offences against family, property, and their own selves will readily betray the state and cannot be allowed to hold public office.

154 With whom does he like to associate? Hegesandros. The singling out of this man (see also on **54–71**) among Timarchos' associates and alleged lovers confirms that he was the one who counted most in contemporary Athens. Aeschines must have felt that if he could remind, or persuade, the jury of Hegesandros' reputation as a man with a highly dubious past and as a bullying and aggressive politician, it would greatly aid the chances of gaining a conviction against his friend.

what oath did you swear? Aeschines is here preparing the ground for the major argument (**166–76**) that the jury must resist Demosthenes' attempts to divert the case from the accusations against Timarchos' personal offences on to the current political situation. Here, as again in **170**, he claims that the heliastic oath which all jurors swore at the start of their year of office (see also on **114**, and also Aesch. 3. 6–7) insisted that they give their verdicts solely on the charges brought by the prosecutor; the same point is made by prosecutors at Dem. 23. 19, 44. 14, 45. 50. Demosthenes, in his speech against Timokrates, has the oath read out to the jury (24. 149–51), and our manuscripts at that point preserve a version of the oath which he read out. As is usual with the documents in our texts, it is uncertain how many , if at all, of the clauses included are genuine (cf. Drerup 1898: 256–64; Lipsius 1905–15: 151–2; Hansen 1991: 182–3); it includes the phrases 'I shall listen to the prosecutor and the defendant, equally to both, and I shall cast my vote on the matter which is raised in the charge'. On the varied rhetorical uses of the oath, see above all Johnstone (1999: 33–42, 60–2).

155–159 *Examples of good and bad youths*

155 too long expounding. This soft and almost apologetic transition from the appeal to the pleasant instruction of the poets leads to a very important section where Aeschines seems to have brought the accusations forcibly home, by an apparently success-ful bid to evoke audience participation against the defendant. To demonstrate by arguments *ad hominem* that the distinction between those boys or youths who kept their reputations for self-control intact and those who failed was in fact actively maintained by public opinion, Aeschines introduces two lists, of attractive youths who had retained a reputation for *sophrosyne* and those who had not. Two of those listed, Timesitheos and Antikles, are expressly described as runners (and the second of them is almost certainly the Olympic victor of a few years later), but it is surely likely that they had all become well known for their exceptional physical attractions, and had acquired multiple pursuers, through some forms of self-display at the *gymnasia* or in athletic competitions; they are the sort of 'naked stars' that all parents allegedly hoped their sons would be (**134**), in whom the whole city takes a keen interest: see generally Winkler (1990: 63–4); Fisher (1998a: 101–2) and P. J. Wilson (2000: 254–6). A similar point about the intensity of community evaluation of the use made by the young of their beauty, conceived as something almost sacred, is made by Isocrates, in his sophistical disquisition in praise of Helen and of the ideal of beauty (10. 58). Though his topic is Helen's beauty, this example is clearly focused on the beautiful young men who may grow up to serve their state; on this see D. Cohen in Hindley and D. Cohen (1991: 188).

156 Kriton the son of Astyochos. This man (*LGPN* 30; *PA* 8828; Davies, *APF* 337: of Kydathenaion) also appears in the list of twenty-three Athenians, who guaranteed money for triremes to be lent to Chalkis in 340, and paid it up in 325/4 (*IG* II² 1623 l. 191–2; *IG* II² 1629, l. 538): see on **65**. At the time of this speech, Kriton was fully adult, well known and respectable, and by 340, if not earlier, he was rich enough to be in effect in the liturgical class.

Perikleides of Perithoidai (*LGPN* 2; *PA* 11804), **Polema-genes** (*LGPN* 1; *PA* 11878), **Pantaleon son of Kleagoras** (*LGPN*

4; *PA* 11600). No identifications of these allegedly distinguished men can be made.

Timesitheos the runner. The name is unusual (*LGPN* 1; *PA* 13648), and this man probably belonged to a liturgical family of the deme Kerameis (discussed by S. Charitonides, 'The First Half of a Bouleutic List of the Fourth Century BC', *Hesperia* 30 (1961), 51; Davies, *APF* 102–3), but which member is not clear. As he is also in the list of the older, well-known men, he is unlikely to be, as Davies thought, the Timesitheos (or Timasitheos) son of Demainetos II (*LGPN* 7; *PA* 13641: himself trierarch in 356/5, and again before 334/3, perhaps actually in 345/4): this Timesitheos is first attested as trierarch in 323/2. Kyle (1987: 226–7), who pointed this out, suggested he was the father of Demainetos II, Timasitheos, who appears on an inscription (*IG* II² 143, new fr. in *Hesperia* 7 [1938], 278 no. 13; *LGPN* 6; *PA* 13640) among a list of men honoured probably for their roles as public arbitrators, which was a post performed in one's sixtieth year (the new fragment adds the key phrase 'resolving disputes' in the epigram praising the honorands). The inscription is dated on letter forms to *c.* 375–360, and so this Timesitheos would be at least *c.* 75 by 346/5, which might perhaps be thought a bit old to be so highlighted; another member of the family cannot be ruled out. If it is the arbitrator, it is possible that his fame as a beauty and as a runner (still mentionable so much later) contributed to the rise in the family's fortunes.

had very many lovers of the greatest moral control (*sophronestatoi*); but still no one ever criticized them. This argument significantly reveals that it was thought possible for a beautiful youth to accept, without endangering his reputation for *sophrosyne*, not just one or two but many lovers; it does not quite make it clear how the trick was done. More was involved, presumably, than a matter of luck, of avoiding malicious gossip or arousing powerful enemies; what counted must have been to avoid the impression of seeming to maintain many lovers at the same time, and even more important (see **75–6**), avoiding the impression of accepting money, expensive gifts, or a lavish lifestyle above one's means. (See also Intro. pp. 42–5, 50–1). In practice, judging by comedy, many attractive youths must have incurred gossip or passing treatment in a play, without too much mud sticking as they grew older: see for example the famous relationship between Kallias and Autolykos, mocked in three plays by Eupolis (the *Flatterers*, and the two *Autolykoses*), but presented as a fine and noble relationship in Xenophon's *Symposion*; and Autolykos survived to have his political career ended by the Thirty. See also Dover (1978: 89–91); Fisher (1998a: 99); Hindley (1999: 76–7, 89).

157 The nephew of Iphikrates, the son of Teisias.
Iphikrates the Athenian general (*LGPN* 4; *PA* 7773; Develin, *AO* no. 1449; Hansen, *Inventory* 49) best known for his development of an effective peltast force, evidently was a self-made man, as many anecdotes of his enemies attacking his low birth, the son of a cobbler, and his own pride in his personal achievements alike attest: see Plut. *Mor.* 187b; *scholia* to Dem. 21. 62; Davies, *APF* 248–52; Parke (1933: 50–7); Pritchett (1974: II, 62–72, 117–25); Gauthier (1985: 125, 177–80); Mitchell (1997: 51, 102–3). He acquired wealth as well as a favourable marriage to the sister (so Davies) of Kotys, a king in Thrace; presumably he, and certainly his son Menestheus and his brother, the Teisias mentioned here and at Dem. 21. 62 (*LGPN* 19; *PA* 13481), performed liturgies. The family's rise to prominence, like that of Chabrias, is more spectacular, but essentially not dissimilar to the success of Aeschines and his brothers. A brother of this Timarchos the son of Teisias, Timotheos (*LGPN* 82), dedicated an altar to Herakles found in the Agora (Agora I 1052, inscription published by B. D. Merrit, *Hesperia* 7 [1938], 92–3; cf. Lambert 1999: 124, with new readings by M. H. Jameson, see Jameson 2000); it gives a short list of names of members of the *genos* Praxiergidai and some other group who shared activities at the shrine. Lambert points to the possibility of a connection of this group with the association of the *thiasoi*, probably of Herakles revealed in *IG* II² 2345, and hence perhaps with the Salaminians; he makes the further tentative suggestion that there may in fact be some family or other connection between the two Timarchoses, and that the nephew of Iphikrates was keen to distance himself from the more controversial older man. But it would be surprising if neither Aeschines nor Demosthenes mentioned any connection, however remote, between the defendant Timarchos and the family of Iphikrates.

Rural Dionysia. The Rural Dionysia was celebrated with a procession and community festivities to Dionysos in mid-winter in a good many, if not all, of the local demes in Attica (see above all the parodic presentation in Aristophanes' *Acharnians* of 425). In at least ten demes, which developed small theatres, repeat productions of tragedies and comedies were staged (see Whitehead 1986a: 215–20; Taplin 1999: 36–7). This passage, and Demosthenes 18. 180 and 262, provide the evidence for comedy and tragedy at a Rural Dionysia festival at Kollytos, a city deme, in the tribe of Aigeis, bordering Melite (Strabo 1. 4. 7) which lies to the west of the *agora*. Kollytos is most plausibly placed to the south of Melite, including some of the area between the Pnyx and the Areopagos (Pritchett 1953: 275–6; D. M. Lewis, 'Notes on Attic Inscriptions II', *BSA* 50 (1955), 16 and n. 40); but areas north of Melite, to the north-west of the *agora*, cannot quite be ruled out, depending on the relationship with the deme Kerameis (W.E. Thompson, 'Notes on Attic Demes', *Hesperia* 39 (1970), 67). No theatre structures have been discovered in either area; conceivably there was never more than a wooden theatre (Whitehead 1986a: 220, n. 266). Demosthenes' story (18. 180) that Aeschines flopped while giving a performance as Oinomaos at Kollytos may have an element of 'revenge', in view of Aeschines' effective use of the alleged comic joke at the same theatre at Timarchos' expense here (see Intro. pp. 14–15); one should contemplate the possibility that Demosthenes invented the anecdote. It may or may not be relevant that a joke made against Demades by Demosthenes, implying that he had just been caught in adultery at Kollytos, suggests that Kollytos might be considered a deme of ill-repute (Plut. *Demosth.* 11).

Parmenon the comic actor. He won a victory at the Lenaia in the mid-fourth century, *IG* II² 2325, 194, and was the subject of an anecdote in Ps. Arist. *Probl.* 948c, and in Plut. *Mor.* 18c. See Ghiron-Bistagne (1976: 350); Stefanis (1988: no. 2012); *LGPN* II.

big Timarchean whores. On the significance of this reference to Timarchos in a comedy for the date of the speech, see Intro. pp. 6–8, and for the previous reputation for immorality of Timarchos, Intro. pp. 57–8. 'Big' may imply full-size (Dover 1978: 39 translates the phrase as 'grown-up *pornoi* like Timarchos'), not young boys; but also is likely here to convey 'famously engaged in large-scale prostitution'. The phrase here could be a direct quotation, since *pornous megalous Timarchodeis* could be a metrical line ('anapaestic dimeter') of a type which appears to have been popular in Middle Comedy (especially in lists of foods), see Arnott,

Alexis 479–80; but it is possible that they were single, but not adjoining, words extracted from a longer sentence, see Wankel (1988: 385); *PCG* VIII *adesp.* 73K/A.

you are the true heir of this practice. The term *kleronomos* essentially means one who has established a claim as heir to an estate (the word is most commonly used therefore in inheritance cases, and see on **30**). The points made here are, first, that Timarchos is fitted by his 'nature' for his long involvement in this 'practice' (on *epitedeuma* in the context, above on **37**); second, he has voluntarily entered on to it and established himself in it; and third, he is the most famous member of this class of 'bad boys', as it were the leading *pornos* of his generation.

Antikles the stadium-runner. The *stadion* was the straight foot-race, or sprint, or the running track along which it was run (roughly 200 metres), or the 'stadium'; as a whole. The sprint was one of the earliest events at the Olympic games, with perhaps something of the privileged status that the 100 metres enjoys at our Olympics, and it was the winner's name in this event which was recorded in the Olympic victor lists which were of great importance in ancient systems of chronology (see e.g. Kyle 1987: 178–80). Two chronological sources indicate that an Athenian Antikles (*LGPN* 11; *PA* 1057; *PAA* 133225; Kyle 1987: 197) won in the foot-race at the Olympics in the summer of 340: Africanus *ap.* Eusebius *Hist.* 1. 206, line 21 in his list of Olympic victors, and Diodoros 16. 77, synchronizing his victory with an Athenian archon and the Roman consuls. This is likely to be the same man, who thus a little later fulfilled his youthful promise to win an Olympic crown. The name, though, is common, and there is no particular reason to associate the runner, as Kyle is tempted to do, with any other homonyms, e.g. either of the two men of this name from Sounion, probably cousins, each recorded as freeing a slave on the 'Attic Manumission' documents (*IG* II^2 1697 18, 20).

Pheidias the brother of Melesias. Both common names, found in 13 and 24 demes respectively, and there are no obvious identifications for this Pheidias (*LGPN* 3; *PA* 14148) or this Melesias (*LGPN* 4; *PA* 9807), though it is tempting to suspect a link with Melesias the famous early fifth-century Athenian athletic trainer mentioned several times by Pindar (*Ol.* 8, *Nem.* 4 and 6), and plausibly identified as the father of the conservative politician Thucydides, related by marriage to Kimon (and probably also related to the historian), who was ostracized in the mid-440s (see Wade-Gery 1958: 243–6; Rhodes 349–51; Davies, *APF* 7268).

giving them praise through desire to win their favour. Aeschines is concerned to be seen to show proper caution here, not to be trying to arouse the interest of these particularly attractive youths; similarly he insists at **169** that he had no improper interest in the boy Alexander, and one may compare comic poets' denials that they used their fame to pick up boys at the *gymnasia* (Ar. *Wasps* 1025–6; *Peace* 762–4, and cf. Eupolis 65 K–A: see Intro. p. 51). In contrast Aeschines accuses Demosthenes (**170–2**, 3. 255) of hunting wealthy and vulnerable young men under the guise of teaching them rhetoric.

158 wishing to avoid enmities. Athenians recognized that they might well make enemies as well as friends, who could be very dangerous (see Dover 1974: 180–4; Blundell 1989: ch. 2); naturally, politically active Athenians attracted enemies even more readily than less active citizens and such enmities were pursued in the courts (see also on **1–2**, **110**, and Rhodes 1998, and S. C. Todd's response, 1998). Considerations alike of civic order and of personal advantage, however, also produced the recognition that one should not make enemies unnecessarily (see Herman 1994; Schofield 1998). Aeschines himself was facing a determined attempt from his enemies to destroy his career, and responding by a similar attack on Timarchos; whether he had particular reasons to mention those whose reputations he attacks here is unclear.

Diophantos, known as the orphan. Diophantos was a common name, occurring in 24 demes, but this particularly uninhibited youth (*LGPN* 5; *PA* 4420) cannot be further identified. This is an especially curious and interesting case; clearly we cannot presume that Aeschines is telling the whole, or indeed any of, the truth (and the *topos* 'Who of you does not know' does not help), but the name of the *paredros* as well as that of the litigant is provided, and if the story was quite inconceivable there was little point in retelling it (see Dover 1978: 30).

who brought the foreigner before the archon. The verb translated 'brought' (*apagein*) might suggest the summary procedure known as *apagoge*, most frequently used to bring various criminals (typically, types of thieves) swiftly to the magistrates known as the Eleven, or to the *thesmothetai*, for summary execution if they admitted the offence, or referral to trial (see on **91**). But no other source refers to an *apagoge* of that type to deal with maltreatment of orphans, and probably here the term refers to an arrest of the accused foreigner after an indictment for maltreatment (*eisangelia kakoseos*) had been laid before the archon: see Hansen (1976: 29).

whose assistant was Aristophon of Azenia. On the role of the 'assistant' *paredros* lending experience and support to magistrates such as the archons, see Kapparis (1998: 382–93); *Neaira* 322–3. He demonstrates that it was not uncommon for more experienced men to undertake such roles, such as the archon's father (see Dem. 2. 178), or well-known politicians, such as Aristophon (on whom, see on **64**); they could have wide powers delegated to them. The best-known case is that of Stephanos, *paredros* to Theogenes (Ps. Dem. 59. 72–4, 80–4), who allegedly inveigled him into marrying his daughter 'Phano'. The *scholia* to Dem. 21. 178 suggest that a *paredros* would sit with an archon hearing cases to do with orphans and inheritance disputes, so it is likely enough that Aristophon was involved in the Diophantos case (see Kapparis 1998: 389).

four drachmai. Assessing the significance of this sum is difficult, not least because it is not made clear whether it is supposed to be a payment for a period, or for one occasion, nor whether it is the whole fee, or a part which allegedly remained unpaid. We hear of the dinner-party insult that the well-known and witty 'parasite' Eukrates, known as the 'Lark' (*korydos*), was once available for the very small sum of an obol, and other evidence that one obol was the conventional, standard, insulting, sum for the cheapest female prostitutes. On the other hand, a much higher sum is mentioned at Lysias 3. 22, but it is similarly hard to interpret: it was apparently alleged that a sexual contract had been entered into between Simon, the speaker's opponent, and the 'Plataean boy' (*meirakion*), amounting to 300 drachmai: this was presumably for Simon's exclusive sexual use of the boy for an extended period (see on Carey, *Lysias* 102–3), but the duration is not stated, and in any case the speaker disputes that it was ever made. Tentatively one might suggest that if four drachmai were the whole fee for one occasion (or a very short period), it might represent a middling sort of price for an attractive youth of citizen family. In general, see Halperin (1990: 107–12); Davidson (1997: 194–200); Loomis 1998: 172).

the laws which command the archon to take concern for orphans. On these laws giving wide-ranging powers (in theory at least) to the eponymous *archon*, see the quotation of the law (conceivably authentic) in Ps. Dem. 43. 75, and also Lys. 26. 12; Dem. 24. 20, 35. 48; Isaeus 7. 30, and Arist. *Ath. Pol.* 56. 6–7, with Rhodes 629–30; Harrison (1968–71: I, 99–104).

while he had himself. There are serious difficulties in understanding this case as presented, and serious distortion may be supposed. If Diophantos was known as 'the so-called orphan', why is he appealing to the archon under the laws designed to protect actual orphans against abuse? Perhaps the claim was that the contract had been entered into before Diophantos came of age, but the case was brought some time later, and his claim to be a suffering orphan was felt to be somewhat fraudulent. But according to Isaeus 10. 10 'boys', like women, were not legally permitted to engage in financial agreements greater than the value of a *medimnos* of barley (perhaps about three drachmai, Carey, *Lysias* 103); though there are grave doubts about this alleged law, or how it was implemented, if at all, in classical Athens—see generally Foxhall (1989); Hunter (1994: 19–29). If Diophantos was still a minor when he alleged the contract was agreed, one must wonder what role, if any, the boy's guardian(s) played in the case, since *prima facie* they should have become liable under the laws protecting boys quoted in **13**. It would seem in any case that the point at which one was registered on the deme's *lexiarchikon grammateion*, and then passed the *dokimasia* in the council (Arist. *Ath. Pol.* 42. 1) was also the moment at which one became in charge of one's property (and could then embark on a prosecution against one's guardian(s), as Demosthenes did, 30. 15), and would also be the point at which one became responsible for sexual decisions (see on **18** and **103**). Conceivably once Diophantos came of age, he became involved in a case against his guardian or guardians, for example on the grounds that they had deprived him of some or all of his inheritance and had hired him out to foreigners; then perhaps one of these men was brought into court, either to give evidence or to face the accusation that he had failed to deliver on this disreputable deal; and the guardians may have responded with the claim that Diophantos had himself made the agreement with the foreigner (hence he may have acquired the soubriquet of the 'the orphan').

If the substance of the case did involve an agreement between a citizen orphan and a foreigner, one may observe that Diophantos, presumably an attractive youth of a deceased citizen father, was either exploited for short-term profit by his guardian(s), or himself decided or was persuaded to accept such a deal, on the grounds that he had no desire for, or chance of, a political career and also little chance of becoming richer while retaining a reputation for *sophrosyne*. The option taken was to exploit his beauty for money, accepting a deal with a foreign client and insisting on payment. Whatever the circumstances, going to law must have been a high-risk strategy, as the jury might react with moral distaste rather than strict observance of the law. Aeschines does not state that the case was thrown out, and it is just conceivable that this had indeed happened, and was well enough known not to need to be emphasized; it is, however, more likely that the case went for Diophantos, or was settled by a compromise. Even so Aeschines calculated that it left enough doubt about the circumstances of Diophantos' relations with the foreigner, and his age at relevant times, for him to enrol him among his list of non-*sophron* boys.

Kephisodoros, known as the son of Molon. Kephisodoros is an extremely common name, found in 43 demes, and no identification offers itself for this youth (*LGPN* 15; *PA* 8346); Molon is a much rarer name (*LGPN* 5; *PA* 10412). But the phrase 'known as' (*ton kaloumenon*) may suggest some form of nickname, rather than that Aeschines is merely giving the real father's name. At Lysias 13. 19 an alleged 'informer' for the Four Hundred in 411 is introduced as 'Theokritos, known as the son of Elaphostiktos (Deer-tattooed)'; the point seems to be that the supposed patronymic denotes his supposed servile origins by indicating a dappled tattoo. If so, there may perhaps be a pun on the supposed father's name, and one might suspect a play with the verb *molunein*—to defile, pollute, get dirty, used in sexual contexts, for example, in Ar. *Knights* 1288, of Ariphrades' filthy habits getting his beard dirty when engaged in *fellatio* in brothels, or Theocritus 5. 87, where the coarse shepherd Lacon recalls with pleasure having 'debauched a young boy' (an *anhebos pais*, not yet reached his full manhood, *hebe*) after a successful day's cheese-making.

Mnesitheos, known as the butcher's son. Again a

common name (16 demes), and no obvious identification; clearly not the man mentioned at **98** (*LGPN* 6). The term I have translated 'butcher', *mageiros*, conveys a person responsible for all aspects of dealing with a domestic animal for a sacrifice, bringing it to the sacred area, killing and butchering it, and cooking the meat for the celebratory group. See G. Bertiaume, *Les Rôles de mageiros* (Leiden, 1982). In this case too, if the designation 'known as the butcher's son' is a nickname, it may reinforce the shame ascribed to these youths, and further emphasize the significance of Timarchos' own nickname, the most explicit of all. The point of the name remains unclear.

159 could you now answer me this question. A splendid example of the invitation to a loud audience reaction, i.e. a chorus of 'the prostitutes'. See on Bers (1985: esp. 6–7 and n. 21), suggesting Aeschines exploits the fact that it is easier to shout a disyllabic *pornoi* (whores) than a quadrisyllabic *eromenoi*, 'beloveds', and Hall (1995: 44). Demosthenes employed a very similar tactic in the Crown speech, inviting the jury to shout their response to the question 'was Aeschines the guest-friend (*xenos*) or the hired man (*misthotos*)' (19. 51–2)

group into which you have chosen to register. Attracting a reputation, and a nickname, to oneself is assimilated to self-assessment into a fixed class or group; the term used (*symmoria*) had been most commonly used in Athens since 378/7 for the groups into which the wealthy Athenians were placed for the purposes of collecting the property-tax (*eisphora*) or (since 357) or organizing and performing trierarchies (see e.g. Gabrielsen 1994).

and desert to the pursuits (*diatribai*) of the free men. The metaphor now seems to move rather to the military services, with the use of the verb *automolein*, desert, with the effect that it was even less open to Timarchos to leave the class he has chosen to join. On *diatribai*, pursuits, see on **132**.

160–165 *Arguments about contracts and agreements*

160 unless he was hired out with a contract. On the growth of written contracts in general in fourth-century Athens, F. D. Harvey, 'Literacy in the Athenian democracy', *REG* 79 (1966), 585–635; W. V. Harris (1989: 69); Thomas (1989: 41–2), and on **171**. The effect of the arguments presented here is that written contracts for a sexual relationship involving some form of payment were very hard if not impossible to enforce in case of breach by either party, if the boy or youth concerned was or would be a citizen. There are only three cases where we hear of contracts in such relationships. The one referred to in Lysias 3, esp. 22–6 involved a youth described as a 'Plataean', whose precise status is uncertain (and it is not clear whether the agreement was supposed to be written or oral): see e.g. Dover (1978: 32) and Carey, *Lysias* 87, suggesting that the youth was probably a slave. Second, the case of Diophantos just discussed, where allegedly a citizen youth did bring a case to court, and incurred a good deal of public ridicule, but may (or may not) have recovered his money; and third the alleged contract now under discussion (see on also Davidson 1997: 96–7). How frequent they were in practice is unclear, but Aeschines does supply cogent reasons why they would generally be avoided.

Aeschines is no doubt right that the law did not require evidence of a written contract. First, whenever this law allowing a *graphe* or a *dokimasia* of the politically active was created, it was not later than Aristophanes, *Knights* (see Intro. p. 53), and written contracts were scarcely known then; second, in the fourth century, it seems likely that most males and females who would be described either as *pornoi/ai* or as involved in *hetairesis* would have worked to verbal agreements rather than to formal contracts, whether for a single payment or a more lasting arrangement (but see now E. E. Cohen 2000). This anticipation of a supposed argument serves, as earlier at **119–24**, to characterize the defence as captious and over-precise, whether the defence in fact intended to use it, or whether this is rather a distortion of the defence's most obvious strategy, to deplore the total lack of any evidence supplied by the prosecution; so, by focusing on the alleged claim that they will demand a written contract, Aeschines diverts attention from their much more reasonable claim that he provide at least some witnesses. The argument also reminds the jury that this law fitted into a wide-ranging and coherent set of laws designed by 'the lawgiver' to preserve the moral basis of the community (cf. on **6**, and Johnstone 1999: 311–13).

when young stood aside from the ambition for noble honours (*philotimia*) because of his shameful pleasures

... share in the honours. This way of putting it brings into the open how attractive youths had in principle to decide very early whether they intended or hoped for a future political career; the dilemma in their position may indeed be that pursuing lover(s) were simultaneously urging them to yield to their desires and promising them help with their future careers. The language emphasizes the centrality of the ideas of honour and shame in these laws and their interpretations; if one commits shameful acts, one excludes oneself from the pursuit of the highest honours from the community, and can (in theory) never recover the chance of such ambition (see also **129, 194–6**).

161 what would the arguments on each side appear to be? Aeschines sets out in **161–4** two scenarios where a man who has hired a youth (the only term in fact used for the younger partner in this section is *neos*, young man; but it is clear that we are not to think of someone below the age of enrolment as a citizen) according to a contract. One is where the hirer has not fulfilled his side of the agreement, and the other one is the reverse; in both cases it is held that the actual terms of the hiring agreement with a youthful citizen will so outrage the jury that the plaintiff, which-ever he may be, will derive no benefit from the case. It is in fact clear from the discussion of the laws in **13–32** that the contract could well be legal, and the whole point of setting up these scenarios is that the prosecutors in each case might have some sort of legal case (see above all Dover 1978: 23–33); but Aeschines then asserts that the older man, even if correct on the issue of the con-tract, might fail to win a fifth of the votes, be thought to have hired the youth 'contrary to the *nomoi*', and might even be 'stoned' (see notes below). Aeschines has consistently applied his misinterpreta-tion of these laws (**72, 87, 90**) to claim that a hirer of an adult Athenian youth has committed serious *hybris*, and as a result might be held liable to the most severe penalties, and these passages have been taken too seriously by some scholars (e.g. D. Cohen 1995: 155–6). In this passage it seems likely that Aeschines is guilty of a contradiction in this establishment of his own scenario (see on Dover 1978: 33–4). He seems to suppose that the imaginary plaintiff would have a theoretical case for redress even though his contract was illegal. It is just possible, however, that he is suggesting no more than that such a man, choosing to parade his hire-agreement before a jury and asking for redress, might see his case thrown out, and risk extra-legal violence ('stoning') from an angry crowd. For this to work, 'against the *nomoi*' here would have to be taken as 'against prevailing social norms and values', not 'against the laws'. Probably, though, he is pressing as far as he can the argument that the action of hiring a youth is unacceptable, and as a result is trying to have his cake and eat it: he hopes the jury will believe both that the hiring was illegal and that a hirer might try to claim in court that it should be honoured, and not see the contradiction. The general argument is probably well founded, however, that such contracts would be very difficult to enforce in practice, given the unpopularity litigants would incur if they admitted to such arrangements (see also Carey, *Lysias* 102–3).

163 'I hired Timarchos . . . which is deposited with Demosthenes'. This vivid way of imagining the scenario pointedly places Timarchos as the 'youth' who might be involved, and also Demosthenes as the third party with whom the contract is deposited. This play thus surreptitiously and amusingly encourages the jury to suppose Demosthenes as a faithful friend and supporter of Timarchos even in his most debauched period as a young man going around with Hegesandros.

will he not be stoned? The mention of this extra-legal expression of a community's sense of appalled outrage (cf. 'lynching') shows Aeschines' awareness that actually the imaginary 'hirer' had not committed a legal offence. The most famous supposed cases of Athenian stonings were confused traditions of punishments meted out to those who proposed surrender to the Persians during Xerxes' invasion (Hdt. 9. 5; Lyc. 1. 122; Dem. 18. 204); see Dover (1978: 31); Thomas (1989: 84–91); for a comic example, Ar. *Ach.* 204–36, 280–96; more generally, for traditions of stoning in Greece, especially in the archaic period, see Parker (1983: 194–6); D. Ogden, 'Cleisthenes of Sicyon, *leuster*', *CQ* 43 (1993), 353–63; Allen (2000: 141–6).

sixth payment for his failure. In certain private actions, where a claim of a certain monetary value was at issue, plaintiffs who failed to win a fifth of the votes (probably so, rather than losing by any margin), had to pay to their opponents a penalty of a sixth of the amount at issue; this penalty was called the *epobelia*, as it constituted one obol per drachma: see Harrison (1968–71: II, 183–5).

164 the wise Batalos. Several more sneers are slipped into this hypothetical case: Demosthenes is again supposed to be helping, this time with the youth; his advocacy is (supposedly) necessary if the case is to be clearly put, and Demosthenes' suitability to work with such cases is emphasized by the reuse of his old nickname (see also on **131**).

which the one acting as an escort must do. Further euphemistic allusions to the supposedly disgraceful acts which the client would demand of the boy or youth he had hired (see on **41**, **51**).

Will not everyone say? Aeschines does not go so far in the case of the hypothetical wronged youth to imply that he might be immediately punished, legally or extra-legally, but merely that he will be told, in a spontaneous outcry in the court (see Bers 1985: 9), that he is now and for ever dishonoured, and cannot even hope to succeed in a private action, or undertake any other public act in the *agora*, though bringing a private action does not seem to have been an action forbidden to those who had 'lived shamefully' (see **19–20, 27**). On exclusion of the dishonoured (*atimoi*) from the *agora* see de Ste Croix (1972: 397–8).

165 One of our citizens (I shall not give his name). The individual here, whom Aeschines alludes to, but will not name, was identified by a writer of varied literary remarks preserved on an early imperial papyrus (*Oxyrynchus Papyri* no. 1012 C II 14) as Androtion the son of Andron (*LGPN* 3; *PA* 913 and 915; *PAA* 129125; Develin, *AO* no. 159; Hansen, *Inventory* 35), who was a mid-fourth-century politician and writer of a history of Athens. The identification was probably based, plausibly enough, on the similarity of the phraseology concerning the provision by the lover of a 'written agreement' here and in Demosthenes' attack, in the speech of the mid-350s on Androtion's alleged offence of *hetairesis* for which Demosthenes—on behalf of his client Diodoros—is promising that a prosecution will be brought (Dem. 22. 21–4, especially the 'written document' mentioned in 23). We have no reason to suppose a case was ever brought, but for the identification, see Jacoby, *FGH* 324 *Introduction* n. 64, and Harding,

Androtion 23. Our version of Demosthenes' speech for Diodoros does not name Androtion's supposed lover; the Antikles with whom the written agreement was deposited is presumably to be taken to be a friend who held the document rather than the lover, and no connection is suggested or need be supposed with either of the other two men called Antikles mentioned in the speech, Timarchos' lover, now in Samos (**53**), or the recently mentioned pretty but pure runner (**157**). The Antikles who was reputedly one of Isocrates' pupils might be suspected (he was mentioned by Isocr. 15. 93), as Androtion was also allegedly a pupil of Isocrates, and his general circle of rhetoricians and pupils, many of whom went going into politics, might be the setting from which the gossip spread (cf. the dubious list of his pupils at Ps. Plut. *Mor*, 837d; on the traditions of ascribing politicians and writers famous teachers and/or lovers, see also J. Fairbrother, 'Fiction in the Biographies of Ancient Writers', *Anc. Soc.* 5 (1974), 232–75.

It is not clear how many of the jury or the bystanders were likely to understand this allusion. Harding, *Androtion* 23, argues that the jury were supposed to remember that Androtion was the 'lover' and also that Demosthenes had written the speech against him along with Diodoros (see on Dover 1968: 161–3). He further suggests that Aeschines intended these remarks as snidely critical of a supposed closer political relationship now current between Demosthenes and Androtion, and supports this view by the speculative argument that at 2. 79 Aeschines is engaged in a veiled attack on Androtion's' proposal to use the stratiotic fund for the crowns to be offered to two Kings of the Black Sea region, Spartokos and Pairisades (*IG* II² 212). This supposed strategy seems very risky, depending as it would do on the confidence that enough of the jury would remember details of a political trial of a decade earlier. It seems more likely, as Aeschines himself claims, that he did indeed wish to avoid giving offence to Androtion by reminding the jury of an earlier scandal, especially if Androtion's position in the current dispute over the embassy was as yet uncertain.

166–176 *Attacks on Demosthenes' attempts at diversion*

166 There will be a lot of Philip. Aeschines speaks, understandably, somewhat cautiously in this section about how Philip's current promises, and hence the peace itself, will turn out to be regarded by the Athenians. Hence he is absolutely insistent that all serious political issues to do with the peace must be excluded from the case (see Intro. pp. 54–6; and Johnstone 1999: 54–60 on the common tension between litigants' competing views of what issues may be raised). Here he mentions them precisely to encourage the jury to watch for, and refuse to consider, such arguments from Demosthenes, and at the same time further to undermine Demosthenes' status as a representative of Athens or a spokesman for her culture. So the focus is on a verbal dispute between the two which is alleged to have taken place at a Council meeting, and was allegedly designed by Demosthenes to affect Aeschines' forthcoming scrutiny (*euthuna*) for his part in the embassy; the dispute concerned the behaviour of the young Alexander. If anything like this did occur at the Council meeting, Demosthenes' purpose will have been to suggest that Aeschines let slip at the meeting that he was already in Philip's pocket, by reacting so strongly to the jokes at the prince's behaviour. For a later example where politicians in the courts sought to arouse hostility against their opponents by irrelevant allegations of excessive pro-Macedonian connections, see Hyper. *Eux.* 19–26.

an uncultured (*amousos*) and uneducated (*apaideutos*) person. As a result of the lengthy discussion earlier (**132–40**), Aeschines now feels able to assert, contrary to his opponents' claim that he is an uncultivated upstart, that it is Demosthenes who lacks literary culture, education, and sophistication.

167 boorish and untimely. Aeschines highlights again the lack of taste and sense in Demosthenes' criticism of Philip and the Peace, and suggests at least that it is too early ('untimely') to assume that the Peace will fail, and to risk antagonizing the King.

disgraceful allegations against the man—he, who is himself no man. As well as the contrast between the mature adult Philip and the boy Alexander, and the repetition of the snide allegations against Demosthenes of sexual indeterminacy, there seems also to be a hint that Philip was an impressive figure of a man.

168 the boy Alexander. Alexander was born *c.* July 356 (Plut. *Alex.* 3), and was therefore not quite 10 when this party supposedly took place, in the spring of 346, his first appearance in history (see Lane Fox 1973: 46). Elaborate dinner-parties were essential elements of life at the Macedonian court, and they came to adopt many cultural features of the Greek formal *symposion* (often attended by visiting Greek intellectuals such as Euripides or Aristotle). On the other hand, hostile Greek perceptions of them emphasize their drunkenness, gambling, and brutishness (see especially Theopompos *FGH* 115 F 224 and 225), and the presence of the king and other 'royals' could create dissonances between the temptation to flatter and the more egalitarian ideology of the feast: see generally E. Borza, 'The Symposium at Alexander's Court', *Ancient Macedonia III* (Thessaloniki, 1983), 45–55 and Davidson (1997: 286–7, 301–4). At the Macedonian court, it is said, no one was permitted to recline at *symposia* until they had killed their first wild boar without a net, and Kassandros, Antipatros' son, who was to be one of the major competing dynasts after Alexander's death, had still not attained this privilege at the age of 35 (Athen. 18a, quoting Hegesandros of Delphi fr. 33; see Bremmer 1990: 139).

how he played the lyre. The prince was brought in, with other royal pages, to show off his paces at this early age, in music, recitations, and debating with his peers. Aelian (*VH* 3. 32) reports Alexander's casual approach to musical practice.

sallies against another boy. the meaning of the rare word *antikrousis* is not quite clear. In Aristotle's *Rhetoric* it indicates a sudden and effective stop to a clause (1409b22) and the verb *antikrouein* a deliberate act of opposition at which one might get angry (1379a13); in the *Politics* (1270a7) the verb is used of the obstacle Spartan women could form to their state, and in Dem. 19. 198, of an obstructive event. Here the reference is probably to brief, sharp, debating points or repartee made by Alexander to a mate. E. M. Harris' assertion (1985: 378) that Alexander was represented as flirting with another boy seems less plausible.

when he was revealing to the Council. This meeting is the one which took place after the return of the Second Embassy to Philip, which set off after the agreement to the peace, and reported back to the Council on 13th Skirophorion 346, at which Demosthenes later claimed that he denounced Aeschines' treachery (19. 17–18); on the implications for the date of the trial, Intro. pp. 3–6.

I . . . became angry at the jokes. The story presumably was that rather tasteless jokes were made at Alexander's expense, or perhaps double entendres discovered in his remarks directed at the other boy; Aeschines claims he was right to object on the grounds that they showed lack of taste and let the city down, but Demosthenes is suggesting excessive partiality ('as if I were a relation').

Demosthenes apparently continued to make offensive jokes against Alexander, and they could rankle and be used against him. After news of Philip's death reached Athens, Demosthenes, encouraging support for Theban resistance to Macedon, referred to Alexander as a boy and as 'Margites': see Aesch. 3. 160; Plut. *Dem.* 23. 2; *Alex.* 11.6; and Marsyas of Philippi, *FGH* 135 F 3. Alexander, when approaching Thebes and hearing of Athens' sympathy for it, recalled Demosthenes' recent insults, calling him a boy in Illyria, and a youth in Thessaly, and claimed he wished 'to prove himself a man in front of the walls of Athens' (Plut. *Alex.* 11). The *Margites*, an epic parody composed in the seventh or sixth century, retailed the adventures of a comic 'hero', a useless idiot, who fled in ignorance from his wedding night, in horror at his wife's genitalia and fear of what her mother might say; he was only persuaded to consummate by the story that his wife had been wounded there and could only be cured by the application of the male member: see the testimonia and fragments in West, *Iambi et Elegi Graeci*[2] (Oxford, 1992), II 69–78, and cf. Hyper. *Lyk.* 7. Demosthenes' point was that the young prince would grow up more like Margites than the hero of the *Iliad*, Achilles, on whom Alexander liked to model himself; and so attacked at once his pretensions, aptitudes, and capacity for full-scale masculinity.

169 I have naturally had no conversation. This (and the phrase 'paying court to the boy' below) seems to hint at another, more serious, albeit more implausible allegation against Aeschines, of making secret sexual overtures to Alexander. Different, more plausible, and serious, allegations of Aeschines' bad behaviour were highlighted in Demosthenes' Embassy speech, of sexual abuse and *hybris* against the Olynthian woman (19. 196–8); Aeschines naturally claims that these allegations produced outrage in himself and among the listeners (2. 4, placed early in the speech for emphasis).

**now have some praise for Philip because of the pro-
pitiousness of his statements.** The period after the making of
the peace was marked by mutual and well-founded uncertainties
concerning the possibilities of further co-operation between Philip
and Athens. The precise references to some arguably favourable
statements or speeches of Philip's depend to some extent on
whether the trial took place in the last months of 346 or very early
in 345 (see Intro. pp. 6–8). Philip did, after some delay, return the
Athenian prisoners (perhaps in the first month of the Attic year
346/5—Ps. Dem. (= Hegesippos) 7. 38; Ellis 1976: 127), but of
course the settlement of the Sacred War and Philip's assumption
of a leading role in the Delphian Amphictiony did more to alarm
many Athenians (see e.g. Ellis 1976: 127–8). Aeschines speaks as if
he yet had good hopes for the value of the peace and his and
Philokrates' part in it (cf. **174**); but the tone is markedly guarded.

paying court to the boy. The term *ektherapeuein*, a rare
strengthening of the much commoner verb *therapeuein*, suggests an
excessive concern to flatter and seek to win over the boy.

170 So in general. Aeschines broadens the attack on Demosthenes in **170–2**, in order to bring in the juiciest of the gossipy
anecdotes currently canvassed against him. The attack seems
totally without relevance to his case against Timarchos, and
contrary in spirit to his protestations against Demosthenes' veer-
ing off the point. Aeschines justifies it by the evident fact that
Demosthenes was to share more or less equally in the defence,
and by the general argument, central to the whole case, that those
who behave dreadfully in their private lives will do so also in
public life, and their arguments are not to be accepted. This leads
to the conclusion that as a dangerous 'sophist', and 'no man',
Demosthenes is not to be trusted as a supporter of Timarchos, but
is himself, like Timarchos, a threat to the whole community.

first because of the oaths. See on **154**, where the first
reference to the jury's alleged commitment in their oath to give
their verdicts in accordance with the specific charge. Other
speeches similarly argue against accepting alternative views of
what the trial is about from defendants: see Dem. 30, 43–6, 23.
124, 36. 61, 58. 36; Lyc. 1. 13; Lys. 22. 7; and Johnstone (1999:
60–2).

on the hunt for rich young orphans. See also 3. 256, where

Demosthenes is criticized for neither hunting wild boars nor training his body, but practising his (rhetorical) skills against those who
possess properties (a reference to his pursuit of rich pupils to
exploit, not a reference to sykophantic litigation, as Christ 1998:
95). A more positive treatment of Demosthenes' concentration of
rhetorical 'exercises' through his initial court cases instead of
athletics is found in Plut. *Dem.* 6. 1–2.

I shall pass over. The standard technique of implying there
are many more scandals, which the accuser will forbear to
mention (*praeteritio*). See on **39, 52, 109, 131**.

mention just one of those who were treated terribly.
This alarming story appears to have been the most long-running
and potentially serious of the allegations against Demosthenes'
private life; it certainly involved an unsolved murder. The story is
referred to also in a number of other passages: Dem. 21. 104–22
and the *scholia*, on which see MacDowell, *Meidias* 9, 325–44,
Aesch. 2. 148, 166, Dein. 1. 30, 47 (and see Worthington 179–81)
and Athen. 592 f. Each offers different versions of a complex tale,
whose truth was presumably hard to disentangle at the time. It
appears that Demosthenes befriended Aristarchos the son of
Moschos (*LGPN* 9; *PA* 1656; *PAA* 164185), and his widowed
mother as well, and taught him rhetoric; an erotic element to their
friendship was naturally alleged. Two men were involved in a
prosecution of Demosthenes for desertion from the Euboian
campaign of 348 (Dem. 21. 103–4 with Aesch. 2. 148); according to
Demosthenes, this prosecution was planned by Meidias in 348/7,
after his assault on Demosthenes in the theatre. They were Nikodemos of Aphidna (*LGPN* 25; *PA* 10868, a common name, and no
other associations seem especially plausible) and Euktemon of
Lousia (*LGPN* 53; *PA* 5800; *PAA* 438275), known as 'dusty', who
was probably the same man as Euktemon, son of Charias, of
Lousia (*PA* 5785; PAA 438280; Develin, *AO* no. 1169) who was an
Athenian member of a board of *naopoioi* at Delphi in a number of
years in the 340s–320s (see MacDowell, *Meidias* 325–60).
Euktemon probably had his name as prosecutor of the charge,
that Demosthenes had left his post in the army in Euboia without
permission, perhaps to fulfil his sudden role as *choregos* for his tribe
at the City Dionysia; but he did not carry it through to a prosecution (Dem. 21. 103).

Nikodemos, whom his enemies doubtless called a sykophant,

and his defenders, as Aeschines here, a private individual defending free speech on behalf of the people, seems also to have been
involved, or conceivably brought a prosecution of his own. He
was killed, allegedly having his eyes gouged out and his tongue cut
out in the process. Aeschines in this speech claims that Aristarchos
did it, but that Demosthenes was also somehow involved, and
achieved a dreadful form of revenge; in the Embassy speech he
accused Demosthenes of sharing in the murder, as does
Deinarchos. Idomeneus (*FGH* 338 F 12, ap. Athen. 592–3) asserted
that Demosthenes did it out of jealous love for Aristarchos, and in
a drunken rage (*paroinein*), which may at least suggest that the
setting of the killing was thought to be a drinking-party or subsequent *komos* (discounted by Worthington 180 on the grounds
that the killing more likely had a political than a sexual motive,
but mixed motives, and drunken quarrelling, may yet have played
their parts). Meidias' initial attempt to encourage Nikodemos'
relatives to prosecute Demosthenes, not Aristarchos, from a
combination of hatred for Demosthenes and his friendly relations
with Aristarchos (Dem. 21. 117), came to nothing. Aristarchos was
prosecuted by the relatives, and went into exile, perhaps under
the permitted procedure of leaving before the end of the trial
(D. M. MacDowell, *Athenian Homicide Law* (Manchester, 1963),
114–15, and on this case MacDowell, *Meidias* 329). If he was guilty,
as seems most likely, it may well have been the enraged assault of
a drunken young hothead, as Aeschines' description of him ('half-
mad') suggests, rather than a calculated killing; whether or not the
prime motive to attack was the desire to defend the honour and
career of his friend and/or lover. At all events, Demosthenes felt
he wished, or needed, to continue to speak of the exiled youth
with sympathy (21. 104; cf. his sympathy for Timarchos at 19. 283–
7), while Aeschines added the further allegations, unsupported by
any evidence, that he appropriated three talents supplied, presumably by the young man and his mother, to sustain him in
exile, and (2. 166) the extra charge that this showed that he had
not been capable of any 'just love' for him, as that was incompatible with the meanness shown by cheating him of the money
(see Dover 1978: 46–7 on the implications of this last argument).

171 He spotted a wealthy household. This (down to the end
of **172**) forms in the Greek one long, tortuous, and rhetorically

very effective sentence, which encapsulates the whole disastrous history of Demosthenes' relations with this family to its dreadful conclusion.

in charge of which was a woman . . . while a young orphan . . . was running the estate. The implications of this situation seem to be that a widow and a son, who presumably is just old enough to take financial decisions himself, i.e. now enrolled as a citizen and past his ephebic service (he is a *meirakion* and there is no mention of a male guardian), may be conceived of as in effect managing (or mismanaging) the estate together; see Foxhall (1989: 36–7); Hunter (1994: 29–33).

pretending to be his lover. This point both looks ahead to the implication (made more explicit in 2. 166) that Demosthenes was to betray and destroy this household, and so cannot have genuinely loved the young man, and reminds the jury that Demosthenes' indeterminate sexuality made him in any case incapable of a proper erotic relationship (see on **131**). Both points of course usefully serve further to undermine his claim to be able to speak with any authority on the central issues of the case, the place of legitimate same-sex relations in Athenian culture and education.

generosity For *philanthropia*, see on **137**. Here the implication is that the affection and concern for the interests of the junior friend was as fake as his erotic pretensions: see Dover (1978: 46–7).

empty hopes . . . showing him a written list. The jury may be supposed to imagine that Demosthenes was offering much that an established rhetorical educational establishment (such as that of Isocrates) could offer, for very reasonable rates, and with the protection of a politician of growing importance, and love and lasting affection, thrown in. Such private training deals may well have been a very important part of 'just *eros*' in the rhetorical and political spheres of 'higher education' as well as in the athletic and gymnastic (see Fisher 1998a: 102–3). The alleged production of a list of names (*katalogos*), presumably of satisfied pupils and perhaps also litigants for whom Demosthenes had composed law-court speeches, like the written contracts discussed earlier, is another indication of the growing use of literacy in Athenian life; but whether it still may have had a somewhat alienating effect on some at least of the jurors who were less used to such forms of communication is hard to say (see Thomas 1989: 41–5, 55–9; D. Cohen 1992: 178–9).

173 Did you put Sokrates to death. Aeschines draws an interesting parallel between Demosthenes' corruption and destruction of his rhetorical pupils, and the most famous previous condemnation by the Athenians of an intellectual and teacher, because they believed he had done much to undermine the moral and religious well-being of a generation of Athenian youth. This example seems designed to suggest that a similar crisis for the education of the young and for the democracy may be looming, and that Demosthenes 'the sophist' is a comparable danger to his pupils and hence to all Athens.

It is generally accepted that the picture of Sokrates as a teacher of serious philosophy and morality and high personal integrity in Xenophon, Plato, and Aristotle is in essentials more accurate than that of the home-spun Athenian version of the most immoral sophists found in Aristophanes' *Clouds*. If so, then the casual reference here to 'Sokrates the sophist' shows the enduring success of the affixing of labels by popular and comic repetition. Despite the efforts of the ancient 'Sokrates industry', through his pupils' ceaseless oral teachings and published pamphlets and dialogues which shared the aims of distinguishing Sokrates from the Sophists, and portraying his trial and execution as a crime and blunder of the democracy (on which see e.g. W. K. C. Guthrie, *Socrates* (Cambridge, 1971), 169–87; T. C. Brickhouse and N. D. Smith, *Socrates on Trial* (Oxford, 1989)), Aeschines, presumably representing a still living popular tradition, presents Sokrates as a dangerous sophist, a threat to his pupils like Kritias and Charmides and others, and through their actions as leaders of oligarchic Athens in 404–3, a disaster for the democracy. He was not alone, as a fragment of Hypereides' speech against the general Autokles (cf. on **56**) seems to have reminded the Athenians that they had punished Sokrates for his words, not his deeds (fr. 65 Jensen, of. c. 360). On the issues of the trial from the Athenians' point of view, however, see above all M. H. Hansen, *The Trial of Sokrates—From the Athenian Point of View* (Copenhagen, 1995), 29–30, who argues, after a telling analysis of the known political acts of Sokrates' Athenian associates (four sound democrats, and at least ten whom the Athenians came to regard as crooks or traitors), that this brief statement in this speech has a good claim to be regarded as the best and least biased source for the Athenian jury's actual reasons for condemning him; and see also G. Vlastos, *Socrates* (Cambridge, 1991), 293–7; Parker 1996: 199–207).

will Demosthenes then beg off his companions. Aeschines uses the term *hetairoi* to refer to Timarchos and any other friends and political associates whom Demosthenes may come to court to get off. As in **110**, one implication is that they are involved in shady political activities, and another perhaps recalls subtly the relationship of *hetairesis* which Timarchos had with so many other older Athenians.

inflicted revenges of that sort. In his speech against Meidias (esp. 21. 70–6), Demosthenes claimed great credit for his restraint, in not seeking direct revenge for the blow and other insults he had received at Meidias' hands, but trying to bring Meidias to justice, and attain his revenge through the democratic courts. Aeschines may well have recalled Demosthenes' use of such arguments; even if, as he himself claims, 3. 51–2, Demosthenes did 'sell' the case before bringing it to court, rather than, perhaps, agree to settle for a small penalty—but see MacDowell, *Meidias* 23–8 and E. M. Harris (1989)—the argument may have been used already in the assembly speech immediately after the offence, and indeed elsewhere, and versions of what Demosthenes would have said may have been already circulating. If so, it must have given him ironic pleasure to allege that at around the same time Demosthenes had been actively involved in a more secretive, and nastily violent, act of revengeful murder. On the debate over the relative values attributed to direct and legal forms of revenge, see D. Cohen (1995); Herman (1994; 1995); Fisher (1998b: 78–86).

private individuals who showed their popular concern by defending free speech. See also on **1, 110**. The point here is complex: it seems to amount to the claim that if the Athenians were right to condemn Sokrates (and thus might be held to have offended against freedom of speech, as they have to later generations), because he was responsible for the rule of the Thirty tyrants which destroyed freedom of speech for all Athenians, then in consistency, they ought equally to condemn Demosthenes, who plotted the removal in the most gruesome of ways from Nikodemos, a democratic spokesman in the courts, of his power of speech; otherwise they might have to reconsider the justice of 'their' earlier version. Even though the trial was more than fifty years earlier, the common convention that all Athenian assemblies and law courts are in effect the same people enables Aeschines to implicate this jury in the earlier verdict, and invite them to hold to 'their' former position of suspicion towards 'sophists'. There seems thus to be a tacit acknowledgement that the trial of Sokrates has become a hotly disputed issue; if the jury were to acquit Demosthenes, who is a more obviously guilty 'sophist', the correctness of their earlier, crucial, decision would be more seriously questioned (see Ober 1989: 171–2 and 1998: 261).

Some of his pupils. This line of argument, placed just after the account of the Aristarchos disaster, neatly suggests to the jury that Demosthenes is still attempting to charm and delude impressionable young men, and may be intended even to warn the pupils of their master's treachery and the fate of Aristarchos. On the vocal audience for important trials, see on **69**, **157**; clearly Aeschines expected his supporters would encourage cheering and shouts at the right moments, but tries to warn the jury against similar moves made by the opposition. There may also be the hint that Demosthenes' pupils might turn out to be as dangerous such as some of Sokrates'; see Rubinstein (forthcoming).

doing deals . . . at your expense. *Ergolabia*, a contract, *ergolabein* to make contracts, are terms found fairly frequently in both literary texts and in inscriptions indicating contracts for specific work made by cities or organized groups: examples include the contracts between the Euboian cities to engage the 'Artists of Dionysos' for their festivals (*IG* XII 207); the contract of employment of a public doctor at Samos (*c.* 200 BC), renewed thanks to the testimony of cured patients (G. Klaffenbach, 'Samische Inchriften', *Atth. Mitt.* 51 (1926), 28–33; and the contract to build the temple of Artemis at Magnesia proclaimed in a dedication by the famous architect Hermogenes (H. von Gaertringen, *Inschriften von Priene* (Berlin, 1906), no. 207). Naturally the word is also applied, with something of a sneer, to sophists and teachers negotiating their fees; at 2. 112 Aeschines puts into the mouth of Demosthenes, as a sign of his flattery of Philip, the disclaimer that he did not praise his memory, as that would be praise of a sophist contracting his fees. Here the allegation ('at your expense') is that Demosthenes will attempt to use his successful deception of the jury as a sales-pitch to attract pupils.

This whole line of argument may be seen as a witty and

contemptuous variation of the frequently used rhetorical *topos* that one's opponent's supporting speakers may try to 'beg off' their friends or political allies, and thereby to show off and increase their power and influence (e.g. Lys. 14. 21–2; Lyk. 1. 139–40, and see also on **132–5**, the attack on 'the General'); Demosthenes has the extra nerve not only to show off in court, but to use a success in court to boost his educational activities. See generally Rubinstein (forthcoming).

transform the case and your understanding. This is the sole point in the speech where Aeschines mentions the issue of current views of the peace; his aim is to make any discussion seem totally irrelevant (see Intro. pp. 54–5), and Demosthenes' attempt to raise the issue merely sophistic and profiteering exhibitionism. The tactic appears to have worked. Demosthenes in the Embassy speech (241–3) confirms that Aeschines did use it, and offers a summary version of the boastful speech Aeschines had attributed to him, even repeating some key words from this passage, namely 'carrying them away' (*apagein*) and 'filched the case' (*hyphairein*) (see below); he then attempts to turn the tables and persuade Aeschines to answer the charges put to him.

174 inspire . . . as soon as he comes forward. An attempt to counter in advance any effect Demosthenes may have, by ludicrously exaggerating the arrogant claims he may be supposed to make in private.

criticizing the peace that was made thanks to Philokrates and me. Aeschines has no apparent qualms in admitting that his support for Philokrates was crucial in making the peace, and that he will have to face the accounting procedure (see Intro. pp. 3–5); but E. M. Harris's statement that Aeschines 'boasts' of his and Philokrates' responsibility for the peace seems too strongly put (1995: 105).

175 provide the sophist. Referring to Demosthenes now contemptuously as the 'sophist' rather than as 'Battalos' or the '*kinaidos*' reinforces the idea that he poses a worse threat to the political community even than Sokrates had. It is notable how far he pursues the idea that any mention of Philip and the demerits of the peace will be to deceive the jury to serve Demosthenes' personal interests. Here the technique involves the dramatic creation of an imaginary speech to be delivered by a gloating (and it will be remembered, effeminate) sophist displaying his contempt for the *demos*. Whereas more usually litigants argue that advocates (*synegoroi*) appear in court to show off and enhance their own honour (see on **132**), Aeschines here more amusingly and more sinisterly suggests it is to benefit his business and his popularity with his pupils; see Rubinstein (forthcoming).

filched the case away. *Hyphaireisthai*: a strong term for surreptitiously purloining or stealing, and a word of which Aeschines is elsewhere quite fond: see 3. 66, 101, 222.

carried them away. For this use of the verb *apagein*, for the act of diverting peoples' attention from one topic to another, see Thuc. 2. 59, 2. 65 (of Pericles' control of the people's emotions), and Plat. *Phaidr.* 262 (an even closer parallel, of sophistic diversion).

Philip and the Phokians. Here alone in this speech is a specific mention of Philip's activities at the time of the making of the peace and subsequently, which Demosthenes and his colleagues were using to undermine confidence in it. For the events of the ending of the Sacred War, and the settlement of the Phokians at the Delphian Amphictiony, see Dem. 5 *passim*; Demosthenes did later at least elaborate his charges against Aeschines in these respects in the Embassy speech, esp. 19. 57–87, 121–30: see e.g. Hammond and Griffith (1979: 343–7); Ellis (1976: 111–28). Aeschines could not, it seems, completely avoid an allusion to the Phokian settlement, so he wrapped it carefully inside this offensive fictional boast.

the defendant started prosecuting, the prosecutor was on trial. Since the defence could argue, with justification, that Aeschines had brought the trial now solely because he was about to be prosecuted by Timarchos at his embassy scrutiny (cf. Dem 19. 286), this tactic might seem more acceptable in this case than in most others.

176 to stand in line together against this practice. Aeschines uses a similar military metaphor in 3. 16, encouraging the jury to deploy the law in line against the shamelessness of his sophistic opponents. See also **135**, the 'raid' which Aeschines claims 'the General' is preparing to launch.

outside the contest; no, as at the horse races (*hippo-***

324 AESCHINES, *AGAINST TIMARCHOS*

dromiai), **drive him down the course of the case.** The metaphor switches and becomes an explicit simile. A Greek contest (*agon*—the term is picked up in 'arguments outside the contest'—*logoi exagonioi*) may be a battle, competitive games, or a legal trial, and by the end of the sentence the jury are likened to judges at the horse-races, trying to make the contestants stick to their own lane (*dromos*). Many Athenian festivals, and especially the Panathenaia, had horse-riding and chariot races. Some took place along the Panathenaic Way in the *agora* (see Kyle 1987: 185–90, and in Neils 1992); the main facility, the hippodrome (*hippodromos*), which need have had little or no architectural features, has not been found, but on the basis of literary and epigraphic references appears to have been eight stades long (= *c.* 1 mile), and was probably located in Phaleron, in the village of Echeleidai, near the sanctuary of Poseidon Hippodromios to which the Salaminioi sacrificed a pig in Boedromion (see the Salaminioi decree, Text no.I 1. 92 = Lambert 1997b, and *Etym. Magn*, s.v., with Ferguson 1938: 24–6; Kyle 1987: 96–7). The chances of crashes and potentially fatal accidents, to jockeys and charioteers, spectators, and certainly the horses, seem to have been pretty high: see N. B. Crowther, 'Reflections on Greek Equestrian Events. Violence and Spectator Attitudes', *Nikephoros* 8 (1994), 121–33. How far the judges were able to prevent contestants from changing lanes to gain unfair advantages or cause accidents, whether on the straight or at the turns, is unclear; but note Ar. *Clouds* 26, where the dreaming horse-man Pheidippides tells a cheating rival to 'stick to your own course (*dromos*)'.

Similarly in the Crown speech, Aeschines tells the jury not to allow Demosthenes to use an old 'wrestling throw' of the law courts; he should not avoid the central issue of the illegality of the crowning proposal, but rather watch his position as carefully as do 'boxers in the gymnastic contests' (3. 205–6). Other arguments or metaphors drawn from the athletic contests and major civic festivals are **26, 33;** 2. 183, 3. 91, 179–80, 189, 246; and for Demosthenes, see e.g. 4. 35, 40 and 18. 318–19. Clearly Aeschines, as well as Demosthenes, liked to display an assumed familiarity with the contests, and in part this may reflect his own claims to be an habitué of the gymnasia. See Intro. pp. 18–19, Ober (1989: 281–3); Golden (1998: 158–9, 2000: 169–72), though both arguably exaggerate the aristocratic or élite overtones of such associations;

it may be preferable to suggest that this familiarity is designed to unite the experience of the orators with that of middling Athenians, whether as spectators and judges, or even as participants.

If you do that, you will not incur contempt. This sentence rounds off this section devoted to destroying Demosthenes' standing as the major and very important advocate (*synegoros*) for Timarchos; it also introduces one of the leading themes of the final concluding section: the law relating to the character of politicians is a good one, and must be maintained in practice.

to be angry at them, but that when they have been committed, you no longer care. The view that it is entirely proper and necessary for a jury to feel and to express its anger naturally runs though the latter part of the speech: see **166, 186, 193**. Anger was defined by Aristotle (*Rhet.* 1378a30–2) as an emotion involving both a feeling of pain and a longing for revenge (*timoria*), and it was generally felt to be an appropriate emotion for jurors to feel against offenders: the view that they should express their anger directly, at offences committed against the whole community, or more vicariously, by granting legal revenge and justice to the wronged plaintiff, is found alike in dramatic representations of the legal system (see Aeschylus' *Eumenides*, e.g. at 705, and, presented more ambivalently, throughout Aristophanes' *Wasps*), in many prosecution speeches (e.g. Lys. 1. 1–4, 13. 1–3, Dem. 54. 42), and in Aristotle's more theoretical analysis (in the remainder of the relevant chapter of the *Rhetoric* II. 2 (1378b–1380a4). A related and constant fear for prosecutors (and hope for defendants) was that initial anger at serious crimes or political misdemeanours or mistakes might become blunted over time, or expended solely on those who came up for trial first; cf. e.g. Kleon's arguments in the Mytilene debate, Thuc. 3. 38. 1, 40. 7; Lys. 19. 6; Dem. 6. 34, and the cases of Philokrates and Kallisthenes (*c.* 362) cited by Arist. *Rhet.* 1380b5–15. On the nexus of issues involved here see T. J. Saunders, *Plato's Penal Code* (Oxford, 1991), 99–100; D. Cohen (1995: 65–70, 82–5); Fisher (1998b: 80–3) and Christ (1998: 154–7).

SECTION V 177–196 Concluding arguments

The conclusion returns with greater intensity to the main themes of the introduction: above all that the existing laws, and especially those defending the ideals of *sophrosyne* and *eukosmia* and protecting the youth of the country, must be upheld, by making an example of Timarchos. See the beginning of the Commentary, and on the principles of ring composition in the forensic speeches, see also Worthington 27–39.

177–179 *The need to maintain the laws*

177 your laws will be excellent and valid. Aeschines probably hits hard with the argument that the laws must be upheld because of a general feeling that prosecutions under this law, involving retrospective judgements of a man's youthful activities, were very rare, and unfamiliar to this jury. Here the theme of giving central priority to the laws is emphasized by a contrast both with the assembly's decrees and with the courts' verdicts. The first contrast reflects the conscious revaluation of their democracy associated with the revision of law-making procedures of the restored democracy of 403, and is consequently found frequently in fourth-century oratory; see e.g. Dem. 23. 86, 24. 139–43; Hyper. *Athen.* 22, with Hansen (1979: 165–77); Allen (2000: 180–1); criticisms of particular verdicts are naturally found when prosecutors bring a different action against an opponent who has won in an earlier case (cf. Dem. 26. 20, 37. 45, Ps. Dem. 47. 15, 59. 5), and as here direct criticism of the jury is mitigated or removed by the emphasis on the lies and rhetorical trickeries of their opponents.

178 since you are intelligent, more so than others. It is common and natural for orators to praise the political sense of the Athenians and their democratic system, and especially sensible to do this when about to utter some (mildly) critical or cautionary remarks to the assembly or jury: cf. Dem. 3. 15, 23. 109; Isaeus 1. 19, Ober (1979: 156–7).

led astray by deceit and pretentious cheating. The terms *alazon* (charlatan, 'pseud'), and *alazoneumata*, the behaviour or tricks of an *alazon*, often suggest not just lies, but pretentious assertiveness or the adoption of a false expertise; in Aristophanic comedy it is applied to sophists, oracle-mongers, pretentious politicians, ambassadors and the like (see the account in Arist. *EN* 1127 a13–b32, with D. M. MacDowell, 'The Meaning of *Alazon*', in

E. Craik (ed.), *Owls to Athens: Essays on Classical Subjects for Sir Kenneth Dover* (Oxford, 1990), 287–92, and also Powell (1995: 250–1) on the description in Plut. *Per.* 12 on the Parthenon as a pretentious and deceitful woman. In fourth-century speeches the term is often used, as here, in connection with the deceit and lies of the speaker's opponents; MacDowell seems to conclude too readily, however, that in these contexts it has lost its association with false pretentions to expert knowledge or superior skills or achievements. In this case, for example, the jury is urged not to give way to abusive rhetoric, and the term *alazoneumata* connects the general point to the reported arrogant claims of the 'sophist' and 'teacher' Demosthenes to use his supposed skill to turn a case upside down. See also Aesch. 3. 101 and 3. 256, where again it is Demosthenes' showy and arrogant rhetoric or his false claims at political successes which are so branded.

179 this custom. Presumably the custom defined just above, of allowing defendants to bring charges against prosecutors.

an argument not accompanied by a morally good life. It is because defendants (or their advisors like Demosthenes) have bad characters that they seek to distort trials by their lies and distortions. This point then helps to justify Aeschines' abuse of Demosthenes' moral character as well as Timarchos'.

180–184 *Moral examples from Sparta and Athens*

180 But not so of the Spartans. Aeschines approaches the idea of citing a Spartan example of public support for *sophrosyne* and hostility to debauched politicians with understandable caution, given the long history of wars and ideological opposition between the two states, and the damage done on occasions to Athens by prominent Laconizers like the Thirty Tyrants. The heat of this opposition had of course been much reduced over the years since the battle of Leuktra (371), when first Thebes, and then Macedon, replaced Sparta as the leading external threats to Athens, when Sparta seemed clearly weaker; so the two states maintained a cautious and largely ineffectual alliance between *c.* 370 and 345. It is noticeable, however, that this anecdote is presented with absolutely no date, no individual names, and no indication of the issue under debate.

The moral, the need to uphold good laws, and avoid being guided by immoral politicians, suits Aeschines' argument especially neatly. This makes a strong case for supposing that it was either invented outright by Aeschines, or was based on a vague, unlocated, anecdote which could be applied to any state with a reputation for good government and respect for age. The story is twice alluded to briefly by Plutarch (*Mor.* 41b and 233f.), and retold in a fuller version at *Mor.* 801c, a discussion of the desirability of statesmen not leading disgraceful private lives. It is found also in a rhetorically expanded paraphrase in Aulus Gellius 18. 3, and mentioned obliquely in Philo 195b. All these, however, can plausibly be supposed to be dependent on Aeschines; in particular Plutarch's slip, at *Mor.* 801c, in giving the decadent Spartan the name Demosthenes, may revealingly display, behind the confusion, his instinctive understanding of Aeschines' intent. It would be unwise, then, to take the story too seriously as a source for the Spartan assembly and the recruitment of the Elders, as is done for example in the course of Ruzé's recent exhaustive examination of Spartan decision-making procedures (1997: 160–1, 231); Rhodes (1997: 492, n. 60) is rightly more sceptical.

It seems clear that by the 340s and 330s it was thought perhaps a little risky, but none the less positively desirable, to appeal to Sparta (or at least to a distanced, traditional Sparta) as a model of discipline and moral order; it struck much the same note as praise of the Areopagos (see on **81**, **91**, and 3. 19–20, 252). The same pattern of praise of the traditional virtues in both old Sparta and the Areopagos are found in Lycurgus, *Against Leokrates*. In general, on fourth-century Athenian speakers' use of Spartan themes, see Fisher (1994: esp. 370–5 on this passage in Aeschines). One may also compare Aeschines' use of the term *syssitoi* in 2. 22, 55, 127, 163 for the solidarity of common meals for the envoys, which may perhaps evoke a Spartan ideal (Bourriot 1995: 439).

a man who had lived shamefully, but was an exceptionally able speaker. This invented character is meant to remind the jury of both Timarchos and Demosthenes, as the final sentence of **181** makes clear. This whole argument was anticipated in **31**.

one of the Elders. The reference is to the Spartan *gerousia*, the body of the *gerontes*, the leading Council in Sparta, composed of twenty-eight men aged over 60, elected for life by the citizens by open voting, in the form of shouting (see Xen. *Lak. Pol.* 10. 1; Arist. *Pol.* 1270b36–1271a20, Plut. *Lyc.* 26).

they regard as the greatest. The *gerousia* had very considerable powers in Sparta, which could in some respects be compared to the powers of the Areopagos in Athens before the reforms of Ephialtes and Pericles. They (sitting with the two kings and five Ephors) formed the highest law court, often, for example, hearing prosecutions against kings such as the trial of Pausanias in 403 (Paus. 3. 5. 2); they held the preliminary debates in preparation for meetings of the Assembly (*probouleusis*). In these ways they exercised some general supervision over Spartan laws and customs (*nomophylakia*). See e.g. de Ste Croix (1972: 353–4); Cartledge (1987: 121–3); Powell (1994: 274–80), on thematic connections between respect for age in Sparta and in Plato's *Laws*; and Ruzé (1997: 225–35). Ten years earlier, Demosthenes had included, among much else hostile to Sparta, criticism of the powers of the members of the *gerousia* as the clearest indicator that Sparta was an oligarchy (20. 105–8): on Demosthenes' attitudes to Sparta see Fisher (1994: 364–70) and Trevett (1999: 189–92, 201–2).

they appoint men to it from those who have been self-controlled (*sophron*) from boyhood to old age. It seems likely that there was no constitutional restriction to particular families, but that the intensely competitive elections were fought between elderly Spartans who commanded the greatest influence and status, whether derived from ancestry, personal achievement, or wealth (Arist. *Pol.* 1270b36–1271a20; notice especially his use of the word *dynasteutike* of the office at 1306a18–19). This theme of the Spartan respect for age connects again with the citation of the (alleged) procedural law of the Athenian assembly giving priority to speakers over 50 and encouraging general respect for age over youth (**23–4**).

would not for a long time inhabit an unravaged Sparta, if they used in their assemblies advisers like that. Sparta was ravaged by the Thebans in 370 (Xen. *Hell.* 6.5; Diod. Sic. 15, 62–7), and this prediction seems a strong hint that the story is to be imagined to be set in the past, when Spartan traditional *eunomia* and respect for age and *sophrosyne* were fully intact. The effects of this would be, first, to minimize the risk of offence in using an example from Sparta, and second, to suggest that the successful invasion of Laconia was both a sign of Spartan decline and a warning to the Athenians.

181 a man not well-favoured at speaking, but conspicuous in war and remarkable for justice and moral endurance. Not exactly a Spartan equivalent of Aeschines, though it might perhaps be intended to encourage Athenians in part to think of his friend Phokion, known as a moderate Laconizer, who spoke for him in the Embassy trial (2. 184, where Aeschines' introduction of his friend emphasizes his military record and his justice); his rhetorical style, however, was admired for its brevity and effectiveness: see Tritle (1988: 22–6); and also Fisher (1994: 360–1).

to express the same sentiments, as best he could. The idea of a poor speaker pedantically repeating the same points seems more than a little ridiculous to us. It may well be that it was intended to amuse the jury as well, who might feel that archaic Spartans were somewhat silly but yet accept the emphasis on age and the good life, and the abuse of Timarchos and Demosthenes. Demosthenes' citation (24. 139–43) of the extremely strict provisions against making new laws at Epizephyrian Locri, and the exception offered to the one-eyed man, is a very similar case (see Fisher 1994: 367–70).

do not receive into their ears the voices of those proved to be cowards and evil. There seems to be the suggestion here that the words of such deviants have a quasi-polluting power of contamination; decent men should cover their ears in protection, as decent Athenians veiled their faces when Timarchos displayed his polluted body in the assembly (**19, 26**).

He would readily have allowed Timarchos or the deviant (*kinaidos*) Demosthenes. Aeschines rounds this improving story off with a powerfully barbed point aimed at his two opponents, and notably saves the damning noun *kinaidos* for Demosthenes, the man with the effeminate clothes and ambiguous sexual practices with his pupils (see on **131** and **171**, and the similar effect achieved at 2. 150–1). One may again (see on **26**) wonder whether Cicero remembered this powerful use of the term when he used the similar term *catamitus* with dramatic effect of Mark Antony, engaged in a frantic dash to effect a passionate reconciliation with his powerful wife Fulvia (*Phil.* 2. 77) which allegedly threw the whole of Rome into panic. It is Cicero's only use of the word, which is a Latinization of Ganymede, coming to the language through Etruscan (Adams 1982: 228; Williams 1999: 55–61), and used, like *cinaedus*, though more sparingly, also for pretty boys who accepted domination or penetrations. The similarity lies in the argument that Antony's frivolous debauchery and devotion to all forms of excess (including marital passion) endangered and shamed the state; calling Antony 'catamite' may both recall his earlier submission to Curio, and also suggest his sexual and political domination by the virago Fulvia, see Williams (1999: 205–6), Corbeill (1997: 110–12).

182 in order that I should not be thought to be courting the favour of the Spartans. This caution confirms the risk involved in praising Sparta, but evidently it was one worth taking. Aeschines switches his ground to give two indications of Athenians' traditional support for the strict sexual morality imposed upon their women.

one of the citizens. This alarming story of a man who punished his errant daughter by locking her up with a horse to produce her death was not invented by Aeschines, but his version is radically edited to suit his purpose. It is recognizably (as the *scholia* observe) the same story as one told of Hippomenes, one of the Kodridai, who is presented either as the last King of Athens, or as one of the ten-year archons of Athens before Drakon and Solon; in these versions the revenge is seen as excessive. The fullest surviving version presents Hippomenes as acting in response to the accusation that the rule of his dynasty was becoming soft; this response was, however, felt to be so cruel, and one typical of a tyrant rather than a king, that the monarchy soon fell, and as a result the archonship was opened up to all the aristocrats (known as the Eupatridai). This story was evidently told by one of the writers of Athenian histories, the Atthidographers, and repeated in the Aristotelian *Constitution of Athens* (Herakleides *epitome*, fr. 1); it is also told or alluded to in Callim. fr. 94–5 Pfeiffer (from the *Aetia*); Diod. Sic. VIII. 22; Nicolaus of Damascus, *FGH* 90 F 49; Ovid *Ibis* 335–8, 459–60; Dio Chrystostom 32. 78 and Suda s.v. *Parhippon kai kore*. On these traditions, see Jacoby on *FGH* 323a F23, esp. IIIb 45–6, and 1949: 149, 364–6; Carlier (1984: 364–6); Seaford (1994: 345); Scafuro (1997: 274, 475). There is no reason at all to believe the story, nor even that it nonetheless reflected pre-Solonian powers for Athenian fathers (Harrison 1968: I, 74; Ogden 1996a: 141–2, against Sissa: 1990, 89). Aeschines has, deliberately, omitted the names of Hippomenes and his daughter Leimone (or Leimonis), and the story's place in the sequence of the end of the monarchy and transition to a more equal state. So he appears to present the action as a severe, yet appropriate, punishment inflicted by an ordinary citizen in the distant past (see also Seaford 1994: 345, for whom this version, like the version where the father is an archon, emphasizes continuity not political change). The story might be told to reveal a clear development between the horrific killing of the king's personal revenge and the state-controlled penalties of social exclusion and humiliation imposed by Solon's laws on unchaste Athenian women cited immediately below (see the treatment by Ghiron-Bistagne 1985: 105–21, though she exaggerates the 'clemency' of the Solonian law, as also does D. Cohen 1991: 123–4). But Aeschines seems not to take that line, but preferred to present them both as admirable. G. Hoffmann (1990: 33–48) and Seaford (1990: 80–3) put this portrayal in contexts of humiliating punishments for women caught in adultery and of other men who imposed strict restrictions on their female dependants. Hoffmann observes that Aeschines' version of the 'horse and the maid', ignores the 'bad ruler' version, and argues that while classical Athenians did not actually practice such cruel penalties, they liked to hear the story, and admire a citizen who put 'an expiatory and exemplary death above a life of shame and prostitution for his disgraced daughter'. One should note, however, that even Aeschines puts an emphasis on how severe attitudes were in the past, and follows this immediately with an account of the rather less strict Solonian legal rules which are still valid; it seems likely that Aeschines was encouraging his hearers to take this horse and maid story (like the Spartan anecdote) half-humorously, as an example of old-fashioned severity, admirable in that at least Athenians then took these issues of *sophrosyne* very seriously, but now seen as extreme, whereas the Solonian laws represented more accurately the proper treatment of daughters or wives who commit adultery (*moicheia*). Nonetheless it is clear that Aeschines has put his more conservative spin on the old story, and made some attempt to conceal the original by removing the names.

**she had not preserved her youthful beauty (*helikia*)
well until marriage.** On the term *helikia* in general, see on **106**;
of women, it usually means 'prime age', i.e. age for marriage, and
sometimes, as here, with the nuance of the appropriate condition
for marriage, i.e. unsullied sexual reputation. See Kapparis, *Neaira*
214–15.

walled her up inside an empty house with a horse. The
idea was that the horse, through starvation and frustration, would
either trample or eat the girl (cf. Diod. Sic. 8. 22; the manuscripts
here have 'through starvation' after 'going to be killed', but that
was—probably rightly—deleted as an explanatory gloss by
Dobree). The Aristotelian version known through Herakleides
epitome adds that the lover was killed by being dragged behind
Hippomenes' chariot. Both methods have a symbolic appropriateness, and can be compared with motifs in other myths, for
example, Hippolytus' death, mangled by his stampeding horses
who were terrified by Poseidon's bull from the sea. The horse, like
the young boy or girl, can have its raw power domesticated, and is
also a powerful image of sexuality; hence any who fail, in whatever ways, to channel their sexuality into the appropriately
socialized setting of marriage may appropriately be destroyed
by horses reverting to raw savagery; see also Ghiron-Bistagne
(1985: 105–21); Padel (1992: 142–4); J. Larson, *Greek Heroine Cults*
(Madison, 1995), 99 on a sequence of myths featuring over-
protective or hostile fathers, though her view that these myths
imply fear of paternal abuse of power rather than too much
concern for daughters' chastity is disputable, and other cases
involving animals in G. Hoffmann (1990: 35–41). Some versions
hint at further sexual elements, either that the girl had loved the
horse (Dio Chrysostom 32. 78), or that the horse raped as well as
ate the girl (*scholia* on Ovid, *Ibis* 459). The names of the characters
are appropriate to the theme of sex and horses: Leimone suggests
leimon 'meadow' and Hippomenes' name may suggest both 'horse-
strength' and also horse-sex-madness (*hippo-manes, hippomanein*, see
also Carlier 1984: 366, n. 251); *hippomanes* is also the name given to
the genital discharge supposedly produced by mares on heat, or a
growth on the forehead of a new-born foal, and to a herb supposed to drive horses mad with lust, and hence used in erotic
magic. The term is, according to Aristotle, applied as an insult to
sex-mad women (Arist. *Hist. Anim.* 572a8–31, 577a8–13; cf. Aelian

Hist. Anim. 4. 11; Virg. *Georg.* 3. 266–83, esp. 280–3; *Aen.* 4. 515–16; Theocr. 2. 48–51 with Stadtler RE VIII, 1878–82; M. Detienne and J. P. Vernant, *Cunning Intelligence in Greek Culture and Society* (Hassocks, 1978), 192–3). On the whole story and for a possible origin of the myth in relation to horse-sacrifice, see V. García Quintela, 'Le dernier roi d'Athènes: entre le mythe et le rite'; *Kernos* 10 (1977), 135–51.

the house-site is standing in your city. On *oikopeda*, see on **84.** This assertion suggests that the story had a certain attraction and resonance for the Athenians, as some old foundations were pointed out as the site where the event had taken place, and the building then razed to the ground. The site (called an *abaton* by Dio Chrysostom) cannot be identified (see also Carlier 1984: 365, n. 247, who suggests it may originally have been a site and a local legend connected with Poseidon Hippios, and Thomas 1989: 199; Scafuro 1997: 274, 475). A. N. Oikonomides' attempt ('The site of the horse and the maid', *Anc. World* 3 (1980), 47–8) to interpret a very fragmentary *c.* first-century *agora* grave-epigram (*IG* II² 13126), which includes the words 'horse' and 'twelve', as a record for tourists of the site of the event in the Agora, rests on extravagantly bold (and in places unmetrical) restorations; he also seems to believe that the event actually took place.

'By the horse and the maid'. The term for 'maid' (*kore*), like *parthenos*, designates a pubescent girl, of marriageable age, or at times a bride, who is expected to be, but is not necessarily, a virgin, cf. Calame (1997: 27–8, 91–3); Sissa (1990: 73–86). Here it is appropriate for a nubile girl who lost her virginity and met death, not a marriage; one may compare the Maiden, *Kore par excellence*, Persephone and her forced marriage to Hades; and Seaford (1987), on the frequent exploration of this theme in tragedy.

183 Solon, the most famous of lawgivers. Returning again to a major theme of the beginning of the speech, 'Solonian' legislation concerned with *sophrosyne* and good order (see on **6–17**, and **22–7**), Aeschines manages to bring in the further laws which regulated marriage by imposing severely humiliating penalties on women. Athenian laws, unlike those of many other states which have placed a high value on female sexual continence, imposed more severe penalties on the male offenders, who might be killed by self-help in certain circumstances, might have direct and humiliating physical punishments applied to the anus, or might be prosecuted under a number of statutes (on which see D. Cohen 1985; 1991; 110–22, Cantarella and Foxhall 1991; J. Roy, 'Traditional Jokes about the Punishment of Adulterers in Ancient Greek Literature', *LCM* 16 (1991), 73–6; C. Carey, 'Return of the Radish, or Just When You Thought it Was Safe to Go Back into the Kitchen', *LCM* 18 (1994), 53–5; K. Kapparis 1995, id., 'Humiliating the Adulterer: the Law and the Practice in Classical Athens', *RIDA* 43 (1996), 53–77, and id., *Neaira* 302–4). The reason for the greater severity of penalties for men may be the sense that, despite the constant threat of women's sexuality and their alleged weak resistance to temptation, it was males who usually took the initiative in such affairs, and who should have had a greater sense of the outrage of the offence (Lys. 1. 1–5, 26 and Ps. Dem. 59. 86, with Carey *Lysias* 75, and *Neaira* 129). The punishments imposing dishonour on women may well have had their origins in community-imposed social exclusion or 'social death' (see Humphreys 1991: 33–4), which were then written into law by Solon.

written . . . about the good order (*eukosmia*) of women. Two senses of *kosmos* run through this account of the penalties imposed on women caught in adultery, and a neat appropriateness connects them. 'Good order' for women denotes general good behaviour, obedience, avoidance of unnecessary speech (see Ps. Dem. 59. 51 and Kapparis, *Neaira* 269–70), and most importantly, as here, chastity before marriage and fidelity to their husbands; women who seriously fall short of this ideal through unchastity or infidelity lose the right to display their own feminine *kosmos*, 'adornment', on their persons. On the ideals of *kosmos* and *eukosmia* in the speech see also Intro. pp. 60–2 and on **8, 34.**

a seducer (*moichos*) The definition of the *moichos* and *moicheia* in Athenian law and legal discourse has been much debated recently. The traditional view (e.g. Dover 1974: 209–10) has been that while in most cases it is consensual sex with someone else's wife (or concubine to whom legitimate children might be born), the term may extend to sex with other dependent women inside the family (e.g. unmarried daughters or sisters). D. Cohen (1984; 1991: 98–132) argued that it was in fact restricted to consensual sex with wives or concubines, but effective counter-arguments to that view have been made by Cantarella (1991: 289–96); Foxhall

(1991: 297–304); Carey (1995: 407–8); Patterson (1998: 114–25); Kapparis, *Neaira* 297.

to attend at the public cult ceremonies. The penalties for errant females are presented in this passage, in Hyper. *Lyk.* 12, and in Ps. Dem. 59. 86 (and at 59. 87 we have a citation of the law which is probably genuine, if incomplete, see Harrison 1968: I, 35–6; Cantarella 1991 and Foxhall 1991; Carey, *Neaira* 129 and Kapparis, *Neaira* 354–7). They were expected to live in permanent disgrace and in an unmarried state (i.e. rejected by their husbands if they had had them), or at best (Hyper. *Lyk.* 12) could only expect to live with a man of lesser wealth or status in an illicit relationship (presumably a form of concubinage, as a *pallake*, see also Verihlac and Vial 1998: 270–2). This private exclusion is matched and marked by this life-time ban on appearing in the many public ceremonials open to women on which see generally S. Blundell, *Women in Ancient Greece* (London, 1995), 160–9; Foxhall (1995) and other essays in Hawley and Levick (1995), and many essays in Blundell and Williamson (1997). These provisions, forcing the husband to divorce an adulterous wife, and imposing these humiliations on all disgraced women, may well have been introduced in fact (despite what Aeschines claims) after Solon's legislation, and later than the laws of citizenship introduced in the mid-fifth century increasing the importance of Athenian parentage on both sides; the restrictions on the women should be seen as properly and precisely parallel to the exclusion of male citizens punished with *atimia* from the *agora* and the sanctuaries. See Kapparis (1995); *Neaira* 359; also Hansen (1976: 56).

D. Cohen's view (1991: 124) that such divorced and disgraced women 'could, and did, remarry', rests on very slender foundations; it seems related to his belief that the prime element of concern in the laws was the threat of adultery to 'public violence and disorder', underplaying any idea of a 'moral' concern for the honour of families and for the protection of legitimacy. One piece of evidence he cites is Electra's tirade against Aegisthos in Eur. *Electra* 920–3; but the generalization in that passage that seducers may be forced to marry the wives they had corrupted (and then find them no more faithful) is designed to fit the example from the mythical royal family of Mycenae, and need not have appeared applicable to the society of the audience. For Athens, one must ask who would wish, or be able, to 'force' the seducer to marry the wife. Secondly, Cohen refers to the account of the remarriage of Neaira's daughter in Ps. Dem. 59; but Apollodoros' argument there is that Phano's remarriage was actually illegal, and only agreed to by Theagenes because he knew nothing of her past history; on the other hand, if one accepts the view that the whole story is very suspicious (see also D. Cohen himself, 1991: 109, n. 32 and Carey, *Neaira* 125–7), it is not evidence for remarriage of a disgraced woman. The legal regulations and their justifications that such women should be permanently prevented from social contact with other married women is in itself a strong sanction against easy remarriage (see next note, and Patterson 1998: 131; Kapparis, *Neaira* 358–9).

public cult ceremonies (*demotele hiera*). This phrase designates those festivals, sacrifices, and sanctuaries which are maintained by public moneys, and hence ones over which the people can easily pass restrictive rules such as this one; they would include deme rites and shrines as well as *polis* sanctuaries, and perhaps those of other sub-divisions of the state such as phratries and *orgeones*. See generally on **21**, and Davies, *CAH*[2] IV. 2, 379–82; Aleshire (1994: 9–16); Parker (1996: 4–7); and Kapparis, *Neaira* 357. Whether such disgraced women, or dishonoured men, would be admitted to more private or even familial rites would probably be left to the members.

that she should not mix with the innocent women and corrupt them . . . thereby dishonouring such a woman and making her life not worth living. These phrases conveniently disclose the official purposes of these rules: because such offences threatened so seriously both the public honour of the family involved and the stability of the community built on legitimate and respectable citizen families (see e.g. Arist. *Pol.* 1253a30–1253b14, 1260b4–26), their punishment was thought appropriate both because it imposed permanent dishonour on them, and protected others from 'contamination'. Though the equivalent passage in Apollodoros' speech against Neaira describes such women as potentially likely to cause 'pollutions and impieties in the temples' (Ps. Dem. 59. 86), this pollution should be seen not as a specifically supernatural contagion (as may some forms of homicide), but rather that their moral impurity and threat to the minds of others may be described as a pollution and as offensive to the gods if they enter their shrines or participate in rituals. See above all Parker (1983: 94–7); Fisher (1992: 79); and Kapparis, *Neaira* 358–9.

tells anyone who meets her. The version of the law in the Neaira speech states more simply 'if she enters the public shrines, let her suffer whatever she may suffer short of death with impunity'. Probably the important element that the woman may no longer 'adorn herself' was included in the law, and omitted as not relevant to his case by Apollodoros (see also Carey, *Neaira* 129). Aeschines has sharpened the 'instruction' of the law to punish such offenders (see also Lys. 1. 27), and added more graphic detail of the violent and humiliating action allegedly encouraged, stripping off clothes and jewellery, and physical beating (see also Kapparis, *Neaira* 355–6). No cases of such direct community revenge are known; but it seems likely to have acted, as Apollodoros suggests, as a fairly powerful deterrent (see Winkler 1990: 61; Patterson 1998: 130–2; but see also Foxhall 1991: 303, and J. Roy, 'An Alternative Sexual Morality for Classical Athenians', *G&R* 44 (1997), 11–22, for suggestions that these penalties for adulteries were often ignored). This may indeed have been another area of concern for citizens in general, but was not one openly discussed in the law-court speeches.

184 the procurers, male and female. For the laws about procuring, see also on **14**. The mention of them again may recall for the jury the various laws concerned with sexual offences allegedly related to Timarchos' acts.

185–196 *The need to protect morality and honour in public life*

185 These then were the decisions. This leads clearly into the final section, emphasizing further the total unsuitability of Timarchos to exercise any rights as a citizen, and the need to uphold (or restore) the law.

The man who has a male body, but who has committed womanish offences . . . the man who committed *hybris* **against himself contrary to nature?** These crucial ways of condemning aspects of homosexual acts as the complete betrayal of masculinity and as hybristic and unnatural acts are introduced as something of a rhetorical climax close to the end of the speech. A number of points need to be noted. First, these arguments suggest a new reason for the apparently irrelevant introduction of laws about adulterous women. If the laws and the 'ancestral traditions' impose permanent dishonour, with extra public humiliation, on adulterous women, at least equal dishonour should be imposed on men who willingly behaved as dissolute women; if not, Aeschines suggests, the consequence would be that the citizens would feel a reluctance to impose the proper humiliations on bad women. One can compare the fears aroused by Ps. Dem. 59. 112–15 of the consequences if Neaira were to be acquitted: see also Patterson (1998: 131).

Second, and more important to his case, is the assertion that what Timarchos did with his lovers was actually worse than the offences of women: women commit their sexual offences in accordance with their natures (the implications here are that women had strong sexual desires, and weak moral control, see also Dover 1974: 98–102; 1978: 67), but Timarchos' behaviour involved *hybris* against himself (on which see on **15–17** above) *contrary* to men's nature. It is clear by comparison with the rest of the speech, and especially **138** (see notes there), that it is only the sexual behaviour of the younger partner's (the *paidika*) that is so characterized, not that of the older lover. This argument is comparable to that in the fragment of Hypereides (fr. 215 Jensen: see Intro. pp. 98–9) which treats as astonishing and appalling if a man ignores nature's clear demarcation of male and female jobs and duties by abusing his own body in a feminine way. These uses of the terms such as womanly, hybristic, and unnatural are not, that is, to be taken as condemnatory of all homosexual acts as unnatural and hybristic, and therefore are to be distinguished from the severe attitude of the later Plato (*Laws* 836–41) or even that attributed to Sokrates and Prodikos by Xenophon (*Symp.* 8; *Mem.* 2. 1, esp. 31–2; for a plausible argument that Xenophon's own views may have been less condemnatory and more nuanced, Hindley 1999). D. Cohen (e.g. 1987: 13; 1995: 155–6) assimilates them too closely.

Third, this passage is of some importance in the debate on the 'passivity' of the 'boyfriend' in 'bad' homosexual relationships (see Intro. pp. 45–50): whether the condemnation of the unnatural and effeminate *'kinaidos'* is based on the assumption that he accepts penetration (e.g. Dover 1978: esp. 100–6); Foucault 1985: 220); Winkler 1990a: 50, 52, or Halperin 1990: 34–5), or whether the emphasis in these denunciations is rather on an insatiability and shamelessness of desires which unites nymphomaniac women and the degenerate men: see Davidson (1997: esp. 167–82); part of his argument is that there has been an excessive emphasis on phallic penetration in discussions of Greek discourses on sex. As seen above (on **38**, **41**, **51–2**, **55**, **70**, **131**), Aeschines avoids explicit mention of specific sexual acts (e.g. anal or oral sex), preferring the appearance of adherence to the convention of decorum in speech in public assemblies combined with a knowing and titillating insinuation. The phrase 'who has committed womanish offences' is ambiguous: it might suggest men offending as women do (which might suggest then excessive and illicit sexual pleasures) or rather men committing acts which are only offensive when men, rather than women, do them. The second seems much more likely to be meant here, since this behaviour is evidently 'worse', because it is 'contrary to nature' when men do them; we are certainly dealing with certain acts performed (or 'endured') by the junior partners in homosexual relationships; the main candidate is clearly anal intercourse. What is objectionable about that may be the mere acceptance of penetration (which would be considered normal for women, but not for men), the mere preparedness of 'boyfriends' to surrender their power of negotiating with their lovers and performing whatever their lovers demanded, in exchange for money or other goods, or eagerly seeking out penetration because they found pleasure in the anus or in buttock-movements (see also above all Davidson 1997: 178–80). Given Aeschines' affected reticence, the language of this passage may not seem decisive. However, since Aeschines has consistently argued that of the pair it is Demosthenes who is the *kinaidos*, with his effeminate clothes and ambiguous sexual practices with his pupils, and Timarchos' insatiable desires concern women, gluttony, and gambling, not what he did with his lovers, the emphasis here (as in **51**, **55**, **94–5**) is not likely to be on Timarchos' desire for the pleasure of anal gratification. The other two elements are both, I suspect, strongly involved. There is certainly a major and explicit concentration on the acceptance, for money, of unspecified sexual acts (and penetration by many different men is surely what would first leap to the jury's minds); and this is repeatedly said to be in a somewhat bizarre expression to 'commit *hybris* against oneself', above all because it involved surrender of autonomous choice for the sake of gain (see on **188** 'selling the *hybris* of his own body'). Yet the coy but repeated references to 'the thing', and here to the 'womanish offences' which Timarchos and those like him agreed to do for their lovers, seems only to be fully explained if admitting penetration is itself presented as a major problem for masculinity, whether or not he took active pleasure in it.

without understanding of our culture (*apaideutos*). Previously (**132**) Aeschines claimed that he, contrary to the 'General's' alleged view, was not displaying his lack of culture (*apaideusia*) by his charge against Timarchos, but on the contrary a proper discrimination between just and self-controlled love and the wrong sort; whereas the bad lover who pursues boys in the wrong way was uncultured (*apaideutos*) and a *hybristes* (**137**). The careful delineation of what is involved in the preservation of Athenian culture is extended here: the argument is that it would be an uncultivated juryman who failed to discriminate between acceptable and non-acceptable behaviour of the boyfriends, and so failed to punish the wrong sort, just as it would be to fail to act even more severely against male, 'unnatural' offenders than they would against female offenders, or worst of all, failed to stop them continuing to act as their political leaders. The adjective works, that is, as a cunning combination of flattery of the jury, of their sophistical understanding of, or even partial participation in, leisured culture, and as a warning of the many serious dangers of allowing a man like Timarchos political prominence. This last point is elaborated in **187**.

186–7 What feeling will each of you have? . . . what are you going to say? Aeschines builds on the earlier representation of the jury as participators in a broad gymnastic, musical, and literary culture (see on **132–44, 155, 185**) and as parents concerned to employ slave attendants, athletic trainers, and teachers to ensure the protection of their boys and young men from illicit approaches from adult males (with implicit references back to the sections on such protection of boys at **9–11**). He then argues the effect of an acquittal will be that the major sanction designed to inhibit *hetairesis* or prostitution among young men who may wish to seek a political life will not be seen not to be operating; in which case he gloomily predicts that the jury's sons will have good reason to object to the restrictions imposed on them for their protection. Naturally, Aeschines assumes that the conclusion drawn from an acquittal would be that the jury did not care to maintain the sanction, not that he actually had failed to provide any evidence for his case. This rhetorical tactic, of inviting the jury to contemplate having to justify a difficult or unpopular verdict when they go home, is found also in a closely similar, if even more dramatic, form in Apollodoros' Neaira speech (Ps. Dem. 59. 109–13 with Kapparis, *Neaira* 405, and see also Lycurgus 1. 141), where it is the jurors' wives who are imagined as interrogating their husbands, and drawing different conclusions from a vote to acquit such a notorious prostitute, depending on their moral character. Again in the Crown speech (3. 245–6) Aeschines imagines jurors' sons being less inclined to take orders from their fathers if they hear they have acquitted a traitor. If in fact (see also Intro. p. 63) Apollodoros was encouraged to bring his case against Stephanos and Neaira by the verdict of this speech, his use of this particular tactic may well have been influenced by Aeschines' successful employment of it a few years earlier.

be overturning our common cultural education? We find here yet another reversal of 'the General's' accusation that Aeschines was subverting the basis of Athenian culture; not only, he claims, are Demosthenes and Timarchos doing this, but so would the jury be if they acquit Timarchos.

those who have the laws entrusted to them are bent down to the acts of shame? This is another powerful way of putting the central point of the crisis for the system when the legislators and political leaders betray their trust. The verb (*katakampo*) means 'bend down', and this seems to be its only occurrence in the Attic orators. The form here may be passive 'are bent/ induced to . . .' that is, presumably, by entreaty (so LSJ[9] s.v.); but much more likely, in view of the emphasis throughout on Timarchos' willingness to submit to anything, is that it is the Greek 'middle voice', that is it means 'bend themselves down to'. This could be understood metaphorically, as meaning 'incline to', 'yield to', but it could also carry a hint of the physical act of 'bending over', with a suggestion of agreeing to anal sex (in the manner of the man labelled 'Bendover' on the 'Eurymedon vase': see Intro. pp. 47–8). If so, right at the end of the speech, Aeschines allows himself to get somewhat closer than hitherto to indicating 'the act' – but carefully through an amusing ambiguity (see also on **38**).

188 I am surprised at this too. The argument is weak, but designed to increase the sense of distaste towards Timarchos. Pimps and brothel-keepers may incur social disapproval, but pimping was not in itself illegal (many or most were doubtless metics), nor was male prostitution; the point at issue was whether the Athenian people really cared to prevent ex-prostitutes from representing the city in politics.

hate the brothel-keepers. Pimping and brothel-keeping (*pornoboskia*) were pre-eminent among the 'shameful' professions (see e.g. Arist. *EN* 1121b40–3; Theophr. *Char.* 6. 5), along with inn-keepers and tax-collectors (on whom see on **119**); not only did they make their living from feeding men's sexual appetites, but they were represented as greedy and exploitative (cf. e.g. Ps. Dem 59. 29–30, on Neaira's madam Nikarete, with Kapparis, *Neaira* 228–9). They also appeared regularly in Middle and New Comedy (e.g. Euboulos' *Pornoboskos*, Nesselrath 1990: 324–5). Aeschines, on unclear grounds (if any), called Ktesiphon, Demosthenes' supporter who proposed to crown him in 336, a bad man and a brothel-keeper (3. 214, 246).

elected by lot to none of the priesthoods of the gods. On these alleged restrictions, and the general presentation of people like Timarchos as falling into a category of 'metaphorical moral pollution' and offensive to the gods, with obvious dangers for the city's policies and safety, see on **19**, and also Arist. *Pol.* 1329 29–30; Ps. Dem. 59. 92, with Parker (1983: 96–7); Kapparis, *Neaira* 372–3; and comparable passages of abuse against allegedly depraved politicians such as Androtion (Dem. 22. 78), and Demosthenes himself, see on **131**.

write in our decrees prayers to the Solemn Goddesses. The Solemn Goddesses (*Semnai theai*, sometimes referred to just as the Semnai) were very closely linked to the Areopagos Hill and Council (on which see **6, 81, 92, 180**); they received cult at their shrine located in a cavern just below the top of the hill to the north-east, which was a place of asylum for those fleeing from their enemies, and was naturally close to where the court itself sat which grew up to hear cases arising from such conflicts: see Wallace (1985: 9–11, 215–18). According to the *scholia* to this passage the court sat for three days each month, each sacred to one of the three Semnai; parties to the Council's proceedings took especially solemn oaths, and some of these, at least, perhaps all, included the Semnai as divine recipients (Dein. 1. 47). Their cult included a sacrifice and procession organized by members of a traditional family or *genos*, the *Hesychidai*, and sacrificial officials (*hieropoioi*) appointed by the Areopagos (see Parker 1996: 298–9). The last play of Aeschylus' trilogy the *Oresteia* (first performed in 458), the *Eumenides*, shows the vengeful underworld powers called the Furies (*Erinyes*), who have played leading and increasingly open roles in bringing about the sequence of kin-revenges in the Argive royal house of Agamemnon, being persuaded by Athena to accept a permanent home near the Areopagos, lasting cult from Athens, and a new role in support of the newly established homicide court. From Aeschylus' time on, they were held in Athens to be virtually identical (cf. e.g. Paus. 1. 28. 6). It has been argued that Aeschylus may have been the first to identify the Semnai and their cult at Athens with the *Erinyes* and the *Eumenides* (A. L. Brown, 'Eumenides in Greek Tragedy', *CQ* 34 (1984), 260–81; A. H. Sommerstein, *Aeschylus' Eumenides* (Cambridge, 1989), 10–12). But this seems over-sceptical; the connections seem very strong between the 'Furies' and these Athenian goddesses with their more euphemistic title who nonetheless inspired dread and worked for revenge, but who had evidently for some centuries (apparently from the time of the Kylonian attempt at a tyranny, see Thuc. 1. 126; Plut. *Solon* 12) worked closely topographically and in spirit with the Areopagos, the oldest ancient Athenian court, to deliver vengeance for the families of the dead within the judicial process of the state: see e.g. Lloyd-Jones, 'Erinyes, Semnai Theai, Eumenides', in E. Craik (ed.), *Owls to Athens: Essays on Classical Subjects for Sir Kenneth Dover* (Oxford, 1990), 2803–11; Seaford (1994: 95–9); Jameson, Jordan, and Kotansky (1993: 77–81); S. I. Johnston, *The Restless Dead: Encounters between the Living and the Dead in Ancient Greece* (Berkeley and Los Angeles, 1999), 267–87, and Allen (2000: 19–23). On the iconography of the Semnai, and their distinctively more benign appearance than that of the *Erinyes*, see *LIMC* III, 839–40, and Paus. 1. 28.

If Timarchos were to be permitted to continue in public life, he would be likely to propose motions for the assembly and sign those actually formulated by others (cf. also Ps. Dem. 59, 43, and see Hansen 1983; 1991: 146–7, 207–8); the point in the addition of the second clause here is presumably that Timarchos will carry on working as Demosthenes' supporter and toady (see also on **191**).

The notion of the prayers in the assembly was introduced early in the speech (**23**), where Aeschines reminded the jury that assembly and Council meetings always began with solemn prayers to the gods along with curses against traitors, bribe-takers, and any who tried to mislead the people, both recited by the herald from texts provided by the clerk (see also Dem. 19. 70–1; Lyc. 1. 31; Dein. 1. 47–8, 2. 14, and the parody of such curses at Ar. *Thesm.* 347–51, with Rhodes 1972: 36–7). All 'orators' who spoke and proposed motions were particularly bound by these prayers and curses. Deinarchos (1. 46–7) makes the point against Demosthenes that because of his bribe-taking, above all in the Harpalos affair, and his other offences, he has made himself liable to all available curses; Deinarchos mentions the 'solemn goddesses', but also specifies that these oaths were taken in relation to the procedures of the Areopagos.

Here the reference seems to be to a practice found occasionally in our epigraphic records of Athenian decrees, whereby the herald was told to pronounce a prayer to specified deities, of the form that if the proposed course of action turned out well, the city would offer these gods a special sacrifice and procession in gratitude. Three fourth-century Athenian examples survive, of which one certainly and one probably mention the Semnai. At *IG* II^2 30, 1–3 = Lalonde, Langdon, and Walbank 1991: no. L3, an early fourth-century decree to do with leasing properties on Lemnos, the only deities to whom the vow is made who can be read on the stone are the twelve gods (and there is space for only one other deity, perhaps Herakles); at *IG* II^2 112 = Tod II 144 = Harding no. 56, a well-preserved decree accepting an alliance with Arcadians, Achaeans, Eleians, and Phliasians in 362/1, a full quota of deities, Olympian Zeus, Athena Polias, Demeter, Kore, the twelve gods and the *semnai theai* are invoked, and a sacrifice and a procession promised; and in a similar vow in *IG* II^2 114 = Tod II 146 = Harding no. 58, in the same year, a decree concerned with sending out klerouchs to Poteidaia, 'the *semnai theiai*' is the most plausible supplement between the twelve gods and Herakles. Aeschines has evidently imagined that Timarchos might propose a decree stipulating such a procedure; and he has selected as recipients of such a prayer those who might be especially offended by Timarchos continuing acting as the city's representative, because they stand for the principles of just retribution. There is likely to be a connection of thought also with the picture of the internalized 'Furies' of insatiable desires which are said in the next section to dominate Timarchos. There may conceivably be the further suggestion that such prayers were likely to be used (or may have been recently used) to attempt to increase the likelihood of Athens' alliances and her peace with Philip turning out well; the suggestion is that to have one such as Timarchos putting his name as proposer to a decree stipulating such a prayer would upset the stern goddesses of retribution.

What would he not sell, when he has sold the humiliation (*hybris*) of his own body? Again a recapitulation of a central point behind the laws: see on **29** and Intro. pp. 40–2.

189 repulsiveness. Here and in **192** the strong term *bdelyria* is employed again, as the final emphasis is on the physical unpleasantness of what he did, and its effects on his body.

Just as we recognize those in athletic training. Again Aeschines has recourse to the argument from men's physical appearance (despite the problems this had given him with Misgolas, see on **49**; and for the argument about Timarchos' body, see on **25, 126**). Here it is asserted that even citizens who do not regularly go and watch people at the *gymnasia* are interested enough, and skilled enough in the techniques of visual assessment and clue-spotting, to spot a man in good athletic condition; see also on **155–9** for the assumption that all Athenians take a keen interest in the physical appearance of those who display their bodies in athletic contests.

even though we are not present at their activities, from their shamelessness, boldness, and practices. The argument has shifted, and in a crucial way. Instead of arguing (in the fashion of the conclusions drawn at **25** from the current raddled state of Timarchos' body) about the lasting physical effects of their activities on the *pornoi*, the prostitutes, Aeschines suggests that their repeated activities have a permanent deleterious effect on their characters (or 'souls'). This is designed to provide a more intellectual justification of one basic assumption behind the law, that voluntary involvement in shameful sexual practices makes men unsuitable characters to lead their city.

condition. The word here (*hexis*, condition) picks up the word used above of athletes (*euhexis*, good condition); *hexis* is commonly

used in fourth-century discussions, both 'ordinary' and philosophical, for settled dispositions of character, usually conceived as
either for good or for bad (cf. e.g. Cairns 1993: 398–411). The
language here, as in many other cases, may suggest a certain
diffusion of general ideas about the formation of character as a
result of one's characteristic acts and habits, from the more philosophical discussions of the sophists and the intellectual schools to
the general public (see Adkins 1978); but Aeschines keeps this
language to a minimum, and the general idea that men's moral
characters were largely formed by habituation in their formative
years rather than by inheritance was widely available in all our
categories of evidence (see on **11**, and Dover 1974: 88–95; 1978:
109).

190 as a result of men like this. To reinforce the point,
Aeschines claims that politicians with shameful pasts have often in
the past ruined their cities and themselves. He gives no examples;
he might have used, as Demosthenes had in the Meidias speech
(21. 143–50), the case of Alkibiades, whose turbulent political
career was intimately connected both with the excesses of his
sexual and social malpractices (see esp. Thuc. 6. 15) and with
Athens' disaster in Sicily and defeat in the Peloponnesian War:
see MacDowell, *Meidias* 358–66, and Wohl (1999: 365–80), who
brings out well the complexities of his varied transgressions
against sexual norms and protocols, in relation to partners of both
sexes.

**Do not believe, Athenians, that the origins of wrong-
doing lie with the gods.** Having presented positively, if briefly,
a more 'philosophical' view of the development of settled immoral
or criminal characters from their own choices and actions,
Aeschines warns the jury against an explanation in terms of the
impetus to crime being an external visitation by one or more
divine powers. From Homer on, Greeks had regularly accepted
the compatibility of explanations of extraordinary or transgressive
human acts in terms both of divine attack and individual responsibility, though arguments about exact allocation of responsibility
remained open (the so-called 'double determination': cf. e.g. on
Agamemnon in the *Iliad*, E. R. Dodds, *The Greeks and the Irrational*
(Berkeley and Los Angeles, 1951), ch. 1, important modifications in
Taplin 1990: 75–6, and *Homeric Soundings* (Oxford, 1992), 98–105,

203–8). Similar views are often expressed in the orators (including Aeschines himself), where the claim that a god must have led a man astray does not in any way lessen the need to see him punished for his crimes: see e.g. Aesch. 3. 117; Lys. 6, 19–20, 22, 26, 34 with the responses of Andoc. 1. 113–14; Dem. 4. 42, 24. 121; Lyc. 1. 92; Dover (1974: 133–8); J. D. Mikalson, *Athenian Popular Religion* (Chapel Hill and London, 1983), 57. Yet here Aeschines asks the jury to dispel these thoughts and attribute Timarchos' and other people's offences solely to their insatiable desires and the effects of their disgusting behaviour. His reason is the wish to emphasize Timarchos' personal guilt, and establish a close connection between his alleged youthful sexual and financial excesses and his current political crimes. There is no need to see here any sign of generally reduced beliefs in such powers, nor any indication of Aeschines' personal views, especially since he has just suggested the disgrace which would be involved in allowing Timarchos and his like to inscribe prayers to the Semnai (who were thought very close to, perhaps identical with, the *Erinyes* or the *Poinai*) on behalf of the city (see Dover 1974: 145–6; Padel 1995: 178).

men who have committed impiety are driven and punished, as in the tragedies, by the Furies with their blazing torches. The Furies, who are here called *Poinai*, vengeances, and elsewhere often *Erinyes* (see also on **188**), are the spirits of divine revenge and punishment, conceived often, as in Aeschylus' *Eumenides*, as black-clothed, repulsive harpies with snakes in their hair or their arms, dripping blood and ooze, and brandishing fiery torches (see Padel 1995: 164–92; Aellen 1994: I, 24–9). The phrase 'driven and punished' clearly covers the double process characteristic of such personified powers, who first impel the impious to commit worse crimes than they (or their ancestors) have already, then ensure their punishment (see Dover 1974: 146, Padel 1995: 177). The word for 'driven—*elaunein*—is used in a similar context at Eur. *IT* 970, and there is probably a connection with *elasteros* or *alastor*, terms for the vengeful dead or their spirits: see Jameson, Jordan, and Kotansky (1993: 116–20).

With his reference to 'tragedies', Aeschines is not only using his own experience as an actor, but also appealing to the audience's knowledge of plays. But it is less clear whether he is here, as usual, appealing to the now 'classical' fifth-century tragedies, which had frequent 'revivals' (see P. J. Wilson 1996: 315–16; we would think above all of the Furies visibly present in Aeschylus' *Oresteia* and in Orestes' mind in Euripides' *Orestes*), or also to more recent contemporary plays and representations of them. Furies associated with Orestes appear on a number of Athenian fifth- and fourth-century vases: see J. Prag, *The Oresteia: Iconographic and Narrative Tradition* (Warminster, 1985), 44–51; Aellen (1994: I, 26–7); Padel (1995: 170), and on a great many South Italian vases associated with many different mythical characters (see Aellen 1994: *passim*). It has been suggested that Aeschines may have been influenced particularly by the *Achilles, Slayer of Thersites* of the fourth-century tragedian Chaeremon (*TrGF* 71 frr. 1–3), especially since Aeschines had used Achilles and Patroklos extensively earlier (e.g. Meulder 1989: 321, n. 53; P. J. Wilson 1996: 327–8 is cautious). This play has been brought plausibly into connection with a complex representation of a scene on a Tarentine volute-krater, now in Boston, of *c.* 350–340, which features a crowded scene of labelled figures: Achilles and Phoinix are inside a tent, outside lies Thersites' trunk with his head nearby, both guarded by Automedon, Achilles' squire; from one side Diomedes, on one version a distant kin to Thersites, approaches menacingly, but is restrained by Menelaus, from the other Agamemnon arrives judiciously, while above sit or stand Athena, Hermes, and a Fury labelled as *Poine* holding a drawn sword; (*Boston Museum of Art* 03.804; *LIMC* I. 1 171, 2, VII. 1, 422–3; discussions by L. Séchan, *Études sur la Tragédie grecque dans ses rapports avec la céramique* (Paris, 1926), 527–31 and Aellen 1994: I, 39, 65). But the connection between Aeschines' praise of the noble love of Achilles and Patroklos and Achilles' later killing of Thersites over an insult for his supposed love for the Amazon Penthesileia is hardly close or appropriate. Aeschines need not have in mind any specific tragedy; and one may note that Timocles' comedy *Orestautokleides* (see on **52**) apparently parodied tragic presentation of a chorus of Furies, in an attack on one of the 'wild and shaggy' pederasts, and that Alexis' *Agonis* (3 K/A), parodies the imaginary Furies haunting Orestes in Euripides' *Orestes* (see on **41**).

191 fill the robber bands, make men board the pirates' boats. We have here, as comparable cases to Timarchos, examples of other criminals and dangers to the state who may be supposed to have been set on their terrible paths by their insatiable love of physical pleasures; the point is to blacken Timarchos further by assimilation to these generally reviled characters, organized criminal bands of outsiders who declare war on society. *Leisteria* are bands of brigands (*leistai*), a term which includes both raiders by land and the better attested pirates who attack from boats. *Epaktrokeleta* is a rare word for a light, fast boat often used by pirates, made up from two words: *epaktris*, a skiff, from *epaktos*, foreign, imported, mercenary—see Xen. *Hell.* 1. 1. 11; Aul. Gell. 10. 25. 5—and *keles*, a swift horse or swift boat. On such organized criminals in fourth-century Greece, see e.g. Aesch. 2. 71–3; Hyper. *Lyc.* 2; P. McKechnie, *Outsiders in the Greek City* (London, 1989), ch. 5; Y. Garlan, *Guerre et économie en grèce ancienne* (Paris, 1989), ch. 8.

they are the Fury for each man, which urges him to slaughter his fellow-citizens, to act as the tyrants' underlings, and to help in destroying democracy. The condemnation becomes even more extravagant, as such criminals are said to be murderers, and act as the supporters of tyrants in overthrowing democracy. Timarchos, the assimilation seems to suggest, is not only a threat to the state as a polluted debauchee and a ridiculous representative abroad, but also is only too likely to be driven into outright opposition to their political system; here again the general points made at the start of the speech are picked up again at the end. The basic pattern of thought here, though it seems extreme, connects with a constant strand in Athenian political rhetoric and thought. One of the major modes of attack on Alkibiades' dangerously anti-social practices, during his lifetime and later (see on **190**), had been to claim they 'proved' he was a natural tyrant, and in fact was aiming at tyranny (see Thuc. 6. 15; Lys. 14; Ps. Andoc. 4, with R. Seager, 'Alcibiades and the Charge of Aiming at Tyranny', *Historia* 16 (1967), 6–18; Murray 1990a, and Wohl 1999: 365–80).

Plato's schematic analysis in book 9 of the *Republic* of the evolution of the 'tyrannical' man, son of the excessively democratic father, has much in common with the main lines of the portrait of Timarchos as it has with that of Alkibiades. Central to Plato's analysis is the same frenetic and insatiable need in the tyrannical man to satisfy all lusts and desires, however immoral and shameless, and important elements in his rake's progress include feastings, *komoi* and *hetairai*, dissipation of his inheritance, crimes of violence and against property, assaults on his parents (571a–76b). The parallels and differences between the two texts are explored well by Meulder (1989) and Davidson (1997: 294–301). Meulder is probably right to argue, against Weil (1955), that they are exploiting, for their different purposes, conventional ideas and prejudices about the tyrannical nature, and that we should not assume that Aeschines owes anything to a reading of the *Republic*. Not all his arguments are valid, however; if Aeschines had read this section of the *Republic*, he would have no reluctance to exploit it just because he was going to label Plato's teacher Sokrates a sophist whose teachings were shown to be dangerous to the democracy. Aeschines, however, avoids mentioning Alkibiades (see also on **190**), and his claims notably assimilate Timarchos to the tyrant's 'underlings', who will help in the pre-paratory murders of citizens and join the anti-democratic coup; while he wishes to suggest that Timarchos alarmingly shares the tyrant's desires, he also denigrates him as not important enough himself to lead an attempt at a tyranny, and the further implica-tion is no doubt that it is Demosthenes who would be the leader (see Meulder 1989: 319–20; Davidson 1997: 301).

While rejecting a specific 'tragic' mode of explanation, Aeschines nonetheless strikes, in his language and his appeal to the experience of the plays, a 'tragic' note of denunciation. Demosthenes often used 'tragedy' or 'speak like a tragedy' [*tragodein*] for the elaborately emotional appeal of his ex-actor opponent, e.g. Dem. 19. 189, 18. 13, 127, 313, with Wankel, on 18. 13; and Hypereides also accuses the prosecutor of Lykophron, and Alexander's mother Olympias, of similar 'tragic' language (Hyper. *Lyk.* 12 and *Eux.* 26). On such use of characters and images from classic tragedies in denunciation, see above all P. J. Wilson (1996: 317–24).

192 the basis for good order (*eukosmia*) in the city. This key idea in the speech, encapsulating the preservation of the division between orderly and non-orderly forms of relationships, and much else besides, is suitably emphasized in the conclusion. See Ford (1999: 246, n. 52).

if he is acquitted, it would be better. As prosecutors commonly do, Aeschines argues that an acquittal would be a disaster for Athens and her democratic system, making the assumption that it would be an unjust verdict: see the comparable moves made in other concluding summing-ups at Dem. 21. 219–25, 24. 142–3, 54. 43. Aeschines puts this line especially strongly, probably because it might have seemed very likely that an acquittal would bring this law into disrepute, if in recent memory it had been the focus of many accusations, but few or no cases.

Before Timarchos came to trial. No other cases are cited under this law, which reinforces the case for supposing this was a rarity, and genuinely seen as a test case.

the best known of all. Aeschines is now, he hopes, confident that he has established the prevalence of existing reports over many years concerning Timarchos' activities, and that much of it had some basis: see on **157**.

at the end it will not be speeches, but a clear crisis that will arouse your anger. The argument is that the acquittal of Timarchos would remove the deterrent value of the law, and the spread of immorality among the young would become so obvious that it would be recognized by the people as a general crisis demanding more serious legislative action, rather than merely control by individual prosecutions. One could suppose (see Intro. pp. 65–7) that the introduction of the *ephebeia* in response above all to the post-Chaironeia crisis was a response in part to a fear that defences against the immorality of the youth needed strengthening.

193 not on a crowd. A rather bizarre picture of the alleged 'crisis' is briefly summoned up, whereby a mass of dissolute youths would need to be dealt with in a group; the actual processes are left conveniently vague, but the frightening picture is designed to reinforce the case for making a decisive example of Timarchos.

preparations and advocates of these men. The plural ('these men') includes Demosthenes as equally or more responsible with Timarchos with planning the case, and providing friends and supporters to plead for Timarchos. For such pleas to the jury to mistrust their opponents' legal expertise, elaborate preparations and lying witnesses and character references, see e.g. also Dem. 21. 112, 29. 28, 30. 3, 40. 9, with Christ (1998: 38–9), and Rubinstein (forthcoming).

I shall not mention any of them. As he had also refrained from identifying 'the General'—though some of those he has in mind may be those he has mentioned in the speech and attempted, without success, to agree to the public testimony he had prepared for them. His alleged reason, that he did not want to encourage men to testify for Timarchos by naming them, is probably specious. Another better reason is that he is enabled to blacken all possible character-witnesses in advance, by claiming, without needing even to rake up any specific items of gossip, that they fall into one of three categories (see **194**): those who, like Timarchos, have ruined their inheritances, those who have committed the same offences of self-prostitution, and those who like to exploit such youths' preparedness to accept such offers. The idea that Timarchos might have respectable relations, friends, or close political associates, men who were neither themselves excessively dissolute nor had been involved in the wrong type of relationships, but were prepared to attest their belief that he was innocent of the charges, is thus cleverly discounted in advance.

194 fall into three groups. A division of one's opponent's defence team into three groups is found elsewhere; at Lysias 14. 16–21 the three are the younger Alkibiades' friends, relations, and some magistrates who may wish to display their own power. Elsewhere, friends and relations may be put together and distinguished from the politicians (e.g. Lys. 30. 31; Lyc. 1. 135 and 138). Aeschines deliberately adopts his more insulting variation (spendthrifts, self-prostitutes, and their 'lovers') and through the surprise achieves additional power for his anticipatory assault: see Rubinstein (forthcoming).

   those who have unstintingly used such people. The term for 'used' (*chresthai*), when applied to social relationships between people, may be general and neutral ('treat as a friend/enemy; have a beneficial social relationship with': see e.g. Isaeus 3. 19), but it may also as here be a euphemistic way of saying 'use sexually', where the victims may equally be women (e.g. Hdt. 2. 181; Isaeus 3. 10; Ps. Dem. 59. 29, 33, 108) or men (e.g. Xen. *Mem.* 1. 2. 29). Here the adverb 'unstintingly' (*aphthonos*) emphasizes, albeit decorously, the sense that these men gave free rein to their sexual appetites. See Kapparis, *Neaira* 263.

195 remember their lives, and tell. Aeschines invites the jury to offer terse 'advice' to his three categories of likely supporters of Timarchos; the point is designed to reinforce the condemnation in advance of all the defendant's supporters, and to seek to ensure that the jury will not listen with any sympathy to what they may have to say. For variation, he switches the order of the groups.

not to go on bothering you, but to stop speaking in public. The first piece of advice, to those who have been '*pornoi*' or involved in relationships which may be construed as *hetairesis*, is in effect to remind 'them' and the jury (rightly, as the *scholia* comment) that these forms of scrutiny are only directed at the active politicians, the 'orators'. On this vital point see also **3, 19, 32, 40, 73**; Dem. 22. 30, with Dover (1978: 30–1); Winkler (1990a: 59–60); and Intro. pp. 51–3.

to work and acquire a livelihood from some other means. To the second group, those who have destroyed their properties, he gives a simple (if unhelpful) instruction, to go out and find a legitimate form of work.

who are the hunters of such young men as are easily caught. 'Hunting' was a natural and easy metaphor to apply to the pursuit of young men who might give in easily, or might run away or prove hard to get; cf. e.g. Plat. *Prot.* 309a, *Phdr.* 241d, and Dover (1978: 87–8); on hunting representations in vase-imagery in relation to erotic relations see A. Schnapp *Le chasseur et la cité* (Paris, 1997), esp. 247–57. The description of this third group makes it clear that they are to be seen as adult male citizens whose settled choice ('inclination', *prohairesis*, see on **41**) in sexual matters is to persuade—by money, gifts, or whatever, but without too troublesome a period of 'pursuit'—attractive boys or youths, preferably of citizen families, to do whatever they demanded (see on **41, 51–2, 55, 70**). In conformity with his relatively gentle treatment of individuals in this class like Misgolas earlier in the speech (see on **41**), Aeschines does not condemn this choice outright ('be not deprived of their inclination'), provided that such men do not seek to corrupt those young citizens who might wish to go into politics, and so either ruin promising careers, or bring the whole system of 'legitimate *eros*' to ruin ('you are not harmed'). There is an implicit condemnation of such an *eros* as one-sided and solely concerned with physical gratification for the lover, but also a grudging toleration of it provided it does not harm the citizen body.

turn themselves to the foreigners and the metics. The categories mentioned here are foreigners, i.e. transient workers or visitors to Attica, and metics, either those who have settled for a period (probably at least a month) in Attica, or freedmen; they had to register in a deme, name an Athenian as their representative (*prostates*), and pay the metic-tax. On metics, see generally Whitehead (1977). Aeschines shows little interest in metics in any of his speeches beyond this generalized contempt: see Whitehead (1977: 52, 55–6, 120).

This brief piece of 'advice' assumes, plausibly enough, that a good many of the more readily available male prostitutes working in brothels, little rooms, or in the murkier parts of the city, or working as 'musicians' or 'dancers' were not of citizen status (see Dover 1978: 31–2; Davidson 1997: 78–80, 90–1). Many, like their female counterparts, were presumably in fact slaves; but the sort of target his 'hunters' were presumably looking for are those with at least some powers of refusal, over whom some rivalries and counter-bidding might be expected, and hence were free or at least freed, or, like the Plataean youth of Lysias 3, for whom two citizens one of whom at least was rich, though perhaps getting less so (3. 20), competed over a long time, may have been of unclear or disputed status (see Dover 1978: 32–3; Carey, *Lysias* 87, 102–3, and on **160**). Demosthenes' defence of the 'Solonian' laws which attempt to prevent those who had engaged in *hetairesis* from entering public life allowed that it was acceptable for citizen boys to remain unpunished, provided they kept quiet (Dem. 22. 30–1); Aeschines seems to go a little further, in advising the active pederasts to avoid citizen youths altogether, to avoid later problems. This argument at the conclusion of the speech may support the view that there was a consciousness of a wider class of youths entering the competitive and dangerous worlds both of the *gymnasia* and politics, see Intro. pp. 58–62 and on **13**

196 You have now heard everything. A set of brief, simple yet solemn sentences round the speech off, and leave the decision with the jury.

I am to be the spectator. Aeschines here shows his awareness of the similarities between the law court and the theatre as public displays which lead to a verdict (see Hall 1995: 54–5), and reminds the jury of their powerful role, able to enact a reversal of fortune in real life.

with your verdicts that the case rests. The case (*praxis*) may be taken to extend beyond this particular trial to the more general issue of the status of this law, and the community's need to define its attitudes to youthful excesses and the morality of the different types of pederastic relationships.

to win more honour (*philotimoteron*) from you by investigating those who break the laws. The final sentence reinforces the idea that more than a single case is at stake: in addition, the point is reiterated that a decision on what the community expects and demands of its leaders is centrally involved. The emphatic 'we' here evidently means the politically active men, the '*rhetores*', and the use of the comparative adverb of *philotimos* ('honour-loving', 'ambitious') is appropriate because the concept of *philotimia* has become crucial to discussions of these reciprocal relations between mass and élite: it is assumed that the leaders spend their wealth, time, and effort to benefit and protect the people and the city's interests, and can expect to be given legitimate honours as the return gift (*charis*) from the people (see also on **129** and **160**, and Whitehead 1983; 1993; Johnstone 1999: 93–108; P. J. Wilson 2000: 144–97). If Timarchos is convicted, the argument seems to be, this will be the signal that the people will after all only accept and honour as its leaders those who have maintained certain standards in their family and private lives, and met their military obligations, and that they will encourage other politicians to see that these standards are preserved. The last conclusion the jury might draw from this statement is that Aeschines himself might be given some reward, in the form of greater consideration from the jury when his own case comes up; that he expected this point to be picked up is suggested by the fact that he used the successful outcome of this trial as just such a ground for a return at 2. 180, where he appealed to fathers and older brothers of the vulnerable young to remember the moral lesson of this prosecution. So the dishonouring of Timarchos should, Aeschines hints, lead to more honour for himself; and so, it may be argued, it turned out, at least in the relatively short term.

APPENDIX

Gambling, Pittalakos, and the genos of the Salaminians

Gambling evidently played an important part in the social life of
many Athenians, and especially no doubt the younger and more
leisured of them. Our understanding of the settings and organization of bird-fights and dicing, however, is very limited. Aeschines'
account of Pittalakos' troubles is an important item of evidence,
but it raises more questions than it answers.

Two late sources state that cock-fighting had an official place in
some festivals. Aelian (*VH* 2. 28) relates how after the victory of
the Persians the Athenians passed a law that there should be cock-
fighting contests on one day a year publicly (*demosiai*) in the
theatre; the origin of the law was that Themistocles observed the
fighting spirit and desire to win of the fighting cocks and thought
the contests would be a spur to young Athenians to *arete*. Solon in
Lucian's *Anacharsis* 37 in support justifies this practice: it is by law
compulsory for the young men to watch cock and quail fights until
the end, in order to encourage them to face dangers in battle with
no less courage than the birds. These anecdotes in themselves are
pretty dubious, but it may nonetheless be possible (cf. Schneider
in *RE*; Fowler 1989: 256–8) that at some times cock-fighting
played an institutional part at the Dionysia and perhaps other
festivals as well. They appear prominently in the iconography.
Fighting cocks were displayed on columns on many Panathenaic
vases. Two cocks appear on the table-cloth of the table at which
are seated the three judges for the Rural Dionysia in the so-called
Calendar frieze now on the Church of *Hagios Eleutherios* in Athens:
see Deubner (1932: 138, 248–50); E. Simon, *Festivals of Athens: An
Archaeological Commentary* (Madison & London, 1983), 101. Another
pair of cocks are held ready for combat by boys as Erotes on the
stone throne of the priest of Dionysos Eleuthereus in the theatre of
Dionysos: see M. Maass, *Die Prohedrie des Dionysostheaters in Athen*
(Munich, 1972), 60–76, who argues for a Lycurgan date for the
throne. It is clear, then, that cock-fighting was a pervasive and
powerful metaphor for the masculine and competitive courage

encouraged in many of Athens' contests and festivals (see Hoffman 1974, and esp. Csapo 1993); the invention of stories about the introduction of public cock-fights at the time of Themistocles might conceivably come from the period of the mid-fourth century when innumerable documents and stories of Athens' glorious past were invented (see Davies 1996). Conceivably cock-fights did become part of the programme at some point during the fourth century; in which case a state-slave might have been involved, for example under the direction of the *epimeletai* (see Arist. *Ath. Pol.* 56. 4), in ensuring that birds were provided. More explicit evidence would make this easier to believe; as Deubner (1932: 138, 248–9) and Pickard-Cambridge (1968: 51) suggest, the representations of cock-fights may well have essentially symbolic value. There may, however, be parallels elsewhere: Pliny *Nat. Hist.* 10. 21 states that there were official cock-fights every year at Pergamon, and that the best cocks came from Rhodes, Tanagra, Media, and Chalcis.

Other possibilities might be that bird-fighting and gambling with dice and knucklebones were part of the peripheral activities of festivals, and also at the *gymnasia*; the facts that bird-fights could be seen as suitably encouraging for the young, that birds were among the most popular love-gifts from men to youths, and that youths would enjoy playing the games, would all fit well enough. Plato (*Lysis* 206e) shows boys at a new *palaistra*, celebrating the Hermaia (see on **10**), and playing with 'all types of knucklebones' at moments of relaxation; knucklebones were particularly associated with children (see Kurke 1999: 290–2, and on **59** and **149**) and Suetonius, *Peri Paidion* ('On Games') 1. 10, p. 65 (ed. by J. Taillardat, Paris, 1997) asserts that Hermes and Pan are the patrons of dicing: Hermes because he is the god of chance, and the god of *gymnasia* and *palaistrai*, whereas Pan, Hermes' son, was often associated with his father in races and other contests (see Taillairdat *ad loc.*, P. Borgeaud, *The Cult of Pan in Ancient Greece* (Chicago, 1988), 134–5, 153–5). This more informal play might not so readily explain any connection with state-owned slaves. It is worth noting, however, that Demosthenes' abuse of crooks and debauchees who had found congenial refuge at Philip's court (2. 18) includes one Kallias who is also described as a *demosios*, along with other similar tellers of jokes and singers of disgraceful songs; and one can compare the account of the association of the sixty jesters, supposedly admired by Philip, who used to meet at the gymnasium and shrine of Herakles Kynosarges (Athenaeus 614d–e).

Another possibility may be the public leisure houses, *leschai*, where men gathered, especially in winter, to chat and tell stories (see in general W. Burkert, 'Lescha-Liškah. Sakrale Gastlichkeit zwischen Palästina und Griechenland, in B. Janowski, K. Koch, and G. Wilhelm (eds.), *Religionsgeschichtliche Beziehungen zwischen Kleinasien, Nordsyrien und dem Alten Testament* (Freiburg, 1993), 19–38; and R. G. A. Buxton, *Imaginary Greece: The Contexts of Mythology* (Cambridge, 1994), 40–4). Some evidence attests public *leschai* at Athens (see also D. M. Lewis 1990: 250): a fifth-century *horos*-stone from the Peiraieus, which marks off 'public *leschai*' (*IG* I^3 1102); a reference in Antiphon's speech against Nikokles' 'On Boundaries' (*Horoi*) (Harp. s.v. *leschai*); two fourth-century *horoi*-stones (II^2 2620a and b) found between the Areopagos and the Pnyx in the deme of Melite; and a fourth-century inscription from Aixone (*IG* II^2 2492, line 23), which stipulates that details of a forty-year leasing contract of land be inscribed on two *stelai*, one to be set up in the temple of Hebe and one in the *lesche* (probably also in the deme). But nothing seems to connect these leisure centres with gambling or bird-fights, or with public slaves.

One final area of speculation may be more worth exploring. Common terms for gambling places and gamblers were *skirapheia* and *skiraphoi*. The earliest appearance is a fragment of Hipponax (129a) the sixth-century iambic poet from Ephesos, where *skiraphoi* are apparently cheats or confidence tricksters; so the term probably did not originate in Athens. A number of late sources, however, tie the terms closely to specific Athenian gambling locations. Eusthathius, the twelfth century AD bishop of Thessalonike, in his Commentary on *Odyssey* 1. 107, supplies the quotation from Hipponax, but also suggests that the term *skirapheia* for gambling places, and *skiraphoi* for gamblers, villains, and gambling tricks, arose from the fact that the Athenians, who were very keen on dicing, played in shrines and especially at the temple of Athena Skiras at Skiron; and that as a result other gambling places were known as *skirapheia*. Harpokration quotes both Theopompos (*FGH* 115 228) and Deinarchos fr. 48 Conomis, a speech against Proxenos (of *c.* 292/1, after his return from exile, see Dionysios of Halicarnassus, *Dein.* 3) for the claim that gambling places could be called *skiraphia*, and Pollux (9. 96) and other lexicographers repeat the view that the Athenians used to dice especially in the temple of Athena Skiras at Skiron. Isocrates (7. 48–9, 15. 286–7) twice described degenerate contemporary youth, more decadent than in earlier times, as 'dicing' or 'spending their time' 'in the *skirapheia*. See the very full citation of sources and discussion in Jacoby's commentary on Philochoros (*FGH* 328 F 14–16).

There were two temples of Athena Skiras, just outside the city, each associated with a particular festival. The one specified by these sources as being 'at Skiron' was evidently the one located to the NW, on the road to Eleusis, to which the priestess of Athena and the priest of Poseidon/Erechtheus would solemnly process, under parasols, at the festival of the *Skira* (see Burkert 1985: 142–9, esp. 145 on the atmosphere of licence at Skiron, with dicing and prostitutes; also Calame 1996: 341–4). The sources perhaps give the impression that the dicing and other amusements there were not restricted to the time of the festival alone, and one might wish to contemplate Pittalakos' gaming activities there.

The other temple of Athena Skiras located at Phaleron is, however, even more tempting. It played a central part in the young men's festival of the *Oschophoria* associated with male transvestism, and Theseus' return to Athens from Crete; it was managed by the *genos* of the Salaminioi, who provided the two youths in women's clothes to carry bunches of grapes (*oschoi*) and others to carry the food (*deipnophoroi*): (Jacoby as above; Deubner 1932; Vidal-Naquet 1986a: 114–16; and above all Calame 1996: 324–64). It seems likely that there were several places, often referred to as *skirapheia*, where young men gathered regularly to dice; as we saw, Isocrates twice (7. 48–9 and 15. 286–7) castigates the most degenerate of young Athenians for wasting their time dicing in gambling dens (*diatribein/kubeuein en tois skirapheiois*). If the area of the Athena Skiras sanctuary at Skiron was the most famous gambling haunt, it seems not at all unlikely that Athena Skiras at Phaleron may have seen similar activities, especially, but perhaps not solely, at the time of the *Oschophoria*. The two shrines were closely associated, by being attached to the same deity and her epithet, and by association with similarly named heroes (Skiros the Eleusinian prophet at Skiron, Skiros a Salaminian King and perhaps also Skiron the Megarian bandit associated with the Phaleron shrine and the Salaminioi: see Kearns 1989: 197–8, but also M. C. Taylor 1997:

49–50). Rituals involving rites of passage of young men, races and Dionysiac processions at the *Oschophoria*, or of the women leaving home to celebrate the *Skira* at Skiron, alike share associations of temporary marginality or subversion; the same ideas are suggested also by the recurrent language of *skir-* words, which carry associations of border country or badlands, and of lime or 'white' earth; the dubious or marginal activities of the young, such as dicing, might fit in well enough.

We cannot of course say that all gambling dens were associated with sanctuaries in this way. It is interesting how the denunciation of young men's debauchery in Isocrates' *Antidosis* (15. 286–7) distinguishes two forms: the unlocalized, and less disgraceful, drinking, social gatherings, idle pursuits, and games, indulged in even nowadays by the most respectable of the young men, and the more public activities indulged night and day by those with 'worse natures'. These debaucheries are said to be such that a decent house slave in previous times would not have dared to do; the youths cool their wine from the water at the Nine Fountains, drink in bars (*kapeleia*), dice in the *skirapheia*, and spend their time hanging round the training-schools for the girl-pipers. Kurke's recent analysis (1999: 284–6) focuses well on the disapproval of the monetarization of pleasures, divorced from traditional social groupings, which she observes in both the more élite discourses such as this and also in law-court speeches (she compares Lys. 14. 27, 16. 11, as well as **42**). The 'better' youths indulge in more private settings, such as the *symposia* of friends, but the more debauched youths purchase their pleasures in the bars and the market-place, abuse the public provision of clean water at the Nine Springs for their nomadic drinking (on their *komoi*), spend time even during the day with the girl-pipers; the argument works well if the gambling dens are privately owned establishments like the bars (*kapeleia*: on these see also Davidson 1997: 52–60); it works equally well, if not better, if some or many of the *skirapheia* were known to be attached to religious shrines: as with the Fountain, there would be a suggestion of a misuse of public or sacred places for extravagant pleasures.

If, then (perhaps a big 'if'), gambling and related activities took place around Athena Skiras at Phaleron, then the quarrel between Hegesandros and Pittalakos may have been located there, and had as much to do with dicing and gambling on the

birds as with sexual rivalries. Various scenarios could be postu-
lated. The strongest element in the story appears to be the attempt
by Glaukon and others to rescue Pittalakos from Hegesandros by
the legal procedure of 'bringing back to freedom' (see on **62**),
especially in view of the fact that Glaukon seems to have provided
testimony. But this evidence may only have supported the case
that Hegesandros had been whipping Pittalakos, and was claiming, illegally, some form of ownership of the man; Glaukon did
not necessarily testify that the cause of the dispute was Pittalakos'
love-sick complaints over the removal of Timarchos from his care.
Further, the details about the breaking up of the tables and equipment and the killing of the birds are vivid and memorable, but
perhaps not the material that would immediately spring to
Aeschines' mind if he were simply inventing stories of erotic
jealousy and fighting. The relative sympathy afforded at times to
Pittalakos in the speech is compatible with the idea that he did
actually have a serious quarrel with the brothers, had a good
claim to be a free man or a freedman, but eventually had to give
up a possible lawsuit. Conceivably, Timarchos was perhaps
involved, but not at the centre of the story; and at its heart rather
was some sort of territorial dispute over the gaming activities
around the Salaminians' shrine in Phaleron. One possibility
might be that prominent members of the *genos* objected to a
spread of these activities near the shrine they controlled; another
might be that they already profited from such activities, and took
offence when one of their ex-slaves began operating his own gaming business on or near their ground, perhaps even using
experience he had acquired while working for them.

If there is any truth in these speculations, it seems significant
that Aeschines never mentions the brothers' membership of the
genos of the Salaminians, or any connection between the brothers
and its cults or the island of Salamis; he could, for example, have
contrasted their behaviour with the image of Solon and his statue,
as he did with Timarchos (see **25**). The reason may be that to
mention the association, even in criticism, might have reminded
the jury of their cultic position and hence social legitimacy, as
members of an ancient and respected body in Athenian society,
which might have counted in their favour. In fact it is Aeschines
who is claiming to defend Athenian traditions.

BIBLIOGRAPHY

a) Editions of Aeschines' Against Timarchos *and related texts*

This translation is based on the latest Teubner edition: Aeschines, *Orationes*, ed. M. R. Dilts. Stuttgart and Leipzig, 1997.
See also other editions:
Éschine, *Discours*, edited by V. Martin and G. de Budé: Budé edition with French translation. Paris, les Belles Lettres, 1927–8.
The Speeches of Aeschines, with an English translation, by C. D. Adams. Loeb edn. London and Cambridge, Mass., 1919.
The ancient lives of Aeschines, summaries (*hypotheses*) and the *scholia* (extracts from ancient commentaries written in the margins of our manuscripts) are all found in: *Scholia in Aeschinem*, ed. M. R. Dilts. Stuttgart and Leipzig, 1992.

b) Books and articles mentioned in the Introduction and (more than once) in the Commentary

ADKINS, A. W. H. (1978), 'Problems in Greek Popular Morality', *CP* 73, 143–58.
AELLEN, C. (1994), *À la Recherche de l'Order Cosmique: forme et fonction des personnifications dans la céramique italiote*. Zurich.
ALCOCK, S. E. and OSBORNE, R. G. (1994) (eds.), *Placing the Gods: Sanctuary and Sacred Space in Ancient Greece*. Oxford.
ALESHIRE, S. (1994), 'Towards a definition of "State-Cult" for Ancient Athens', in Hägg (1994) (ed.), 9–16.
ALLEN, D. S. (2000), *The World of Prometheus: The Politics of Punishing in Democratic Athens*. Princeton.
AUSTIN, M. M. (1981), *The Hellenistic World from Alexander to the Roman Conquest*. Cambridge.
BARBER, E. M. W. (1991), *Prehistoric Textiles: the Development of Cloth in the Neolithic and Bronze Ages*. Princeton.
———(1994), *Women's Work, The First 20,000 Years*. New York and London.
BELOCH, J. (1912–27), *Griechische Geschichte²*. Strassburg, Berlin, and Leipzig.
BERS, V. (1985), 'Dikastic *Thorubos*', in Cartledge and Harvey (1985) (eds.), 1–15.
BLASS, F. (1898), *Die attische Beredkamseit*. 3 vols. 2nd. edn. Leipzig.
BLUNDELL, M. W. (1989), *Helping Friends and Making Enemies: A Study in Sophocles and Greek Ethics*. Cambridge.

BLUNDELL, S. and WILLIAMSON, M. (1997) (eds.), *The Sacred and the Feminine*. London.

BOEGEHOLD, A. L. (1972), 'The establishment of a Central Archive at Athens', *AJA* 76, 23–30.

————(1995), *The Athenian Agora. Vol. XXVIII: The Lawcourts at Athens*. Princeton.

BOEGEHOLD, A. L. and SCAFURO, A. C. (1994) (eds.), *Athenian Identity and Civic Ideology*. Baltimore and London.

BONFANTE, L. (1989), 'Nudity as a Costume in Classical Art', *AJA* 93, 543–70.

BONFANTE, L. and VON HEINTZE, H. (1976) (eds.), *In memorial Otto J. Brendel*. Mainz.

BOSSI, K. (1995), 'Male Nudity and Disguise in the Discourse of Greek Histrionics', *Helios* 22, 3–22.

BOSWELL, J. (1980), *Christianity, Tolerance and Homosexuality*. Chicago and London.

BOURRIOT, F. (1976), *Recherches sur la nature du génos*. 2 vols. Lille.

————(1995), *Kalos Kagathos—Kalokagathia: D'un terme de propaganda de sophistes à une notion sociale et philosophique*. (Spudasmata 58). 2 vols. Hildesheim, Zurich, and New York.

BOWIE, A. M. (1997), 'Tragic Filters for History: Euripides' *Supplices* and Sophocles' *Philoctetes*', in Pelling, C. B. B. (1997) (ed.), 39–62.

BREMMER, J. (1980), 'An Enigmatic Indo-European Rite: Pederasty', *Arethusa* 13, 279–98.

————(1989), 'Greek Pederasty and Modern Homosexuality', in Bremmer (1989) (ed.), 1–14.

————(1989) (ed.), *From Sappho to de Sade*. London.

————(1990), 'Adolescents, *Symposion* and Pederasty', in Murray (1990) (ed.), 135–48.

————(1991), 'Walking, Standing and Sitting in Ancient Greek Culture', in Bremmer and Roodenburg (1991) (eds.), 15–35.

BREMMER, J. and ROODENBURG, H. (1991) (eds.), *A Cultural History of Gesture*. Ithaca, New York.

BRUNT, P. A. (1969), 'Euboea in the time of Philip II', *CQ* 19, 245–65.

BUCKLER, J. (1980), *The Theban Hegemony*. Cambridge, Mass.

————(1989), *Philip II and the Sacred War*. Leiden.

BUFFIÈRE, F. (1980), *Eros adolescent*. Paris.

BURCKHARDT, L. A. (1996), *Bürger und Soldaten: Aspekte der politischen und militärischen Rolle athenischer Bürger im Kriegswesen des 4. v. Chr.* Historia Einzelschriften 101. Stuttgart.

BURKERT, W. (1983), *Homo Necans*. Berkeley and Los Angeles.

————(1985), *Greek Religion*. Oxford.

CAIRNS, D. (1993), *Aidos: The Psychology and Ethics of Honour and Shame in*

Ancient Greek Literature. Oxford.

CALAME, C. (1996), *Thésée et l'imaginaire athénienne*. 2nd edn. Lausanne.

——— (1997), *Choruses of Young Women in Ancient Greece. Their Morphology, Religious and Social Functions*. Lanham and London.

——— (1999), *The Poetics of Eros in Ancient Greece*. Princeton.

CANTARELLA, E. (1989), 'L'Omosessualita nel diritto Ateniense', *Symposion 1982: Vortrage zur griechischen und hellenistiche Rechtsgeschichte,* 153–76. Cologne.

——— (1991), 'Moicheia: Reconsidering a problem', *Symposion 1990: Vortrage zur griechischen und hellenistiche Rechtsgeschichte,* 289–96. Cologne.

——— (1992), *Bisexuality in the Ancient World*. New Haven.

CARAWAN, E. M. (1985), '*Apophasis* and *Eisangelia*: The Role of the Areopagos in Athenian Political Trials', *GRBS* 26, 115–40.

——— (1998), *Rhetoric and the Law of Draco*. Oxford.

CAREY, C. (1994a), 'Legal Space in Classical Athens', *G&R* 41, 172–86.

——— (1994b), 'Comic Ridicule and Democracy', in Osborne and Hornblower (1994) (eds.), 69–84.

——— (1995), 'Rape and Adultery in Athenian Law', *CQ* 45, 407–17.

——— (1998), 'The Shape of Athenian Laws', *CQ* 48, 93–109.

CARGILL, J. (1981), *The Second Athenian League: Empire or Free Alliance*. California.

——— (1995), *Athenian Settlements of the Fourth Century BC*. Mnemosyne Suppl. 145. Leiden.

CARLIER, P. (1984), *La Royauté en Grèce avant Alexandre*. Strasbourg.

——— (1996) (ed.), *Le IVᵉ siècle av. J.-C.: approches historiographiques*. Paris.

CARNES, J. S. (1998), 'This Myth Which Is Not One: Construction of Discourse in Plato's *Symposium*', in Larmour, Miller, and Platter (1998) (eds.), 104–21.

CARTER, J. B. (1997), '*Thiasos* and *Marzeah*: Ancestor Cult in the Age of Homer', in Langdon (1997) (ed.), 72–111.

CARTER, J. M. (1971), 'Athens, Euboea and Olynthos', *Historia* 20, 418–29.

CARTLEDGE, P. A. (1981), 'The Politics of Spartan Pederasty', *PCPS* 27, 17–36.

——— (1998), 'The *machismo* of the Athenian Empire—or the Reign of the *phaulus*?', in Foxhall and Salmon (1998b) (eds.), 54–67.

CARTLEDGE, P. A. and HARVEY, F. D. (1985) (eds.), *Crux: Essays Presented to G.E.M. de Ste Croix*. Exeter.

CARTLEDGE, P. A., MILLETT, P. C. and TODD, S. C. (1990) (eds.), *Nomos: Essays in Athenian law, Politics and Society*. Cambridge.

CARTLEDGE, P. A., MILLETT, P. C. and VON REDEN, S. (1998) (eds.), *Kosmos, Essays in Order, Conflict and Community in Classical Athens*. Cambridge.

CAWKWELL, G. L. (1978), *Philip of Macedon*. London.

———— (1960), 'Aeschines and the Peace of Philocrates', *REG* 73, 416–38.

———— (1962), 'Aeschines and the Ruin of Phocis in 346', *REG* 75, 453–9.

CHRIST, M. R. (1998), *The Litigious Athenian*. Baltimore and London.

CLAIRMONT, C. (1993–5), *Classical Attic Tombstones*. Kilchberg.

CLARKE, W. M. (1978), 'Achilles and Patroclus in Love', *Hermes* 106, 381–96.

COHEN, D. (1983), *Theft in Athenian Law*. Munich.

———— (1984), 'The Athenian Law of Adultery', *RIDA* 31, 147–65.

———— (1985), 'A Note on Aristophanes and the Punishment of Adultery in Athenian Law', *ZSS* 102, 385–7.

———— (1987), 'Law, Society and Homosexuality in Classical Athens', *P&P* 117, 3–21.

———— (1991a), *Law, Sexuality and Society*. Cambridge.

———— (1991b), 'Sexuality, Violence and the Athenian Law of Hubris', *G&R* 38, 171–88.

———— (1995), *Law, Violence and Community in Classical Athens*. Cambridge.

COHEN, E. E. (1992), *Athenian Economy and Society: A Banking Perspective*. Princeton.

———— (2000), '"Whoring under Contract": The Legal Context of Prostitution in Fourth-Century Athens', in Hunter and Edmondson (2000), 113–48.

COHN-HAFT, L. (1956), *The Public Physicians of Ancient Greece*. Northampton, Mass.

COLE, S. G. (1993), 'Procession and Celebration at the Dionysia', in Scodel (1993) (ed.), 25–38.

———— (1998), 'Domesticating Artemis', in Blundell and Williamson (1998) (eds.), 27–44.

CONNOR, W. R. (1971), *The New Politicians of Fifth-century Athens*. Princeton.

———— (1990) (ed.), *Aspects of Athenian Democracy*. Copenhagen.

CORBEILL, A. (1997), 'Dining Deviants in Roman Political Invective', in Hallett and Skinner (1997) (eds.), 99–128.

COULSON, W. D. E., PALAGIA, O., SHEAR, T., and FROST, F. (1994) (eds.), *The Archaeology of Athens and Attica under the Democracy*. Oxford.

COX, C. A. (1998), *Household interests: Property, Marriage Strategies, and Family Dynamics in Ancient Athens*. Princeton.

CROSBY, M. (1950), 'The Leases of the Laurion Mines', *Hesperia* 19, 189–312.

CROWTHER, N. B. (1985), 'Male "beauty" contests in Greece: the *Euandria* and *Euexia*', *AC* 54, 285–91.

Csapo, E. (1993), ' "Deep Ambivalence": Notes on a Greek Cockfight', *Phoenix* 47, 1–28, 115–24.

——(1997), 'Riding the Phallos for Dionysos: Iconology, Ritual and Gender-Role De/construction', *Phoenix* 51, 253–95

Daux, G. (1958), 'Notes de lecture' *BCH* 82, 358–67.

Davidson, J. (1993), 'Fish, Sex and Revolution in Athens', *CQ* 43, 53–66.

——(1997), *Courtesans and Fishcakes*. London.

Davies, J. K. (1971), *Athenian Propertied Families*. Oxford.

——(1981), *Wealth and the Power of Wealth in Classical Athens*. London and New York.

Deacy, S. and Pierce, K. F. (1997) (eds.), *Rape in Antiquity*. London.

de Bruyn, O. (1995), *Le Competence de l'Aréopage en matière de procès public*. Historia Einzelschriften 90, Stuttgart.

Delorme, J. (1960), *Gymnasium. Étude sur les monuments consacrés à l'éducation en Grèce*. Paris.

de Ste Croix, G. E. M. (1972), *Origins of the Peloponnesian War*. London.

Deubner, L. (1932), *Attische Feste*. Berlin.

Develin, R. (1985), 'Age Qualifications for Athenian magistrates' *ZPE* 61, 149–59.

——(1989), *Athenian Officials 684–321 BC*, Cambridge

de Vries, K. (1997), 'The "Frigid Eromenoi" and their Wooers Revisited: A Closer Look at Greek Homosexuality in Vase Painting', in Duberman (1997), 14–24.

Dickie E. (1996), *Greek Forms of Address from Herodotus to Lucian*. Oxford.

Diller, A. (1979), 'The Manuscript Tradition of Aeschines' Orations', *Illinois Classical Studies* 4, 34–64.

Dillon, M. P. J. (1995), 'Payments to the Disabled at Athens: Social Justice or Fear of Aristocratic Patronage', *Anc. Soc.* 26, 126–57.

Donlan, W. (1973), 'The Origin of *kalos kagathos*', *AJP* 94, 365–74.

Dorjahn, A. P. (1927), 'Poetry in Athenian Courts', *CP* 22, 85–93.

——(1929/30), 'Some Remarks on Aeschines' Career as an Actor', *CJ* 25, 223–9.

Dover, K. J. (1968), *Lysias and the Corpus Lysiacum*. Berkeley and Los Angeles.

——(1974), *Greek Popular Morality in the Time of Plato and Aristotle*. Oxford.

——(1978), *Greek Homosexuality*. London.

——(1988), *The Greeks and their Legacy*. Oxford.

Dowden, K. (1989), *Death and the Maiden*. London.

——(1992), *The Uses of Greek Mythology*. London.

Dreher, M. (1995), *Hegemon und Symmachoi: Untersuchungen zum Zweiten Athenischen Seebund*. Berlin and New York.

Drerup, E. (1898), 'Über die bei den attischen Rednern eingelegten

Urkunden', *Jahrbuch. für classische Philologie* Suppl. 24. 221–366.

DUBERMAN, M. B. (1997) (ed.), *Queer Representations: Reading Lives, Reading Cultures*. New York.

EADIE, J. W. and OBER, J. (1985) (eds.), *The Craft of the Ancient Historian*, Lanham and London.

EASTERLING, P. E. (1997), 'From Repertoire to Canon', in Easterling (1997) (ed.), 211–27.

————(1997) (ed.), *The Cambridge Companion to Greek Tragedy*. Cambridge.

————(1999), 'Actors and Voices: Reading between the Lines in Aeschines and Demosthenes', in Goldhill and Osborne (1999) (eds.), 154–66.

EDER, W. (1995) (ed.), *Die Athenische Demokratie im 4. Jahrhundert v. Chr.: Vollendung oder Verfall einer Verfassungsform?* Stuttgart.

ELIOT, C. W. J. (1962), *Coastal Demes of Attica*. Toronto.

ELLIS, J. R. (1976), *Philip II and Macedonian Imperialism*. London.

FERGUSON, W. S. (1938), 'The Salaminioi of Heptaphylai and Sounion', *Hesperia* 7, 1–74.

FINLEY, M. I. (1973) (ed.), *Problèmes de la terre en Grèce ancienne*. Paris and La Haye.

FISHER, N. R. E. (1990), 'The Law of *hubris* in Athens', in Cartledge, Millett, and Todd (1990) (eds.), 123–38.

————(1992), *Hybris*. Warminster.

————(1993), *Slavery in Classical Greece*. London.

————(1994), 'Sparta Re(De)valued: Some Athenian Public Attitudes to Sparta between Leuctra and the Lamian War', in Hodkinson and Powell (1994) (eds.), 347–400.

————(1995), '*Hybris*, Status and Slavery', in Powell (1995) (ed.), 44–84.

————(1998a), 'Gymnasia and social mobility in Athens', in Cartledge, Millett, and von Reden (1998) (eds.), 84–104

————(1998b), 'Violence, Masculinity and the Law in Classical Athens', in Foxhall and Salmon (1998b) (eds.), 68–97.

————(1999), ' "Workshops of Villains": Was there much Organised Crime in Classical Athens?', in Hopwood (1999) (ed.), 53–96.

————(2000), 'Symposiasts, Fisheaters and Flatterers: Social Mobility and Moral Concern', in D. Harvey and J. Wilkins (2000) (eds.), *The Rivals of Aristophanes*, 355–96. London.

FISHER, N. R. E. and VAN WEES H. (1998) (eds.), *Archaic Greece*. London.

FLENSTED-JENSEN, P., NIELSEN T. H. and RUBINSTEIN, L. (2000) (eds.), *Polis and Politics: Studies in Ancient Greek History Presented to Mogens Herman Hansen*. Copenhagen.

FORD, A. (1999), 'Reading Homer from the Rostrum: Poems and Laws in Aeschines' *Against Timarchus*', in Goldhill and Osborne (1999) (eds.), 231–56.

FORSEN, B. and STANTON, G. (1996) (eds.), *The Pnyx in the History of Athens.* Helsinki.

FOUCAULT, M. (1985), *The History of Sexuality.* Vol. 2: *The Use of Pleasure.* London and New York.

————(1986), *The History of Sexuality.* Vol. 3: *The Care of the Self.* London.

FOWLER, D. P. (1989), 'Taplin on Cocks', *CQ* 39, 257–9.

FOXHALL, L. (1989), 'Household, Gender and Property in Classical Athens', *CQ* 39, 22–44.

————(1991), 'Response to Eva Cantarella', *Symposion 1990: Vorträge zur griechischen und hellenistiche Rechtsgeschichte,* 297–303. Cologne.

————(1995), 'Women's Ritual and Men's Work in Ancient Athens', in Hawley and Levick (1995) (eds.), 97–110.

————(1998), 'The Politics of Affection: Emotional Attachments in Athenian Society', in Cartledge, Millett, and von Reden (1998) (eds.), 52–67.

FOXHALL, L. and LEWIS, A. D. E. (1996) (eds.), *Greek Law in its Political Setting: Justifications not Justice.* Oxford.

FOXHALL, L. and SALMON, J. B. (1998a), *Thinking Men: Masculinity and its Self-Representation in the Classical Tradition.* London and New York.

————(1998b), *When Men were Men: Masculinity, Power and Identity in Classical Antiquity.* London and New York.

FRÉZOULS, E. and JACQUEMIN, A. (1995) (eds.), *Les Relations Internationales.* Paris.

GABRIELSEN, V. (1994), *Financing the Athenian Fleet.* Baltimore and London.

GARLAN, Y. and MASSON, O. (1982), 'Les acclamations pédérastiques de Kalami', *BCH* 106, 3–22.

GAUTHIER, P. (1985), *Les Cités grecques et leurs bienfaiteurs. BCH* Suppl. XII. Paris.

GAUTHIER, P. and HATZOPOULOS, M. B. (1993), *La Loi Gymnasiarchique de Beroia.* Athens.

GEDDES, A. G. (1987), 'Rags and Riches: the Costume of Athenian Men in the Fifth Century', *CQ* 37, 307–31.

GHIRON-BISTAGNE, P. (1976), *Recherches sur les acteurs dans la Grèce ancienne.* Paris.

————(1985), 'Le cheval et la jeune fille ou de la virginité chez les anciens grecs', *Pallas* 22, 105–21

GLEASON, M. (1995), *Making Men: Sophists and Self-Presentation in Ancient Rome.* Princeton.

GOLDEN, M. (1990), *Children and Childhood in Classical Athens.* Baltimore and London.

GOLDEN, M. (1984), 'Slavery and Homosexuality at Athens', *Phoenix* 38, 308–24.

———(1998), *Sport and Society in Ancient Greece*. Cambridge

———(forthcoming), 'Demosthenes and the Social Historian', in I. Worthington (ed.), *Demosthenes*. London and New York.

GOLDEN, M. and TOOHEY, P. (1997) (eds.), *Inventing Ancient Culture: Historicism, Periodization and the Ancient World*. London and New York.

GOLDHILL, S. (1994), 'Representing Democracy: Women at the Great Dionysia', in Osborne and Hornblower (1994) (eds.), 347–70.

———(1998), 'Seductions of the Gaze', in Cartledge, Millett, and von Reden (1998) (eds.), Cambridge, 105–24.

———(1999), 'Programme Notes', in Goldhill and Osborne (1999) (eds.), 1–29.

GOLDHILL, S. and OSBORNE, R. G. (1999) (eds.), *Performance Culture and Athenian Democracy*. Cambridge.

GOULD, J. (1973), '*HIKETEIA*', *JHS* 93, 74–103.

GRAHAM, J. W. (1974) , 'Houses of Classical Athens', *Phoenix* 28, 45–54.

GRASBERGER, L. (1883), *Die Griechischen Stichnamen*. Wurzburg.

HABICHT, C. (1997), *Athens from Alexander to Actium*. Harvard.

HÄGG, R. (1994) (ed.), *Ancient Greek Cult Practice from the Epigraphic Evidence*. Stockholm.

HALL, E. (1995), 'Lawcourt Dramas: The Power of Performance in Greek Forensic Oratory, *BICS* 40, 39–58.

HALLETT, J. P. and SKINNER, M. B. (1997) (eds.), *Roman Sexualities*. Princeton.

HALLIWELL, S. (1991), 'Laughter in Greek Culture', *CQ* 41, 279–99.

HALPERIN, D. (1990), *One Hundred Years of Homosexuality*, London.

———(1997), 'Questions of Evidence: Comments on Koehl, De Vries and Williams', in Duberman (1997) (ed.), 39–54.

HAMMOND, N. G. L. and GRIFFITH, G. T. (1979), *A History of Macedonia: II.* Oxford.

HANSEN, M. H. (1974), *The Sovereignty of the People's Court in Athens in the Fourth Century BC and the Public Action against Unconstitutional Proposals.* Odense.

———(1975), *Eisangelia: The Sovereignty of the People's Court in Athens in the Fourth Century B.C. and the Impeachment of Generals and Politicians.* Odense.

———(1976), *Apagoge, Endeixis, and Ehpegesis against Kakourgoi, Atimoi and Pheugontes*, Odense.

———(1983), 'The Athenian "Politicians", 403–322 BC', *GRBS* 24, 33–55.

———(1984), '*Rhetores* and *Strategoi* in Fourth-Century Athens', *GRBS* 25, 151–80

————(1985), *Demography and Democracy*, Copenhagen.

————(1987), *The Athenian assembly in the Age of Demosthenes*. Oxford.

————(1989a), 'Solonian Democracy in Fourth-Century Athens', *CM* 40, 71–99.

————(1989b), *The Athenian Ecclesia II*. Copenhagen.

————(1990), 'The Size of the Council of the Areopagos and its social Composition', *C&M* 41, 73–7.

————(1991), *The Athenian Democracy in the Time of Demosthenes*. Oxford.

————(1994), 'The 2500th Anniversary of Cleisthenes' Reforms and the Tradition of Athenian Democracy', in Osborne and Hornblower (1994) (eds.), 25–37.

————(1996a), 'The Ancient Athenian and the Modern Liberal view of Liberty as a Democratic Ideal', in Hedrick and Ober (1996) (eds.), 91–104.

————(1996b), 'Reflections on the Number of Citizens Accommodated in the Assembly Place on the Pnyx', in Forsen and Stanton (1996) (eds.), 23–33.

HANSEN, M. H. and RAAFLAUB, K. (1995), *Studies in the Ancient Greek Polis*. Historia Einzelschriften 95. Stuttgart.

HARRIS, E. M. (1985), 'The Date of the Trial of Timarchus', *Hermes* 113, 376–80.

————(1986), 'The Names of Aeschines' Brothers-in Law', *AJP* 107, 99–102.

————(1988), 'When was Aeschines born?', *CP* 83, 211–14.

————(1989), 'Demosthenes' Speech against Meidias', *HSCP* 92, 117–36.

————(1990), 'Did the Athenians Regard Seduction as a Worse Crime than Rape?', *CQ* 40, 370–7.

————(1992), review of MacDowell, *Meidias*, *CP* 87, 71–80.

————(1994), ' "In the Act" or "Red-Handed"? *Apagoge* to the Eleven and *Furtum Manifestum*', in *Symposion 1993 – Vorträge zur griechischen und hellenistischen Rechtsgeschichte*. 10, 169–84. Bohläu.

————(1995), *Aeschines and Athenian Politic*. Oxford.

HARRIS, W. V. (1989), *Ancient Literacy*. Cambridge, Mass.

HARRISON, A. R. W (1968–1971), *The Law of Athens*. Vols. I and II. Oxford.

HARVEY, F. D. (1985), '*Dona ferentes*: Some Aspects of Bribery in Greek Politics', in Cartledge and Harvey (1985) (eds.), 76–117.

————(1990), 'The Sykophant and Sykophancy: Vexatious Redefinition?', in Cartledge et al. (1990) (eds.), 103–22.

HAWLEY, R. and LEVICK, B. (1995) (eds.), *Women in Antiquity: New Assessments*. London.

HENDERSON, J. (1991), *The Maculate Muse*. 2nd edn. New Haven.

HERDT G. (1984) (ed.), *Ritualized Homosexuality in Melanesia*. Berkeley and Los Angeles.

——————(1987), *The Sambia: Ritual and Gender in New Guinea*. New York.

——————(1994), *Guardians of the Flutes, Vol. 1: Idioms of Masculinity*. 2nd edn. Chicago.

HERMAN, G. (1993), 'Tribal and Civic Codes of Behaviour in Lysias 1', *CQ* 43, 406–19.

——————(1994), 'How Violent was Athenian Society?', in Osborne and Hornblower (1994) (eds.), 99–117.

——————(1995), 'Honour, Revenge and the State in Fourth-century Athens', in Eder (1995) (ed.), 43–60

——————(1996) 'Ancient Athens and the Values of Mediterranean Society', *Mediterranean Historical Review* 11, 5–36.

HESK, J. (1999), 'The rhetoric of Anti-rhetoric in Athenian Oratory', in Goldhill and Osborne (1999) (eds.), 201–30.

HESKELL, J. (1997), *The North-Aegean Wars*. Historia Einzelscriften 102. Stuttgart.

HINDLEY, C. (1994), '*EROS* and Military Command in Xenophon', *CQ* 44, 347–66

——————(1999), 'Xenophon on Male Love', *CQ* 49, 74–99

HINDLEY, C. and COHEN, D. (1991), 'Law, Society and Homosexuality in Classical Athens, a Debate', *P&P* 133, 170–89–94.

HODKINSON, S. (1998), 'Lakonian Artistic Production and the Problem of Spartan Austerity', in Fisher and van Wees (1998) (eds.), 93–117.

HOFFMANN, G. (1990), *Le Châtiment des Amants dans la Grèce classique*. Paris.

HOFFMANN, H. (1974), 'Hahnenkampf in Athen. Zur Ikonographie einer attischen Bildformel', *RA* 195–220.

HOLST, H. (1926), 'Demosthenes' speech-impediment', *SO* 4, 11–25.

HOPPER, R. J. (1953), 'The Attic Silver Mines in the Fourth Century BC', *ABSA* 48, 200–54.

——————(1968), 'The Laurion Mines: a Reconsideration', *ABSA* 63, 293–326.

HOPWOOD, K. (1999) (ed.), *Organised Crime in Antiquity*. London.

HUBBARD, T. K. (1998), 'Popular Perceptions of Elite Homosexuality in Classical Athens', *Arion* 6, 48–78.

HUMPHREYS, S. C. (1985a), 'Lycurgus of Boutadae: an Athenian Aristocrat', in Eadie and Ober (1985) (eds.), 199-252.

——————(1985b), 'Social Relations on Stage: Witnesses in Classical Athens', *History & Anthropology* 1, 313–69.

——————(1990), 'Phratores in Alopeke, and the Salaminioi', *ZPE* 83, 243–6.

——————(1991), 'A Historical Approach to Drakon's Law on Homicide', *Symposion 1990: Vortrage zur griechischen und hellenistiche Rechts-geschichte*, 17–45. Cologne.

————(1999), 'From a Grin to a Death', in Porter (1999) (ed.), 126–46.

HUNTER, V. J. (1990), 'Gossip and the Politics of Reputation in Classical Athens', *Phoenix* 44, 299–325.

————(1994), *Policing Athens: Social Control in the Attic Lawsuits, 420–320 B.C.* Princeton.

HUNTER, V. J. and EDMONDSON, J. (2000) (eds.), *Law and Social Status in Classical Athens*. Oxford.

HUPPERTS, C. A. M. (1988), 'Greek Love: Homosexuality or Pederasty? Greek Love in Black Figure Vase-Painting', *Proceedings of the Third Symposium on Ancient Greek and Related Pottery*, 255–68. Copenhagen.

INSTONE, S. (1990), 'Love and Sex in Pindar: Some Practical Thrusts', *BICS* 37, 34–42.

JACOB, O. (1928), *Les esclaves publics à Athènes*. Liège.

JACOBY, F. (1949), *Atthis*. Oxford.

JAMESON, M. H. (2000), 'An Altar for Heracles', in Flensted-Jensen, Nielsen, and Rubinstein (2000), 217–28.

————, JORDAN, D. R., and KOTANSKY, R. D. (1993), *A Lex Sacra from Selinous*. Durham, NC.

JEFFERY, L. H. and MORPURGO-DAVIES, A. (1970), '*Poinikastas* and *Poinikazen*: BM 1969. 4–2. 1, A New Archaic Inscription from Crete', *Kadmos* 9, 118–54.

JOHNSTONE, S. (1999), *Disputes and Democracy: The Consequences of Litigation in Ancient Athens*. Austin, Tex.

JONES, J. ELLIS (1975), 'Town and Country Houses of Attica in Classical Times', in H. Mussche, P. Spitaels, and F. Goemaere-De Poercke (eds.), *Thorikos and the Laurion: Misc. Graeca*, Ghent. 63–136.

JUST, R. (1989), *Women in Athenian Law and Life*. London.

KAPPARIS, K. (1995), 'When Were the Athenian Adultery Laws Intro-duced?', *RIDA* 42, 97–122.

————(1998), 'Assessors of Magistrates in Classical Athens' *Historia* 47, 382–93.

KEARNS, E. (1989), *The Heroes of Attica*. London.

KENNEDY, G. (1963), *The Art of Persuasion in Greece*. London.

KEULS, E. (1995), 'The Greek Medical Texts and the Sexual Ethos of Ancient Athens', in van der Eijk, Horstmanshoff, and Schrijvers (1995) (eds.), 261–74.

KILMER, M. F. (1993a), *Greek Erotica*. London.

————(1993b), 'In Search of the Wild Kalos-name', *EMC/CV* 12, 173–99.

————(1997a), 'Painters and Pederasts: Ancient Art, Sexuality and Social History', in Golden and Toohey (1997) (eds.), 36–49.

374 AESCHINES, *AGAINST TIMARCHOS*

KILMER, M. F. (1997b), ' "Rape" in Early Red-figure Pottery', in Deacy and Pierce (1997) (eds.), 123–41.

KINDSTRAND, J. F. (1982), *The Stylistic Evaluation of Aeschines in Antiquity*. Stockholm.

KNIGGE, U. (1991), *The Athenian Kerameikos*. Athens.

KNOEPFLER, D. (1981), 'Argoura. Un toponym eubéen dans la Midienne de Demosthène', *BCH* 105, 289–324.

————(1984), 'La decret d'Hegesippe d'Athènes pour Érétrie', *MH* 41, 152–6.

————(1995), 'Une paix de cent ans et un conflict en permanence: étude sur les relations diplomatiques d'Athènes avec Érétrie et les autres cités de l'Eubée au IVᵉ siecle av. J.-C', in Frézouls and Jacquemin (1995) (eds.), 338–46.

KOCH-HARNACK, G. (1983), *Knabenliebe und Tiergeschenke: iher Bedeutung im päderastischen Erziehugnssystem Athens*. Berlin.

————(1989), *Erotische Symbole: Lotus Blüte und gemeinsame Mantel auf griechishe Vasen*. Berlin.

KOEHL, R. (1986), 'The Chieftain Cup and a Minoan Rite of Passage', *JHS* 106, 99–110.

————(1997), 'Ephoros and Ritualized Homosexuality in Bronze-Age Crete', in Duberman (1997) (ed.), 7–13.

KURKE, L. (1999), *Coins, Bodies, Games, and Gold: The Politics of Meaning in Archaic Greece*. Princeton.

KYLE, D. G. (1984), 'Solon and Athletics', *Ancient World* 9, 91–105.

————(1992), 'The Athletic Events', in Neils (1992) (ed.), 80ff.

————(1987), *Athletics in Ancient Athens*. Leiden.

LALONDE, G. V., LANGDON, M. K, and WALBANK, M. B. (1991), *Inscriptions: Horoi, Poletai Records, Leases of Public Lands*. Agora Vol. XIX. Princeton.

LAMBERT, S. D. (1993), *The Phratries of Attica*. Ann Arbor.

————(1997a), *Rationes Centesimarum: Sales of Public Land in Lykourgan Athens*. Amsterdam.

————(1997b), 'The Attic *Genos* Salaminioi and the Island of Salamis', *ZPE* 119, 85–106.

————(1999), '*IG* II² 2345, Thiasoi of Herakles and the Salaminioi', *ZPE* 101, 93–130

LAMBIN, G. (1982), 'Le Surnom *BATALOS* et les mots de cette famille', *RPh* 56, 249–63.

LANE FOX, R. (1973), *Alexander the Great*. London.

————(1994), 'Aeschines and Athenian Politics', in Osborne and Hornblower (1994) (eds.), 137–55.

LANG, M. (1976), *Graffitti and Dipinti*, Agora, Vol. XXI. Princeton.

————(1990), *Ostraka*, Agora, Vol. XXV. Princeton.

LANGDON, S. (1997) (ed.), *New Light on a Dark Age*. Columbia .

LANNI, A. (1997), 'Spectator Sport or Serious Politics: *hoi periestekotes* and the Athenian Lawcourts', *JHS* 117, 183–9.

LARMOUR, D. H. J., MILLER, P. A., and PLATTER, C. (1998), *Rethinking Sexuality: Foucault and Classical Antiquity*. Princeton.

LAUFFER, S. (1979), *Die Bergwerklssklaven von Laureion*. 2nd edn. Mainz.

LAVRENCIC, M. (1988), 'ANDREION', *Tyche* 3, 147–61.

LEITAO, D. D. (1995), The Perils of Leukippos: Initiatory Transvestism and Male Gender Ideology in the *Ekdusia* at Phaistos', *CA* 14, 130–63.

LEWIS, D. M. (1958), 'When was Aeschines Born?', *CR* 8, 108.

————(1959), 'Attic Manumissions', *Hesperia* 28, 203–38.

————(1968), 'Dedications of *phialai* at Athens', *Hesperia* 37, 368–80.

————(1973), 'The Athenian Rationes Centesimarum', in Finley (1973) (ed.), 187–214.

————(1990), 'Public Property in the City', in Murray and Price (1990) (eds.), 245–64.

LEWIS, S. (1996), *News and Society in the Greek Polis*. London.

LIND, H. (1988), 'Ein Hetärenhaus am Heiligen Tor?', *MH* 45, 158–69.

LIPSIUS, J. H. (1905–15), *Das attische Recht und Rechtsverfahren*. Leipzig.

LISSARRAGUE, F. (1999), 'Publicity and Performance: *kalos* Inscriptions in Attic Vase-Painting', in Goldhill and Osborne (1999) (eds.), 359–73.

LLOYD, A. (1996) (ed.), *Battle in Antiquity*. London.

LOOMIS, W. T. (1998), *Wages, Welfare and Inflation in Classical Athens*. Ann Arbor.

LORAUX, N. (1986), *The Invention of Athens: The Funeral Oration in the Classical City*. Cambridge, Mass.

LUDWIG, P. (1996), 'Politics and Eros in Aristophanes' Speech: *Symposium* 191e–192a and the Comedies', *AJP* 117, 53–62.

MCDONNELL, M. (1991), 'The Introduction of Athletic Nudity: Thucydides, Plato and the Vases', *JHS* 111, 182–92.

MACDOWELL, D. M. (1978), *The Law in Classical Athens*. London.

————(1990), *Demosthenes: Against Meidias*. Oxford.

MACTOUX, M.-M. (1988), 'Lois de Solon sur les esclaves et formation d'une société esclavagiste', in Yuke and Doi (1988) (eds.), 331–54.

MANVILLE, P. B. (1990), *The Origins of Citizenship in Ancient Athens*. Princeton.

MASSON, O. (1990) *Onomastica Graeca Selecta*. Paris.

MERITT, B. D. (1952), 'Greek Inscriptions: 5', *Hesperia* 21, 355–9.

MEULDER, M. (1989), 'Timarque, un être tyrannique dépeint par Éschine', *Les Études classiques*, 18, 317–22.

MILLER, M. C.(1997), *Athens and Persia in the Fifth Century BC*. Cambridge.

MILLER, S. G. (1991), *Arete: Greek Sports from Ancient Sources*. 2nd edn. Berkeley and Los Angeles.

MILLER, S. G. (1995), 'Old Metroon and Old Bouleuterion in the Classical Agora of Athens', in Hansen and Raaflaub (1995), 133–58

MILLETT, P. C. (1989), 'Patronage and its Avoidance in Classical Athens', in Wallace-Hadrill (1989) (ed.), 15–47.

————(1990), 'Sale, Credit and Exchange in Athenian Law and Society', in Cartledge, Millett, and Todd (1990) (eds.), 167–94.

————(1991), *Lending and Borrowing in Ancient Athens*. Cambridge.

————(1998), 'Encounters in the Agora', in Cartledge, Millett, and von Reden (1998) (eds.), 222–4.

MITCHEL, F. W. (1961), 'The Cadet Colonels of the Ephebic Corps', *TAPA* 92, 347–57.

————(1970), *Lycurgan Athens*. Cincinnati.

MITCHELL, L. G. (1997), *Greeks Bearing Gifts: The Public Use of Private Relationships in the Greek World, 435–323 BC*. Cambridge.

MORGAN, T. (1998), Literate Education in the Hellenistic and Roman Worlds. Cambridge.

MUNN, M. (1993), *The Defence of Attica*. Berkeley, Los Angeles, and Oxford.

MURRAY, O. (1980), *Early Greece*. London.

————(1990a), 'The Affair of the Mysteries: Democracy and the Drinking Group', in Murray (1990) (ed.), 149–61.

————(1990b) ' The Solonian law of *hubris*', in Cartledge, Millett, and Todd (1990) (eds.), 139–46.

————(1990) (ed.), *Sympotica: A Symposium on the* Symposion. Oxford.

MURRAY, O. and PRICE, S. (1990) (eds.), *The Greek City from Homer to Aristotle*. Oxford.

NEILS, J. (1992) (ed.), *Goddess and Polis: The Panathenaic Festival in Ancient Athens*. Princeton.

————(1994), 'The Panathenaia and Kleisthenic Ideology', in Coulson *et al.* (1994) (eds.), 151–60.

NESSELRATH, H. H. (1990), *Die attische Mittlere Komödie*. Berlin and New York.

NORTH, H. (1952), 'The Use of Poetry in the Training of the Ancient Orator', *Traditio* 8, 1–33.

NYE, R. (1999) (ed.), *Sexuality*. Oxford Readers. Oxford.

OBER, J. (1985), *Fortress Attica. Defence of the Athenian Land Frontier, 404–322 BC*. Leiden.

————(1989), *Mass and Élite in Democratic Athens*. Princeton.

————(1994), 'Power and Oratory in Democratic Athens: Demosthenes 21 *against Meidias*', in Worthington (1994) (ed.), 85–108.

————(1995), 'Greek *horoi*: Artefactual Texts and the Contingency of Meaning', in Small (1995) (ed.), 91–123.

————(1996), *The Athenian Revolution*. Princeton.

————(1998), *Political Dissent in Democratic Athens*. Princeton.

OBER, J. and HEDRICK, C. (1996) (eds.), *Demokratia: A Conversation on Democracies, Ancient and Modern*. Princeton.

OGDEN, D. (1996a), 'Homosexuality and Warfare in Ancient Greece', in Lloyd (1996) (ed.), 107–68.

————(1996b), *Greek Bastardy*. Oxford.

————(1997), *The Crooked Kings of Ancient Greece*. London.

OMITOWOJU, R. (1997), 'Regulating Rape: Soap Operas and Self Interest in the Athenian Courts', in Deacy and Pierce (1997) (eds.), 1–24.

OOST, S. I. (1977), 'Two Notes on Aristophon of Azenia', *CP* 72, 238–42.

OSBORNE, M. J. (1981–3), *Naturalization in Athens*. Vols. I–IV. Brussels.

OSBORNE, R. G. (1985a), *Demos: The Discovery of Classical Attica*. Cambridge.

————(1985b), 'Law in action in classical Athens', *JHS* 105, 40–58

————(1987), 'The Viewing and Obscuring of the Panathenaea Frieze', *JHS* 107, 98–105.

————(1990a), 'Vexatious Litigation in Classical Athens: Sykophancy and the Sykophant', in Cartledge, Millett, and Todd (1990) (eds.), 83–102.

————(1990b), 'The *Demos* and its Divisions in Classical Athens', in Murray and Price (1990) (eds.), 265–93.

————(1991), 'Pride and Prejudice, Sense and Subsistence: Exchange and Society in the Greek city', in Rich and Wallace-Hadrill (1991) (eds.), 119–46.

————(1993), 'Competitive Festivals and the Polis: A Context for Dramatic Festivals at Athens', in Sommerstein *et al.* (1993) (eds.), 21–37.

————(1994), 'Archaeology, the Salaminioi, and the Politics of Sacred Space in Archaic Attica', in Alcock and Osborne (1994) (eds.), 143–60.

————(1998a) 'Men without Clothes: Heroic Nakedness and Greek Art', in Wyke (1998) (ed.), 504–28.

————(1998b), 'Sculpted Men of Athens: Masculinity and Power in the Field of Vision', in Foxhall and Salmon (1998a) (eds.), 23–42.

OSBORNE, R. G. and HORNBLOWER, S. (1994) (eds.), *Ritual, Finance, Politics: Athenian Democratic Accounts Presented to David Lewis*. Oxford.

OSTWALD, M. (1955), 'The Athenian Legislation against Tyranny and Subversion', *TAPA* 96, 103–28.

————(1986), *From Popular Sovereignty to the Sovereignty of Law*. Berkeley and Los Angeles.

PADEL, R. (1992), *In and Out of the Mind. Greek Images of the Tragic Self*. Princeton.

————(1995), *Whom Gods Destroy: Elements of Greek and Tragic Madness*. Princeton.

PARKE, H. W. (1933), *Greek Mercenary Soldiers from the Earliest Times to the Battle of Ipsus*. Oxford.

PARKER, R. C. T. (1983), *Miasma. Pollution and Purification in Early Greek Religion*. Oxford.

————— (1996), *Athenian Religion: A History*. Oxford.

PATTERSON, C. B. (1998), *The Family in Greek History*. Harvard.

PATZER, H. (1982), *Die Griechische Knabenliebe*. Wiesbaden.

PELLING, C. B. B. (1990) (ed.), *Characterization and Individuality in Greek Literature*. Oxford.

————— (1997) (ed.), *Greek Tragedy and the Historian*. Oxford.

PERCY, W. A. III (1996), *Pederasty and Pedagogy in Archaic Greece*. Urbana and Chicago.

PERLMAN, S. (1964), 'Quotations from Poetry in Attic Orators of the Fourth century B.C.', *AJP* 85, 155–72.

————— (1973) (ed.), *Philip and Athens*. Cambridge.

PICKARD-CAMBRIDGE, A. W. (1926), *Demosthenes and the Last Days of Greek Freedom, 384–322*. New York and London.

PICKARD-CAMBRIDGE, A. W. (1968), *The Dramatic Festivals of Athens*. 2nd edn., revised by J. P. A. Gould and D. M. Lewis. Oxford.

PIÉRART, M. (1971), 'Les Euthunoi athéniens', *AC*, 526–73,

POOLE, W. (1990), 'Male homosexuality in Euripides', in Powell (1990) (ed.), 108–50.

PORTER, J. I. (1999) (ed.), *Constructions of the Classical Body*. Ann Arbor.

POWELL, A. (1990) (ed.), *Euripides, women and sexuality*. London.

————— (1994), 'Plato and Sparta: Modes of Rule and Non-rational Persuasion in the *Laws*', in Powell and Hodkinson (1994) (eds.), 273–322.

————— (1995), 'Athens' Pretty Face: Anti-feminine Rhetoric and Fifth-century Controversy over the Parthenon', in Powell (1995) (ed.), 245-72.

————— (1995) (ed.), *The Greek World*, London.

POWELL, A. and HODKINSON, S. (1994) (eds.), *The Shadow of Sparta*. London.

PRICE, A. W. (1989), *Love and Friendship in Plato and Aristotle*. Oxford.

PRICE, S. R. F. (1999), *Religions of the Ancient Greeks*. Cambridge.

PRITCHETT, W. K. (1953), 'The Attic Stelai. Part I', *Hesperia* 22, 225–99.

————— (1956), 'The Attic Stelai. Part II', *Hesperia* 25, 178–317.

————— (1974), *The Greek State at War, Vol. II*. Berkeley and Los Angeles.

RAAFLAUB, K. (1996), 'Equalities and Inequalities in Athenian Democracy', in Ober and Hedrick (1996) (eds.), 139–74.

RASMUSSEN, T. B. and SPIVEY, N. (1991) (eds.), *Looking at Greek Vases*. Cambridge.

REINMUTH, O. (1971), *The Ephebic Inscriptions of the Fourth Century BC*.

Mnemosyne Supplement 14. Leiden.

RHODES, P. J. (1972), *The Athenian Boule*. Oxford.

——(1982), 'Problems in Athenian *Eisphora* and Liturgies', *AHAH* 7, 1–19.

——(1994), 'The Ostracism of Hyperbolus', in Osborne and Hornblower (1994) (eds.), 85–98.

——(1998), 'Enmity in Fourth-century Athens', in Cartledge, Millett, and von Reden (1998) (eds.), 144–61.

RHODES, P. J. (with D. M. LEWIS) (1997), *The Decrees of the Greek States*. Oxford.

RICH, J. and WALLACE-HADRILL, A. (1991) (eds.), *City and Country in the Ancient World*. London.

RICHTER, G. M. A. (1929), 'Silk in Greece', *AJA* 33, 27–33.

——(1965), *Portraits of the Greeks*. 3 Vols. London.

ROBERTS, J. T. (1982), *Accountability in Athenian Government*. Madison.

ROBERTSON, B. G. (2000), 'The Scrutiny of New Citizens at Athens', in Hunter and Edmondson (2000), 149–74.

ROY, J. (1998), 'The Threat from the Piraeus', in Cartledge, Millett, and von Reden (1998) (eds.), 191–202.

RUBINSTEIN, L. (1998), 'The Athenian Political Perception of the *idiotes*', in Cartledge, Millett, and von Reden (1998) (eds.), 125–43.

——(forthcoming), *Litigation and Co-operation in Classical Athens*.

RUZÉ, F. (1997), *Délibération et pouvoir dans la cité grecque de Nestor à Socrate*. Paris.

SCAFURO, A. (1997), *The Forensic Stage: Settling Disputes in Graeco-Roman New Comedy*. Cambridge.

SCHAEFER, A. C. (1885–7), *Demosthenes und seine Zeit*. 2nd edn. Leipzig.

SCHAPS, D. (1977), 'The Women Least Mentioned: Etiquette and Women's Names', *CQ* 27, 323–30.

——(1979), *Economic Rights of Women in Ancient Greece*. Edinburgh.

SCHMITT-PANTEL, P. (1992), *La Cité au Banquet*, Paris

SCHNAPP, A. (1997), *Le chasseur et la cité*. Paris.

SCHOFIELD, M. (1998), 'Political Friendship and the Ideology of Reciprocity', in Cartledge, Millett, and von Reden (1998) (eds.), 37–51.

SCHÜLLER, W. (1982) (ed.), *Korruption in Altertum*. Munich and Vienna

SCODEL, R. (1993) (ed.), *Theater and Society in the Classical World*. Ann Arbor, Michigan.

SEAFORD, R. A. S. (1987), 'The Tragic Wedding', *JHS* 107, 106–30.

——(1990), 'The Imprisonment of Women in Greek Tragedy', *JHS* 110, 76–90.

——(1994), *Reciprocity and Ritual: Homer and Tragedy in the Developing City-State*. Oxford.

SEALEY, B. R. I. (1967), *Essays in Greek Politics*. New York.

———— (1993), *Demosthenes and his Time*. New York and Oxford.

SEKUNDA, N. V. (1990), 'IG II² 1250: A Decree concerning the *Lampadephoroi* of the tribe Aiantis', *ZPE* 83, 149–82.

———— (1992), 'Athenian Demography and Military Strength 338–322BC', *BSA* 87, 311–55.

SERGENT, B. (1986a), *Homosexuality in Greek Myth*. Boston.

———— (1986b), *L'Homosexualité initiatique dans l'Europe ancienne*. Paris.

SHAPIRO, H. A. (1981), 'Courtship Scenes in Attic Vase-painting', *AJA* 85, 133–43.

SHEAR Jr., T. Leslie (1995), 'Bouleuterion, Metroon and the Archives at Athens', in Hansen and Raaflaub (1995) (eds.), 157–98.

SILK, M. S. (1996) (ed.), *Tragedy and the Tragic*. Oxford.

SINCLAIR, R. K. (1988), *Democracy and Participation in Athens*. Cambridge.

SISSA, G. (1990), *Greek Virginity*. Cambridge, Mass.

———— (1999), 'Sexual Bodybuilding: Aeschines against Timarchos', in Porter (1999) (ed.), 147–68

SLATER, N. W. (1998), 'The Vase as Ventriloquist: *Kalos*-Inscriptions and the Culture of Fame', in E. A. Mackay (ed.), *The Oral Tradition and its Influence in the Greek and Roman World*. Mnemosyne Suppl. 188. Leyden. 143–63.

SMALL, D. B. (1995) (ed.), *Methods in the Mediterranean*. Leiden.

SMITH, A. C. (1999), 'Eurymedon and the Evolution of Political Personifications in the Early Classical Period', *JHS* 119, 128–41.

SOMMERSTEIN, A. (1996), 'How to Avoid Being a *Komodoumenos*', *CQ* 46, 327–56.

SOMMERSTEIN, A., HALLIWELL, S., HENDERSON, J. J., and ZIMMERMANN, B. (1993) (eds.), *Tragedy, Comedy and the Polis*. Bari.

SPARKES, B. A. (1996), *The Red and the Black: Studies in Greek Pottery*. London.

SPIVEY, N. (1991), 'Greek Vases in Etruria', in Rasmussen and Spivey (1991) (eds.), 131–50.

STAFFORD, E. J. (2000), *Worshipping Virtues: Personification and the Divine in Ancient Greece*. London.

STEFANIS, I. E. (1988), *Dionysiakoi Technitai*. Heraklion.

STEINER, D. (1998), 'Moving Images: Fifth-century Victory Monuments and the Athlete's Allure', *Class. Ant.* 17, 123–53.

STEWART, A. (1997), *Art, Desire and the Body in Ancient Greece*. Cambridge.

STRAUSS, B. S. (1991), 'Athenian Exiles and Diaspora in the Peloponnesian War', *First International Congress on the Hellenic Diaspora*. Amsterdam. I, 61–71.

STROUD, R. S. (1974), 'An Athenian Law on Silver Coinage', *Hesperia* 43, 157–88.

————(1999), *The Athenian Grain-Tax Law of 374/3 BC*. Hesperia Supplement 29. Princeton.

STYLIANOU, P. J. (1998), *A Historical Commentary on Diodorus Siculus, Book 15*. Oxford.

TAPLIN, O. P. (1990), 'Agamemnon's Role in the *Iliad*', in Pelling (1990) (ed.), 60–82.

————(1993), *Comic Angels and other Approaches to Greek Drama through Vase-Painting*. Oxford.

————(1999), 'Spreading the Word through Performance', in Goldhill and Osborne (1999) (eds.), 33–57.

TAYLOR, M. C. (1995), 'A Fourth-Century Honorary Decree of the Athenian *Demos* on Salamis', *ZPE* 107, 289–95.

————(1997), *Salamis and the Salaminioi*. Amsterdam.

TAYLOR, M. W. (1991), *The Tyrant Slayers: The Heroic Image in Fifth-Century B.C. Athenian Art and Politics*. 2nd edn. Salem.

THOMAS, R. (1989), *Oral Tradition and Written Record in Classical Athens*. Cambridge.

————(1992), *Literacy and Orality in Ancient Greece*. Cambridge.

————(1994), 'Law and the Lawgiver in the Athenian Democracy', in Osborne and Hornblower (1994) (eds.), 119–33.

THOMPSON, H. A. (1982), 'The Pnyx in Models', *Hesperia* Suppl. 19. Princeton. 133–47.

THOMPSON, H. A. and WYCHERLEY, R. E. (1972), *The Athenian Agora Vol. XIV: The History Shape and Use of an Ancient Civic Center*. Princeton.

THOMPSON, W. E. (1983), 'Chares at Phlius', *Philologus* 127, 303–5.

THORNTON, B. S. (1997), *Eros. The Myth of Ancient Greek Sexuality*, Boulder.

THORP, J. (1992), 'The Social Construction of Homosexuality', *Phoenix* 46, 54–61.

TODD, O. J. (1938), '*Tritagonistes*: A Reconsideration', *CQ* 32, 30–8.

TODD, S. C. (1990a), '*Lady Chatterley's Lover* and the Attic Orators', *JHS* 110, 146–73.

————(1990b), 'The Purpose of Evidence in Athenian Courts', in Cartledge, Millett, and Todd (1990) (eds.), 19–40.

————(1993), *The Shape of Athenian Law*. Oxford.

————(1996), 'Lysias *Against Nikomakhos*: The Fate of the Expert in Athenian Law', in Foxhall and Lewis (1996) (eds.), 101–31.

————(1998), 'The Rhetoric of Enmity in the Attic Orators', in Cartledge, Millett, and von Reden (1998) (eds.), 162–9.

TREVETT, J. (1992), *Apollodoros, Son of Pasion*. Oxford.

————(1999), 'Demosthenes and Thebes', *Historia* 48, 184–202.

TRITLE, L. (1988), *Phokion the Good*. London.

VAN DER EIJK, P. J., HORSTMANSHOFF, H. F. J., and SCHRIJVERS, P. H.

(1995) (eds.), *Ancient Medicine in its Socio-Cultural Context*. Amsterdam and Atlanta.

VERIHLAC, A.-M. and VIAL, C. (1998), *Le Mariage Grec*. *BCH* Suppl. 32. Paris.

VIDAL-NAQUET, P. (1986a), *The Black Hunter*. Baltimore and London.

———(1986b), 'The Black Hunter Revisited', *PCPS* 32, 130–45.

VIVIERS, D. (1994), 'La Cité de Dattalla et L'Expansion Territoriale de Lyktos en Crète Centrale', *Bulletin de Correspondance Hellénique* 118, 229–59.

VLASTOS, G. (1973), *Platonic Studies*. Princeton.

———(1987), 'Socratic Irony', *CQ* 37, 79–96.

VON BLANKENHAGEN, P. H. (1976), 'Puerilia', in Bonfante and von Heinze (1976) (eds.), 44–6.

VON REDEN, S. (1995), 'The Peiraeus – a World Apart', *Greece & Rome*, 24–37.

———(1998), 'The Well-ordered *polis*: Topographies of Civic Space', in Cartledge, Millett, and von Reden (1998) (eds.), 170–90.

WADE-GERY, H. T. (1958), *Essays in Greek History*. London.

WALLACE, R. W. (1985), *The Areopagos Council , to 307 B.C.* Baltimore and London.

———(1994), 'Private Lives and Public Enemies: Freedom of Thought in Classical Athens', in Boegehold and Scafuro (1994) (eds.), 127–55.

———(1996), 'Law, Freedom and the Concept of Citizens' Rights in Democratic Athens', in Ober and Hedrick (1996) (eds.), 105–19.

———(2000), ' "Investigations and Reports" by the Areopagos Council', in Flensted-Jensen, Nielsen, and Rubinstein (2000), 581–95.

WALLACE-HADRILL, A. (1989) (ed.), *Patronage in Ancient Society*. London.

WANKEL, H. (1982), 'Die Korruption in der rednerischen Topik und in der Realität des klassischen Athen', in Schüller (1982) (ed.), 29–47.

———(1988), 'Die Datierung des. Prozessus gegen Timarchos (346/5), *Hermes* 116, 383–6.

WEIL, R. (1955), 'Éschine, lecteur de Platon', *REG* 68, xii.

WENDER, D. (1973), 'Plato: Misogynist, Paedophile and Feminist', *Arethusa* 6, 75–90.

WEST, M. L. (1992), *Ancient Greek Music*. Oxford.

WHITEHEAD, D. (1977), *The Ideology of the Athenian Metic*. Cambridge.

———(1983), 'Competitive Outlay and Community Profit: *Philotimia* in Democratic Athens', *C&M* 34, 55–74.

———(1986a), *The Demes of Attica*. Princeton.

———(1986b), 'The Political career of Aristophon', *CP* 81, 313–19.

———(1993), 'Cardinal Virtues: The Language of Public Approbation in Democratic Athens', *C&M* 44, 37–75.

WHITLEY, A. J. M. (1998), 'Literacy and Law-Making: The case of Archaic Crete', in Fisher and van Wees (1998) (eds.), 311–31.

WILLIAMS, C. (1999), *Roman Homosexuality: Ideologies of Masculinity in Classical Antiquity*. New York and Oxford.

WILSON, N. G. (1983), *Scholars of Byzantium*. London.

WILSON, P. J. (1991), 'Demosthenes 21 *against Meidias*: Democratic Abuse', *PCPhS* 37 164–95.

———(1996) , 'Tragic Rhetoric: The Use of Tragedy and the Tragic in the Fourth Century', in Silk (1996) (ed.), 310–31.

———(1997), 'Leading the Tragic Khoros: Tragic Prestige in the Democratic City', in Pelling (1997) (ed.), 81–108.

———(1999), 'The *aulos* in Athens', in Goldhill and Osborne (1999) (eds.), 58–97.

———(2000), *The Athenian Institution of the* Khoregia: *The Chorus, the City and the Stage*. Cambridge.

WINKLER, J. J. (1990a), *The Constraints of Desire*. London.

———(1990b), 'The Ephebes' song: *Tragoidia* and *Polis*', in Winkler and Zeitlin, 20–52.

WINKLER, J. J. and ZEITLIN, F. (1990), *Nothing to do with Dionysos?* Princeton.

WOHL, V. (1999), 'The *eros* of Alcibiades', *Classical Antiquity* 18, 349–80.

WOOTEN, C. W. (1983), *Cicero's* Philippics *and their Demosthenic Model*. Chapel Hill and London.

———(1988), 'Clarity and Obscurity in the Speeches of Aeschines', *AJP* 109, 40–3.

WORTHINGTON, I. (1994) (ed.), *Greek Rhetoric in Action*. London.

WYCHERLEY, R. E. (1957), *The Athenian Agora Vol. III. The Testimonia*. Princeton.

WYKE, M. (1998) (ed.), *Gender and the Body in the Ancient Mediterranean*. Oxford.

YUKE, T. and DOI, M. (1988) (eds.), *Forms of Control and Subordination in Antiquity*. Leiden.

INDEX

homosexual 6, 36–41, 56–7, 64,
  159–61, 179, 183, 185, 208,
  210–13, 220–1, 227–9, 257–60,
  270–1, 300–1, 306, 341–3, 352–5
  prices 303–4
  prostitutes' tax 257–9
  under contract 306–11
Poseidon 210, 255, 333–4
prayers at assemblies 146–7, 345
probole (initial procedure) 158–9,
  176–8
procheirotonia (initial vote) 147
procuring 36–7, 135–8, 338, 343
prohairesis (choice, inclination) 173–4,
  354–5
prohedroi (presiding officers) 147–8,
  163, 241–2
Promethia 134
property-sales 230–40
prosecutors 3–5, 21–3, 119–22,
  138–40, 144–5, 153, 162–3, 168,
  193–5, 202–3, 206–7, 219,
  247–50, 254, 275–6, 304–11,
  316–18, 324–5
  see also lawcourts, politicians,
  sykophantes
prostitutes, see *porneia*
prytaneis (standing committee of
  Council) 12, 163
Ps. Demosthenes 43, *against
  Makartatos* 139–40
Ps. Demosthenes 50, *for Polykles* 194
Ps.-Demosthenes 59, *against Neaira*
  63–4, 167, 185, 189, 220–1, 303,
  335–8, 339, 342
public cult ceremonies 144–5, 335–7
Pydna 4–5
Pyrrhandros of Anaphlystos 221–2
Pytheas 19, 48–9

quail-fighting 187–8, 196, 357

radish, punishment for adulterers
  47, 334–5

rape 37–8, 44, 47, 140–1, 333
Report, see *Pheme*
reticence, of language in forensic
  speeches 42, 56, 166–8, 184,
  208, 220–1, 282, 340, 342
revenge 119–20, 122, 162, 247, 248,
  290, 320, 325, 332
Rhamnous 271
rhetores (orators), *see* politicians
ring-composition 118–19, 326
rites of passage 27–31

Sacred War 3–4, 54, 315
  sacred wreaths 144–5
sacrifice at assemblies 146–7
Salaminioi, *genos* of 152, 188–9,
  200–1, 203, 207, 232, 264, 299,
  324, 360–2
Salamis 151–2
Samos, klerouchy on 186–7
Sannion the chorus-trainer 14
schools, schoolmasters 9, 12, 36–7,
  128–30, 175, 287
Scipio Aemilianus 213
seduction, see *moicheia*
Semnai theai (Solemn Goddesses)
  343–6, 347–9
sexual identities 25–8, 34–6
  see also homosexual relations
shame, values of appealed to in
  speech *passim*, and esp. 36–64,
  121–2, 157–9, 191–3, 208, 211,
  223, 235, 249, 259, 270–2,
  307–8, 327–9, 334–8, 346
silk, silkworms 233–4
silver mines, mining leases 238–91
Simmias, actor 14
skirapheia (gambling, gambling
  places) 360–2
slaves, slavery, slavish acts 26, 37,
  44–5, 58–9, 62, 129–30, 131,
  141–2, 164, 174, 189–93, 198,
  208, 232–4, 266, 283–4